This book offers a reappraisal of Churchill's role as Britain's wartime leader, and in particular reconsiders his response to the dominant strategic challenges of his first year as prime minister. Based on a detailed examination of the public and private records of both political and military leaders, Dr Lawlor analyses what were often conflicting views and reactions to events. She suggests that Churchill's own position reflected the uncertainties, differences and vacillations of his colleagues, and that he was a far more sophisticated and astute politician than he allowed himself to appear.

The first part of the book considers the various reactions among the British leadership to the fall of France and the Battle of Britain. To the strategic complexities were added Churchill's own complex relations with the conservative party and his predecessor, Neville Chamberlain. The second and third parts analyse the discussions and decisions which led to British action in the Middle East and to sending military support to Greece; they consider how Greece became as central as Turkey to Britain's position in the Middle East – a change which was to have repercussions for the final post-war settlement.

Churchill and the politics of war, 1940–1941

Churchill and the politics
of war, 1940–1941

Sheila Lawlor

CAMBRIDGE
UNIVERSITY PRESS

Published by the Press Syndicate of the University of Cambridge
The Pitt Building, Trumpington Street, Cambridge CB2 1RP
40 West 20th Street, New York, NY 10011–4211, USA
10 Stamford Road, Oakleigh, Melbourne 3166, Australia

First published 1994
Reprinted 1995

Printed in Great Britain by Athenaeum Press Ltd, Gateshead, Tyne & Wear

A catalogue record for this book is available from the British Library

Library of Congress cataloguing in publication data

Lawlor, Sheila.
Churchill and the politics of war, 1940–1941 / Sheila Lawlor.
  p.   cm.
Based on the author's thesis (Ph.D.) – University of Cambridge.
Includes bibliographical references.
ISBN 0 521 44545 0
1. World War, 1939–1945 – Great Britain.
2. Churchill, Winston, Sir, 1874–1965.
3. World War, 1939–1945 – Diplomatic history.
I. Title.
D759.L32   1994
940.53'2241 – dc20   93–28733   CIP

ISBN 0 521 44545 0 hardback

CE

For J.A.M.M.

Contents

Acknowledgements

This book developed from initial work for a Ph.D. thesis in the University of Cambridge on 'British Politics and Strategy during the Second World War'. I should like to thank Sir Harry Hinsley, who supervised the thesis and record my thanks to the late Desmond Williams who helped with the choice of subject. I am especially grateful to Maurice Cowling, Donald Cameron Watt and Philip Williamson who kindly read and commented on earlier drafts of the manuscript and gave valuable advice. During the course of writing this book Christopher Andrew, Derek Beales, Tim Blanning, Gabriel Gorodetsky, Sir Michael Howard, Harold James, the late Elie Kedourie and Norman Stone have made helpful suggestions and comments. I have also been helped by the comments and criticisms of hosts and members of the seminars and societies to which I read earlier versions of chapters – those in Cambridge under the aegis of Derek Beales, Christopher L. Brooke, Owen Chadwick, Sir Geoffrey Elton and Sir Harry Hinsley, and those in London under the aegis of Donald Watt and John Turner and Kathleen Burke at the late A.J.P. Taylor's seminar.

I should like to thank William Davies of Cambridge University Press for his help and encouragement. I am grateful to the readers engaged by the Press for their helpful and detailed suggestions and comments. I should also like to thank Jean Field of the Press for her scrupulous copy-editing.

I should like to thank Frances Hawkins and Francesca Murphy for their help with word-processing the manuscript.

I am grateful to the Controller of H.M. Stationery Office for permission to consult and quote from Crown Copyright records and to the owners and trustees of copyright materials from the private collections listed on pp. 260–2 for permission to use and quote from this material. I am grateful to the librarians, archivists and custodians of the records listed on pp. 260–2 and especially to the staff of the Public Record Office London, to the staff of Birmingham University Library, the Bodleian Library Oxford, the Borthwick Institute York, Cambridge University Library, the

Cambridge History faculty library, Churchill College Cambridge Archives Centre, the House of Lords Record Office, the Centre for Military Archives of King's College London, the John Rylands University Library of Manchester. Especial thanks are due to Corelli Barnett, Ben Benedikz, John Mason.

I am grateful to the Master and Fellows of Sidney Sussex College, who elected me first to a research studentship and then to a research fellowship and to the Master and Fellows of Churchill College, Cambridge and to the Bodossakis foundation for electing me to a research fellowship. These posts provided conditions conducive to, and support for, research and writing. I have also been helped by the Cambridge history faculty in acquiring microfilms and by scholarships awarded by the Robert Gardiner Memorial foundation.

My outstanding debts are of a wider order: to my parents for their constant support and generosity and to John Marenbon on whose advice and help – both practical and critical – I have depended.

Abbreviations

The following abbreviations have been used throughout the footnotes:

GENERAL

AOCinC	Air officer commanding-in-chief
AOCinCME	Air officer commanding-in-chief RAF Middle East
BEF	British Expeditionary Force
CAB	War cabinet files
cabinet	War cabinet conclusions (minutes)
CA	Confidential annex
CAS	Chief of the air staff
CIGS	Chief of imperial general staff
CNS	Chief of naval staff
CinC	Commander-in-chief
CinCME	Commander-in-chief Middle East (or general officer commanding-in-chief Middle East)
CinC Medn	Commander-in-chief Mediterranean
CsinCME	Commanders-in-chief, Middle East, RAF Middle East and Mediterranean
COS	Chiefs of staff ('Chiefs of staff' refers to the conclusions (minutes) of meetings)
DMO	Director of military operations at the war office
DO	Defence committee (operations) ('defence committee' refers to the conclusions of the defence committee)
FO	Foreign office
HQ	Headquarters
HQME	Headquarters Middle East
HQRAFME	Headquarters Royal Air Force, Middle East
PM	Prime minister
PPS	Parliamentary private secretary
PREM	Prime minister's office, records
RAF	Royal Air Force

SOS	Secretary of state
VCAS	Vice-chief of the air staff
VCIGS	Vice-chief of imperial general staff
VCNS	Vice-chief of naval staff
WO	War office
WP	War cabinet memoranda

UNPUBLISHED MATERIAL

Abbreviations for the public records in the Public Record Office are noted in the bibliography on p. 260. Abbreviations for private collections are by name unless otherwise designated below. The diaries of Brooke, Cadogan, Eden and Nicolson have been consulted in manuscript as well as in published form. See the bibliography on pp. 260–6.

AVAR	Papers of the 1st Viscount Alexander of Hillsborough, Churchill College, Cambridge
BBK	Papers of the 1st Baron Beaverbrook, House of Lords Record Office
BL Add. MS.	London, British Library Additional manuscript
Brooke	Manuscript papers of Field Marshal Lord Alanbrooke, Liddell Hart Centre for Military Archives, King's College, London
Croft	Papers of the 1st Baron Croft, Churchill College, Cambridge
DC	Papers and copies of documents in the Royal Air Force Museum, Hendon, relating to Air Chief Marshal Sir Arthur Longmore
GHS	Papers of Sir Geoffrey Shakespeare, Imperial War Museum
Halifax	Papers of the 1st Earl of Halifax, made available at York and at Churchill College, Cambridge
HFX MCF	As above, on microfilm in Churchill College, Cambridge
Hky	Papers of the 1st Baron Hankey, Churchill College, Cambridge
IOL MS.	London, India Office Library, manuscript
IRW	Papers of Lieutanant-General N.N.S. Irwin, Imperial War Museum
LG	Papers of the 1st Earl Lloyd George of Dwyfor, House of Lords Record Office
LH	Papers of Sir Basil Liddell-Hart, Liddell Hart Centre for Military Archives, King's College, London

MM	Papers of Field Marshal Sir Archibald Montgomery-Massingberd, Liddell Hart Centre for Military Archives, King's College, London
NC	Papers of Neville Chamberlain, Birmingham University Library
PJGG	Papers of Sir James Grigg, Churchill College, Cambridge
SB	Papers of the 1st Earl Baldwin, Cambridge University Library
ZNK	Papers of the 2nd Marquess of Zetland, India Office Library

PUBLISHED MATERIAL

Abbreviations for published diaries or extracts, diary notes or letters are as follows:

Avon, *The Reckoning*/Eden diary	The Earl of Avon (Anthony Eden), *The Reckoning*, London, 1965
Channon diary	R. Rhodes James (ed.), *Chips: The Diaries of Sir Henry Channon*, London, 1967
Colville diary	John Colville, *The Fringes of Power: Downing Street Diaries 1939–1945*, London, 1985
Connell, *Wavell*	John Connell, *Wavell. Scholar and Soldier to June 1941*, London, 1964
Into Battle	Winston S. Churchill, *Into Battle. War Speeches by the Rt. Hon. Winston S. Churchill, C.H., M.P.*, compiled by Randolph S. Churchill, London, 1941
Kennedy, *Business of War*	John Kennedy, *The Business of War* (ed. Bernard Fergusson), London, 1957
Letters	N. Nicolson (ed.), *Harold Nicolson. Diaries and Letters 1939–1945*, London, 1967
Pownall diary	Brian Bond (ed.), *Chief of Staff. The Diaries of Lieutenant-General Sir Henry Pownall*, vol. I: *1933–1940*, vol. II: *1940–1944*, London, 1972, 1974

Reith diary

Charles Stuart (ed.), *The Reith Diaries*, London, 1975

Second World War, I

Winston S. Churchill, *The Second World War*, vol. I: *The Gathering Storm*, London, 1948

Second World War, II

Winston S. Churchill, *The Second World War*, vol. II: *Their Finest Hour*, London, 1949

Second World War, III

Winston S. Churchill, *The Second World War*, vol. III: *The Grand Alliance*, London, 1950

Sherwood, *Hopkins*

Robert E. Sherwood, *The White House Papers of Harry L. Hopkins. An Intimate History . . .*, vol. I: *September 1939–January 1942*, London, 1948

Unrelenting Struggle

Winston S. Churchill, *The Unrelenting Struggle. War Speeches by the Rt. Hon. Winston S. Churchill, C.H., M.P.*, compiled by Charles Eade, London, 1942

Introduction

Politics and strategy

This is a book about political matters. It is about how Churchill became established as prime minister in succession to Neville Chamberlain, and how he and his government saw and tackled the great issues of the war as they emerged during the remainder of 1940 and early 1941: Hitler's attack on France and its subsequent fall; the Battle – and defence – of Britain; the defence of Egypt and the Middle East; diplomatic relations with Greece, the Balkans and Turkey, and the question of military intervention there. The book concludes with the decision, reluctantly reached by the cabinet in March 1941, to send British troops to Greece.

The book concentrates on the the first months of Churchill's wartime leadership – from his becoming prime minister in May 1940 to his committing British troops to Greece in March 1941. For most of the period Britain was fighting alone. The war, therefore, and Churchill's leadership, had a character different to that of the later years when first the Soviet Union, and then the United States and Japan entered the war, in June and December 1941 respectively. None the less, the views about the nature of British interests, which were to dominate the closing stages of the war, had their origins in this early period.

Churchill established his dominance over the conservative party and in the country during these months, and set about securing British interests – first the security of Britain and then that of the Middle East. This led to a series of political, diplomatic and strategic views and interventions in the course of which the Balkans came to be seen as central to the British position. In particular Greece came to be seen as the alternative to Turkey as the pivot on which Britain's Middle Eastern position depended. And although a number of political, diplomatic and strategic considerations lay behind military intervention in Greece, its long term implications were more definite. Because Greece was seen to have become central to Britain's strategic and political position, inclusion of Greece in Britain's sphere of interest in the ultimate settlement of Europe was paramount –

1

even at the cost of having to cede Poland or its eastern European neighbours to the Soviet Union. Such a policy had implications for Britain's other interests – for example in the Far East and the Pacific – and for her relations with the Soviet Union and the United States. The Far East and the Pacific were to be subordinated to the demands of the Mediterranean and Middle East. At no stage was it believed that the navy could be sent in any force to protect possessions in the Far East or Pacific from the Japanese threat. Nor could specific promises be made to Australia or New Zealand on this count. Britain would look to and depend on America to regain these possessions in the Far East, and if necessary wait until the peace settlement. Similarly with the Soviet Union: while it became clear in the months after Hitler attacked the Soviet Union in June 1941 that ideological differences were not to stand in the way of an accommodation with the Soviet Union, and thus pragmatism rather than ideology was to guide relations, none the less even after the Soviet Union became an ally there was next to nothing to spare for her.

While this book therefore restricts itself to the first months of Churchill's leadership – when Britain was fighting alone – and does not examine the wider sweep with which Churchill came to be associated, it suggests that the subsequent view of what constituted British interests had its origins during this period, and that Churchill's approach was more complex and idiosyncratic than his own history would imply.

The context of the book is the unstated question of how far the new administration formulated a coherent plan in response to Hitler's extension of the war to his western front. Implied in this question is another: how far did the nature of its response differ from that of the regime it had replaced, over and beyond how it was said or thought to do so? How did Churchill's administration perceive the nature of Britain's traditional interests – the integrity of the island and the preservation of her empire? How far was this combined with, or subordinated to an often incoherent reaction to changing circumstances?

The changing circumstances to which Churchill and his colleagues had to respond have, since the war, become the familiar terrain of the initial phase of the 'real war': the invasion of France and its subsequent fall; the German air attack on Britain ('the Battle of Britain'); and the defence of Egypt, initially against Italian aggression westwards from Libya and subsequently from German intentions. At the time the lines – and the response to events – were less clear; and even what in retrospect appear as the major landmarks of the war at the time were superseded, or affected by a number of considerations which often seemed to those responsible to be every bit as central: the war at sea; relations with – and help from – the United States; the Soviet Union; the vexed question of relations with

Vichy France, de Gaulle and the Free French, or Franco's Spain; and the underlying problems of supply and production, the wartime economy and the organisation of the country for war.

All of these topics, like everything to do with the Second World War, have been much discussed over the last fifty years. What is there new to say about them? In order to answer this question, and to move from defining the subject of this book to stating its aim, it is necessary to look at the historiography of both the 1930s and 1939–41.

Historiography

The 1930s: appeasement and revisionism

In the aftermath of war, historical views of the 1930s owed much to the alleged contrast between Churchill and his predecessors. The contrast rested on the assumptions which took shape once Churchill came to power: that throughout the 1930s his predecessors in government had been wrong in failing adequately to stand up to Hitler; and that when he emerged in 1940 as a resolute prime minister he was to take the difficult diplomatic and strategic choices avoided by his predecessors. This view was implied at the time by those of Chamberlain's critics who, for a variety of reasons, supported Churchill. And though initially reticent about castigating his predecessors himself, Churchill was less so when he came to write his history of the Second World War. He set his account in the context of the mistakes of the interwar years.

That approach, in which discussion of the Second World War is set in the context of the failings of politicians in the 1930s, became the model for academic as well as non-academic historians. It involved discussion of the decade in terms of the weakness of the leaders – particularly Baldwin and Chamberlain – in standing up to Hitler, their lack of sophistication in foreign affairs, the malign influence of the treasury, the attempt to set Nazi Germany against the Soviet Union. In 1965 Donald Watt noted that the stereotype which bedevilled even academic discussion pre-dated the release of the sources and indeed stretched back to the outbreak of war. Academic discussion had, in the first post-war decades, been a matter of stereotypes – for instance, Chamberlain 'as a Birmingham business man, ignorant of foreign affairs, ... easily gulled by Hitler' and in the pocket of the treasury and influenced by the anti-communist views of certain con-servatives.[1] Watt noted that the views of both British and German policies

---

[1] D.C. Watt, 'Appeasement: The Rise of a Revisionist School?', in *The Political Quarterly*, 36 (1965), 191–213.

were not the result of scholarship, but had been given currency by those involved in the events on the right or left long before documentation was available. On the right were 'patriotic–chauvinist Germanophobe realists of the Churchill–Amery–Sir Lewis Namier school' but also 'right-wing social patriots of the Labour Party ... Dalton, Bevin ... Wedgwood'. On the left (or liberal) side were the 'political left ... all brands of collectivist, from liberal advocates of collective security to socialist and communist collectivists.' During the war, Watt explains, their views were popularised in the Gollancz series, *Guilty Men, Tory M.P., Your M.P., Brendan and Beverley* and subsequently 'adopted lock, stock and barrel by the historians who wrote after 1945, drawing on the flood of captured Nazi documents and justificatory memoirs.'

Watt argued the need for 'a serious revision of the orthodox view' – an orthodoxy which by now has run its course in academic writing. Diplomatic and strategic issues have been considered in terms of their integral place in domestic politics, which itself involves a variety of considerations often overlooked in books devoted expressly to foreign policy. The works of Maurice Cowling, David Dilks, Keith Middlemas and John Barnes, R.A.C. Parker, George Peden and Philip Williamson are among the studies which have been most resolute in seeing off the orthodoxies about the 1930s.[2] Although this is not the place to consider this discussion of the 1930s,[3] the question should be raised: does the fact that the interpretations of the 1930s which provided the context for discussion of the war no longer stand mean that now classic interpretations of the war must be reconsidered?

The effect of the revisionist historiography of the 1930s on the war years has been problematical. This is partly the result of the role of Churchill and his supporters. Theirs was an anti-establishment stance: they were the radicals fighting the forces of reaction, they were responsible for bringing in a new order. Churchill and his supporters set much of the tone not only for the 1930s but for the war on a multitude of counts which rested on the common assumption of battling against reaction.

---

[2] For instance see Maurice Cowling, *The Impact of Hitler: British Politics and British Policy, 1933–40*, Cambridge, 1975; David Dilks, 'Appeasement Revisited', *University of Leeds Review*, 15 (1972), 28–56 and (ed.), *Retreat from Power: Studies in Britain's Foreign Policy of the Twentieth Century*, vol. I, London, 1981; Keith Middlemas and John Barnes, *Baldwin. A Biography*, London, 1969; R. A. C. Parker, 'Economics, Rearmament and Foreign Policy: The United Kingdom before 1939 – A Preliminary Study', *Journal of Contemporary History*, 10 (1975), 637–47; G. C. Peden *British Rearmament and the Treasury, 1932–1939*, Edinburgh, 1979; P. Williamson, *National Crisis and National Government: British Politics, the Economy and Empire, 1926–32*, Cambridge, 1992. See also the other works by these historians listed in the bibliography.

[3] But see pp. 25–30, for a brief account of the 1930s in the light of this work.

Politicians, generals and officials came to be considered in terms of belonging to the new order, or were dismissed as members of the backward-looking old. The upshot has been that much of the running, after 1940, has been made by those whose accounts arise out of that premise: not only participants (politicians, generals, civil servants and advisers), but also those historians who examine the nature of the new order – of whom Paul Addison remains master.[4] So ingrained have such ideas become that they have even been used to explain Churchill's strategic failures and the weakened position of Britain in the twentieth century. For example, one popular genre identifies the difficulties of the country as stretching beyond the interwar years to the Victorian past: political leaders are alleged to be the maladjusted products of Victorian values whose beliefs had been fashioned by irrelevant education, religion, morality; and that even the heroic Mr Churchill was the victim of the accumulated consequences of the past and could do little to arrest their unfolding.[5]

Churchill's history

The first volume of Churchill's war history addresses the weaknesses of the interwar years, made good, it is implied, by Churchill when the forces of destiny brought him to office. Churchill's tone, the qualities with which he and others tended to endow his leadership, the alleged moral advantage which he was implied to command, have continued to leave their mark on accounts of the war. This survey will therefore begin with Churchill's own history of *The Second World War*.

Churchill's express intention in writing the history of the Second World War was to pin the story of great events on the experiences of one man – himself. The method and subject was, he believed, particularly apt, since he had led the government for five years and, as prime minister, issued documents amounting to 'nearly a million words' which would provide an account of events as seen 'by one who bore chief responsibility for the war'.[6] His chosen method, he explained, followed that employed by Defoe in *Memoirs of a Cavalier*.

Although Churchill's records were contemporary to the events he discussed and provided what he described as a 'current account', none the less they were inspired by, and composed with, an eye to history – as

---

[4] Paul Addison, *The Road to 1945: British Politics and the Second World War*, London, 1975; see below, p. 14.

[5] Corelli Barnett, *The Collapse of British Power*, London, 1972 and *The Audit of War: The Illusion and Reality of Britain as a Great Nation*, London, 1986.

[6] *Second World War*, I, p. ix.

supporters and critics alike noted; Churchill was preoccupied with 'getting the record straight for posterity'. He did not keep a diary and once advised against doing so because it would subsequently reflect changes of opinion or decision. After the outbreak of war he wrote assiduously to his colleagues on issues which he might more easily have discussed with them at daily meetings. Chamberlain, the recipient of many such letters, considered that Churchill was writing for history. (Churchill, however, took the line that such letters enabled him to put his knowledge at the disposal of colleagues and avoid arguments at cabinet.)[7]

The detailed version of events which Churchill came to compose after the war existed in outline when he became prime minister in 1940. But neither the outline nor the fuller, later version, adequately reflect his views and perceptions at the time, or his appreciation of and response to the complexities and subtleties of politics and war. In retrospect Churchill looked upon the war as 'the unnecessary war'.[8] It was the result of his predecessors' failure to stop Hitler, despite his own repeated warning of danger. And the forces of destiny called him to the highest office in May 1940 – to save his country and deliver his people.

Churchill devotes most of the first volume of *The Second World War* to describing the failure of his predecessors to stop Hitler and thus prevent a Second World War. Although he criticises the weakness of Britain's leaders in the years immediately after 1918 and castigates the victors for the policies they pursued towards Germany, Churchill describes the 1920s as a period of 'marked improvement and recovery'.[9] He had high hopes for peace at the time: 'nor in the event was I proved wrong. War did not break out till the autumn of 1939.'[10] However, when MacDonald came to power, the conservative party failed, in opposition, to confront the labour government on imperial and national issues; and, in government, was privy to the worsening scene. MacDonald closed his eyes and ears to the disquieting symptoms in Europe. Baldwin, it seemed, thought the hope of the conservative party lay in accommodation with the labour and liberal forces. Churchill broke with Baldwin in 1931 over India, and he continued to warn against disarmament and urged concentration of air defences to a government and opposition 'so sunk in lethargy and [slackness] that ... warnings [were] ineffective'.[11] In Churchill's view, Baldwin considered that the British people wanted peace; and Baldwin was an astute party manager who wanted a quiet life and was venal in his desire

---

[7] Lord Moran, *Winston Churchill. The Struggle for Survival 1940–1965*, London, 1966, p. xvi; David Dilks, 'The Twilight War and the Fall of France', in Dilks, *Retreat from Power*, vol. II, pp. 42–4; *Second World War*, I, pp. 409–12.

[8] *Second World War*, I, p. x.　　[9] Ibid., p. 23.　　[10] Ibid., p. 46.

[11] Ibid., pp. 31, 64, 66, 76.

to hold on to office whatever the cost – even that of not defending his country. He broke his word on rearmament and could not make up his mind.[12]

Churchill recounts how he himself had wanted international pressure brought to bear on Germany to carry out decisions of the League of Nations. He advocated a policy of rearmament and wished the government to act with firmness and resolve through the League.[13] But Chamberlain, who succeeded Baldwin in 1937, wanted, Churchill suggests, to get on good terms with the dictators and come to terms with the totalitarian powers in a search for peace. The upshot was a series of mistaken policies formulated against the background of Chamberlain's limited outlook, inexperience on European matters, and foolish attitude of rebuttal to the United States.[14] Even after the outbreak of war, Churchill suggests, Chamberlain's administration (in which he himself was included as first lord of the admiralty) was insufficiently wholehearted and single-minded.[15] France and Britain remained impassive and Churchill's own plans for an offensive naval war were undermined.

This, on Churchill's account, is the background against which he became prime minister. The themes it establishes – the short-sightedness and indecisiveness of his predecessors, contrasted with his own prescience and resolve – are central to Churchill's own presentation of the three topics which will be examined in the three parts of this study: Churchill's reaction to the invasion and fall of France, Holland and Belgium, the Battle of Britain and his simultaneous handling of opposition to him in his own party in 1940; the nature of interest in Turkey and the Balkans and the decision to fight in the Middle East in late 1940; and the decision to intervene in Greece in March 1941. It is worth looking in some detail at how Churchill himself treats each of these subjects: first, because his treatment provides the basis for most subsequent accounts (even those which, on the surface, are very different); and, second, because the account he gives of his views and motives differs interestingly from his perception of matters at the time, as they will be reconstructed from contemporary documents in the chapters which follow.

In his discussion of the events leading up to Chamberlain's resignation, Churchill stresses two themes: that he had behaved towards Chamberlain with impeccable loyalty, and that his succession to the prime ministership came to him as the award of destiny. He had not intrigued; rather, the highest office had come to him as a matter of course. His leadership

[12] Ibid., pp. 165, 177, 181, 195–9, 216.   [13] Ibid., pp. 195–9, 181–2, 189.
[14] Ibid., pp. 226–9.
[15] Ibid., pp. 361–5, 367.

marked the end of party or political considerations and differences; and the country was behind his leadership. He recalls, for example, that during the Narvik debate he took his share of responsibility – having been closely involved and having had a full part to play. He tackled the labour opposition for bearing their share of responsibility for the events and he urged Chamberlain to stay on and strengthen his government. Moreover, it was only after he had done his utmost to persuade Chamberlain to stay, Churchill suggests, that it occurred to him that he might have to lead.[16] Indeed, the only encouragement he gave to this course was to keep silent during one, albeit vital, interview. And so, Churchill intimates, without intrigue or effort, the highest office fell to him: 'I felt as if I were walking with destiny and all my life had been but a preparation for this hour.' But it was also a reward for having been right: 'My warnings over the last six years had been so numerous ... and were so ... vindicated ... I could not be reproached either for making the war or with want of preparation for it'.[17]

Churchill goes on to explain how the reservations about him held by many conservatives were superseded by events. In any case, he says, they amounted to no more than the traditional loyalty of the party to its chosen leader.[18] Nor did he stoop to demagogic demand to purge the 'guilty men'. He was, he implies, statesmanlike and judicious. He won the support, not only of the conservatives, but of the liberal and labour parties, and the trade unions (implied by his including Bevin in the government). Not only did he bring political cohesion and unity, but he established an efficient machinery for conducting the war. This ultimately involved, he implies, his directing the war, aided by the chiefs of staff, while the war cabinet concentrated on home and party matters – and interfered less and less in operational ones.[19]

Churchill is particularly keen to emphasise those characteristics which endowed him and his leadership with particular qualities and which he implies marked him out from predecessors and contemporaries alike: defiance in face of adversity; readiness to take risks rather than play safe; and a determination to fight on and never surrender.

These themes dominate Churchill's account of the battle of France, its fall and the events of the summer of 1940 – the Battle of Britain and the preparations to resist invasion. Churchill recalls how, even towards the end of their struggle, he urged the French to continue to resist and to fight on, if necessary from Africa. Britain would, whatever happened, continue to fight and of that, he maintained, there was no question. No inquiries

[16] Ibid., pp. 583, 593–4.   [17] Ibid., p. 601.   [18] *Second World War*, II, p. 9.
[19] Ibid., pp 10–12, 16–20.

could, he instructed, be made of Hitler's peace terms and, he maintained, the question of whether they would fight on alone 'never found a place upon' the war cabinet agenda. 'It was taken for granted and as a matter of course.'[20]

Churchill stresses that this course was announced repeatedly; after Dunkirk and again after the French collapse.[21] The will to fight – and not to avoid difficult decisions – was illustrated by the 'hateful' decision to sink French vessels in North African ports rather than allow them to fall into German hands. Churchill suggests that the action made it clear to the world, and to the United States, that Britain would not give up. The same air of single-mindedness and resolution characterised preparations to resist invasion and strengthen the defences of the country; and despite the almost insuperable obstacles, 'the buoyant and almost imperturbable temper' of the country – which he himself 'had the honour to express' – may well have 'turned the scale'.[22] So successful were the preparations that the country, Churchill records, grew stronger 'from day to day.'[23] Such strength and confidence, manifest in the preparations and readiness to defeat invasion, the naval superiority and the acquired air superiority, are all conveyed as being the results of his leadership.

When he goes on to deal with his own replacement of Chamberlain as party leader, Churchill does so in the context of an account which suggests that there were no domestic differences and no political factions. Harmony and loyalty reigned supreme. Chamberlain was commended for his loyalty and courage; and was only eventually forced to retire because of grave illness. The account does not allude to any difficulty over the retirement. Churchill, prompted by the social and political implications of the Blitz of London, decided to make changes in the government – bringing in Herbert Morrison and moving John Anderson.[24]

When he comes to discuss British policy in the Middle East in 1940, Churchill puts forward the view that he and Eden were in strong agreement. The differences which subsequently arose about deploying troops to fight were the result of misunderstanding and Churchill's ignorance that an offensive was on the cards. Once he learned, he was 'delighted ... it should ... have ... first claim upon our strained resources'. He set to work, wiring Wavell to prepare to exploit it and pressing the Turks to take action should Bulgaria facilitate a German attack on Greece. He was, he says, 'so pleased' with the prospect of an offensive that he did

[20] Ibid., pp. 146, 152, 157–61, 172–4.   [21] Ibid., pp. 197–8.
[22] Ibid., pp. 206–12, 226–7.
[23] Ibid., pp. 213–24, 225–46.   [24] Ibid., p.326.

not worry about the result. He does not hint at any impatience with Wavell, or pressure put on him, beyond urging pursuit once the operation began.

Nor does Churchill's account of the conflicting demands of Greece after the Italian attack suggest that there was any great difficulty, division or political imperative. Churchill refers to the treaty of 1939, which 'we were bound to honour'; his attitude, according to the letters he prints, was tough. The Greek situation must dominate – but the problem was the Middle East command. 'How far short was the action taken by [it] of what was ordered and what we all desired.'[25]

When he comes to discuss the decisions and events leading to intervention in Greece in 1941, in face of the German attack, Churchill emphasises his open-mindedness to developments in the Balkans and Mediterranean theatre. Indeed his, he implies, was the wisest approach. There could be no easy or clear-cut decisions about reacting to German intervention in the Balkans, contrary to what critics at the time, and subsequently, might imply. These critics, Churchill suggests, do not see the wider picture or appreciate the strategic aims prompted by Hitler's moves in south-east Europe and the consequences for Russian action.[26]

According to Churchill, the general policy was that the Greek–Turkish situation should have priority after Tobruk, and a Turkish and Balkan front be formed; hence the offer of air forces to the Turks on 31 January and the decision to despatch Eden to the Middle East on a mission, the object of which was 'the sending of speedy succour to Greece'. Churchill himself continued to be whole-hearted – and he explains his second thoughts as the result of the incompleteness of the available information before certain wires from Eden arrived which referred to the unanimity of those on the spot to help the Greeks.[27] Moreover Eden's decisions – and consequently the approval of Churchill and his colleagues in London – rested on military, rather than political, considerations and on the fact that the Greeks had resolved to resist, irrespective of whether they were to receive help. Churchill, however, goes on to emphasise that – even at the stage of full cabinet approval on 24 February – strategic options remained open. The only definite steps taken had been to gather the largest possible strategic reserve in the Balkans and to make plans to transport an army to Greece.[28] Preparations could have been stopped by a single order – and, indeed, given that the Greeks had by late February departed from the Athens agreement, Britain could certainly have sought release from it.

Churchill's line is that there was no confusion or rushed reaction and

---

[25] Ibid., pp. 472–3, 485–6.   [26] Second World War, III, London, 1950, pp. 4–10, 25–7.
[27] Ibid., pp. 30–3, 60–3, 90–2.   [28] Ibid., pp. 62–9.

that options remained open. Britain was not cornered into any rash intervention. By early March he considered that the time had come to decide on whether to send the army of the Nile – a decision bound up with forming a Balkan front. He refers to the support for such a course (despite the risks, of which they were well aware) from the advisers on the spot who would bear the brunt; and he implies that there were no other options with regard to Turkey and Yugoslavia.[29] Although the situation by 5 March had changed for the worse, none the less those on the spot did not consider it hopeless. For them the right decision had been taken, and the temporary change of heart in London was, on this basis, overcome. At the cabinet on the 7th there was, Churchill explains, no division, no hesitation. He 'personally' felt that the 'the men on the spot had been searchingly tested' and the united cabinet resolved, without hesitation, to go ahead.[30]

As a close examination of the contemporary documents will show, Churchill's account obscures or denies much of the conflict, doubt and indecision evident at the time, and also tends to justify his own role. Yet it is Churchill's history which is reflected in much subsequent interpretation of these events.

The legacy of Churchill's history

The turn of events in 1940 and the exigencies of war left their mark on how contemporaries and later generations wrote about it. There has been, virtually, a Churchill school, which has transcended time and type, sharing the general tone in which Churchill described his leadership, if not implicitly that with which he described his predecessors. The school is catholic. It includes dissentients who may have accepted the dominant status quo yet grumbled or dissented on a number of counts; enthusiasts, particularly from amongst the new establishment, who assumed for themselves the Churchillian characteristics said to mark the new order; radicals who shared the implied view that Churchill was overturning a reactionary and debilitating order; populists who found more in the nature of that order than merely failing to stand up to Hitler; and utopians who saw in the composition, sentiment, intelligence and pursuits of the new order the opportunity for social and economic transformation.

The school has included Churchill's own contemporaries – politicians, advisers, professionals – and his and their biographers; it has included from the outset antagonists to the pre-war established order and pro-tagonists of the progressive coalition or the ideas which, it was alleged, began with Churchill in 1940.

[29] Ibid., pp. 84–7.   [30] Ibid., p. 94.

Of the biographers, Martin Gilbert remains the doyen. His account was determined by the brief he inherited from the original biographer, Randolph Churchill, that Winston Churchill should be 'his own biographer',[31] and by an unreconstructed view of the 1930s. Gilbert's aim, therefore, is to let the Churchill papers and supporting documents speak for themselves. Gilbert's account, though fuller than Churchill's own in The Second World War, does not differ in tone except to make, rather than assume, its subject's magisterial case. The themes and characterisation of the subject reflect those established by Churchill and his supporters at the time and in retrospect: the wartime heroism, courage, resolution and defiance of the man who dominated grand strategy and mastered the most minute of details. Gilbert does not question Churchill's own account, according to which political disharmony disappeared when he became prime minister, and he remained in office by virtue of popular and parliamentary acclaim. The biography is more explicit than its subject was in documenting the support for Churchill. He was 'at the helm of destiny' (Violet Bonham Carter), had a special 'courage' (Lloyd George), a 'wonderful vitality' and would be 'impossible' to replace (Brooke) and gave 'incomparably the most brilliant [leadership]' in memory 'save perhaps that of Mr Gladstone' (Lambert). And where the biography modifies the established view, it is to enhance Churchill's reputation yet further. The cavalier approach which Churchill tended to convey about his tackling of events (except when he wished to convey circumspection, as in the case of Greece) has been refined by Gilbert's introduction of qualities such as prudence and caution with which Churchill balanced his resolve and strategic direction: loyalty to an ally, though absolute as in the case of France in 1940, did not result in the reckless sacrifice of resources, while Churchill's doubts about Greece revealed statesmanlike prudence.

The accounts by or about officers in the services also tend to suggest that events were dominated by Churchill and to imply that the successful belonged to the new order which he brought with him. Arthur Bryant, biographer of General Sir Alan Brooke, chief of staff from December 1941, characterises relations between Churchill and Brooke as 'a partnership in genius'.[32] Churchill is depicted as standing head and shoulders above his compatriots, whilst Bryant's Brooke is something of a pastiche of the wartime hero, his characteristics apparently complementing those

---

[31] Martin Gilbert, *Finest Hour: Winston S. Churchill 1939–1941*, London, 1983, and *Road to Victory: Winston S. Churchill 1941–1945*, London, 1986.
[32] Arthur Bryant, *The Turn of the Tide 1939–1943*, London, 1957.

of Churchill, for whom his admiration was unconcealed: tenacity in resisting decisions with potentially dangerous military consequences; impatience with the failure to prepare adequate defences at home; holding out for the right course and scepticism about the politicians. It is the same with the biography of Portal,[33] chief of air staff from 1940. Any flaws in Churchill's temperament and judgement are seen as being 'more than counterbalanced by the prime minister's courage, determination, dynamism and broad sweep of ideas'.[34] Like Brooke, Portal, it is implied, belonged to a new category of men promoted by Churchill to positions of authority and amongst whose number Churchill liked to count himself: those unencumbered by reaction or the constraints of belonging to any particular establishment.

Other military writers, though critical of Churchill, accept none the less his dominance of events. For Major-General John Fuller, Churchill's regrettable deficiencies of temperament, judgement and vision led to a series of strategic failures and missed opportunities. Churchill 'was a man cast in the heroic mould, a berserker ever ready to lead a forlorn hope or storm a breach'.[35] For Generals Wavell and Auchinleck (the subject of John Connell's biographies)[36] Churchill's unquestioned dominance and temperament had considerable disadvantages. Manifestations of resentment were sporadic and centred on doubts about Churchill's appreciation of events, on his lack of judgement, his failure to grasp detailed tactical matters and his interference with military operations in the field. Connell, critical on his own account, and reserved on his subjects' accounts, none the less treats Churchill in the manner in which Churchill tends in his history to view himself – as the *Generalissimo*,[37] reflecting at the same time the implicit criticism made of Churchill by his generals. A similar impression is conveyed by the various contributors to John Keegan's book on Churchill's generals. Churchill is presented as a figure who would have 'really ... preferred to exercise command himself, at all times and in all places' and whose generals – certainly those with whom

[33] Denis Richards, *Portal of Hungerford, London*, 1977. See pp. 167, 178–9, 193.

[34] Ibid., pp. 183–5.

[35] J.F.C. Fuller, *The Conduct of War, 1789–1961*, London, 1961, p. 253. Or see Fuller's more dispassionate summary of the Greek campaign which concluded that the campaign had been 'a political one. It should never have been fought', J.F.C. Fuller, *The Second World War 1939–45*, London, 1948.

[36] John Connell, *Auchinleck. A Biography of Field-Marshal Sir Claude Auchinleck*, London, 1959; John Connell, *Wavell. Scholar and Soldier: To June 1941*, London, 1964, and *Wavell. Supreme Commander: 1941–3* (edited and completed by M. Roberts), London, 1969.

[37] Connell, *Auchinleck*, p. 268: '[Churchill] was the *Generalissimo*; soldiers were there to obey his orders, and if they did not, they could be dismissed, broken or shot.'

this book is concerned – did or did not accommodate themselves to what have become the somewhat stereotyped Churchillian ways.[38]

Central to the various military accounts is the predominant role of Churchill, who, it is implied by his supporters, ushered in a new order, the qualities of which were in contrast to the old. The stereotypes of the unreconstructed 1930s therefore remain, if only to provide the context for the new men.

Another book which, for very different reasons, tends to entrench the orthodoxy about 1940 and its implications is Paul Addison's *The Road to 1945*.[39] Addison's is a masterly study of radical politics, which is based on the assumption that 1940 saw the overthrow of the old order. The book is concerned with the progressive origins – inside and outside parliamentary politics – of the 1945 labour victory. Though not concerned with the strategic decisions of the war, he considers the organisation of the home front and the balance of power. Churchill's wartime coalition represented the end for pre-war conservatism. Those who had rejected the policies pursued by Chamberlain, and who had created an intellectual climate in opposition to the social and economic orthodoxies espoused by him, came into their own. When, after the outbreak of war, Chamberlain failed to put in place effective central planning machinery for wartime economic and industrial policy, that was the beginning of 'the eclipse of conservatism in World War 11'. The scene is set for Addison's examination of how, once Churchill became prime minister, social and economic progressivism in and out of government became the new orthodoxy.

In his study of *The Churchill Coalition and Wartime Politics*,[40] Kevin Jefferys refines Paul Addison's thesis. He suggests that the wartime swing to the left, particularly in terms of the balance within the coalition, was in practice less radical than contended by Addison. There was, he says, far less of a 'consensus' between the parties (based on a radical, reforming coalition ministry). Rather the 'central features [of the post-war settlement] were forged after – and not before – the election of 1945 . . . The war . . . made possible the creation of a brave new world; it did not make it certain'.

Jeffery's argument rests on a number of contentions about the nature of

[38] *Churchill's Generals*, ed. John Keegan, London, 1991. See esp. pp. 15, 56–9, 72, 74–8, 101.
[39] Paul Addison, *The Road to 1945: British Politics and the Second World War*, London, 1975; see also (but mainly for a later period) his 'Churchill in British Politics 1940–55', in J.M.W. Bean (ed.), *The Political Culture of Modern Britain: Studies in Memory of Stephen Koss*, London, 1987 and his *Churchill on the Home Front, 1900–1955* (London, 1992).
[40] Kevin Jefferys, *The Churchill Coalition and Wartime Politics, 1940–1945*, Manchester, 1991, especially pp. 4–7, 9–30, 36, 54–5.

wartime politics and policy. Central is his view that neither the fall of Chamberlain nor the succession of Churchill were inevitable, and that the divided allegiances amongst conservatives made for Churchill's maintaining continuity with the past. Churchill, he says, became prime minister largely because he had exploited the unexpected political crisis of April and May 1940. The conservative majority in parliament thereafter 'only reluctantly came to terms with the new Prime Minister and ... enhanced status of the Labour party'. Although Churchill's particular qualities were vital, none the less he was 'fortunate in being able to extend his authority so rapidly', helped by Chamberlain's 'unexpected departure' and the despatch of Halifax to Washington.

General academic historiography

One of the historians most active in reconsidering the interwar years, David Dilks, has also turned his attention to the war, and in a 1975 survey of Churchill's leadership, combined the view of Churchill's being a great man with one modifying the image passed down. Here Dilks addressed the significance of the discussions about peace at cabinet meetings on 26–27 May 1940. Dilks's conclusion that Chamberlain and Halifax did not fundamentally disagree led to his questioning 'the traditional belief that Churchill from the moment of his accession ... was determined to fight until the whole of Europe was liberated'. What mattered to both was the preservation of British interests. In a subsequent essay Dilks maintained that instead of the irreconcilable differences implied by 'the stern strictures' passed by Churchill himself upon his predecessor in *The Gathering Storm*,[41] relations between both Chamberlain and Churchill were characterised by mutual confidence, loyalty and affection; that they did not differ significantly in their views about the war; and that although they disagreed about Narvik, neither anticipated a German counter-strike or imminent attack.

Dilks's thesis has implications for a review of how far Churchill's view of Britain's interests reflected that of his predecessors. Certainly, the scholars who have tackled the detailed issues suggest far less difference than the Churchillian history (see below pp. 15–18). The tone set by R.A.C. Parker in considering the underlying causes and consequences of events suggests some degree of continuity between Churchill's administration and that of his predecessors. Parker's *Struggle for Survival*[42] sets

[41] 'The Twilight War and the Fall of France: Chamberlain and Churchill in 1940'. The essay originally appeared in *Transactions of the Royal Historical Society*, 5th series, 28 (1978),and in a different form in in Dilks (ed.), *Retreat from Power*, vol. II, 1981.

[42] R.A.C. Parker, *Struggle for Survival. The History of the Second World War*, Oxford, 1989.

out to consider the history of the war, how it was won and lost, its causes and consequences, by examining decisive episodes. In 'Britain Alone' he discusses the period from May to June 1940.[43] His dispassionate and elegant account distinguishes between the particular characteristics of Churchill's administration, and the continuity with its predecessor. For example, air power and aircraft production, essential to repel the German air attacks, had by the critical stage of late August and early September exceeded that of Germany, as a result of the priority given to the RAF by Baldwin and Chamberlain's government (and to fighters by Chamberlain's) and the work of Inskip, Kingsley Wood and Lemon. All of these provided the capacity which the new aircraft production minister, Beaverbrook, exploited.

Otherwise, recent scholarship, while incisive in qualifying individual parts of the story, has been cautious about modifying the overall political framework, based as this broadly is on the apparent contrast in all things and attitudes between Churchill and his predecessors. Scholars who have been refining historical understanding of the central, component parts of the war have not, on the whole, dissented from the broad Churchillian picture. As a result the momentum gathered by the scholarly investigations of individual subjects has not been matched where the question of Churchill's overall role – and whether it has been rightly or wrongly represented – is concerned. This may be partly on account of the sources (see below pp. 19–22): many of the official and private records tend not to provide evidence on which to elaborate the nature of activities and interventions. Not only is it not in the character of official records to suggest the immediacy with which decisions and discussions occurred, or to reveal the dissent and divisions on which they were based. But even the private papers – letters and diaries – of the time were constrained by the demands made by war on discretion and patriotism. Later historians have exercised similar discretion, rightly showing for the war years no inclination towards debunking – a vulgar thing in itself and, for this period, one which might convey a perverted sympathy for the forces of darkness or, at the least, a lack of patriotism.

The impact on the war of the historiographical review of the 1930s has therefore been muted. Revision has, for the most part, concentrated on the scholarly examination of individual issues in the context of the period itself. The perceived role of Churchill has been reconsidered in terms of the individual political and strategic issues arising during the war. For example scholars have re-examined a variety of subjects from the question of a negotiated peace to the different policy and strategy adopted for

[43] Ibid., pp. 44–60.

individual theatres or countries: France, Holland and Belgium; the relationship between Britain and America and the nature of the alliance; policy towards Spain, Vichy, the Soviet Union, the Pacific. The upshot of such investigations has been to suggest an approach by Churchill's administration at once more measured, more complicated, less clear in tone and substance than that conveyed to posterity by Churchill's own history or its school.

For example, David Reynolds's re-examination of Anglo-American relations and the wider considerations governing peace and war results in his modifying the categorical position suggested by Churchill's memoirs. Reynolds argues that the differences between the different 'camps' were far less extreme than often believed and that Churchill's private position on the range of issues from negotiated peace to relations with the United States was far less clear than his public stance.[44]

Elsewhere studies of individual areas of policy convey more uncertainty, hesitation and doubt than the official version, and they also modify in certain substantive details the older certainties of wartime history, implying greater similarity between the pre- and post-1940 regimes than has hitherto been fashionable.

Elisabeth Barker, who considered the decision to intervene in Greece in the wider context of policy in south-east Europe, reflected on the wider strategy, politics and diplomacy at issue. But whereas Churchill countered the critics by denying that the operation was a rash mistake without chance of success, she maintained that from the start it was seen as a 'military gamble', justifiable in the light of wider policy.[45] The differences which in Churchill's account appeared as no more serious than considerations rightly raised by those essentially in agreement, were identified as both more complex and contentious by David Carlton in his critical study of Eden. Carlton contends that Churchill and Eden not only differed, but reversed roles on the Greek question. Churchill was at first an enthusiast for intervention, but by March 1941 he had become more cautious. Eden, reluctant at first, became eager for military intervention. Behind policy towards Spain there also lay uncertainty, the result of differences between the foreign office and others, hesitation, doubt and a residue of 1930s sentiment. Denis Smyth's study of the first months of

---

44 David Reynolds, *The Creation of the Anglo-American Alliance, 1937–1941: A Study in Competitive Co-operation*, London, 1981, pp. 104, 176; David Reynolds, 'Churchill and the British 'Decision' to Fight on in 1940: Right Policy, Wrong Reasons', in R. Langhorne (ed.), *Diplomacy and Intelligence during the Second World War: Essays in Honour of F.H. Hinsley*, Cambridge, 1985, pp. 147–67. For Reynolds's further discussion of these things see his entry in the bibliography.
45 Elisabeth Barker, *British Policy in South-East Europe in the Second World War*, London, 1976, pp. 96–103; see also below, pp. 168–9.

Churchill's leadership, shows how Halifax and Hoare, the ambassador to Franco's Spain, opposed proposals which might provoke Spanish belligerency; and Hoare furthermore incurred the hostility of the left for his policy of economic inducements to Spain to keep neutral – appearing to be tantamount to the appeasement of fascist Spain.[46]

No recent book on Churchill has generated such public controversy as John Charmley's provocative biography, which has been taken by supporters and detractors alike to offer a thorough revision of accepted views about Churchill, and at last to remove the trappings of myth which Churchill wove around his own conduct.[47] But for the early years of the war, the treatment is uncontroversial;[48] indeed it reflects the framework and context established by Churchill himself, though it reconsiders some of the assumptions and modifies some of the views in the light of recent scholarship.

Churchill is considered in the context initially set out in *The Second World War*. Charmley's Churchill was the figure which history made him out to be in terms of belligerency, rhetoric, will. He was an 'emblematic prime minister . . . a symbol of resistance and defiance' who established his rapport with the 'nation' through his speeches and rhetoric. He stood out in contrast to the old appeasers (notably Halifax) and won the moral high ground because he was an anti-appeaser. He 'staked his own survival as prime minister upon a strategy of "no surrender"', the 'badge of his administration'; and he imposed his will and his vision on those about him. Less flatteringly, he emerged as dictatorial, dominating colleagues and generals alike on matters civil and military.

In some respects Charmley questions the accepted picture. For example, he argues that the 'myth' of 1940 should not conceal the fact that peace moves continued. He suggests that the three-pronged overall strategy – repelling invasion, superior air power and transatlantic reinforcements – was flawed. Churchill was wrong in thinking the United States was ready to enter the war (though Charmley adds that, privately, Churchill was not so certain about US readiness). He also indicates that Churchill's uncertain support amongst conservatives meant that for six months he was not in command of his own party: he was subsequently helped by Chamberlain's death, Halifax's despatch to the United States and the collapse of the allied front in France. None the less, Churchill

---

[46] David Carlton, *Anthony Eden: A Biography*, London, 1981, pp. 168–81; see also below, pp. 168–9. Denis Smyth, *Diplomacy and Strategy of Survival: British Policy and Franco's Spain 1940–1941*, Cambridge, 1986.

[47] John Charmley, *Churchill: The End of Glory. A Political Biography*, London, 1993.

[48] Ibid., pp. 371–452. See especially pp. 396–8, 401–8, 412, 418–19, 421–5, 428–30, 432–6, 439, 441–6, 450–1.

tended, according to Charmley, to act as though war had banished politics.

Aims, sources and method

There are, then, many studies of this period which have drawn extensively on the specialist, departmental and relevant political sources in order to illuminate, in considerable detail, the background of advice and information against which decisions may ultimately have been reached on a specific subject. The concern of their authors is to examine the way in which advice, decision, intervention and thinking unfolded on a given subject, irrespective of its centrality or dominance at any given moment.

The aim of this book is different. Its starting-point is the politics rather than the policy of the war. It reconstructs the way in which events appeared to those responsible, how they reacted and how their individual reactions were translated, by way of agreement, conflict and misunderstanding, into wartime decisions about strategy. The fine balance of interest, ideals and calculation which characterised the higher politics of peacetime became, if anything, more marked during the war, when those responsible could rely on even fewer certainties. It cannot be assumed that, because Britain was at war, Churchill's administration was any more cohesive, successful or morally better in terms of perceiving and pursuing national interests than its predecessors.

The book considers the central issues of the war as they emerged – the battle for and fall of France, the Battle of Britain, the defence and security of Egypt and the Middle East. It does not, therefore, set out to concentrate on individual areas of policy, diplomacy or strategy. Nor is this book about party politics, though the first part discusses how, in May 1940, Churchill lacked the whole-hearted support of his party, and how he overcame this. Nor does it examine the balance of parties inside and outside parliament or government, the role of the labour party or the broader area of social and economic policy. Nor will it discuss the official workings of the official wartime machine or the working out of detailed military policy in the different theatres, whether in the air, on land or at sea; nor the continuous diplomatic relations with individual countries.

This book is based on the private papers of those involved and on the public records.[49] The character of the private papers – the letters and diaries – written by the principal participants is as various as their authors are numerous. Of the war cabinet, the conservative members, Chamber-

---

[49] For details of the unpublished and published sets of papers, see below, bibliography, unpublished primary sources, and published primary sources.

lain, Halifax (and later Eden) were preoccupied by the international
events which faced the country. They had responsibility, knowledge,
experience and a view (often a changing one) and they continued to
matter (Chamberlain until he became ill). The Chamberlain papers
include his letters – to his sisters and step-mother – and his diary and offer
much detail for the first months of Churchill's leadership during the battle
for and fall of France, Holland and Belgium. Halifax's papers include a
diary and, though brief, modify and refine the official papers and Churchill's record; and among Eden's papers and notes are detailed accounts of
his discussions in Cairo, Athens and Angora and a note of his discussions
with Churchill (and colleagues), the substance of many of which were
published in the course of his autobiography. Beaverbrook, Hankey and
Dalton left collections which are valuable sources for particular issues,
and other members of the government, including Alexander, Attlee,
Bevin, Grigg, Lloyd, Sinclair and Woolton, left less for this period.

Of the records left by officials and advisers, Cadogan's diary is indispensable throughout the period (and Dilks's edition leaves nothing
out); and the diaries or other papers of the chiefs of staff, officers and
officials in London, diplomats, and commanders in the field (Brooke,
Portal, Newall, Dowding, Cunningham. Longmore, Keyes, Ismay, Palairet, Wavell – and papers by Dill and P und found in othe: collections),
both unpublished and published, are helpful for understanding the nature
of action and advice and the constraints to which the advised were
subjected on different occasions.

The private papers supplement, modify, and convey different emphases
or nuance to the public records. But for wartime politics, the public
records are also central, since the cabinet and its committees (meeting
formally or informally) provided the forum for discussion, advice and
decision about the war. The minutes of the cabinet itself, of the defence
committee and chiefs of staff committees (CAB) often include a record of
the individual contributions to discussion and provide a constant (if
somewhat abbreviated) source for what was central and how it was talked
about, and what was decided. They have been augmented and supplemented by the records of the prime minister's office, war office and the foreign
office particularly for the signals which passed between London and
Cairo or Athens and the record of discussions by those concerned on the
spot.

The public and the private sources for the war complement each other,
and sometimes they overlap. Private sources may sometimes be less
private than in peacetime; for while they may convey the details of
discussions, nuance and difference or the individual reaction to events
absent from official records, they may also exclude sustained reference to

disputes or decisions, or hypotheses about war on account of security. For one area, however, the papers, diaries, letters and collections of the politicians (Baldwin, Balfour, Brabazon, Cripps, Croft, Crookshank, Elliot, Hannon, Headlam, Linlithgow, Hoare, Lloyd George, Margesson, Monckton, Nicolson, the Selbornes, and Wallace, in addition to those already mentioned) are the only source. They alone reflect the political balance which increasingly tilted (and was helped to tilt) in Churchill's favour, showing how Churchill's position, which initially depended on a flimsy coalition of interests – labour, liberal and a minority of tory MPs – came to be secured by majority conservative support.

There is, finally, Churchill's own collection, the Chertwell papers up to 1945, which were opened only in 1993. For the period 1940–1 they do not provide a picture of Churchill or the war substantially different from that indicated by the other collections on which this book has been based. Rather, they complement and reinforce the interpretation here (in this book), which is based on other collections, and illuminate further the context in which Churchill operated.

For the 1940–1 period, the Chertwell papers include a variety of material: correspondence of a personal and political character; constituency material; speeches; and of ial material relating to the prime minister's office and to the war ce net. They provide a cross-section of Churchill's first year as prime minister: war cabinet papers and correspondence; official telegrams and minutes relating to different strategic (e.g. the Middle East) and diplomatic matters; summaries of intelligence; personal correspondence from his many admirers and friends of over fifty years – in politics and social life and the army; correspondence with colleagues about matters arising during the war and about specific issues (e.g. the Duke of Windsor).

Like the other private collections for the period, the Churchill collection includes, and often duplicates, official as well as more personal or private material. As in the others, the overall tone reflects something of the constraints on, and loyalties demanded of, politicians in wartime. The nature of the higher political life and direction of events is, by contrast with pre-war material, understated, and so far as the documents go, barely acknowledged. The Chertwell papers complement the other contemporary collections in this respect, and reinforce a view derived from them of the irrepressible and sophisticated nature of Churchill's political finesse; his links with those who continued the battle against Chamberlain; his masterminding of the party machine; his warm relations with the labour party and trade unions; and the trouble taken and personal attention given to every old friend from private, social, domestic or political life (often overlapping categories) in a correspondence, juxtaposed between official, political, personal. Some of the material can be found in other collections; some is in manuscript – but may exist in part elsewhere because a copy may have been taken or because it was summarised in diaries.

Churchill was later to recall that during the war he had written nearly one million words. Yet from his own pen there are few clues as to the private reactions and views which tend normally to contrast or modify the official record and position. Moreover, by force not merely of character, but of practice and intention, Churchill may have left a stronger mark on the official record than did many other contemporaries. Churchill's own contributions, both written and to discussion, were often rehearsed and made with a view to history. For most of his political life he had been writing history; and to friend and foe he appeared to be preparing the record of his own role in and for history. Speeches to the cabinet, the Commons, or to his friends and ministers were carefully rehearsed, as were his written notes and directions, and often went through a number of drafts, the final one being that published. Or, where other ministers or politicians tended to raise a subject one with another during the many informal opportunities which occurred, for example, before and after cabinet and other committee meetings, Churchill wrote formal letters, often more than one, a habit which was thought to be designed for the history books.

This cast of mind helped set the tone for the war not only in terms of the official record, but of his own. Churchill's papers, or those concerning political and strategic matters of which he was the author are consistent in this respect. Those in the Chertwell Trust are no exception. The impression of determination and political will is reinforced, but, strangely for a political collection, particularly that of the prime minister, there is little direct evidence that Churchill was other than the figure he became in his own history.

Using these sources, the following chapters will attempt to reconstruct the individual views of Churchill himself, and of those in the war cabinet responsible for the conduct of war – Chamberlain; Halifax, and later Eden; their advisers and officials, the three chiefs of staff, the war office and the generals, officials and diplomats in the the Middle East; the service ministers; and others – members of the government and backbench MPs. In addition to discussing the individual positions, the following chapters seek both to represent the way in which individual attitudes and stances continued to alter, and to consider the differences between the different groups, factions, interests. In order to represent the changes of nuance as well as of view, the text is built on short extracts from the contemporary sources, the smaller parts intended to contribute to the sum of the whole. The individual quotations have been fitted together as in a mosaic to provide the wider picture. Through the short extracts which have been reproduced it is hoped that the individual positions will emerge as they might have done at the time.

After a brief look backwards to the 1930s, the book begins with Churchill's coming to power. Part 1 considers how the context was set in the first months of Churchill's office for the populist view of Churchill as man of destiny under whose leadership the country, and the politicans, automatically united, seeming to bless that fate which gave them an inspired leader. It suggests that at the outset Churchill was not seen as the man of destiny presented in his own history, *The Second World War*. His coming to power – and staying there – did not result from the workings of fate or come about by universal demand. He was a shrewd politician who painstakingly overcame the opposition both within the party and outside it. He so balanced his position that he neither antagonised Chamberlain and his supporters, substantiating suspicion of disloyalty, nor stopped those who continued to hate Chamberlain from persisting with their illusion that he was one of them. His reaction to Hitler's attack on the west, the fall of France and the Battle of Britain, which combined strong rhetoric with, in practice, a Chamberlainite restraint in the use of scarce resources, made for greater political dominance.

Part 2 discusses British policy with regard to the Middle East from September 1940, when attention switched to that theatre, until December of that year, when Wavell launched Operation 'Compass' against the Italians. It considers the politics of strategy – the way in which the decisions about the war emerged from the vacillations and differences of those responsible. Churchill, though dominant, rarely had the decisive voice. Whereas he was cautious, often preferring to do nothing and wait on events, others were sometimes more hasty to act. For instance, it was Air Marshal Longmore who took the decision to divert aircraft from the Middle East after the Italians attacked Greece. But Churchill's caution was not apparent even to his closest colleagues. Eden and Wavell, for example, whose energies were directed towards the desert operation, did not realise that Churchill's (to them worrying) support for the Greeks was little more than rhetorical.

Part 3 examines the changing attitudes as attention shifted from the Middle East to the Balkans from January to March 1941 in face of a threatened German descent south-eastwards. It shows how, behind the British decision to intervene, political and military considerations were inextricably confused. The politicians and their advisers in London did not unite in favour of intervention on the basis of the many diplomatic or political arguments alone. Rather, they were prepared to accept a *fait accompli*, given the assurances by the commanders that military success was not impossible. For their part, the military commanders had initially accepted the prospect of military intervention only because they believed that such a course was inevitable for political and diplomatic reasons. In the long term, these controversies would have an important effect: Greece, rather than Turkey, became central to British interests in the Mediterranean and Middle East, so that by the end of the war Churchill seemed more ready than Chamberlain had ever been to sacrifice relations with eastern Europe, just so long as he could preserve a sphere of influence in Greece.

Retrospect

This book opens with Churchill's coming to power as prime minister in May 1940. Although he had been brought into government after the outbreak of war in September 1939, he had been out of office for the previous decade. Since the First World War, the character of politics had been determined, not by Churchill, but by Baldwin and Chamberlain. They had led the conservative party since 1923; and they had either led or dominated government throughout that time – except for the short periods of Ramsay MacDonald's labour administrations. In the 1920s this had been a matter of conservative governments between 1922 and 1929 interspersed with MacDonald's brief period of office in 1924, and after the labour government of 1929–31, the national government of the 1930s was very much under the conservative aegis. Though led until 1935 by MacDonald, the real influence was thought to lie with Baldwin. Once MacDonald stepped down in 1935 Baldwin took over as prime minister until 1937 when he, in turn, stepped aside for Neville Chamberlain.

Much of Churchill's support in May 1940 came from those who had throughout the 1930s set themselves against the national government in general or Neville Chamberlain in particular: the labour party which had gone into opposition and expelled MacDonald when he formed a national government; the Lloyd George liberals who withdrew support after a general election was called and the main group of Samuelite liberals who withdrew after the 1932 Ottawa agreement; those conservatives who, for a variety of reasons, continued to set themselves apart from their leaders; and the cross party groups of critics and sceptics which met after the outbreak of war. Indeed, the vehemence of personal and political reaction to Chamberlain – which ultimately helped Churchill – owed much to perceptions of Chamberlain's role as an architect of the national government and its economic policy.

The national government had been formed by MacDonald with conservative and liberal support in August 1931, after the labour cabinet failed to agree on measures to balance the budget and resigned. The majority of the labour parliamentary party went into opposition and expelled MacDonald and Snowden. George Lansbury became leader and Clement Attlee, his deputy, succeeded him in 1935. But the labour opposition did badly at the polls, reduced to 46 MPs in the 1931 general election, though recovering – to 154 – in 1935. The party remained in opposition until 1940 when it joined Churchill's coalition. Whatever the differences between the labour leaders – Attlee, Morrison, Bevin, Dalton, Cripps – and the different groups, there remained two sources of unity throughout the 1930s: rejection of MacDonald (seen as having betrayed the labour movement at the instigation of the bankers and the conservative architects of the national government) and antipathy to Chamberlain.

The liberal party, having abandoned the appearances of unity for which it strove in the 1920s, initially supported the national government in 1931. But Lloyd George and his family group withdrew when the election was called; and Samuel who had led the party into the national government (in Lloyd George's absence) also withdrew his group in 1932 on account of the Ottawa agreement. A third group led by John Simon continued to support the national government (having made overtures to the conservatives in the run up to the crisis). Like the labour party, the liberals did badly during the 1930s, though they might have already lost the fight to be second party to labour in the 1920s – falling from 158 seats in 1923 to 59 in 1929 (72 in 1931). In 1935 the official liberal group was reduced to 16 and Samuel lost his seat. Sinclair, who had been Churchill's ADC during the First World War, took over the leadership, and brought his party into government under Churchill in the 1940 coalition.

Although those who opposed Chamberlain in May 1940 and supported Churchill did so for a variety of reasons, in retrospect the explanations tended to be couched primarily in terms of rejecting Chamberlain's (and Baldwin's) policy of appeasement. Baldwin was thought to have failed to confront the dictators; and the case against him, and against his successor, Chamberlain, rested on the view that the policy of appeasement encouraged the dictators and led to war. With a different course the dictators could have been stopped before 1939. Instead there had been insufficient support for or confidence in the League of Nations; failure to employ collective security and sanctions; refusal to deal with Italy, no less than Germany. Such beliefs about missed opportunities were supplemented by additional considerations – the view that rearmament led to war or that there should be more rearmament; the view that Britain should be willing to threaten, or indeed resort to, war; the view that the Soviet Union should be courted, and drawn in to an old-fashioned four power pact.

Since the 1960s historians have modified this account of the decade leading up to the war – an account which Churchill had made very much his own. Baldwin and Chamberlain have been considered, not as the naive and ineffectual leaders Churchill implied, but rather as leaders whose calculations were endowed with a realism about the international balance and the nature of British interests and a shrewdness about domestic political sentiment often absent from the aspirations of their opponents. They saw the problem in terms of Britain's national – and global – interests which were threatened by three potential aggressors – Germany, Italy, Japan – in three different theatres: given the state of British defences, these could not be taken on at the same time. They did not presume (as their critics did) that the League of Nations provided the solution, or that the prospect of a collective answer to international aggression would materialise. Financial and military constraints, the consequences of the ten-year rule (under which Britain's defences were to be arranged on the basis that there would be no major war for ten years), and the political climate at home (pacifist and opposed to rearmament) made Churchill's position and that of his supporters appear unconvincing and incoherent.

Baldwin, after 1932, resolved to press ahead with air rearmament, carrying opinion with him by warning his compatriots of the dangers the country faced. He may have failed to give sufficient lead, as critics were later to claim; but, as he explained a propos the run up to the 1935 election, had he gone further it would have led to the defeat of his party which promised too few arms, and the return of the socialists who would have no rearmament.

From the 1935 election until the outbreak of war, the issues were increasingly perceived to be a matter of foreign policy and defence: the Italian attack on – and defeat of – Abyssinia in 1935–6; the German occupation of the Rhineland in 1936; the Anschluss with Austria in 1938; and the threat to Czechoslovakia posed and executed by Hitler. For the government the choices were narrow: either to deal piecemeal with the dictators so as to avoid hostility from three enemies on three different fronts – Japan, Italy, Germany – or to call their bluff. There was no reason to believe that the League or collective security would work. Baldwin did not resort to such a solution over the Italian invasion of Abyssinia, nor indeed to any other; and the upshot was the controversial Anglo-French agreement followed by Hoare's resignation, and, in due course the defeat of Abyssinia and the flight of the Emperor. Chamberlain made clear his scepticism about the League when, after Mussolini's victory, he urged successfully that economic sanctions be dropped.

Chamberlain succeeded Baldwin as prime minister in 1937. He believed that they could not 'provide simultaneously for hostilities with Japan and Germany'. He resolved on a policy of rearmament (based on financial strength) and a policy of separating – and dealing separately with – the dictators on the grounds of military prudence. Britain was in no position to take them all on together; and war should be avoided until the country was strong enough to win. This did not, Chamberlain used to stress, mean that war should be avoided at all costs. It did mean that the unpalatable realities which governed policy should be recognised (as had, for example, happened in the case of Mussolini's overrunning Abyssinia): that there would not be popular support for a war entered into lightly; that Britain was not in a position – at least not for the moment – to challenge, militarily, the aggressors; and that no threats should be made unless Britain were determined (and until she was in a position) to carry them out. Thus Chamberlain continued negotiations with Italy and lost Eden in consequence; reached an agreement at Munich over Czechoslovakia, which he did not see as an occasion for war, and lost a further minister, Duff Cooper. In the event, the Germans occupied Czechoslovakia as Chamberlain was pursuing a policy of guaranteeing (with the French) individual eastern European and Danube countries: Poland, Greece, Romania. He did not, however, follow the advice of those critics who wanted the Soviet Union brought into a grand alliance; and as a result he was held responsible for driving Stalin to sign a pact with Hitler and thereby leaving Hitler free to go to war without the worry of covering his other flank.

The historians of recent decades have, therefore, considered Baldwin's and Chamberlain's foreign policy in terms both of its complications, and of the realism or lack of sentimentality with which Baldwin and Chamberlain perceived and pursued Britain's interests. By contrast, political opponents at the time came to articulate their opposition in terms of antipathy to reactionary policy whether social and economic at home or appeasement abroad. The opponents – liberals, labour and conservative dissidents – disagreed, for example, with the policies of financial orthodoxy. Instead of a balanced budget, argued Lloyd George and his following (including some tory dissidents), there should be an expansionist economic policy based on deficit budgeting to stimulate the economy and tackle unemployment. Chamberlain, seen as a rigidly orthodox chancellor and prime minister, inspired cross party antipathy on such grounds.

But this and other objections tended to be lost under the the subsequent tendency to portray opposition in terms of antipathy to appeasement. Amongst the conservatives Churchill, for example, who had parted company with his leaders over India, subsequently appeared to be at odds with them on account of their inertia towards the dictators; Eden appeared to have become disaffected because of Chamberlain's appeasement of Italy in the spring of 1938; Duff Cooper, who resigned as first lord of the admiralty after Munich, believed they should have fought; Harold Macmillan, who supported a course of collective security through the League and voted against the abandonment of sanctions against Italy in 1936, espoused Keynsianism – a managed economy and an expansion of the welfare state – along with his friend, the tory MP Bob Boothby, on the lines advocated by Lloyd George. This group, barring Churchill and Eden, was to remain outside the government after the outbreak of war in 1939, and to vote against Chamberlain with the labour and liberal opposition in the Narvik debate; its members were known as 'glamour boys' or 'tory rebels' and were linked with Churchill. As dissidents their numbers could extend to include Churchill's personal circle of friends, followers and advisers, Brendan Bracken MP, Desmond Morton, Frederick Lindemann and Roy Harrod.

After Munich, it was to this group that labour feelers were directed, prompted by Stafford Cripps who, at one stage, hoped for an anti-Chamberlain alliance of tories, liberals and themselves or an international anti-fascist front which included the Soviet Union. The labour opposition seemed to have in common with the conservative rebels a number of sentiments: loyalty to the League; support for collective security; support for sanctions as a means to deter aggression. (The labour party, in addition, opposed rearmament and conscription and included pockets of the latent pacificism which had characterised the independent labour party.) There was also a shared, and increasing, antipathy to Chamberlain. After the outbreak of war Attlee made it clear that the labour opposition would not join the government under Chamberlain (although it was not entirely clear that some of the leaders – Alexander, Morrison and Greenwood – might not relent). The liberal opposition under Sinclair also refused to join (at least on the terms offered) – although about thirty national liberals led by Simon and Hore-Belisha continued to support the government (though Hore-Belisha resigned from the government in January 1940).

Although labour and the liberals refused to join the government after the outbreak of war, Churchill and Eden were included, and as a result separated by office from the twenty or so backbench MPs who remained critical of Chamberlain. Amery now presided over the critics (his offer to join the goverment having been rejected). For them and for the labour and liberal members, Chamberlain remained the focus of personal and political attack (with Simon and Hoare) – for having failed to prevent war by the 'wise collective organisation of peace', as Morrison put it during the Narvik debate, and for failing to organise matters effectively when at war. An all-party action group of MPs met under the leadership of the national liberal MP, Clement Davies (who resigned the government whip in December 1939), some of its members pressing the example of Lloyd George in the previous war; and under Lord Salisbury a watching committee established in April 1940, served as an additional focus for the discontented.

Churchill, who had become first lord (bringing into the the admiralty Lindemann as head of a new statistical section and Roy Harrod as an economist) proposed a number of naval initiatives. They were designed to bring not only tactical victory, but also the propaganda advantage of appearing to seize the initiative at a time of stalemate after the rapid defeat of Poland in September 1939. One such scheme involved mining the Rhine; a second stopping the transport of iron ore from Sweden to Germany. Churchill's own account of his activities as first lord suggests that his original plans and intentions were thwarted by colleagues; and the proposal to stop the iron ore, which ultimately became the Narvik expedition – called after the Norwegian port which it was intended to seize – had been much delayed and much altered. Narvik failed; the British forces failed to land and were driven back into the sea. In the House of Commons, the adjournment debate on 7 and 8 May turned into a 'Narvik debate', or rather one in which Chamberlain came under attack from his opponents (including the conservative critics led by Amery) for his uninspired leadership and inadequate preparation of the country for war. Though he did not lose the vote, his majority was reduced; and, having sought once again, but without success, to broaden his government by including the liberal and labour opposition, he decided to resign. Of the two possible successors, Churchill and Halifax, Churchill's claims triumphed and on 10 May he became prime minister.[1]

[1] This account draws on: Sidney Aster, *The Making of the Second World War*, London, 1973; Maurice Cowling, *The Impact of Hitler: British Politics and British Policy, 1933–1940*, Cambridge, 1975; Dilks (ed.), *Retreat from Power*; Michael Howard, *The Continental Commitment: The Dilemma of British Defence Policy in the Era of Two World Wars*, London, 1972; Middlemas and Barnes, *Baldwin*; Simon Newman, *March 1939: The British Guarantee to Poland: A Study in the Continuity of British Foreign Policy*, Oxford, 1976; R. A. C. Parker, 'British Rearmament, 1936–1939: Treasury, Trade Unions and Skilled Labour', *English Historical Review* 96 (1981), 306–43, R. A. C. Parker, 'Economics, Rearmament and Foreign Policy: The United Kingdom before 1939 – A Preliminary study', *Journal of Contemporary History*, 10 (1975), 637–47; G. C. Peden, *British Rearmament and the Treasury 1932–39*, Edinburgh, 1979; D. C. Watt, *How War Came: The Immediate Origins of the Second World War, 1938–1939*, London, 1989; Williamson, *National Crisis and National Government*.

Part I

Churchill, the conservative party and the war

It is curious that history repeats itself. Bonar refused to become Prime Minister in '15 [*sic*] when Lloyd George formed the first coalition; and I understand that Halifax refused for very much the same reason vis-à-vis Winston. Each would have been overshadowed by a Man of Destiny. Winston got a poor reception in the House compared with Neville; and in the House of Lords Neville's name was received with a full-throated cheer, whereas Winston's name was received in silence. It is quite clear from the speed with which he made his arrangements that the intrigue had been going on for some time, and that plans had already been laid; and his appointments are being heavily criticised in private.

Davidson to Baldwin, 14 May 1940

If only we had had another year of preparation we should have been in a far stronger position and so would the French. But anyway, and whatever the outcome, it is clear as daylight that if we had had to fight in 1938, the results would have been far worse. It would be rash to prophesy the verdict of history but if full access is obtained to all the records, it will be seen that I realised from the beginning our military weakness and did my best to postpone if I could not arrest the war. But I had to fight ... against both labour and liberal opposition ... who denounced me for trying to maintain good relations with Italy and Japan, for refusing to back Republican Spain against Franco and for not ... standing up to ... Hitler at each successive act of aggression. It is they who ought to be held responsible for this fight, but they don't admit it naturally and perhaps they will succeed in covering up their tracks ...

Chamberlain to Ida, 25 May 1940

1   The opposition to Churchill and its causes

When he came to write his history of the Second World War, Churchill described his becoming prime minister in terms of destiny:

Thus, then, on the night of the 10th of May ... I acquired the chief power in the State ... I went to bed at about 3 a.m. I was conscious of a profound sense of relief. At last I had the authority to give directions over the whole scene. I felt as if I were walking with destiny, and that all my past life had been but a preparation for this hour and for this trial. Ten years in the political wilderness had freed me from ordinary party antagonisms. My warnings over the last six years ... were now so terribly vindicated, that no one could gainsay me. (Winston S. Churchill, *The Second World War*, volume I, *The Gathering Storm*)

Churchill's retrospective sentiments on becoming prime minister – relief, a sense that fate had marked him out, detachment from the normal party antagonisms – were shared by many at the time in parliament and the country. But many contemporaries on the conservative side did not concede his claims on destiny. Though he did not acknowledge that the antipathies which he had evoked on many counts had not vanished, he recalled the louder cheer for Chamberlain when both men entered the House of Commons for the first time after he had become prime minister. In his first weeks as prime minister he failed to dispel the scepticism (if not muted hostility) of his own side on a number of counts: his alleged intrigue and impatience to become prime minister; his poor judgement, disorderly mind and erratic habits; his choice of men; his very conservatism, linked as this was to suspicions of disloyalty to his party and his links with the opposition. His contemporaries saw many analogies with Lloyd George's replacing Asquith in 1916; and the lessons of that analogy did not escape Churchill. He cultivated the restraint which had helped to bring him to office both in his treatment of his predecessors and in his refusal to give vent, publicly, to his views on their deficiencies.[1]

The pages which follow consider the critical reaction to Churchill from his own side. Much of the criticism reflected long-standing views of

[1] Colville diary, 1 June 1940; Davidson to Baldwin, 14 May 1940, SB 174: 275–7.

Churchill. Some of it came from those, like Halifax and Chamberlain, on whose support he counted for his own survival. Some of it came from backbenchers with a more important past than the future which Churchill envisaged for them. Such observations – often trivial in themselves – are presented here in order to suggest that the unease which Churchill had long evoked did not die down immediately he became prime minister, and as a prelude to considering how he established himself securely as leader.

As first lord of the admiralty, Churchill was suspected of having been part of the campaign to replace Chamberlain. The admirals thought it had been going on for some time. Lord Chatfield, the former chief of naval staff and minister for coordination of defence, thought the 'struggle for power and place [had been] carefully engineered over many months'. Admiral Cunningham, commander in chief of the Mediterranean, and former deputy chief of naval staff, noted that Churchill had got 'what he has been intriguing for'. Neither they nor the former party chairman and Baldwin's friend, Lord Davidson, were taken in by Churchill's impeccable behaviour when he separated himself from the government's critics during the Narvik debate which followed the failure of the British expedition to Norwegian ports. Chatfield thought it 'a "put up show"' and Davidson thought it clear 'that the intrigue had been going on for some time, and that plans had already been laid'. Churchill was thought to be 'loving every moment of it [the debate] which was bringing him to power'.[2]

Nor was it clear that Churchill was an adequate replacement for Chamberlain, with whom he was contrasted unfavourably; not that he was sufficiently judicious or orderly in mind and habits; nor that he could command loyalty. Lord Hankey, chancellor of the Duchy of Lancaster – and former secretary to the cabinet and committee on imperial defence – thought Chamberlain both 'well nigh indispensable as PM' and the 'only man who can hold Winston' whose 'judgement [was] not 100% reliable'.[3] Sir Alexander Cadogan, permanent under-secretary at the foreign office was 'not at all [sic] sure of Churchill' and did not think they could get a better PM than Chamberlain.[4] Churchill's mind, methods and failure to concentrate worried Halifax who had 'seldom met any body with stranger gaps of knowledge or whose mind works in greater jerks'. A 'long and rather discursive discussion' left him 'rather uneasy as to Winston's methods' as well as the hours he kept; and it drove Halifax 'to despair

[2] Chatfield to Hankey, 'Monday' (13 May 1940), Hky 4/32; Cunningham to his aunt, 11 May 1940, BL Add. MS. 52558; Davidson to Baldwin, 14 May 1940, SB 174: 275–7.
[3] Hankey to Hoare, 12 May 1940, BBK C/308; Hankey to Chamberlain, 9 May 1940, NC 7/11/33/96.
[4] Halifax diary, 13 May 1940; Headlam diary, 10 May 1940; Cadogan diary, 9 May 1940.

when [Churchill] work[ed] himself into a passion of emotion when he ought to make his brain think and reason'. Never had he seen 'so disorderly a mind' and there was 'no comparison between Winston and Neville as Chairman' and 'if it came to the point our ways would separate'.[5] Chamberlain was 'much distressed by [Churchill's] apparent inability to concentrate on the business' and by his 'readiness to go off on side issues of little importance'. There was, it was said 'no grasp of the situation as a whole'.[6] Cadogan found Churchill too 'rambling and romantic and sentimental and temperamental' and Chamberlain to him was 'still the best of the lot'. Churchill could be 'rather theatrically bulldoggish' and during a crisis endorsed 'any wild idea'.[7] The king, after the first week of Churchill's government, had apprehensions about his administrative methods and did not find him sufficiently forthcoming – neither 'very easy to talk to' or 'willing to give him as much time or information as he would like'. He had 'difficulty in making contact with Winston'.[8]

To Sir Henry (Chips) Channon, the Chamberlainite diarist, who thought 'fantastic the turn of the wheel', Churchill lacked the 'great dignity of Neville' and there was 'always the quite inescapable suspicion that he love[d] war which broke Neville Chamberlain's better heart'.[9] Sir John Dill whom Churchill appointed chief of imperial general staff, was said to entertain doubts both about Churchill's having war-mongered in the 1930s and about his cashing in on it now.[10]

Churchill's appointments were held against him. They seemed to testify to his lack of judgement and exacerbated the unease provoked by suspicions of treachery to Chamberlain, his disloyalty to the party and the dubious nature of his conservatism.

The war cabinet, which was ready on the night of the 10th, had five members: three conservatives, Churchill, Chamberlain and Halifax and two labour men, Arthur Greenwood (without portfolio) and Clement Attlee (lord privy seal). Halifax remained foreign secretary, Chamberlain became lord president of the council.

Other government appointments, outside the war cabinet, included a proportion of posts for labour, liberals and tory rebels. The service

---

[5] Halifax diary, 11, 12, 13, 27, 30 May, 19, 24 June 1940.
[6] Chamberlain restricted his critical observations to a diary entry; and unlike colleagues, restrained himself for four months. Chamberlain diary, 14 Sept. 1940.
[7] Cadogan diary, 26, 29 May, 22 June 1940.   [8] Halifax diary, 5, 18 June 1940.
[9] Channon diary, 6, 18, 20 June 1940; see also Chamberlain's reference to the burden of giving directions 'that would bring death and mutilation and misery to so many', in Chamberlain to Hilda, 17 May 1940, NC 18/1/1156. See also below, p. 55 note 33.
[10] Reith diary, chapter 5, 'John Reith and the Second War (1)' 16 Aug. 1940; Dill to Montgomery-Massingberd, 13 July 1940, MM 160/12; Headlam diary, 7 Aug.1940.

ministries were thus divided: the war office went to Anthony Eden, a former leader of the rebels; the admiralty to the labour party's A.V. Alexander; and the leader of the liberals, Sir Archibald Sinclair, became secretary of state for air. Elsewhere it was the same story. Labour was further strengthened in the government by Herbert Morrison, minister of supply, Ernest Bevin, minister of labour and national service and Hugh Dalton, minister for economic warfare. The leader of the conservative anti-Chamberlain group since the outbreak of war, Leo Amery, was given the India office, and its chief member, Duff Cooper, became minister for information. Other acolytes were given jobs, junior – Brendan Bracken, Bob Boothby and Harold Macmillan; and senior – Beaverbrook and Wood. Beaverbrook became minister for aircraft production. Kingsley Wood, an alleged fellow-intriguer, became chancellor of the exchequer. Sir John Simon and Sir Samuel Hoare were dropped.

There was bemusement about the appointments in general and hostility towards particular ones, exacerbated by the feeling that there had been something of a revolution. Chamberlain considered Churchill to be 'surrounded by a very different crowd' from that to which he was accustomed. He had no confidence that the new administration would be more effective than the last. Indeed they could not be given the 'real reason' for failure to take the initiative: 'comparative weakness because we haven't yet ... caught up with the German start [and] that fact remains'.[11] Other critics doubted whether the changes in general were an improvement on what went before. At best the new men had little experience; at worst they seemed to be chosen without reason, as if at random.

Lord Hankey, who remained chancellor of the Duchy of Lancaster, worried at the sudden replacement at a time of crisis of 'the eight key leaders by men without experience of war or ... public affairs (other than very sordid politics) most of whom ... consistently opposed all war preparations'. He did not 'feel any confidence in the new administration'.[12] Cadogan, though glad Halifax remained at the foreign office, thought the 'other cabinet changes none too good'. Chatfield considered the new people 'a collection of wild men' who would be 'odd bed fellows'. He thought Churchill seemed 'to have challenged fate by the selection of some of his colleagues'; and Channon was surprised that Lloyd George had not been 'offered a decorative post': 'stranger people ha[d] drawn

---

[11] Chamberlain added: 'the stories of the method of government making ... are disagreeably reminiscent of Lloyd Georgian ways'. Chamberlain to Mary, 11 May 1940, NC 1/20/1/198; Chamberlain to Ida, 11 May 1940, NC 18/1/1155.
[12] Hankey to Hoare, 12 May 1940, BBK C/308.

numbers in this mad lottery'.[13] The feeling was that the cabinet as a whole was 'not a very inspiring body'.[14]

Individual appointments provoked criticism on the grounds of inadequate experience, ability, vision, strength or purpose. In the war cabinet itself, Attlee and Greenwood seemed an addition of dubious advantage. Greenwood, Chamberlain thought, would be 'amiable and agreeable enough' but could not 'contribute much else'. He seemed to Dalton to be 'very slow and . . . in danger of being run by his officials'. His inclusion, and that of Attlee instead of Simon and Hoare, suggested to Halifax that 'certainly we shall not have gained in intellect'.[15] Attlee in the House of Commons seemed negligible 'poor stuff. He'll never be a prime minister' according to Captain Harry Crookshank, financial secretary to the treasury. Sir Cuthbert Headlam, a conservative backbencher (and chairman of the northern counties conservative area), echoes these descriptions: 'poor stuff – feeble, inaudible, ineffective'.[16]

Of the service ministers, Eden at the war office seemed (though not universally) the most plausible, and Sinclair at the air ministry the least. While Chatfield thought that Eden 'may do well', the permanent under secretary at the War Office, Sir (Percy) James Grigg, thought him 'a poor feeble little pansy'. Lord Trenchard, the distinguished Marshal of the Royal Air Force, refused to serve as commander-in-chief under Eden.[17]

Alexander's appointment as first lord of the admiralty, according to Davidson 'won't be popular'; and Headlam, after hearing him in the house was not impressed and thought he would 'play second string to Winston'.[18] Sinclair at the air ministry seemed to Halifax 'a major disaster', to Davidson 'terrible'; and to Hankey it was a source of astonishment that 'an untried wholly inexperienced politician' should replace Hoare at 'the key service'. Chamberlain had always had 'a very poor opinion of Sinclair and had told Winston so but Winston gave him this appointment because he didn't want him in the war cabinet'; and Beaverbrook considered the appointment 'thoroughly bad'.[19]

[13] Cadogan diary, 11 May 1940; Chatfield to Hankey, undated c. 13 May 1940, Hky 4/32; Chatfield to Hoare, c. 13 May 1940, Templewood XII:4; Channon diary, 13 May 1940.
[14] Headlam diary, 18 June 1940; Wallace diary, 26 June 1940.
[15] Chamberlain to Churchill, 11 May 1940, NC 7/9/82; Halifax diary, 11 May 1940; Dalton diary, 18 June 1940; Wallace diary, 7 Aug. 1940.
[16] Crookshank diary, 11 June 1940; Headlam diary, 18 June 1940.
[17] Grigg to Grigg, 15 July, 6 Oct. 1940, PJGG 9/6/8, 9/6/9; Chatfield to Hankey, 'Monday' (13 May 1940), Hky 4/32; Reith diary, 5 Aug. 1940.
[18] Headlam diary, 9 July 1940; Davidson to Baldwin, 12 May 1940, SB 174:273–4.
[19] Halifax diary, 12 May 1940; Halifax to Hoare, 8 July 1940, Templewood XIII:20; Davidson to Baldwin, 12 May 1940, SB 174:273–4; Hankey to Hoare, 12 May 1940, BBK C/308; Chamberlain to Hilda, 15 June 1940, NC 8/1/1161; Chamberlain diary, 15 June 1940.

Wood, at the exchequer, was thought to be mediocre and suspected of disloyalty to Chamberlain.[20] Beaverbrook was hardly liked or trusted. Halifax had been amused by a friend's 'horror' at Beaverbrook's appointment, but thought 'in these days one can't be too particular'; Headlam 'utterly distrusted[ed] the man and ... ha[d] little faith in his so called "dynamic" qualities'; and, after almost three months of the new government, Dill found that 'Beaverbrook and others of the PM's galère made him shudder, as they would any decent fellow'; and Headlam claimed that 'Everyone is agreed that personally he [was] a crook.'[21]

Apart from the doubts as to what the new labour colleagues would contribute because of lack of ability or experience or both, or whether they would strengthen the government, Bevin came out better than Morrison. Bevin worked 'hard for the war and a little harder for socialism', and despite 'rather woolly talk' he had 'practical ideas'.[22] Morrison by contrast was said by Harold Balfour, under-secretary of state for air, to be 'definitely no good' and by Macmillan to be 'a timid man'; and, in his own party, Sir Walter Citrine thought him 'the least satisfactory of the labour ministers' and 'much too tangled with his officials'.[23]

Worst of all were 'the glamour boys' – the conservative rebels whose 'only merit ha[d] been long subservience to Winston', or so it was thought. They had been disloyal or connived at treachery, and yet Churchill had rewarded them. Channon was struck by how 'the glamour boys', now 'so prominent and powerful, after being fallow for so long [were] a makeshift and shoddy lot. Their only merit had been long subservience to Winston ... Morton an Oppenheim character ... Lindemann the Berlin-born scientist and snob ... Roy Harrod a theoretical, oriental-looking don'.[24]

Bracken became Churchill's PPS and a privy counsellor, which, there was 'general agreement' was 'little short of a scandal' and the king had been 'much surprised and ... disturbed at being invited to make ... Bracken a privy counsellor'[25] and had made his feelings clear to Churchill through his private secretary.[26] Cooper, the minister for information, was not according to Beaverbrook '"in touch with the public" and had

20 Reith diary, 22 June 1940; Dalton diary, 22 July 1940; Crookshank diary, 2 Sept. 1940; Lloyd George to Stevenson, 4 Oct. 1940, pp. 237–40.
21 The friend to whom Halifax referred was Victor Cazalet. Halifax diary, 15 May 1940; Headlam diary, 11 July, 1 Aug. 1940; Reith diary, 3 Aug. 1940; Butler to Hoare, 6 Sept. 1940, Templewood XIII:17:160.
22 Beaverbrook to Hoare, 27 June 1940, BBK C/308; Cadogan diary, 14 Aug. 1940; Hankey to Chamberlain, 4 Oct. 1940, NC 13/18/85; Dalton diary, 3 Oct. 1940.
23 Dalton diary, 14 Aug. 1940; Wallace diary, 4 Oct. 1940; Crookshank diary, 8 Oct. 1940; Headlam diary, 24 June 1940.
24 Channon diary, 3, 10 Oct. 1940.
25 Halifax diary, 5 June 1940; Headlam diary, 18 June 1940.
26 Colville diary, 1 June 1940.

the outlook of a small and unrepresentative set in ... society'; and he very quickly came to fail both with the newspapers who 'suspect[ed] him of a desire to marshal ... [them] under his orders' and with the public for sending his son to New York and not displaying 'more ... faith in our ability to beat off attack and stand together as a united race'. His attempts 'to dragoon the press and regiment the people ... made him a target for the newspapers'.[27] Macmillan was 'too self centred, too obviously cleverer than the rest of us. He never will let the other man have his say and he invariably knows everything better than the other man.'[28]

Their jealousies and ambition rather than their patriotism were thought to have led to the attack on Chamberlain and the disloyalty to the party. Chamberlain himself resented their wrong-minded explanation of events. For him, Britain's weakness was largely due to the refusal to rearm of those who were now attacking him. Moreover, the delay in going to war which they now deplored had been to Britain's advantage: in another year Britain would be 'in a far stronger position and so would the French ... and whatever the outcome ... it [was] ... clear that if [they] had [had] to fight in 1938 the results would have been far worse'. Nor did the serving members seem to realise 'that though you can double your TA with the shake of the pen, you can't do the same with the equipment'.[29] But the attacks by his opponents on his conduct of peace and war seemed to be as much the result of their envies and desire for office, as of their patriotism. Not only were certain MPs 'the Amerys, Duff Coopers and their lot ... savaged by a sense of frustration because they could only look on', but Chamberlain had failed to take account of 'the seekers after office, the forty thieves outside and the Quislings inside the government'. The result was the 'exhibition of personal and party passion' during the debate, and the 'scene of disgusting jubilation ... [with] fellows like Harold Macmillan yelling themselves hoarse' after it. Moreover the personal dislike of Simon and Hoare 'had reached a pitch'; and this combined with Chamberlain's 'handling ... Labour roughly, his failure to handle the press at all, his coldness to his backbench friends, and ... his own bidding his hand about Norway' – perhaps 'most important ... [though] not directly responsible for the parliamentary revolt'.[30]

These promotions provoked comparison with Lloyd George and 1916. They led both to regret at the ousting of the 'real' conservatives in favour

[27] Chatfield to Hankey, undated, c. 13 May 1940, Hky 4/32; Beaverbrook to Hoare, 27 June 1940, BBK C/308 and 14 July 1940, Templewood XIII:17; Nicolson diary, 3 Aug. 1940; Butler to Hoare, 20 July 1940, Templewood XIII:17.
[28] Headlam diary, 24 June 1940.   [29] Chamberlain to Ida, 25 May 1940, NC 18/1/1158.
[30] Chamberlain to Ida, 11 May 1940, NC 18/1/1155; Davidson to Baldwin, 12 May 1940, SB 174: 273–4; Reith diary, 8 May 1940.

of 'the jackals' and to resolve to keep the party together on the back-
benches until after the war, when it would emerge with a new leader. The
conservative rebels were 'Quislings', the 'political fifth column' or 'the
Treachery Bench'; they had, it was thought, 'a great deal to answer for'; it
was like 'old times ... seeing the vultures gathered together whispering in
corners'; 'the glamour boys ha[d] all got jobs'; Eden and Margesson were
'equal first as head of the Quislings'; and the criticism 'amongst those ...
personally devoted to [Chamberlain] at [his] treatment and ... the way
the "Treachery Bench" has been given office ... would certainly have
broken out if there had been any change in the leadership'.[31] There were
more direct allusions to 1916. The 'crooks [were] on top as they were in
the last war'; 'the method of government making ... [was] disagreeably
reminiscent of Lloyd Georgian ways' and there was a danger that
Churchill would 'build up a "Garden City" at No. 10, full of the most
awful people'.[32]

Churchill was 'putting in the jackals and ousting those who had done
well of ... the respectable rump of the conservative party'; and 'all those
faithful to the Baldwin-cum-Chamberlain tradition' would be dropped;
there was 'a definite plot afoot to oust ... all the gentlemen of England
from the government, and even ... the House of Commons'; and it would
be 'years before a really conservative government comes in again'.[33]

Yet there would be no split in the party: Chamberlain would co-
operate as leader and he hoped 'that the party will loyally accept the
change and follow [his] example' – but only for the war. With Chamberlain, Halifax and Wood giving 'some sort of respectability to the firm ...
[they] ought ... to keep the party together and compact on the backbenches'; and though it should support the government in the prosecution of
the war, afterwards it must 'play its part, and ... look carefully for and
... nurse the next leader of the party from amongst its own ranks'. Meanwhile, they 'must keep [their] powder dry [so] ... that when the war is
over ... [they can] re-establish some moral standards in the new world of
politics'.[34]

The disagreeable implications of Churchill's rewarding the rebels at the
expense of those 'faithful to the Baldwin-cum-Chamberlain tradition'
were compounded by their connection, and his own, with the labour
party. His success had not only been at the expense of a 'really conserva-

---

[31] Davidson to Baldwin, 12, 14 May 1940, SB 174: 273–4, 275–7; Hankey to Hoare, 12 May
1940, BBK C/308; Chamberlain to Hilda, 17 May 1940, NC 18/1/1156.
[32] Chamberlain to Ida, 11 May 1940, NC 18/1/1155; Cadogan diary, 11 May 1940;
Davidson to Baldwin, 14 May 1940, SB 174; 275–7.
[33] Davidson to Baldwin, ibid.; Channon diary, 18, 29 May 1940.
[34] Chamberlain to Hilda, 17 May 1940, NC 18/1/1156; Davidson to Baldwin, ibid.

tive government' now, but also at the expense of one in the future;[35] the socialists would triumph, having gained and exploited the advantage during the war. For this Churchill would be held responsible.

The circumstances of Chamberlain's fall and Churchill's success suggested that the labour party was largely responsible, though put into that position by the conservative rebels. From the outset 'the Tory rebels ... ha[d] been in the closest touch with A[ttlee] and G[reenwood]' and the intention was 'to get a number of their own men in key positions'; Dalton and Macmillan had begun 'to do this sort of thing after Munich' now nearly two years ago; Amery was said to have refused the offer of office 'if he would bring his rebels in' under him. The meeting of rebels under Amery on 9 May resolved to support any prime minister enjoying 'the confidence of the country and ... able to form an all party government'; and as labour would not enter 'if Chamberlain, Hoare and Simon remain', then they must go; and those present would not 'join or support any government which did not contain members of the labour and liberal parties'.[36] The rebel demand, therefore, was primarily for the inclusion of the labour and liberal parties. The resignation of Chamberlain was the means to this end. If met, the demand would have an additional advantage. Chamberlain's departure would seem, not the result of intrigue, but rather a move to facilitate the patriotic inclusion of the labour party in government.

The labour party's seizure of the moment was similarly couched in patriotic terms. Chamberlain and Halifax agreed in advance that 'the chances of labour serving under [Chamberlain] ... were negligible'. Though Chamberlain inquired whether in principle they would join the government 'under the present prime minister or ... under other leadership' he and Halifax had already agreed that 'the chances of [their] serving under [him] ... were negligible'. He found Attlee and Greenwood 'a bit evasive' and they 'eventually' said they did not think they could 'get their party ... to serve' under him; and the national executive next day confirmed unanimously that it would serve 'in a new government which under a new prime minister would command the confidence of the nation'.[37]

Chamberlain's resignation, therefore was, and was seen to be, partly the result of the labour party's refusing to serve under him. Given that 'The Labour people ... would join ... but not under him' Chamberlain 'did not think delay was possible'; and his decision to resign at once followed the labour party's giving authority to Attlee and Greenwood 'to

[35] Davidson to Baldwin, 14 May 1940, Baldwin 174: 275–7; Channon diary, 18 May 1940.
[36] Dalton diary, 9, 10 May 1940; Nicolson diary, 9 May 1940.
[37] Halifax diary, 9 May 1940; Dalton diary, 10 May 1940.

agree to a coalition, but not under Neville'.[38] Churchill offered labour 'two seats out of five in a new war cabinet ... [and] one out of three defence ministries', together with a number of offices for members of the party; and Labour's national executive, on the recommendation of Attlee and Greenwood, agreed. Yet, like Churchill, their remaining in power depended on Chamberlain's staying on. He would remain in the war cabinet, though with no department. Both Attlee and Greenwood urged the party to accept this: 'To get Chamberlain out altogether was impossible ... [and] would create such ... embitterment among his friends' as to make the life of the new government 'brutish and short'; and it was 'generally recognised' that the case for keeping Chamberlain somewhere in the government was 'overwhelming'.[39]

But the desire to oust him did not stop with his resignation. While Churchill would have given him the exchequer, that was 'impossible', Chamberlain thought, on account of 'Labour': he would have 'seemed an obstacle to all they wanted' and they would quickly have made his position untenable; 'the only chance of letting their passions die down' was to take a post which did not bring him 'into conflict with them'. The same went for the leadership of the house.[40] Churchill, therefore, not only owed his position partly to the labour party and should 'have ... some feeling of appreciation' but was further bound to them in a federation which balanced the need to keep Chamberlain with the desire to oust him.

Labour recognised that and the conservatives resented it – particularly given the impact it would have on the fortunes of the party after the war. Dalton was struck by the conservative antagonism to Churchill. On 18 June he thought it 'noticeable' in the commons that Churchill was cheered 'much more loudly by the Labour party than by the general body of Tory supporters'; their 'relative silence ... [was] regarded as "sinister"' and it was thought that 'many Tories [felt] ... quite out of it now ... [that] the Labour party ha[d] ... too large a share both in office and the determination of government policy'. But it was 'clear' that Chamberlain must not be pushed out, 'for he would be a centre of disaffection and a rallying point for real opposition'. Nor did that change, for it seemed even six months after coming to power, that 'there was much stronger and firmer support for the PM among our [labour] people than among the Tories'.[41] The conservatives noted and resented the association from the outset. Halifax had been 'struck by the chilly reception of Winston's assumption

38 Halifax diary, 10 May 1940; Hoare typescript notes, 'Friday' (10 May 1940), Templewood XIII:3, p. 4; Cadogan diary, 10 May 1940.
39 Dalton diary, 11, 12, 27 May, 18 June, 9 Oct. 1940.
40 Halifax diary, 11 May 1940; Chamberlain to Hilda, 17 May 1940, NC 18/1/1156.
41 Dalton diary, 18 June, 9 Oct. 1940.

of office' by the House of Lords, which 'no doubt was to be expected and is the price paid for labour'.[42] Moreover the labour party was making capital for itself out of the change of government, to the indignation of various conservatives. The 1922 committee considered in late July 'the unscrupulous use . . . by the political labour party of the work of certain members of the government' when a leaflet circulated in Birmingham claimed 'that everything was in a muddle until May 12th and the success of the present government was exclusively due to the "Labour Big Four": Attlee, Greenwood, Bevin and Morrison'. Lord Wigram, permanent lord in waiting to the king, thought that 'the Labour Government will get into power at the end of the war . . . already they [were] patting themselves on the back and saying they are winning the war'; and the unionist MP, Sir Geoffrey Ellis, warned Baldwin that 'our own old conservatives . . . [were] rather watchful . . . while giving full support [were] a little apprehensive that Bevin and Morrison [were] rather running away with [Churchill] . . . and trying to secure the labour position for post war purposes' an apprehension which he thought 'well founded'.[43]

Churchill, therefore, did not become prime minister of war-time Britain – in the view of his conservative colleagues – as the representative of destiny. Reservations as to his judgement and doubts, not merely as to his own conservatism, but to his impact on the party, persisted. He had sided with the party's enemies and those whom the better judgement of Baldwin and Chamberlain had dropped or kept out of office since 1931. Though there was no direct evidence of intrigue before the debate there was the feeling that his succession was the result of design rather than destiny. Those who had conspired on his behalf were rewarded; and the combination of Churchill with the traitors, tory rebels and the labour party did not augur well for the country or the party. But the conservatives intended to follow Chamberlain's lead and support the government for the duration of the war; meanwhile they would remain compact on the back-benches, preparing the new leader for the new moral world after the war.

Churchill, however, was to change all that. Though the doubts about his judgement continued to find expression over his men, or, more seriously, his direction of the war, he came to dominate the country and the party. He was helped by events themselves – the fall of France, Holland and Belgium and the attack on Britain herself – and by his own reaction to them. His earlier characteristics of reaction and bombast were

---

[42] Halifax diary, 13 May 1940.
[43] Wallace diary, 31 July 1940; Wigram to Linlithgow 15 Aug. 1940, IOL MSS. Eur. F 125/162 ; Ellis to Baldwin, 7 Aug. 1940, SB: 174.

transformed into patriotism and resolution. Yet Churchill's judgement and appreciation of events differed little in substance from that of the men whom he replaced. What did differ was its expression. For Churchill, no less than for Chamberlain, Britain could do little more than hope and try to hold out; but it was not clear at first that she could do so without any help. That, however, was not forthcoming.

Nonetheless Churchill *seemed* to the professionals to be rash and cavalier in his dispersal of resources – willing first to throw all into France and then to consider Egypt or its outposts in Greece, Crete or even Turkey – at the expense of the survival of this island. But there was no substance behind the appearance. Churchill, like Chamberlain, refused to gamble recklessly on Britain's limited assets. When he seemed to be rash, deploying them on hopeless adventures, he had in fact calculated what could reasonably be lost in order to achieve some higher purpose – whether delaying the collapse of France so that Britain could prepare, or assisting the Greeks to satisfy world opinion and to maintain the balance of power in the Middle East by bolstering Turkey. However, Churchill allowed the appearance of rashness to remain and concealed the careful calculations which lay below some of his decisions. For what his critics described as rashness was, he sensed, his peculiar asset. In public it would appear as courage and decisiveness. Without it, he knew, he would not remain in power.

2   Events and reactions – 1: The German attack on France and its aftermath

The fall of France

Events, and Churchill's reaction to them, served to set him apart from his contemporaries. On 10 May, the day Churchill became prime minister, Hitler invaded Holland and Belgium. Reports were confused at first, but there was no minimising the gravity of the situation. Within five days the Germans had broken through at Sedan and the road to Paris was open. Nothing it seemed would stop Hitler, particularly as the French high command was reported to be paralysed and to have no will to resist. But unless the German advance could be stayed, British troops would be in mortal danger – for the French army would collapse and the BEF would be cut off. By the 18th it did seem that the French would collapse – and within three days a German mechanised column was heading for Boulogne. The Germans had also reached Calais and there was no sign of a French counter attack. Two days later, on the 24th, the French had almost given up and agreed to the evacuation of the British forces, which would begin that night. But they continued to demand support (particularly in the air) and and they also requested an approach to Mussolini, over which the cabinet differed given the need to keep the French in the fight for as long as possible.

French demands for aircraft and for a great allied attack continued throughout early June – but by the 12th there was little doubt in Britain about French resistance being at an end. The French government had left Paris on the 10th, retreating first to Tours, then to Bordeaux on the 14th, the day Paris fell. On the night of the 16th, Reynaud resigned and was succeeded by Pétain, who sought terms from the enemy. When on the 17th France stopped fighting, attention turned to the fate of the French fleet and the danger of its falling into German hands.

Churchill's reaction

Churchill's reaction to events marked him out, by contrast with his colleagues, as resolute, determined, courageous. Whereas they seemed to lose heart throughout the six weeks when France was attacked, overrun and finally fell, Churchill appeared to remain defiant. And though he may not have been completely certain that Britain could hold out or that she would exclude any peace approach, he seemed to declare that she would never surrender; and that she would not abandon the French (see below pp. 46–7, 49–51, 85–6).

Churchill maintained that the Anglo-French alliance must be upheld and insisted that the evacuation and further support would have a direct bearing on the alliance. They must, he urged, continue the evacuation 'as long as possible' for the success or failure of efforts 'to rescue the remnants of the French army might have great results on the alliance'. The commander on the spot must continue for 'as long as the front held, even at the cost of naval losses'.[1] His reaction to Reynaud's wire of 2 June even during the flight from France asking for further help – reorganised units from the BEF and fighter aircraft – was 'to tell the French that we would send three divisions' though he would await the appreciation of the chiefs of staff. He did not consider the proposals of the chiefs, to send two divisions, 'sufficient'; wanted to promise a third; and proposed to tell the French that the BEF should be reconstituted, that British undertakings would be fulfilled within six months of the dates first given, that two divisions would be sent 'at once' and that a third would follow if the French could provide the artillery. As for the air, despite the decision at the cabinet that while existing air forces in France might be brought up to full strength, 'it would be impossible to send ... further fighter squadrons', Churchill seemed resolved to do so. He seemed to be 'trying hard to send out fighters to help them'; he 'raised again the possibility of sending more' (on the 4th) and 'bullied the CAS unmercifully'; and though the decision 'was not altered in the end', Churchill, it was feared, would 'have his way'.[2]

From the start when the Germans broke though at Sedan he pledged that 'even if France was beaten and England in ruins we would go on till we beat them'; and he maintained that 'our intention is, whatever

---

[1] COS, 1 June 1940, COS(40)162, CAB 79/4.

[2] Cabinet, 2, 3 June 1940, CA to WM (40)152 and WM (40)153, CAB 65/13. At the moment there were six bomber and three Hurricane squadrons in France; and though the cabinet agreed that no further fighters could be sent at the moment, this might be considered at a later date. Cadogan diary, 4 June 1940; Chamberlain diary, 4 June 1940.

happens, to fight on to the end in this Island ... in no conceivable circumstances will we consent to surrender'.[3]

The likely collapse of France opened up by 25 May the prospect of a French appeal for peace to Mussolini. In London the cabinet was divided about the effect, and sceptical about the value of such an appeal. The question was whether it might be tried as a means of encouraging the French.

Churchill's attitude to a negotiated peace has been the subject of scrutiny, prompted partly by the feeling that he was more robust in refusing to consider peace after the outbreak of war, than, for example, Chamberlain or Halifax. In *The Second World War* Churchill alludes both to his single-mindedness -- 'I had ... repeatedly declared our resolve to fight on alone' – and to the fact that making peace with Hitler or abandoning the struggle 'were never thought worth a place upon the Cabinet agenda, or even mentioned in our most private conclaves'.[4]

Certainly at the outset, when France was falling, Churchill appeared more robust than Halifax or Chamberlain – though on closer examination there was not so much difference of substance. Churchill opposed joining the French in putting out feelers, which Halifax did not (for Halifax's position see below, pp. 72–6). By 25 May, when France was on the verge of collapse, he seemed to accept that France and Britain should go their separate ways. If France went out of the war, she must ensure that British troops (and their arms) were allowed to leave France, and that no attack on Britain would take place from French soil. Whereas France would soon be at the end of resistance and 'would ... be offered decent terms by Germany', Britain would not. Britain still had powers of resistance and attack, but she must avoid the position of begging Mussolini and Hitler to 'treat us nicely. We must not get entangled in a position of that kind before we had been involved in any serious fighting' and he [Churchill] 'disliked any move towards Musso[lini]'.[5]

Churchill's view predominated (for the different emphases of Halifax see pp. 48, 73–6) helped by the news on the following day, that Roosevelt agreed to make an approach to Mussolini on his own initiative. The feeling at the cabinet now was that a direct approach by France and Britain to Mussolini would confuse the issue, might be resented by Roosevelt and 'was likely to create an impression of weakness'. On the 28th the cabinet rejected a further French proposal for a direct approach

[3] Crookshank diary, 15 May 1940; Churchill to Roosevelt, 20 May 1940, *Second World War*, II, pp. 50–1.

[4] Cabinet, 27 May 1940, WM(40)141, CAB 65/13.

[5] Defence committee, 25 May 1940, DO(40)9, CAB 69/1; Cabinet, 26 May 1940, WM (40) 140, CAB 65/7; Chamberlain diary, 26 May 1940.

to Mussolini and a reply would be based on a draft by Chamberlain and Halifax. The cabinet also rejected Reynaud's suggestion for a joint Anglo-French appeal to the United States which might tend to 'confirm American fears as to our weakness and not produce the desired effect'.[6]

But the differences which had initially seemed to emerge between Halifax and Churchill on whether to join with the French were not substantial. For example, neither believed that Hitler would offer terms acceptable to Britain. Churchill did not think it likely that Hitler would offer terms which they could accept; but if they 'could get out of this jam by giving up Malta and Gibraltar and some African colonies we would jump at it. But the only safe way was to convince Hitler that he couldn't beat us.' (Halifax would make it clear that Britain could not accept terms which would undermine her independence, see below pp. 72–6.) Churchill maintained that while he 'would not join France in asking for terms but if ... told what the terms offered were, he would be prepared to consider them'. Nor were there differences of substance on the question of fighting on – despite the tendency in retrospect to associate resolution to fight on particularly with Churchill. Churchill was not unique in anticipating that Britain would continue to fight on alone – and indeed would be better off without the French. Chamberlain believed they would fight on. There is little evidence to suggest Halifax believed otherwise. His attitude to terms was neither related to his confidence in the country's future resistance nor necessarily affected by it. Rather, terms were, for him, a diplomatic instrument to prevent the French having cause to complain; and in any case they could always be rejected if unsatisfactory. Churchill's anticipations (at least as publicly expressed) about Britain's continuing to fight on were unique. Little distinguished Churchill's expectations from, for example, those of Chamberlain. Each, at times, entertained grim anticipation of what lay ahead (see pp. 56, 65). But each also maintained that without the French Britain stood a good chance of fighting it out alone. Chamberlain did not see that the Germans could attempt to invade without achieving air superiority, which they did not yet have by the end of May. Churchill suggested that if France went out of the war, she might become a neutral 'and it was not certain that Germany would insist on retaining all the ports in Northern France. She might be so anxious to divide France from us that she would offer France very favourable terms of peace.' The 'peace talk', therefore, of late May was in the context of how the politicians proposed to hearten the French, not of whether they believed they should seek peace before defeat. Nor did they see French

---

[6] Cabinet, 27 May 1940, WM(40)142, CAB 65/7; cabinet, 28 May 1940, WM(40)145, CAB 65/7.

survival as necessary to British survival. The point at issue was how to stop the French recriminating when they fell. The principal difference between Churchill on the one hand, and Halifax and Chamberlain on the other, was over the deployment of peace feelers as a means to an end. Churchill (with Sinclair, Attlee and Greenwood) considered that such a move would be futile, or worse than futile, in that it would do no good to British integrity and prestige.[7]

Churchill's courage struck his colleagues. Halifax was 'much impressed by Winston's courage' which continued to be 'very good [although] ... there [was] no minimising the gravity of the position'; and Dalton thought him 'quite magnificent, the ... only man ... for this hour'.[8] His visits to the French roused them; and he was thought to have given them 'a valuable fillip'; 'encouragement by promising to share their tribulations'; his presence was 'simply invaluable and may turn out to be the one thing which keeps the French going'.[9] For his part he would continue to support them; not only with promises, but with the resources and equipment which they continued to demand.

Churchill's determination to do so struck his colleagues as reckless and dangerous. Whereas they urged that resources would be necessary to defend this island and must not be squandered in France, Churchill insisted that the Anglo-French alliance be upheld, whether by the specific policy of continuing the evacuation for as long as possible or by the general one of meeting the demands for help, whether in the air or with troops.

Yet Churchill's intentions were more complex than his colleagues allowed. They were influenced by the balance between his desire to keep the French in the fight for as long as possible with his doubts about sustaining the battle. On 5 June he urged the speedy despatch of further troops, the first elements of which should leave the next day and he also argued for 'immediate ... [air] assistance to France'.[10] Even when, within five days, it became known that the French government and military headquarters had left Paris and Churchill had postponed a visit to France on the advice of Campbell, he would not countenance the prospect of France falling. When he left on the 11th to see the French he resolved to keep them in the fight, give 'general support' and discuss 'future plans'. Everything 'must be done to keep France in the fight'; and the French

[7] Chamberlain diary, 26 May 1940; cabinet 27 May 1940, WM(40)141 and WM(40)142, CAB 65/13, CAB 65/7.
[8] Halifax diary, 17, 19, 23, 24 May 1940; Dalton diary, 24, 28 May 1940.
[9] Halifax diary, 1, 13, June 1940; Wallace diary, 13 June 1940; Dalton diary, 15 June 1940.
[10] COS, 5 June 1940, COS(40)168, CAB 79/6; notes of meeting, 11.00 a.m., 5 June 1940, CAB 127/13.

must 'continue to defend every yard of their soil ... use the full fighting force of their army ... and as soon as the divisions can be equipped ... they will be despatched to France'.[11]

But, simultaneously, he had had doubts as to whether the French could be sustained. He wondered on 1 June 'if we can hold them'; hinted on the 4th that Britain might have to fight alone; and though he intended to see how France could be helped 'without hurting ourselves mutually' he did not know whether it would be 'possible to keep France in the war or not'.[12] By the 8th it seemed to him that they must either regard the battle as 'decisive for France and ourselves and throw in the whole of our fighter resources' or recognise that though of 'great importance' the present battle 'would not be decisive ... for Great Britain'; even if France were 'forced to submit' Britain 'could continue the struggle ... provided ... [her] fighter defences ... were not impaired'.[13] Churchill considered that 'it would be fatal to yield to French demands' and jeopardise 'our own safety'.[14] But although he again reverted to wanting to do all to keep the French in the fight, his visit convinced him that France 'was near the end of organised resistance'; although he would do what he could for them in what he thought would be their last battle, 'a chapter in the war was now closing' and 'effective resistance as a great land power was coming to an end'.[15]

Churchill, therefore, had seemed resolute about helping and continuing to help the French. Not only did he intend to keep the French in the fight, but he would be seen to be resolute, to stand by an ally and stand up to the Nazis, so much so that he worried his colleagues – whether the politicians or the air staff – who dreaded further depletion of the meagre resources in this island. But they did not see – and he did not encourage them to do so – that his protagonism was tempered by calculation. Not only did he wish to be seen to stand by an ally, but he needed to gain time for Britain to prepare. As long as the chance existed of holding the French, that must be done and the price paid. But though the price might seem high it was unlikely to remain so: for if the French did fight on, the gain in time for Britain would be of immeasurable advantage; and if the French were first to falter and then to fall, they would not be in any position to demand so much and the amount would accordingly decrease. This was what happened. Although Churchill did press for more even after the French

---

[11] Halifax diary, 11 June 1940; Churchill to Roosevelt, 11 June 1940, *Second World War*, II, pp. 116–17; cabinet, 12 June 1940, WM (40)163, CAB 65/13.
[12] Pownall diary, 1 June 1940; Halifax diary, 4 June 1940; Wallace diary, 4 June 1940; Churchill to Mackenzie King, 5 June 1940, WSC, 11, pp. 128–9.
[13] Defence committee, 8 June 1940, DO(40)14, CAB 69/1.   [14] Ibid.
[15] Cabinet, 12 June 1940, WM(40)163, CAB 65/13.

seemed most likely to fall[16] (when the government and staff left Paris) once it was clear that organised resistance was at an end, there was no question of further assistance, and in any case it would make no more difference to holding out. Churchill could now turn away from the French having done, and having been seen to have done his utmost to help and to stand by his ally for as long as it was at all possible to do so.[17] There could be no recrimination either from the French, or, at home, from those who had hounded Chamberlain for his failure to stand up to Hitler.

Churchill and the French fleet

In addition to her armies, which proved so ineffective against Hitler's forces, the French had naval forces which (with the exception of some vessels in British ports) were mainly in the North African ports of Casablanca, Mers el Kebir/Oran and Alexandria, and in Toulon and Dakar. Churchill was resolved to prevent this fleet from falling into German hands, irrespective of the cost, and despite the reservations of the navy and the politicians. This attitude was another factor which re-dounded to his standing as the resolute leader determined to take the necessary steps – however unpleasant – to defeat Hitler.

As soon as the French began to think of making terms with Germany, Churchill had been resolute that the French fleet should not fall to Hitler; and had been prepared to suspend his objections to the French making a separate peace so long as the fleet sailed to safe waters. But the fleet did not sail and the armistice terms provided no guarantee that it would not fall to the Germans, from whom Churchill was determined to secure it, if necessary by its destruction. In a matter 'so vital to the British empire' the French promises not to surrender could not be relied upon. Rather they must 'make certain of the two modern battleships Richelieu and Jean Bart'. A strong force would be sent. And 'if the captains refused to parley they must be treated as traitors'; there must be no escape and rather than their falling to the enemy 'we should have to fight and sink them'.[18] Churchill persisted with the general view (expressed at the cabinet on the 24th) that all should be done to get hold of the four big ships and 'if we could not get them into our possession, we should make sure that they were scuttled' – despite reluctance on the part of the navy. Although Pound maintained that 'the only real chance of success lay in a surprise

---

16 Ibid.
17 Cabinet, 13 June 1940, WM(40)165, CAB 65/13; Defence committee, 14 June 1940, DO(40)16, CAB 69/11; note of meeting of PM, First Lord, First Sea Lord, and VCNS, 17 June 1940, AVAR 5/4/26.
18 Ibid., note of meeting; Cabinet, 22 June 1940, WM(40)176, CAB 65/13.

attack ... at dawn' that 'might result in the loss ... of six of our battleships' which seemed 'a heavy price to pay for the elimination ... of the force de Rade', Churchill was resolute.[19] The French 'had handed it over on paper' already; he could no longer take 'any cheerful view of French resistance outside Europe' and felt that Britain would 'have to face the prospect of an unfriendly France'; 'the sooner this operation was carried out, the better'. The operations took place on 3 July, principally in Oran and its main port Mers-el-Kebir: there the French refused terms and a 'heavy engagement ... [took] place ... in the harbour' as a result of which all the French warships were 'put out of action ... [except] ... one of the Strasbourg class'. However, in Alexandria negotiations led to an agreement where the French ships were 'placed ... in a condition in which they could not fight'.[20]

The operation against the French had, Churchill implied during his speech to the Commons, been a matter of duty, and the resolute action necessary to secure those 'righteous purposes' for which they were fighting. Although militarily the result may have been 'none too good', Churchill's account – in which unflinching resolution to fight with vigour was bound up with moral righteousness and duty – won 'a good reception' and was enthusiastically applauded. The statement was 'characteristic ... a theme after his own heart ... The stirring story of the fight and how we had routed the treacherous French'; the routing was bound up with his own determination and resolution to 'prosecute the war with the utmost vigour ... until the righteous purposes for which we have entered upon it have been fulfilled'; now was 'no time for doubt or weakness' and 'we shall not fail in our duty, however painful'. It concluded 'with a tremendous demonstration everyone standing up cheering'; and when 'the House rose, cheered, waved order papers – as ... so often seen [to] do for Neville ... [Churchill] suddenly wept'.[21]

---

19 Churchill told the cabinet at 10.30 p.m on 24 June that the suggestion that the French might scuttle their ships could not be relied upon, particularly once the German occupation of French territory was complete. See cabinet, 24 June 1940, WM(40)178, 179, 180, CAB 65/13.
20 Wallace diary, 25 June 1940; Beaverbrook to Hoare, 27 June 1940, BBK C/308; Cabinet, 30 June 1940, CA to WM(40)188, CAB 69/13; Cabinet, 3, 4, 5 July 1940, WM(40)192, 193, 194; CAB 65/8 and CAB 65/14; Defence committee, 3 July 1940, DO(40)19, CAB 69/1.
21 *Into Battle.* London, 1941, 4 July 1940, pp 239–46; Cadogan diary, 4 July 1940; Chamberlain diary, 4 July 1940; Crookshank diary, 4 July 1940; Channon diary, 4 July 1940.

The events of 1940: the reaction of Chamberlain, Halifax, Cadogan and others

Churchill's reaction to the invasion and fall of France was, in a sense, unique. Whereas amongst his colleagues (both politicians and professionals), there was a sense of doom and horror at what seemed to be the helplessness of Britain in face of the inevitable unfolding of events, Churchill seemed more quickly to regain buoyancy. Moreover what appeared to be his courage marked him out for his colleagues: they tended to perceive in him a contrast to their own views of the fate of the country; and they tended to allow doubts about Churchill to be replaced – at least in part – by admiration. In any case patriotism required that all reservations be cast aside in time of such extreme crisis.

Whereas Churchill did not *seem* to allow the French defeat to discourage him or undermine his resolution, Chamberlain and Halifax – the other two conservatives in the cabinet – possibly with more reason seemed engulfed by the seriousness of events. Chamberlain's increasing horror at the gravity of events superseded the possibility of personal considerations of bitterness and resentment. In the face of the 'terrible', 'black', 'too awful' developments, he could not keep up his objections to the new 'crowd'; he resolved to put differences behind him, was struck by Churchill's courage and accepted his invitation to remain party leader, for unity was all that mattered now. Unlike Churchill he hated war with its attendant 'death and mutilation and misery' and was overwhelmed by it; unlike Churchill throughout the battle in France he thought the French hopeless: they would not fight, yet had the effrontery to make further demands for help which if not met resulted in recrimination. Unlike Churchill, Chamberlain did not consider that they *should* be met and was 'glad' when Churchill decided that in fact they would not be met. He thought the French 'terrible allies' and that they would be 'better off without them'. It was a matter of fighting on alone, for they could not count on early American support. Egypt, Turkey and Spain had already run out, or were about to do so. Britain's fate depended on repelling invasion. If that failed she could not stop the German army.[22]

The German attack in the west had prompted Chamberlain to put off the domestic crisis 'till the war situation was calmer'.[23] Although his critics saw this as a ruse to cling to office, Chamberlain's reaction to events then seemed of a piece with that subsequently, when he was overcome by their gravity. The invasion of Holland and Belgium had discouraged him from considering 'changes in the government while ...

[22] See below, pp. 53–6.   [23] Halifax diary, 10 May 1940.

[we are] in the throes of battle' and he 'would much rather have gone out altogether' but these events made him feel it was his duty to set an example of unity'.[24] Though the House of Commons had not shown 'its best side in the recent debate', nonetheless 'subsequent events ha[d] put all that in the cupboard'. The news from the front filled him with dread, as did its implications for England. It was, on the 15th, 'terrible' when Reynaud telephoned after the German breakthrough at Sedan: 'We are beaten. We have lost the battle. The way to Paris is open.' It was 'worse' on the 16th, for the French were 'all giving way without fighting' and the British army would have to retire 'if it [were] not to be cut off from the French'. Chamberlain did 'not see how we could [fight on without them]'; by midnight it was 'terrible'; and a message from Churchill in Paris warned that 'unless [the] German advance can be stayed [the] French army will collapse and BEF will be cut off'. The news seemed always 'to be bad' with each decision 'at best ... a choice between desperate risks' and the anxiety of the last days harrowing.[25] All of Chamberlain's world had 'tumbled to bits in a moment'. The 'national peril' had 'so swamped all personal feeling that no bitterness remain[ed]'; and Chamberlain accepted on the 18th Churchill's invitation to remain party leader for this would best allow him 'to help ... in serving the cause of national unity'.[26]

There was no relief. The withdrawal and evacuation of the BEF, the fall of France and the nakedness of Britain left Chamberlain with little hope. The 'scene' continued to 'darken every hour'; the French 'did nothing to help' and the British would 'have to abandon the Belgians' though even so 'we may not be able to save the BEF'.[27] By 20 May there was 'nothing to relieve anxiety' and the Germans were 'pushing towards the channel'.[28] The position at Boulogne was, on the 21st 'desperate'; and if the French did not fight, British communications would be severed and the position of the BEF be 'grave in the extreme'.[29] The 23rd was 'another black day' and by the 24th Chamberlain feared 'we shall lose Calais and the men who are in it'; the 26th was 'the blackest day of all ... [with] no possibility of an offensive by the French from the South', and though it was the 'national day of prayer' Chamberlain 'could hardly attend the service with the load on ... [his] mind'.[30] He did not see what could be done, did not see the

[24] Chamberlain to Beaverbrook, 10 May 1940; (copy), BBK, C/80; Chamberlain to Mary, 11 May 1940, NC 1/20/1/198.
[25] Chamberlain to Zetland, 14 May 1940, ZNK x 10; Chamberlain diary, 15, 16 May 1940; Chamberlain to Hilda, 17 May 1940, NC 18/1/1156.
[26] Chamberlain to Churchill, 18 May 1940, NC 7/9/89; Chamberlain to Hilda, ibid. Chamberlain to Linlithgow, 23 May 1940, IOL Eur. MSS. F 125/153(a)65.
[27] Chamberlain diary, 19 May 1940.   [28] Ibid., 19, 20 May 1940.
[29] Ibid., 20, 21 May 1940.
[30] Ibid., 23, 24, 26 May 1940.

point of an approach to Mussolini whom he did not think could 'be bought off'.[31] Although the evacuation began from Dunkirk on 28th, the news that the Belgians would seek an armistice now opened the British flank and made it 'unlikely that any substantial number of the BEF will get away' and the small chance of 'extricating them' had 'now almost vanished'. There were 'terrible tales' of the bombing of troops awaiting to get off and of prisoners and wounded being 'shot in cold blood': it was, for Chamberlain, all 'a horrible story'.[32]

Whereas Churchill gave the impression that 'he love[d] war', it 'broke ... Chamberlain's better heart'. Before war broke out Chamberlain had not thought he could remain had he to give directions 'that would bring death and mutilation and misery to so many'; and even though he now found it perhaps providential that his being overturned 'coincided with the entry of the real thing', that did not stop his feeling when 'writing letters of sympathy to relatives of men killed in action [that] it [was] too awful to have to do this twice in a lifetime'.[33]

Chamberlain throughout the crisis could not avoid the view that the French were to blame; they had 'done nothing to help'; had been 'giving way without fighting'; there seemed to have been 'hardly any mistake that [they] did not make'; they 'invariably started retiring about six hours' before the arranged time and constantly left the British without cover; their generals were 'beneath contempt' and the soldiers 'with some ... exceptions ... would not fight and would not even march'; nor, even when the Germans had broken through, would they 'recognise facts and ... give the order to retire while there is yet time'.[34] It was, therefore, madness, to 'strip ourselves till we are defenceless'. Fighter command had been 'in despair at the way our defences [were] being sacrificed without any decisive effect on the battle in France' and Chamberlain was 'glad to say' that Churchill on the 8th 'refused to send more fighters'. Though 'their generals always seem[ed] to lose their heads and their courage when danger comes, they never ceas[ed] calling on us for more aid ... [and] though we strip ourselves ... they menace us if we demur'.[35] Whereas for Churchill the French must be kept in for as long as possible and there must be no recrimination, for Chamberlain they were 'terrible allies', and he was 'glad' when Churchill decided to send no more fighters; by 15 June 'nothing short of a definite promise of military intervention by USA

[31] Ibid., 26 May 1940.   [32] Ibid., 27, 28 May 1940.
[33] Channon diary, 20 June 1940; Chamberlain to Hilda, 17 May 1940, NC 18/1/1156; 15 June 1940, NC 18/1/1161.
[34] Chamberlain diary, 16, 19 May, 9 June 1940; Chamberlain to Hilda, 1 June 1940, NC 18/1/1159.
[35] Chamberlain diary, 8, 9 June 1940.

would prevent [them] asking for an armistice'. 'Nothing [would] hold the French army, which [was] broken at the top.'[36] All that mattered now was that their fleet should not fall to Hitler; but despite Darlan's pledge that it would 'never be surrendered' Chamberlain did not 'feel as confident about it' as he would like. He hoped the German terms would 'drive the French government into holding out in the ... colonial empire which would be much better than total surrender'. But it 'behaved abominably in breaking its treaty obligations' and was 'likely to accept the German terms'.[37] It was 'now a puppet government' and 'the willingness of the French navy to ... fight on our side'[38] could not be counted upon. Britain, though 'alone' by the end of June, was 'at any rate free of ... the French who ha[d] been nothing but a liability' and 'it would have been far better if they had been neutral from the beginning'.[39]

Chamberlain's recriminations against the French and his reflections that Britain would be better without them, did not lead to high hopes for help from elsewhere in the future. The attack on the fleet at Oran produced, in his view, a 'distressing effect on Anglo-French relations' and Chamberlain was relieved that the 'full agreement' at Alexandria 'remove[d] fear of further bloodshed'.[40] He expected 'no substantial aid [to be] forthcoming from [the] USA'.[41]

Turkey had 'defaulted on her obligations'; Egypt was 'evasive' and Spain 'said to be on the point of coming in against us'. Chamberlain thought 'things look blacker than ever and we are hurrying to the crisis'. Britain's 'fate depend[ed] on [her] capacity to prevent invasion, as in Napoleon's day, but with many circumstances altered to our disadvantage'. If that failed (though the Germans could not try it without air superiority) then 'we have not sufficient force to repel and defeat the German army'.[42]

At the foreign office Halifax thought that there was 'no minimising the gravity of events', though he seemed prepared to try. While he found the news 'black', 'depressing', gloomy and that Churchill's deficiencies hardly mattered by contrast, his view of the French holding and their being helped to do so was affected by his hope that they might. Halifax had greater anxiety than Churchill but more optimism than Chamberlain, and, for that matter, than Cadogan in the foreign office whose fatalism was sharper than Chamberlain's.

[36] Ibid., 9, 15 June 1940.
[37] Ibid., 15 June 1940; Chamberlain to Ida, 21 June 1940, NC 18/1/1162.
[38] Chamberlain diary, 24, 27 June 1940.
[39] Chamberlain to Hilda, 29 June 1940, NC 18/1/1163.
[40] Chamberlain diary, 4 July 1940.   [41] Chamberlain diary, 17 June 1940.
[42] Ibid., 12 June 1940; Chamberlain to Hilda, 15 June 1940, NC 15/6/49.

For Halifax events were so black that nothing else – including his irritation with Churchill – mattered. The news from France and the cabinet discussions were from the outset 'bad', 'depressing' and 'gloomy' and he could not 'get rid of this feeling at the pit of [the] stomach' or the sense of 'a very black day'.[43] He had little confidence either in the French whom he believed, by May 18, had 'got their tails down' or faith in Churchill's 'slightly more optimistic diagnoses' next day (the 19th).[44] If Hitler got to Paris they would 'be immediately confronted with menacing peace terms, supported by the blackmailing Mussolini'; by 23 May there was 'no minimising the gravity of the position' and by the 25th 'nothing cheerful ... about the news from France'; the French push had 'not amounted to much' and the Germans had 'walked through' the French army – 'on which everybody ha[d] been willing to build'.[45] In face of such danger he could ignore his objections to Churchill's extravagant reactions: for though he tended to despair of Churchill's working himself 'into a passion of emotion' at meetings 'none of [that] really mattered in comparison to the military events'.[46]

But Halifax was prepared to believe that the French might hold, or might be helped to do so; and 'the degree of help ... [to be given] the French by land and air' in early June was a 'difficult' matter, the 'reconciliation of claims ... not easy'.[47] Like Churchill his view that the French were fighting reflected his hope that they would on account of the implications for England. The news on 7 June was 'fairly good so far' and the French were 'holding and fighting': 'every day that they hold good is a great day gained, because they must be inflicting heavy losses on the German armoured divisions'. Though 'really fighting [on the 11th] ... they [would] have to give ground' but were 'making the Germans pay heavily'.[48]

Once the French were out Halifax, like Churchill, believed they would be better without them but that they must not let the fleet fall into German hands. By 12 June, after Churchill's visit to France, it did not look to Halifax as if 'the least probability of saving Paris [existed]; or that the French would put up 'much show once their present line [was] gone'. Pétain's taking over raised 'all one's worst fears' and what ever happened they 'could not ... allow ... the French fleet to fall into German hands' even if it meant that 'France will declare war on us'.[49] But he had been more disposed than Churchill to 'exhaust every means of persuasion before using force' and urged that they should 'concentrate all ... efforts

[43] Halifax diary, 16, 18, 20, 25, 28 May 1940.   [44] Ibid., 18, 19 May 1940.
[45] Ibid., 19, 23, 25 May 1940.
[46] Ibid., 25 May 1940.   [47] Ibid., 3 June 1940.   [48] Ibid., 7, 11 June 1940.
[49] Ibid., 12, 17 June, 3 July 1940.

on making the parleys [with the French admirals] a success'.[50] The action was 'a most beastly business' – though he did 'not think there was any choice': but it was 'an incredible freak of diabolic fortune that we have been brought to this pass'.[51]

At the foreign office, the view of events was even less measured. Cadogan was filled with dread by the German advance through France. For him these were 'very critical days' with 'nothing but bad news' and 'things never looked blacker'; they were 'the blackest days [he] ha[d] ever lived through', but with 'doubtless worse to come'; with 'nothing much to be done and no decision taken'. 'These days [were] dreadful'.[52] The French were within a week of the attack 'evidently cracking' and the prospect lay ahead of French capitulation and Britain being 'left alone'. Never did he think 'one could endure such a nightmare' with the possibility of 'Germany conquer[ing] us', the French high command 'in complete confusion and helpless', the news 'black as black' – 'an appalling situation'.[53] Nor was there any news of a counter-offensive essential to 'avert complete disaster'; though Reynaud did not say that France would 'capitulate ... all his conversation [went] to show that he [saw] no alternative'; and it was 'a strain – daily and hourly looking the ugliest facts in the eye' with 'very little light [to be seen] anywhere'.[54] Cadogan had been unsympathetic to the French 'howling for assistance' (and even a 'token' would, in his view, be 'so much down the drain'). It would not 'do any good' and he would 'sooner cut loose and concentrate on defence of these islands ... We should really be better off.' He was 'glad' it was decided 'not to send our fighter protection over to France' – though if there were any sign of their fighting he would 'take a risk'. He hoped the British were 'not uncovering [themselves] to help a helpless France' and would 'like to see the French put up a much better show' before he would 'risk all to help them'.[55] They must concentrate on their 'own defence and the defeat of Germany, instead of dribbling away to France all that we have that is good – and losing it'.[56]

Cadogan, therefore was struck at the outset by the increasing blackness of events and the impossibility of preventing them: unlike Churchill or Halifax he would not waste any further help on the French, for unlike them he held out little hope.

Other politicians, too, were gloomy about the seriousness of events and the dangerous consequences for Britain. Defeat in France would be

---

[50] Ibid., 17 June 1940.   [51] Ibid., 4 July 1940.
[52] Cadogan diary, 12, 13, 15, 16, 17 May 1940.
[53] Ibid., 17, 18, 19, 21, 22 May 1940.   [54] Ibid., 23, 24, 25, 26, 27 May 1940.
[55] Ibid., 2, 3, 4 June 1940.
[56] Ibid., 12 June 1940.

followed by invasion. Davidson thought they were 'in for a very stiff summer. The Germans ... [were] throwing in their maximum strength, in order ... ultimately to get at us.'[57] Channon thought the bombing of Amsterdam and the Hague 'beyond belief for horror'; and observed the French defeat with its dangerous implications for the defence of England. Within a week of the attack departmental heads were being warned that French resistance could not 'be counted upon for more than a fortnight [and] ... that Paris will fall shortly'. To Channon it seemed that the war would be over by September 'the Germans will either win or be exhausted' and they were 'now at our door'; France would make a separate peace which would, or so Channon thought on 28 May, be followed by invasion 'next week'.[58] To Wallace, it seemed that mistakes had been made and the position seemed by 22 May 'very confused' with news of the German units 'very close to the channel ports'; and 'the danger of invasion very much nearer'.[59] To Reith who thought the position on 21 May 'about as bad as it can be' with the Germans at Abbeville, Amiens, Arras, 'things on the western front [were] ... very parlous indeed and we are like [sic] to lose the channel ports and the BEF is all in danger'. The evacuation was to start on 27th but it was 'awful and awful the slaughter that will be done in the process'.[60] To Crookshank the German advance south of Sedan had been critical; the subsequent 'French news bad' with advancing German columns, concluding with the surrender by the Belgians which left the BEF and the French encircled, with little or no chance 'either of feeding them or getting them out'.[61]

Some, at first, made these events a cause of blame for Churchill. The French were culpable and so, indirectly, was Churchill because of the misplaced importance he and his associates placed on the French alliance making for 'nonsense' being talked on the subject: 'the trouble [was] that all this clique (Winston, Duff, FO, etc.) ha[d] never realised the weakness of France, and still scarcely appreciated the truth'.[62]

But that was abstract criticism. It had little to keep it alive after the French were out. The other doubts and reservations tended to be subsumed by the gravity of events. The overrunning of France and the danger of invasion replaced concern with Churchill as the principal preoccupation, and it also seemed right that it should. For all that now mattered was the national interest and differences must be set aside.

[57] Wallace diary, 13 May 1940; Davidson to Baldwin, 14 May 1940; SB 174:275.
[58] Channon diary, 14, 17, 18, 23, 24, 29 May 1940.
[59] Wallace diary, 18, 19, 22, 24 May 1940.   [60] Reith diary, 20, 21, 27 May 1940.
[61] Crookshank diary, 17, 21, 28 May 1940.
[62] Headlam diary, 12 June 1940; see Hankey to Chamberlain, 17 June 1940, Hky 4/32, for the French as 'our evil genius from the Paris Peace Conference until today'.

Churchill therefore not only began to assume his position as the man of destiny by his own resolution and speeches in face of the crisis: but he did so by convincing others of that resolution (almost to the extent of their considering him reckless) though privately balancing what appeared to him to be right with what he knew to be possible. His position stood out in contrast with theirs. Where he was determined, seemed confident and anxious to fight on – even in France when it seemed all was lost, they did not conceal dread at the unfolding of events and the fatal implication for England. But that very dread made his critics far more anxious to forget or suspend their doubts: for the national peril, not party differences, must now dominate.

3   Events and reactions – 2: The Battle of Britain

The Battle of Britain and the danger of invasion

The fall of France put England into straits not known since the days of the Armada: the analogy made by Churchill reflected Hitler's control of the Channel ports.[1] From that position, Hitler would first knock England out by air attack and then launch a seaborne invasion; and, indeed, within ten days of France's accepting the German terms, the Luftwaffe started their raids and the Battle of Britain had begun. The danger of invasion was to dominate until October. But the intensity of the battle fluctuated; and there was no certainty about when Hitler intended to launch his invasion, though there was little doubt that he was planning one.

The air battle seemed to fall into three distinctive periods: the early days in July of lighter raids, the object of which was puzzling, for they were certainly not the 'real thing'; the escalation of attack in early August with some heavy battles, but dying down by the end of the month with the odd plane 'just buzzing'; and the culmination in September with the heaviest and most sustained attack. As the battle became more intense, so too did fears of an imminent invasion.

When the air raids began in early July, they were expected; and there were, as the air staff warned 'grounds for expecting' imminent invasion – 'nothing ... definite ... [but] indications from a number of directions which pointed to [its] imminence ... which would be insane to ignore'.[2] By 2 July the air raids had increased, though there were fewer at night and none yet in London. By 6 July there had been no change in this pattern 'a lot of raids ... everywhere ... but in London' where each night one was expected but 'never seem[ed] to materialise'.[3] On the 7th the main daylight attack was concentrated against the south coast and the shipping in the

---

[1] Brooke diary, 22 July 1940.
[2] Cabinet, 1 July 1940, WM(40)189, CAB 65/8; defence committee, 3 July 1940, DO(40)19, CAB 69/1.
[3] Cabinet, 3 July 1940, WM(40)192, CAB 65/8; Beaverbrook to Hoare, 6 July 1940, Templewood XIII:17[39].

61

straits of Dover; on the 10th one was off Manston and the other intercepted between Dover and Dungeness, with 14 certain enemy losses
(probably 22) and 4 British.[4] Although Dowding, the commander-in-chief
of fighter command had 'no doubt that our fighters were still on top of the
enemy', there was the feeling that, as Chamberlain put it, these raids were
not 'the real thing . . . little damage ha[d] been done to life or property' by
mid July.[5] There were subsequently more serious casualties in the
Channel with heavier engagements involving 100 German aircraft (on
25th and 28th) when it was thought that 'the German aim was to harass
our convoys' yet it was not clear what the Germans were up to.[6] Despite
'various good indications that they [were] going to attack . . . why ha[dn't]
they done so'; and what were they doing 'with these mostly half hearted
air raids'.[7]

After the end of July the attacks increased in number and size, not only
on the south and south-east coasts – Dover, the Isle of Wight and the
Thames estuary – but with waves of aircraft penetrating up to thirty miles
inland. By 9 August the fighting had escalated: that off the Isle of Wight
on the 8th, the cabinet was told, was 'the biggest air action . . . so far . . .
off our coasts involving at least 300 aircraft',[8] with an estimate of 18
British losses and 52 (confirmed) enemy ones. On the 12th there were five
air raids against Portland and Weymouth on a 200-mile front with 200
enemy aircraft and two waves of 100 enemy aircraft attacked convoys in
the Thames estuary.[9] The raids on 13 August, the cabinet was told, were
'on a heavier scale than any yet . . . on a front from Weymouth to the
Thames estuary . . . some of them [having] penetrated . . . 25 to 30 miles
inland' though they had all been intercepted with 'heavy losses' to the
enemy and few casualties to 'ourselves'.[10] The 17th was, according to
Halifax, 'a quieter day' and by the 19th the feeling prevailed that 'we have
. . . got the best of this first round'.[11] Although a scare on the 18th of
parachutists landing led to fears in Wallace's department that 'the
invasion had begun' and to the instructions for 'manning . . . the outer
London defences', it was felt by the 21st that the heavy waves of attack
were over. The cabinet heard that attacks were 'merely confined to small
raids usually by single air craft along the east and south east coasts . . .

[4] Cabinet, 8 July 1940, WM(40)197, 11 July 1940, WM(40)200, CAB 65/8.
[5] Cabinet, 9 July 1940, WM(40)198, CAB 65/8; Chamberlain to Hoare, 15 July 1940,
    Templewood XIII:17.
[6] Defence committee, 26 July 1940, DO(40)23, 29 July 1940, DO(40)24, CAB 29/7; cabinet,
    29 July 1940, WM(40)214, CAB 65/8.
[7] Cadogan diary, 29 July 1940.   [8] Cabinet, 9 Aug. 1940, WM(40)223, CAB 65/8.
[9] Cabinet, 12 Aug. 1940, WM(40)224, CAB 65/8 (British casualties of 20 Hurricanes, 5
    Spitfires; enemy approximately 60).
[10] Cabinet, 14 Aug. 1940, WM(40)226, CAB 65/8.   [11] Halifax diary, 17, 19 Aug. 1940.

[which] seldom penetrated more than 25 miles inland'.[12] While the raids did not stop entirely, they were small 'lone raids, playing against morale' – designed 'to keep everybody disturbed ... [but] only using odd planes ... buzzing round London and the suburbs'.[13] The impression by the end of August was that 'though the Germans had done a lot of damage in different parts of the country they ha[d] not done as much as they would have liked, nor as much as we ha[d] done to them ... [and nor had they] ... seriously interfered with our production'. The civilian air raid casualties for the month were approximately 700 killed and 781 seriously injured; and the cabinet saw 'no reason why these ... should not be announced publicly'.[14]

But in September the battle escalated, culminating in the heavy and sustained blitzkrieg at the end of the month; and the prospect of invasion seemed more persistently imminent. The raids began to increase on the 4th and 5th, particularly on the London area. On the 7th came what to Halifax was the biggest raid yet in London: 'They got the docks and did a good deal of damage [and] a lot of casualties in the East End.' Cadogan was struck by the 'terrific explosions [during the night] ... awful noise ... bombs in Pont Street, Victoria Street and Westminster [and the] frightful blaze in the docks', Brooke by 'the whole sky being lit up by the ... fires in London dock'.[15] The planes on the 8th were 'coming over now in quick succession'; and the cabinet on the 9th decided (on Brooke's suggestion) to evacuate the towns on the east and south east coast of non-essential civilian population, voluntarily and without publicity in the newspapers.[16] That evening nearly 400 aircraft crossed the coast, though they were broken up by British fighters and turned back; but there was an attack on London that night when several fires were started and the next day 'a good deal of desultory raiding [by] ... day and bad bombing ... at night'.[17] It seemed to 'all the fighting men ... that Hitler intend[ed] to try the invasion in ... the next few days' – and the prospect of invasion continued to dominate.[18] The 13th was 'one of the many days thought to be the ... invasion date', while the 'weather, tides etc [sic] were right for invasion' on the 14th; though 'still no invasion' on the 16th there were

[12] Wallace diary, 18 Aug. 1940; cabinet, 22 Aug. 1940, WM(40)232, CAB 65/8.
[13] Halifax diary, 28 Aug. 1940; Cadogan diary, 31 Aug. 1940; Crookshank diary, 27 Aug. 1940; cabinet, 22 Aug. 1940, WM(40)232, CAB 65/8.
[14] Halifax diary, 31 Aug. 1940; cabinet, 2 Sept. 1940, WM(40)239, CAB 65/9.
[15] Halifax diary, 5, 7 Sept. 1940; Wallace diary, 6 Sept. 1940; Cadogan diary, 6, 7 Sept. 1940; Brooke diary, 8 Sept. 1940.
[16] Cadogan diary, 8 Sept. 1940; Cabinet, 9 Sept. 1940, WM(40)245, CAB 65/9.
[17] Churchill to Chamberlain, 9 Sept. 1940, NC 7/9/95; cabinet, 10 Sept. 1940, WM(40)246, CAB 65/9; Halifax diary, 10 Sept. 1940.
[18] Chamberlain diary, 10 Sept. 1940.

'continued raids ... bombs in Burlington arcade, Bond Street, Berkeley Square [and] Park Lane'; despite the high winds on the 17th 'a mild hurricane' which 'storm[ed] up the Channel well' and scattered invasion barges, the raids none the less continued and there were 'constant ... warnings all day and all night', and they continued over the next days.[19] Invasion was again expected on the 23rd but did not come; the night of 24/25 was 'rather ... worse ... than usual' and 'the Germans went for north and west London ... Queen's Hall, St Margaret's Westminster got it ...'.[20]

The raids continued with the same intensity through the last days of September: and on 1 October Churchill warned the junior ministers that the 'invasion "menace" still remain[ed] and [would] so long as the Germans ha[d] in that long row of ports transports enough to put half a million men' in the Channel and North Sea on any night they chose. Nor, he told the House of Commons on the 8th, would 'the mists and storms which enshroud our island in ... winter ... by themselves prevent the German bombers'. In any case Pound believed it 'impossible to say that any particular period in the winter was free from conditions suitable for invasion' and preparation against invasion would continue'.[21]

Nonetheless the coming of winter would make invasion, if not impossible, at least unlikely. By 1 October 'people ... [thought] invasion either postponed or abandoned'.[22] Churchill, despite his warnings about the invasion menace, considered that 'as the weather [broke] and the season advance[d] the invasion must surely seem to them more and more difficult'. It seemed that it had been 'definitely projected for September 15' but at the last minute called off.[23] The chiefs of staff when they considered on the 3rd the diversion of light naval forces 'from anti-invasion work to the protection of trade' generally thought that as far as a successful invasion went 'in the long and possibly foggy nights of the winter ... that conditions of fog had more advantages than disadvantages for us'.[24] Brooke, the commander of home command, was 'beginning to think that the Germans may after all not attempt it'; and he told the chiefs of staff on the 7th that he realised that 'the threat of invasion had probably ... receded'.[25] Now that they were in October – as Churchill told the Commons on the 8th – and 'the weather becomes very uncertain

19 Crookshank diary, 12, 13, 14 Sept. 1940; Brooke diary, 17, 18, 19, 20, 22 Sept. 1940; Cadogan diary, 17 Sept. 1940.
20 Cadogan diary, 23 Sept. 1940; Brooke diary, 23, 25 Sept. 1940.
21 Halifax diary, 30 Sept. 1940; Dalton diary, 1 Oct. 1940; House of Commons, 8 Oct. 1940, *Into Battle*, pp. 279–91; Chiefs of staff, 3 Oct. 1940, COS(40)334, CAB 79/7.
22 Channon diary, 1 Oct. 1940.   23 Dalton diary, 1 Oct. 1940.
24 Chiefs of staff, 3 Oct. 1940, COS(40)334, CAB 79/7.
25 Brooke diary, 3 Oct. 1940; Chiefs of staff, 7 Oct. 1940, COS(40)338.

... there are not many ... intervals of two or three days together in which river barges can cross the narrow seas and land upon our beaches'.[26]

Churchill's reaction

Churchill's reaction to the Battle of Britain and the prospect of invasion marked him out as Britain's wartime leader. His view and appreciation of the events may not have greatly differed from that of his colleagues, but it seemed to do so. Privately, for example, he thought it doubtful after Dunkirk that he would live to see the better days that were bound to come; and in late July he wondered whether 'England has ever been in such straits since the Armada days'.[27] But Churchill's public reaction to the air attack and the likelihood of invasion revealed no trace of doubt or apprehension. It was characterised by some of the qualities which had emerged during the crisis in France: courage, resolution and defiance – now bound up with a resolve to defend England with her special life and liberties and never to surrender even though 'we be rotting senseless in the grave'. What Churchill did was to combine the practical organisation of the country to resist invasion with a fighting rhetoric. Not only would there be no surrender, but he was confident that Britain could and would defeat not only the invasion attempt, but Hitler and Hitlerism. In this he struck supporters and doubters alike as having 'wonderful courage', or being 'grand' or 'magnificent'.

From the outset Churchill had made the claim that attempted invasion would follow the fall of France. The attack, he implied, had been expected; and therefore events in France did not put England into an unexpected position, nor one for which she had not prepared. Churchill maintained that he felt less afraid of a German attempt at invasion than he did at their piercing the French line at the Somme and the fall of Paris.[28] The danger of 'concentrated air attack ... coupled with parachute and air borne landings' had existed since the outbreak of war; and 'the French could never have saved us from it'; nor could he see 'why we should not be able to meet it'.[29] German concentrations would be attacked in their invasion ports and the country organised to resist attack.

Not only did he suggest that Britain had in no sense been caught out; he also indicated that the country was on the offensive. He wanted raids on the French coast so the Germans 'could be made to wonder where they

---

[26] House of Commons, 8 Oct. 1940, *Into Battle*, pp. 279–91.
[27] Churchill to Baldwin, 4 June 1940, SB 174:264; Brooke diary, 22 July 1940.
[28] Churchill to Ismay, 2 June 1940, *Second World War*, II, pp. 123–4.
[29] Churchill to PM Australia, 16 June 1940, *Second World War*, II, pp. 172–4.

were going to be struck next, instead of forcing us to try to wall in the Island.'[30] The first line of defence was the enemy ports against which bombing attacks should be directed. An expedition should be destroyed before setting sail; he warned – for example, in the case of enemy shipping at St Nazaire and Bordeaux – of the consequences should this method of defeat fail; and he wanted a naval operation prepared for the destruction of shipping in Biscayan ports.[31] He continued to urge action against the French ports such as Calais and Boulogne which would 'affect the morale of German trooops assembled ... to invade this country'. Despite the view that the bombers should concentrate on military targets in Germany, he maintained it would be 'assuming a great responsibility' to allow 'invasion concentrations to accumulate in the Channel ports without taking action against them'. Few people 'would care to court an invasion in the hopes of being able to deal with it satisfactorily once it had been launched'.[32] The first line of defence was the enemy's ports; the second 'the vigilant patrolling of the sea to intercept any invading expedition'. If additional action were needed to deter an attempt on the western approaches, then the naval patrols might be increased – or a minefield laid.[33] But he did not overrule the navy which warned of losses should British ships be sent to attack the enemy concentrations passing 'westward down the French coast ... opposite this country'; but rather referred to the need to strengthen 'the vital stretch of coastline ... from North Foreland to Dungeness'.[34]

In addition to his schemes to stop the Germans 'forcing us to wall in the island' by planning attacks, raids and patrols against their invasion forces, Churchill was determined to encourage boldness in home defence. He was determined that the impact of the bombing on civilians be reduced. He returned, for example, from a visit to Ramsgate in late August with plans for compensation schemes 'impressed with the necessity of ... compensation in order to let the whole country share ... with those parts ... particularly battered'; and he would make a statement to the Commons on compensation for air-raid victims.[35] He wanted reforms in the air-raid warning system; had strong views on the size of the London warning area and 'referred to the folly of waking people at Barnet when

30 Churchill to Ismay, 4 June 1940, *Second World War*, II, p. 214;
31 Defence committee, 19 July 1940, DO(40)20, CAB 69/1; 22 July 1940, DO(40)21, CAB 69/1.
32 Cabinet, 9 Sept. 1940, WM(40)245, 26 Sept. 1940, WM(40)259, CAB 65/9; Churchill to Trenchard, 26 Sept. 1940, Trenchard 1V/54/20/2, MFC 76/1.
33 Defence committee, 19 July 1940, DO(40)20, CAB 69/1; Churchill minute 'Defence Against Invasion', 5 Aug. 1940, *Second World War*, II, pp. 257–60.
34 Cabinet, 11 Sept. 1940, WM(40)247, CAB 69/15.
35 Halifax diary, 29 Aug. 1940; cabinet, 2 Sept. 1940, WM(40)239, CAB 65/9; House of Commons, 5 Sept. 1940, Parl. Deb. 5th series, vol. 365, cols. 39–50.

aeroplanes [were] ... to bomb Croydon or of rousing Staines when Dagenham is in danger'; and he thought the discrepancies between the rules for civil servants and those for munitions workers during air raids should be resolved to 'enable the work to proceed and ... prevent serious casualties'.[36]

Churchill's view that invasion could be countered – either in the enemy ports themselves before it was launched, or by organising the country to minimise the effects of the bombing – was combined with exhortations to be vigilant. At no stage would he concede that the danger of invasion had passed, though its prospect 'became more remote with the winter weather'.[37] Even after the slackening of the attack in late August he maintained that the German scheme was 'to hammer Kent promontory flat and then attempt invasion'; that Hitler had not yet 'struck his full blow'; that there was cause for apprehension given how the battle had developed into a 'combat between fighters and fighters and we were getting through our reserves ... at a dangerous rate'.[38] Nor did he concede that the coming of the autumn and winter weather would necessarily put a stop to an invasion; he saw fog 'which was more likely in the autumn, as a great ally to an invader ... especially as fog was usually accompanied by a calm sea'; the danger of invasion would 'not disappear with the coming of winter' and 'actual invasion must be regarded as perpetually threatened, but unlikely to materialise as long as strong forces stand in this island'.[39] No one, he told the Commons on 5 September 'must suppose that the danger ... ha[d] passed'; and he did not 'agree with those who assume[d] that after the 15th ... we shall be free from the menace ... There must not be ... any relaxation of effort'; and on the 17th he warned that they must expect the enemy to make his attempt 'at what he judges to be the best opportunity' and therefore 'all our preparations must ... be maintained in a state of vigilance'.[40]

The miltary men's reactions

Those in command of the armed forces did not share Churchill's confidence about meeting invasion or its becoming less likely. Even after the

---

[36] Wallace diary, 2 Sept. 1940; Chiefs of staff, 14 Sept. 1940, COS(40)310, CAB 79/6; Hansard, ibid.

[37] Churchill to Chamberlain, 21 Oct. 1940, NC 7/9/93.

[38] Cabinet, 30 Aug. 1940, CA to WM(40)238, CAB 65/14; Cadogan diary, 29 Aug. 1940; Churchill to Roosevelt, 28 Aug. 1940, *Second World War* 11, pp. 382–3.

[39] Cabinet, 2 Sept. 1940, CA to WM(40)239, CAB 65/16; Churchill memorandum, 'The Munitions Situation', WP(40)352, 3 Sept. 1940, CAB 66/11; House of Commons, 8 October 1940, *Into Battle*, pp. 279–91.

[40] House of Commons, 5, 17, September 1940, *Into Battle*, pp. 263–71, 276–8.

politicians began to discount it, the military men to continued to expect it and feared that there would be difficulty withstanding it. For the war office England's resistance to invasion was bound up with the fate of France and it was feared that French failure would have grave implications for Britain. On 3 June, Croft, under-secretary of state for war, noted that 'our power to defend ourselves and to win the war [was] weakened 30% by our loss of the channel ports'. And, whatever happened, 'we must keep the French in'. Each day the French held, Britain had 'an extra fortnight to prepare for her own defence'.[41]

Dill, by the end of June, was 'like all the other soldiers ... very worried and anxious about the invasion feeling that the troops are not trained and may not be steady when the test comes'.[42] He continued to expect invasion sooner or later. In mid July he thought Hitler would next move on 'Ireland and Scotland ... [and] that the direct attack on England will [not] be made until he ha[d] tried to draw us off a bit'; by the end of July that he would 'have a go at Ireland soon, and possibly Iceland and the Orkneys and Shetland'. Although by 7 August he felt 'a bit happier' about the army he did not attempt 'to minimise the extreme gravity of the situation and ... expect[ed] a full-blooded invasion any day'.[43] By early September he thought the 'indication of impending attack before September 15th [were] accumulating'; supported the evacuation of the east coast towns on the 9th and with 'all the fighting men ... agreed that Hitler intends to try the invasion ... in the next few days'.[44]

Brooke, responsible for home command, was alarmed at the weakness of British defences and continued to fear invasion and doubt the country's ability to resist. He was struck, in late June, by 'the nakedness of [the southern] ... command' particularly given the new position in western France; and was generally 'bewildered ... as to what has been going on ... since the war started ... the shortage of trained men and equipment [was] appalling'.[45] On 1 July he failed to see 'how we are going to make [the] country safe against attack'; the more he saw 'the nakedness of our defences' the more appalled he was 'untrained men, no arms, no equipment ... yet ... masses of men in uniform ... after ten months of war'.[46] His tours of inspection exacerbated his fears: 'a great deal more time to complete defensive arrangements' was needed; and 'a lot of work [was]

[41] Croft memorandum, 13 June 1940, Croft 2/4; Croft appreciation, 3 June 1940, Croft 2/4.
[42] Chamberlain diary, 1 July 1940.
[43] Dill to Montgomery-Massingberd, 13 July 1940, MM 160/12; Dill to Montgomery-Massingberd, 27 July 1940, MM 160/13; Headlam diary, 7 Aug. 1940.
[44] Brooke diary, 3 Sept. 1940; cabinet, 9 Sept. 1940, WM(40)245, CAB 65/9; Chamberlain diary, 10 Sept. 1940.
[45] Brooke diary, 26, 30 June, 1 July 1940.   [46] Brooke diary, 1, 2 July 1940.

still required' for the beach defences where they were 'painfully thin on the ground'. Even after inspecting the York area in late July from Scarborough to Bridlington 'where a lot of good work ha[d] been done' he none the less felt 'overcome with the job . . . like a man trying to swim up a very strong current and doubtful whether he is making any headway'.[47] Brooke had not become more confident; he was, rather 'less . . . as to our powers of meeting invasion'; and given the way in which aircraft now 'seriously undermined' the naval position which could 'no longer ensure the safety of this island against invasion' a much heavier task was thrown on the army. By September he wished he had 'more completely trained formations . . . But for the present there [was] nothing to be done but to trust God and pray for his help'; and he found 'the suspense of waiting . . . very trying especially when . . . familiar with the weakness of . . . defences'. Even then the exposed coastline was being held with only twenty-two divisions 'of which only about half . . . [were] fit for any form of mobile operations' – by contrast with the front in France held jointly by the French and British just half its length and 'with 80 divisions and a Maginot line'.[48]

Brooke's fears about the weakness of the country were compounded by his continuing to believe in imminent invasion. From early July when he felt 'certain that we can only have a few weeks left before the Bosche attacks' he continued to expect an early attempt; though the 12th, 'the probable date of invasion', passed as did the month of July without an attack 'it remain[ed] to be seen whether he would attack in August'.[49] Though no attack came in August the reports and the enemy's preparations continued to point to invasion; and throughout September Brooke expected an attempt constantly. On the 7th he thought 'all reports look[ed] like invasion getting nearer. Ships collecting, dive bombers concentrated, parachutists captured' and he sent out the order for a 'state of readiness in Eastern and Southern command'.[50] On the 8th there were 'further indications of impending invasion [with] everything pointing to Kent and East Anglia as the two . . . threatened points'; and the reports suggested 'invasion starting between the 8th and the 10th'; on the 9th he recommended 'in view of . . . the enemy's preparation for invasion' the evacuation of the towns from Ramsgate to Brighton, which in the event of invasion 'would be subject to intensive bombing'; on the 11th he noted further 'evidence of impending invasion . . . all day, more ships moving west down the Channel . . . cypher messages'; and though it was 'possible

---

[47] Ibid., 13, 15 July 1940; Brooke to Cynthia Brookeborough, 25 July 1940, AB:1W:M.
[48] Brooke diary, 26 July, 8, 15 Sept. 1940.   [49] Ibid., 2, 12 July, 1 Aug. 1940.
[50] Ibid., 7 Sept. 1940.

... it may be only a bluff to hide some other ... stroke'; none the less, 'the next day or two [were] bound to be very critical'.[51] He spent the morning of the 13th 'studying increasing evidence of impending invasion' and thought, by the evening that 'everything looked[ed] like [one] starting tomorrow from Thames or Plymouth'. He wondered whether the 'ominous quiet' next day meant they had 'completed their preparations [and were] ... giving their air force a last brush ... will he start tomorrow ...'? On the 15th, though there was 'still no move' 'everything remain[ed] keyed up for an early invasion and the air war [went] on unabated'. The 'coming week must remain a critical one, and it [was] hard to see how Hitler [could] retrace his steps and stop this invasion'.[52] Though 'still no invasion' over the next few days, there was 'every indication' that there would be one.[53]

Although Brooke believed that 'the indications point[ed] towards working up to something definite' he had by 25 September begun to be less certain: it was, then 'very hard to fathom what he really intends to do and whether he still contemplates invasion'; and by the 29th he believed that the next week would 'bring the matter ... to a head', for Hitler could not 'leave it much later than this week'.[54]

Until then he had feared the possibility of an invasion and was not confident that it could be withstood: since the fall of France he had continued to believe an attempt imminent, culminating in his expecting the attack practically throughout September, when the battle was at its height and the reports suggested the invasion barges were collecting ready to be launched. At no stage had Brooke been confident of withstanding invasion. At the outset, inspecting the defences with the untrained and unarmed men left him wondering what had been going on since the war began; and from then on he wished for 'more completely trained formations' but there was 'nothing to be done but to trust God'. But without armed and trained men there was no defence against Hitler, in Brooke's view, for the coming of air power had undermined the role of the navy in securing the island.

Pound, the chief of naval staff, though more confident both about meeting invasion, and of its being less likely once the weather changed in September, also continued to expect it. In mid-August, for example, he thought it looked 'as if an operation against Iceland, Shetlands, North of Scotland or Ireland might be staged in [the] next few days'; and on 2

51 Ibid., 8, 11 Sept. 1940; cabinet, 9 Sept. 1940, WM(40)245, CAB 65/9.
52 Brooke diary, 13, 14, 15 Sept. 1940.
53 Ibid., 16, 17, 18, 20 Sept. 1940.
54 Ibid., 25, 28, 29 Sept. 1940. He had wondered whether it was 'all a bluff to pin troops down in this country while he prepares to help Italy invade Egypt', diary, 14 Sept. 1940.

September that 'the indications pointing to invasion had never been more positive than ... at the present time'. On the 20th, when he noted 'a most gigantic concentration of shipping and barges from the Scheldt to Havre' he 'firmly believe[ed] invasion will be attempted.[55] But for Pound the danger would diminish once the weather broke with the equinoctial gales. He thought that in the six weeks up to 20 July 'tremendous strides ha[d] been made ... in preparing the country'; and was then sure it would 'not be an easy proposition' for the Germans. By mid-August he thought the air force was 'doing magnificently' and did not see 'how the morale of the German Air Force [could] stand up against the losses ... inflict[ed] on them'; and the German air superiority in September in the Channel did not, in his view 'mean they ha[d] generally obtained air superiority'.[56] Although in early September, 'the indications pointing to invasion had never been more positive', these would not last. Invasion would not necessarily be helped by autumnal fog and a calm sea; for the use of barges and small fishing craft was possible 'on so few days ... they could not form part of any expedition which started on a pre-arranged date'. While it was 'difficult to give any date after which the weather would deteriorate seriously ... after the equinoctial gales, about 21st September, the weather was uncertain'.[57]

Pound seemed more confident than Brooke about withstanding invasion, but he continued to expect it; and he continued to be dominated by its prospect; by the shipping which collected in the invasion ports; by the German air supremacy in the Channel – with its implications for the navy – a matter which also concerned Admiral Drax, Commander-in-chief Nore. Without supremacy in the Channel it was impossible to send ships out in daylight or for the navy to interfere with the Germans. Without fighter protection Pound considered it 'unsafe for a destroyer to be at sea by day anywhere between Portland and Dover'. (Drax was more worried by what could happen in the event of invasion: for he was 'not satisfied that when his destroyers went into action against an enemy invading force, the co-operation of our fighters was assured'.)[58]

[55] Pound to Cunningham, 14 Aug., 20 Sept. 1940, BL Add. MSS 52561; cabinet, 2 Sept. 1940, CA to WM(40)239, CAB 65/15.
[56] Pound to Cunningham, 20 July, 13 Aug., 20 Sept. 1940, BL Add. MSS 52560 and 52561; cabinet, 2 Sept. 1940, CA to WM(40)239, CAB 65/15.
[57] Cabinet, 2 Sept. 1940, CA to WM(40)239, CAB 65/15.
[58] Pound to Cunningham, 20 Sept. 1940, BL Add. MSS 52561; defence committee, 22 July 1940, DO(40)21, CAB 69/1.

The politicians' reactions

Whereas the commanders and chiefs of staff continued, unlike Churchill, to expect invasion and to be dominated by the air battle, this was not the case with the politicians. The views of his cabinet colleagues as to the likelihood of an invasion and the prospect of repelling it increasingly coincided with Churchill's own real views (as opposed to those he suggested in his public speeches). Indeed, his attitude and views on the prospect of invasion (as on subsequent issues) were closest to those of Halifax and Chamberlain – at least until Chamberlain left London on grounds of ill-health.

From the outset Halifax looked on the French battle in terms of its implications for England; he expected an attempt at invasion, then became confident that it would not come. Although sympathetic to the French request in May to approach Mussolini, Halifax did not believe in that or subsequent peace moves: in his view the combination of England's strength and the difficulties which Hitler would encounter must, ultimately, prevent him.

His view during the French battle that 'every day ... they hold ... is a ... great day gained' came to be balanced by the feeling that there were limits as to what could be done for the French in view of 'the struggle ... [we] must shortly anticipate' at home and the danger of invasion.[59] Until mid-July Halifax did not doubt that invasion would be attempted, though he could not be sure from where. On 11 June it looked to him 'as if the Germans [were] collecting ships on the Norwegian coast' and Hambro, President of the Norwegian Parliament, thought it 'more likely ... from there than from Holland', as being under less close observation.[60] For Halifax the question remained not whether Hitler would launch it but when and from where. Unlike Churchill who was 'inclined to doubt whether he [would] ... do it', Halifax could not 'find much room for doubt'. Hitler was 'bound to' and the question was 'whether we can hold the position till winter'. By mid-July the new date was said to be 1 August 'coupled with a suggestion that it will not be England, but ... Ireland'.[61]

Hitler did not arrive and Halifax, who had already begun to wonder whether he would come, now became confident that he would not. Hitler must be sure of success, for unless he could 'achieve a complete success quickly ... it [was] tantamount for him to failure'.[62] But Hitler could not be sure given the increasing strength of the defences and the difficulties he

[59] Halifax diary, 7, 14 June 1940.   [60] Ibid., 11 June 1940.
[61] Halifax to Hoare, 8, 17 July 1940, Templewood XIII:20.
[62] Halifax to Hoare, 8 July 1940, Templewood XIII:20.

would encounter. On 13 July, after a tour of inspection in the north-east, Halifax felt 'much happier'; and he did not think it looked 'a very good military proposition' from Hitler's point of view. By late July the position 'from the army point of view ... [was] improving day by day'; and by mid-August those who knew were 'well satisfied with the development of our fighter strength'.[63] Hitler could not invade until he had 'completely paralysed our air force' which by mid August he had not: on the contrary Britain had got 'the best of this first round.[64] Nor, during the escalation of the air battle in September did Halifax expect invasion. On the 8th, despite 'a great deal of talk ... about [its] imminence' and the next few days being thought 'appropriate from the point of view of moon and tides' Halifax 'still doubt[ed] whether Hitler [would] attempt it unless he ha[d] ... air superiority which ... he [did] not look like getting.[65] Though he wondered on the 15th whether the large German air-raid was 'the first curtain raiser of invasion' he nonetheless could not see the project from Hitler's point of view 'in very attractive terms'; and despite the persistent 'great expectation about invasion', his own doubts persisted'.[66] By 26 September he could not 'exclude the possibility that Hitler is deliberately scaring us with invasion in order to check reinforcements to Egypt where the main blow is to be delivered'.[67] This view strengthened his instinct against a negotiated peace.

Although Halifax had been sympathetic to French demands for an approach to Mussolini in late May, that had been in the context of the fall of France: Halifax had wanted to avoid giving the French cause for recrimination. Although he himself did not believe in such an approach, and did not in substance differ from Churchill about it, it was probably his conciliatory attitude (albeit to the French) at that stage which led to Halifax's being associated with a peace-move party. Once the French were out of the fight, Halifax rejected the peace feelers, though possibly his increasing gusto coincided with his confidence about the country's prospects. He recalled that the only basis for a settlement had already been made clear just after the outbreak of war in 1939 by Chamberlain – that Hitler could always stop the war by restoring to liberty those countries he had violated. This position was endorsed once again by the cabinet in September 1940.

Halifax's attitude to the French request – when France was falling – for

[63] Halifax diary, 13, 25 July, 13 Aug. 1940.
[64] Halifax diary, 31 July, 19 Aug. 1940. By mid-August the air force had good reason to be 'very well satisfied with their achievement' and Halifax began to think that the German air force must be concealing their figures from Hitler; ibid 13, 14, 19 Aug. 1940.
[65] Halifax diary, 8 Sept. 1940.
[66] Ibid., 15, 24 Sept. 1940; Halifax to Chamberlain, 18 Sept. 1940, NC 7/11/33/81.
[67] Halifax to Hoare, 26 Sept. 1940, Templewood XIII:20.

a peace approach to Mussolini was sympathetic, provided Mussolini was left in no doubt about where Britain stood. He did not oppose an approach, not because he expected something to come of it, but because he did not wish to give the French the chance to recriminate. He did not, on 26 May, 'think it [the approach] will do any good, but ... [did] not want to give the French an excuse for complaining'. He thought they 'might say to Mussolini that if there was any suggestion of terms which affected our independence, we should not look at them'. If Mussolini were to look at matters from the perspective of the balance of power, then they might consider Italian claims – and he was to circulate a draft to the cabinet for discussion next day. He did not (like the French ambassador himself) on the 27th, 'believe in' the approach desired by Reynaud to Italy but he agreed to put it before the cabinet – which he duly did. By then, the feeling tended to be against an approach to Mussolini by France and Britain – partly in view of Roosevelt's intervention. Churchill (supported by Attlee, Sinclair and Greenwood) considered that an approach would be futile, and that it would do no good to British prestige. Although Chamberlain proposed, successfully, that rather than give a blank refusal to the French, a reasoned reply arguing on the basis of Roosevelt's intervention should be used, Halifax was put out by Churchill – whom he thought talked 'frightful rot' – also Greenwood. He had raised the matter of a peace offer: would Churchill consider or discuss terms which Hitler might offer to France and England? On the 28th, after the further French appeal 'to us to ask Mussolini to be more reasonable we thought this perfectly futile after all that has been attempted and following on his flat refusal to listen to Roosevelt's last approach'.[68]

Halifax subsequently was reluctant to be drawn into consideration of those peace feelers which reached him. No reply, he suggested on 10 July, should be sent to the minister in Switzerland who reported a 'feeler' made by Berlin through Dr Carl Burckhardt, acting president of the Red Cross. Burckhardt had been told that Hitler was hesitating 'before attacking England because he still clung to the hope of ... arrangement with the British Empire'. The minister himself had counselled against replying and the cabinet had agreed.[69] Again, with the support of his colleagues, he rejected the offer made by the Swedish king to mediate between Germany and Britain in early August, as he did in September the advances of

---

[68] Halifax diary, 26, 27, 28 May 1940; cabinet, 26 May 1940, WM(40)140, CAB 65/7; 27 May 1940, WM(40)142 CAB 65/7, CAB 65/13.

[69] Cabinet, 10 July 1940, WM(40)199, CAB 65/8 and Kelly to foreign office, 8 July 1940 appended. Four days later, in his broadcast on 14 July, Churchill reiterated 'But be the ordeal sharp or long, or both, we shall seek no terms, we shall tolerate no parley; we may show mercy – we shall ask for none', *Into Battle*, pp. 247–51.

Weissauer 'said to be a secret emissary of Hitler'.[70] Nor did Halifax take up Hitler's speech to the Reichstag of 19 July which, he thought, seemed to leave matters 'very much where they were. He [Hitler] of course had never wanted the war and it is everybody's fault but his.' There was 'very little to be made of it' and despite Lothian's requesting Halifax not to include in his broadcast 'anything ... which might close the door to peace,' Halifax was 'perfectly firm' as far as the broadcast went. Nor would the request for a debate in the House on questions arising out of the speech be met and the cabinet agreed that the press 'should be discouraged from suggesting that there was anything in ... Hitler's speech which called for an official reply from this country'.[71]

Halifax rejected the peace moves and negotiations, on grounds both of policy and of tactics – his support for the approach to Mussolini in May having been a matter of not giving the French the opportunity to recriminate. His position was not so different to Churchill's; and, once the French were out of the war tended to coincide with Churchill's, the cabinet tending to support the rejections. In general Halifax saw 'no reason why Germany should not take her place in a new and better Europe' if she 'g[ot] rid of Hitlerism' – the view taken at the outset of the war but dropped 'on the insistence of the French'.[72] But specifically there could be no peace discussed until Germany restored what she had taken. The line laid down by Chamberlain in the House of Commons on 18 October 1940 set the context: 'the peace ... must be a real peace by which the freedom and independence of nations was secured'. Germany must provide 'effective guarantees by deeds, not words ... the restoration of freedom to France and to the other countries deprived of it as well as the effectual security of Great Britain and the British Empire'.[73] Tactically the time was not right for negotiations. The Germans, Halifax thought, had 'got to be knocked about before they will be in any mood to learn any lesson'; and if they did get rid of Hitler 'all the better': but 'at least we

[70] Cabinet, 8 Aug. 1940, WM(40)222, CAB 65/14; 11 Sept. 1940, WM(40)247, CAB 65/15.

[71] Hitler, during his address to the Reichstag on 19 July, claimed that he considered it his duty to appeal 'once more to reason and common sense to Great Britain ... I see no reason why this war must go on', *The Times*, 20 July 1940; Halifax diary, 19, 20 July 1940; Nicolson diary, 22 July 1940; cabinet, 24 July 1940, WM(40)211, CAB 65/8.

[72] See above, pp. 73–5, notes 69–72. For a Germany without Hitlerism see Cabinet, 26 July 1940, WM(40)213, CAB 65/8.

[73] The reply to the king of Sweden referred to Chamberlain's statement in the House of Commons of the previous 18 October 'that the peace on which ... [the] government [was] determined must be a real peace, by which the freedom and independence of nations was secured'. Before any proposals could be considered, Germany must give 'effective guarantees by deeds, not words ... [to] ensure ... the restoration of freedom to France and to the other countries which have been deprived of it'. Reply to the king of Sweden, appended to cabinet, 8 Aug.1940, WM(40)222, CAB 65/14.

want them to learn that war does not pay them. And to stop the sort of terms that Hitler would be likely to contemplate now would definitely look ... as if war did not pay too badly.'[74] Besides there could be no response to Hitler's offers, the substance of which remained that he was 'prepared to call it off provided he could keep what he had got'; for it would, in Halifax's view 'be very damning to have it on record that we had sent a temporising reply to any offer of this kind'.[75]

Like Halifax Chamberlain at first expected an invasion attempt, but came to consider that it would not come; each week made it more difficult for Hitler – who could not risk failure. Nor would Chamberlain consider peace moves or parleys – though at the time of the French request for an approach to Mussolini he wanted the French let down gently. His position had been made clear in October 1939 in his statement to the House when he insisted that Hitler must restore to freedom those countries he had violated before there could be any peace. Like Halifax and Churchill he did not see that anything would be gained from talks, though like Halifax he was more willing to treat the French request for an approach to Mussolini in May with some sympathy as a means of encouraging the French. Chamberlain had made up his mind about Hitler: and whatever the circumstances, even in her darkest hour, there would be nothing for Britain to gain. And once that hour had passed there was even less reason to contemplate any feelers.

Chamberlain expected an attempted invasion after France fell; and continued to do so until late July. At the outset he expected it 'pretty soon', though he felt it might come 'in an unexpected form'.[76] By early July the reports seemed pretty specific. On the 1st they all pointed to invasion, 'this week'; on the 3rd they suggested Britain would be 'attacked from the air by 20,000 planes coming over in waves of thousands' and that after ten days, resistance would be at an end and 'seaborne invasion [would] take place'; on the 6th it seemed that 'the attack ... would be ready by the 15th'.[77] By that date the reorganisation of the German Air Force would be complete and Chamberlain was in no doubt that preparations were being carried out and 'the indications point[ed] to its being attempted very shortly'.[78]

Though by 7 July Chamberlain did not himself discount an attempt, he knew there were 'a good many who doubt whether Hitler will risk it', including Churchill. By the 11th the invasion had not come; and

[74] Halifax diary, 19 Aug. 1940.
[75] Ibid.; cabinet, 11 Sept. 1940, WM(40)247, CAB 65/15.
[76] Chamberlain to Ida, 21 June 1940, NC 18/1/1162; Chamberlain diary, 28 June 1940.
[77] Chamberlain diary, 1, 3, 6 July 1940.
[78] Chamberlain to Ida, 7 July 1940, NC 18/1/1164.

there was still, on the 15th – 'one of the days prophesied' – 'no movement'. Chamberlain suspected 'these mysterious threats ... [were] spread
from Berlin ... to confuse and ... terrify' and he was, therefore, 'not
surprised that nothing ha[d] happened'.[79] By the 14th he had become
'disposed to think that the immediate prospect of invasion on a big scale
had dimmed considerably'; and though something was 'brewing in
Norway ... the target might be Iceland, the Faroes, the Shetlands ...
Scotland or Ireland' and by the 22nd he did not think Hitler 'ready' for
invasion.[80] Chamberlain was away for much of the remainder of the
summer but even in September, on his return when the air battle had
escalated and 'all the fighting men ... agreed [as they did on the 10th]
Hitler intends to try the invasion in the ... next few days', he had and
continued to have his doubts.[81] Hitler, he thought, 'would hardly attempt
it unless he was very sure of success: a failure would be 'so disastrous' a
conclusion to which Chamberlain 'always return[ed] to'. Hitler must be
'very sure of success' and Chamberlain did not see how he could have
'that certainty unless he can first subdue the RAF' which he had not yet
done nor was it clear how he was 'going to'.[82]

Chamberlain, like Halifax, had become less sure that there would be an
invasion attempt as he became more confident of the problems Hitler
would encounter. Even in late June the aircraft squadrons were 'stronger
than ever', while the fall of France had its advantages, in freeing Britain
from her obligations to the French who have been nothing but a liability'
and in America the nomination of Wilkie as Republican candidate was 'a
gleam of light'.[83] As time passed invasion became increasingly unlikely:
and by mid July Chamberlain was confident that 'every week that passes
... [made] it more difficult', and the preparations to resist had made
'remarkable progress'; the prospect 'of being able to hold out through the
autumn look[ed] much rosier than ... a few weeks ago'; 'another 3 or 4
months' production ... and ... we can make ourselves disagreeable in
many ways and many places'.[84] By 22 July the extra time gained to 'go on
strengthening our defences' made Chamberlain wonder whether Hitler
had not 'some other plan'; and returned as he continued to do 'to the
same conclusion that failure would be so disastrous that he could hardly

---

[79] Ibid.; Chamberlain diary, 11, 15 July 1940; Chamberlain to Hoare, 15 July 1940,
     Templewood XIII:17. [54].
[80] Chamberlain to Hilda, 14 July 1940, NC 18/1/1165; and 22 July 1940, NC 18/1/1167.
[81] Chamberlain diary, 10, 11 Sept. 1940; Chamberlain to Ida, 15 Sept. 1940, NC 18/1/1168.
[82] Chamberlain diary, 11 Sept. 1940; Chamberlain to Ida, 15 Sept. 1940, NC 18/1/1168.
[83] Chamberlain diary, 21 June 1940; Chamberlain to Ida, 21 June 1940, NC 18/1/1162;
     Chamberlain to Hilda, 29 June 1940, NC 18/1/1163.
[84] Chamberlain to Hilda, 14 July 1940, NC 18/1/1165; Chamberlain to Hoare, 15 July 1940,
     Templewood XIII:17. [54].

attempt it unless sure of success' and 'the risks involved in ... failure [had] induced Hitler to look elsewhere e.g. to Egypt for his next stroke'.[85] Chamberlain had, since mid-July, speculated on the prospect of Hitler's preparing instead for 'a spectacular advance ... through Turkey, Palestine and Syria to Egypt and the Suez Canal or through Spain to Gibraltar and French North Africa'.[86] Though he could see no sign of either imminent invasion or a move to Africa Chamberlain considered it 'certain that [Hitler] can't sit still and do nothing'; and he continued to return to the view that the risk of failure had 'induced Hitler to look elsewhere e.g. to Egypt for his next stroke'.[87]

Like Halifax, from expecting invasion Chamberlain had come to doubt it, partly because Hitler would find it an increasingly difficult proposition. Like (though less so than) Halifax, Chamberlain had not been unsympathetic to the French desire in May for an approach to Mussolini, and was subsequently sceptical of Hitler's peace feelers: these would not receive a response unless there was a change of heart (of which he had 'seen no sign'). For Chamberlain the basis for any peace had been set out the previous autumn and that basis remained – that Hitler must restore to freedom those countries which he had overrun.[88]

At the outset Chamberlain did not believe that anything would come of a French approach to Mussolini. But like Halifax he did not want to give the French the chance to recriminate and did not think anything would be lost by such a step (terms could be rejected). An approach would not do any 'practical good' but it would 'deny the French the opportunity of condemning the British'; and it would be better to give the French a 'reasoned reply' using the arguments of the Roosevelt intervention rather than a blank refusal. In his view Reynaud's proposal would be 'of no avail' (already the reports were that Hitler had excluded Mussolini from involvement in future arrangements for France) but there was, none the less 'no harm in trying Musso and seeing what the result was. If the terms were impossible we could still reject them'. Chamberlain's support was a matter of tactics *vis-à-vis* the French: designed to avoid giving cause for future recrimination by France. Privately he thought they would be better without the French (see pp. 53–6) and thought the country would fight on alone. About its prospects he had a grim, if measured, sang froid. If France were to collapse then the 'greatest danger was invasion both by sea and air', and Germany would 'try to invade but before she could do so she

<hr>

[85] Chamberlain to Hilda, 22 July 1940, NC 18/1/1167; Chamberlain to Ida, 15 Sept. 1940, NC 18/1/1168; Chamberlain diary, 11 Sept. 1940.

[86] Chamberlain to Hilda, 14 July 1940, NC 18/1/1165;

[87] Chamberlain to Ida, 20 July 1940, NC 18/1/1166; Chamberlain diary, 11 Sept. 1940.

[88] See note 73 above. Chamberlain to Ida, 15 Sept. 1940, NC 18/1/1168.

would require a greater measure of air superiority over us than she now possessed'. It would, he thought 'be best for us to fight on ... [and] ... keep the German[s] at bay till other forces can be mobilised, perhaps in U.S.A.'. He had told the high commissioners that though our dangers were clear, 'Germany would have her difficulties also and even fighting single handed we might well outlast her'. Even if France went out of the war there was, he would tell them, 'no prospect of our giving in. We had good reason to believe that we could withstand attack by Germany', and were resolved to fight on. And though he did not hold out hopes of the United States immediately helping, he considered that Germany did not yet have sufficient air strength to succeed. On the 28th, a further message from Reynaud was received 'asking us to agree to his making a specific offer to Musso, an offer which seemed to us derisory in itself and inopportune'. After a 'rather strong discussion ... in[the] Cabinet ... [they] finally agreed on a reply drafted by me'.[89]

Chamberlain, then, even in late May at the height of the crisis, considered that Britain should fight on alone and that Germany had not, as yet, sufficient air superiority to invade. He did not oppose a peace move by the French to Mussolini in order to avoid recrimination and because unsuitable terms could always be rejected.

Throughout the summer he continued to maintain that there was nothing to be gained from treating with Hitler, who had not changed and would not change: from the abbreviated version of Hilter's speech of 19 July on the wireless it seemed 'to have gone the familiar round of distorted history, megalomania, self righteousness and threats'.[90] Hitler had 'only repeated the same old distortions of history, the same abuse and threats and an even more astonishing exhibition than usual of his power of self deception' – so much so that he would have done nothing to encourage Lloyd George or any peace party.[91]

Chamberlain considered that there could be no peace until Hitler changed heart; and as he did not seem to do so there would be none. Moreover given the increasingly weak position of Hitler's invasion there would be no ostensible reason for Britain to contemplate peace as a result of fear – though for Chamberlain, unlike Halifax and Churchill, there could not, especially during the blackest days of the fall of France, have been any question of peace, for Britain could not influence or impose the terms: and Chamberlain's expectations of dying – rather than submitting

---

[89] Chamberlain diary 26, 28 May 1940; cabinet 27 May 1940, WM(40)141, CAB 65/13; WM(40)142, CAB 65/7.
[90] Chamberlain diary, 19 July 1940.
[91] Chamberlain to Ida, 20 July 1940, NC 18/1/1166.

– though less dramatically couched did not differ from Churchill's pledging never to surrender though they be rotting senseless in the grave. Given that position even at Britain's weakest moment, it was unlikely that Chamberlain's attitude to peace would be modified by events; and given the increasing unlikelihood of invasion, Chamberlain's reluctance to countenance talks correspondingly increased. By mid-September there was no sign of 'a change of heart' from Hitler, whose feelers suggested 'an attempt to get victors' terms without paying for them'. 'As long as that [is] the case they will get no response here.'[92]

After the superficial differences of May (which were really about the best way to deal with the French) Chamberlain's views and those of Halifax and Churchill coincided: confidence that there would be no invasion (first because it would be repelled and then because Hitler would not come) and opposition to, or reluctance to consider, the prospect of negotiated peace. This view was also shared by other politicians – junior ministers, backbench MPs, senior ministers amongst both 'new' and 'old' men: the only difference was that they could acknowledge such confidence but Churchill could not.

Amongst those who had reservations about Churchill at the outset, views about invasion and Britain's prospects were harmonious: Davidson was, after the French fell, 'inclined to think that provided we hold out against the Blitzkrieg in sea and in the air during the next three months' England would have air superiority and command of the sea. Europe, by the winter, would be in an 'absolutely parlous condition', though there were grounds for confidence with the expeditionary, air and light naval forces back from France. He thought there was 'a feeling of satisfaction that we are going to fight this thing out'.[93] Hankey, who towards the end of June had been 'very anxious' and worried by the damage to destroyers and loss of equipment and the extrication of the army from France 'in the form only of bodies' was, by 19 July more confident: 'vast strides' had been made; the army had been 'rebuilt and re-equipped, the mobile armament [was] going along particularly well ... an ... amount ... done on the coast ... damaged destroyers repaired ... air force ... magnificent'.[94] Headlam, after seeing Dill on 7 August, had been told that training was 'improving and supplies ... coming in more adequately'; and Wallace considered when the French went out of the war that 'it may be

92 Ibid., 15 Sept. 1940, NC 18/1/1168.
93 Davidson to Baldwin, 21 June 1940, SB 174:288–9.
94 Hankey to Hoare, 19 July 1940, Templewood XIII:17[66]. Though in September he considered the 'most urgent' needs still to be 'to deter or repel invasion, to defeat the attack on our trade and to continue the air attacks on Germany and Italy', Hankey appreciation, 3 Sept. 1940, Hky 11/3.

that we are better on our own' – though he did think in early August that Hitler could 'hardly dare not to make some attempt to implement his promises to his own people' (about invasion). Moore-Brabazon in early July could not 'see an invasion being any good at all'; for after 'all [the] triumphs abroad it would be ridiculous for [Hitler] to gamble on us and lose'.[95] So too with those who had supported Churchill from the outset. Amery, who at first had been 'desperately alarmed at the possibilities which might follow if the French threw in their hand' and had been preoccupied with invasion, came by August to be confident. While he continued to find it 'very difficult' to make out whether there would be one or what Hitler's plan was, he doubted whether 'even Hitler will venture an invasion of any kind now' and though an expedition 'to the Shetlands or Hebrides may ... still be in the picture ... even that might be very risky'.[96] Beaverbrook too by early July had begun to doubt invasion. He did not 'believe' on the 4th that Hitler would 'try invasion'; was 'altogether sceptical' about it; and concerned instead about 'a German Drang Nach Osten through Salonika, Syria, Palestine, Egypt, Suez Canal and Red Sea'.[97] Bracken was confident by 4 August that 'the defences of this island are rapidly improving'. 'If [the] Nazi invaders hope for an easy conquest they will get the worst of shocks.'[98] Nicolson thought by 10 July that Hitler seemed 'to be funking the great attack upon England'; he was 'at the end of his success' and though an invasion was expected for the weekend of 13 July, 'after that the stars [would be] against him' though he also thought on the 20th that they would 'probably invade us within the next few days'.[99] Sinclair remained confident about British air superiority.[100]

The less confident were the exceptions: and here it was often a matter not so much of lack of confidence in the face of invasion, but of persistent uncertainty as to whether it would come. Crookshank for whom in June 'all look[ed] black but we must go on cost what it may', worried at the food losses through sinkings and air-raids and also wondered whether, on

[95] Headlam diary, 7 Aug. 1940; Wallace diary, 17 June, 7 Aug. 1940; Moore-Brabazon to Hoare, 6 July 1940, Templewood XIII:17 [39].
[96] Amery to Churchill, 13 June 1940, PREM 3/176; Although he thought on 20 September it 'still very difficult to make out whether we are to have an invasion or not'. Amery to Linlithgow, 27 Aug. 1940, 20 Sept. 1940, IOL MSS Eur. F 125/9.
[97] Chamberlain diary, 4 July 1940; Chamberlain to Ida, 7 July 1940, NC 18/1/1164. This did not mean that Beaverbrook would allow resources to be diverted elsewhere; see, e.g., Amery to Linlithgow, 2 Sept. 1940, IOL MSS Eur. F 125/9; Beaverbrook memorandum, 24 Sept. 1940, WP (40)386, CAB 66/12.
[98] Bracken to Hoare, 4 Aug. 1940, Templewood XIII:17 [111].
[99] Nicolson diary, 20 July 1940; Nicolson to Sackville-West, 10, 11 July 1940, Letters pp. 97–8.
[100] Dalton diary, 22 June 1940.

23 September there would be 'invasion tonight'.[101] Eden, though he may
have been subjected to greater influence by the generals than his colleagues, agreed in early September than the indications had 'never been
more positive than ... at ... present' and Dalton recorded at the same
time, after a visit to bomber command, that it was 'still thought in high
quarters that the invasion would be attempted, Dill [being] particularly
sure about this.'[102] There was the modified view that Hitler could hardly
'get out of it'; or general anxieties about specific defence issues – occasionally extending to reservation about Churchill – Nancy Astor's view in
early July that 'everybody in command at Plymouth was incompetent and
... put there because it [was] ... thought a safe place'; or Selborne who
was at the same time 'very worried about home defence' and not reassured
by seeing Churchill 'whom he thought complacent and a lot of whiskies
and soda [sic]'.[103]

Churchill's real views about the threat of a German invasion were,
then, widely held amongst his fellow politicians (especially Halifax and
Chamberlain), though not by the military: initial anxiety that Hitler could
not be prevented from taking over the country, soon succeeded by
increasing confidence that an invasion could be resisted and then that the
invasion would not come; and hostility to any negotiated peace, at first
because it would be foolish to negotiate from a position of weakness, then
because it was foolish to negotiate once the threat of invasion had passed.
However, in his public statements, Churchill *appeared* to be unique in his
attitude to the threat from Hitler: unflinching both in his courage and in
his insistence on the need for vigilance. Churchill's rhetoric of resolution
disguised both his early fears of defeat and his later confidence that the
threatened invasion would not come.

Reactions to Churchill's leadership

Churchill's schemes – to attack invasion shipping in enemy ports and to
organise the country to withstand the effects of the bombing – and his
exhortations to be vigilant were not, then, entirely supported by the
politicians or professionals directly concerned. But they came to be seen
as part of the general bearing of resolution first manifest in Churchill's
reaction to the fall of France, and then seen in his speeches in face of the
bombing and the danger of invasion. Churchill's speeches throughout the

---

101 Crookshank diary, 17 June, 23 Sept 1940.
102 Cabinet, 2 Sept. 1940, WM(40)239, CAB 65/15; Dalton diary, 3 Sept. 1940.
103 If it did not come by the end of August, it would be too late. Nicolson to Sackville-West,
    13 Aug 1940, Nicolson, *Letters*, p. 104; Halifax diary, 2 July 1940; Crookshank diary, 4
    July 1940.

summer of 1940, whether in the House of Commons or over the air, not only made for popularity in the country, but for readier acquiescence in his leadership amongst the politicians, even those who otherwise had reservations about him as prime minister. The reaction of the politicians extended from exultation to admiration; and it seemed to supersede (if temporarily) that of doubt.

Churchill's protagonists remarked on his speeches from the outset. Beaverbrook had described that to the French at Tours as 'magnificent in its eloquence, tact and firmness'; Dalton thought that to the House of Commons on 18 June, just after they sued for peace, 'a grand speech – defiant, reasoned and confident'; Harold Nicolson felt after the Dunkirk speech 'so much in the spirit of [his] great speech that [he] could face a world of enemies', and he 'thank[ed] God for him' on 14 July after hearing him again: he really 'has got guts, that man'.[104]

The expression was more moderate amongst the conservatives in the government and on the backbenches, though the line was the same. Halifax, for example, thought the broadcast of 14 July (when Churchill had pressed his pledge that 'be the ordeal sharp or long, or both, we shall seek no terms, we shall tolerate no parley; we may show mercy – we shall ask for none') 'was excellent'; and after Churchill's helping him with his broadcast one week later he had 'never met a greater artist in language'. Churchill's commending the fighter pilots in his speech to the Commons on the 20th: '"seldom has so much been owed by so many to so few" [*sic*] stated the thing admirably'.[105] Chamberlain thought his speech on 18 June (once the French battle seemed over) 'a real tonic [which] has done much to keep up morale even though there were a few passages in it which had been better omitted.'[106]

The back-bench conservatives and junior ministers were also struck. Headlam thought his speech of 18 June 'very fine and courageous': and though 'not one of his admirers ... [had] ... never believed in his judgement or his fitness for the office which he now [held]'. Churchill was, he thought 'in many ways ... the right man for the present situation ... his personality [was] ... what count[ed] at the moment'; he 'certainly command[ed] the respect of the House of Commons' and was 'very popular' in

---

104 Chamberlain diary, 13 June 1940; Dalton diary, 18 June 1940; Nicolson to Sackville-West, 6 June, 14 July 1940, *Letters*, pp. 91, 99.

105 Halifax diary, 15, 21 July; Halifax to Hoare, 23 Aug. 1940, Templewood XIII:20 [28]; the words used were 'Never in the field of human conflict was so much owed by so many to so few', House of Commons, 20 Aug. 1940, *Into Battle*, pp. 252–62. Cadogan thought it a 'clever, and successful' speech, Cadogan diary, 21 Aug. 1940.

106 Chamberlain to Ida, 21 June 1940, NC 18/1/1162.

the ... country'.[107] Crookshank was struck by the speeches – on 20 June 'a fine speech' in secret session and on 20 August 'a good speech by Winston'.[108] Wallace thought Churchill's statement after Dunkirk 'an absolutely magnificent peroration'.[109] So did Channon who thought it 'an important and moving statement ... [in which] he was eloquent ... oratorical, and used magnificent English'. He continued to be struck by Churchill's command of the House: on 18 July he was 'superb, magnificent ... as he answered questions and later made the very important statement about the Far East; and he successfully quashed the leftish opposition's eagerness for war in the east as well as everywhere else'; on the 23rd he thought Churchill 'in roaring spirits ... and gave slashing answers which he had himself drafted, to foolish questions and generally convulsed the house'. He was, Channon thought 'at the very top of his form now and the house is completely with him, as is the country' – a position which did not change given Brook's account of his tour of defences with Churchill: 'His popularity [was] astounding, everywhere crowds rush up to see him and cheer him wildly, encouraging him with shouts of "stick it".'[110]

Though the soldiers may have had their own objections to Churchill's military initiatives – or his judgement – they were impressed by his courage. To Dill, the chief of the imperial general staff, he seemed in 'great fighting form'; 'full of fight and ... always prepared to accept risks' and did 'not lack courage'. Altogether Dill thought him 'grand'.[111] To Pound – though he had had 'pretty difficult times' with Churchill who was 'occasionally impervious to arguments and sweeps them aside' – Churchill was, nevertheless, 'so magnificent in many ways'. He was 'the ideal leader of the nation in these times ... [and] one must put up with his idiosyncracies'.[112] Brooke, responsible for home command, found Churchill in mid-July 'in wonderful spirits and full of offensive plans for next summer'; and later 'full of the most marvellous courage ... full of offensive thoughts for the future'.[113]

Churchill and 'no surrender'

The idea of Churchill's 'courage' ('offensive' spirit, 'magnificen[ce]') was bound up with his constant reiteration in public and in private that there would be no surrender. This theme, therefore, deserves special attention.

[107] Headlam diary, 18 June 1940.   [108] Crookshank diary, 20 June, 20 Aug. 1940.
[109] Wallace diary, 4 June 1940.
[110] Channon diary, 4 June, 18, 23 July 1940; Brooke diary, 12 Sept. 1940 .
[111] Dill to Montgomery Massingberd, 9 June, 13 July 1940, MM 160/11 and MM 160/12.
[112] Pound to Cunningham, 20 Sept. 1940, BL Add. MS 52561.
[113] Brooke diary, 17, 22 July, 12 Sept. 1940.

Publicly Churchill reiterated the point in his speeches. He set the tone after the Dunkirk evacuation: We shall go on to the end ... we shall defend our island, whatever the cost may be ... we shall never surrender.' In September his message was unchanged: the armed forces had behind them 'a people who will not flinch or weary of the struggle – hard and protracted though it will be'. Churchill reiterated throughout the summer of 1940 the same line, often indeed the same phrase, as he did with the pledge (first made after Dunkirk but repeated in subsequent speeches) to persist 'if necessary for years, if necessary alone'.[114] There would be no peace 'be the ordeal sharp or long ... we shall seek no terms, we shall tolerate no parley'. The aim was 'victory. That is our task' and 'we shall persevere along our course, however the winds may blow'.[115] Churchill did not modify the line, even in private. There were tactical consider-ations: a declaration 'that we were firmly resolved to continue the war in all circumstances would prove the best invitation to the United States ... to lend us their support'.[116] Besides they had no choice: there was 'no alternative ... except to fight it out or else we shall be first despoiled and then enslaved'.[117] There would be no inquiries as to 'terms of peace with Hitler' and he would 'never enter into any peace negotiations with Hitler': not only would Britain 'never surrender' but 'our war aim ... remained the total defeat of Hitler'.[118]

Churchill continued to affect confidence, to this end. From the outset he had insisted, for example, that Britain could resist invasion, should it come, and had drawn on specific events to justify such an attitude. He was after Dunkirk 'much more confident against invasion than ... a week ago. After all ... the BEF [was] in this country now'.[119] The British situation had, in his view, been 'vastly improved by [the] miraculous evacuation of BEF, which [gave] ... an army ... more than capable, when re-equipped, of coping with any invasion': and the 'growing forces in this country should suffice to resist invasion'.[120] He told the cabinet on 12 June that he viewed 'the new phase with confidence'; and he reminded the junior ministers later of the 'long standing doctrine that raids may succeed but

---

114 House of Commons, 4 June 1940, broadcast 11 Sept. 1940, *Into Battle*, pp. 215–23, 272–5.
115 Broadcast, 14 July, House of Commons 20 Aug., 5 Sept. 1940, *Into Battle*, pp. 247–51, 252–62, 263–71.
116 Cabinet, 12 June 1940, WM(40)163, CAB 65/13.   117 Dalton diary, 14 June 1940.
118 Churchill to Mackenzie King, 24 June 1940, in *Second World War*, II, p. 200, Churchill to Eden, 28 June 1940, ibid., p. 152, Cabinet, 13 June 1940, WM(40)165, CAB 65/13.
119 It would, as he explained to the junior ministers, be tactically unsound to waver. For if he did 'for a moment – all [his] colleagues in the government, would turn and rend [sic] me'. Dalton diary, 3 June 1940.
120 Churchill to Mackenzie King, 5 June 1940, *Second World War*, II, pp. 128–9; cabinet, 15 June 1940, WM(40)167, CAB 65/13.

... large scale invasion of this island (was) impossible'. Though there would be 'violent attacks ... if ... beaten off at first they cannot succeed later'. And when the French went out of the war he claimed that if they could 'with ... resources concentrated, hold the devils for two or three months there [was] quite a chance ... the situation [might] turn in our favour'.[121] By early July he was urging the fighting services and civil departments that while 'every precaution must be taken ... there are no grounds for supposing ... more German troops can be landed in this country ... than can be destroyed or captured'; strong grounds existed for confidence: the RAF was 'in excellent order and at the highest strength ... yet', while the army at home had never been 'so strong as now'.[122] By August he was sceptical about invasion – though not in public and was inclined to think that the German announcement that the invasion of Britain would not be undertaken until the Balkan question was settled 'might well be an excuse to get out of an enterprise now regarded as too hazardous'.[123] In any case he was 'feeling much more confident than two months ago ... defences ... hav[ing] been immensely improved'; and though he did not think the air battle had yet, by 21 August 'reached its climax ... the Germans [were] showing signs of weakness'; he was already contemplating certain changes once the battle was decided; and the prospect of invasion became more remote with the winter weather.[124] By early September, though he did not allude to it publicly, he was confident the Germans were unlikely to invade. Though he warned of the need for vigilance – particularly given that the invasion if it were tried could not be 'long delayed' because 'the weather may break at any time' – he no longer believed Hitler would try it.[125] Not only was the RAF 'stronger than ever'; but it was, as he told his colleagues on the 11th 'by no means impossible that the Germans would in the end decide not to launch an attack ... because they were unable to obtain ... domination over our fighter force'.[126] And, despite the escalation of the air battle he did not believe by September that 'the present conditions of bombardment' would 'continue at their present [height] for many weeks'.[127]

By that time – almost five months after his becoming prime minister – Churchill's reaction to the Battle of Britain and the threat of invasion had served to characterise his leadership and to strengthen his claims to be

---

[121] Cabinet, 12 June 1940, WM(40)163, CAB 65/13; Dalton diary, 14 June 1940; Halifax diary, 17 June 1940.
[122] Churchill minute appended to WM(40)192, 3 July 1940, CAB 65/8.
[123] Wallace diary, 2 Aug. 1940.
[124] Dalton diary, 12 Aug. 1940; Churchill to Chamberlain, 21 Aug. 1940, NC 7/9/93.
[125] Broadcast, 11 Sept. 1940, *Into Battle*, pp. 272–5.
[126] Cabinet, 2 Sept. 1940, WM(40)239, CAB 65/9; 11 Sept. 1940, WM(40)247, CAB 65/15.
[127] Churchill to Chamberlain, 24 Sept. 1940, NC 7/9/98.

England's wartime prime minister, even for antagonists in his own party. The idea of Churchill the 'magnificent' leader of 'courage' and 'grandeur' partly resulted from the practical stratagems he devised to put paid to the feeling that the Germans were 'forcing us to ... wall in the island', and partly from the rhetoric which pledged not only that Britain would fight but that her aim was victory. Churchill, though never invigilant, was confident, first of withstanding defeat, and ultimately of victory.

Churchill's refusal to consider peace terms, his holding out for – and being confident of – victory, was less unique than it seemed to be. It derived not so much from a unique resolution but from the considerations which he shared with Halifax and Chamberlain (see pp. 47–9, 73–80). Without his particular rhetorical dressing, Churchill's views would hardly have been distinct. Britain would fight on, not merely because it was the right course, but because it was the only one. Tactically it mattered to Britain's standing (particularly with the United States) that she be seen to persist with the war and not parley with Hitler; practically there was nothing to gain from talking. Not only could Hitler not be trusted, but he would be in a position to impose whatever terms he liked on England which would be 'first despoiled and then enslaved'. Nothing could be lost therefore by fighting on. The very worst (lying 'senseless rotting in the ground') would be no worse than Hitler's despoiling and enslaving, with the advantage that the chance of victory remained. Churchill's decision to fight on was more reasonable and had more in common with that of Chamberlain and Halifax than his rhetoric might suggest, but it was his rhetoric which, in the summer of 1940, had begun to cast him into his wartime caricature. Although this caricature helped to establish him as leader and particularly as leader of the conservatives, among the sources for his rhetoric were Churchill's predecessors, Baldwin and Chamberlain. Churchill's successful leadership owed much to his sharing their apprecations of the past and evoking it in terms he had learned from them.

4   Chamberlain, Churchill and the conservative party

It was not only by his reaction to events in France and to the battle of Britain that Churchill changed the view of himself, and overcame the opposition, particularly amongst the conservatives, and prevented a split in the party. He also did so by balancing his own manipulation of the feeling against Chamberlain (amongst rebel tories, the labour party, independent members and Lloyd George) with meticulous displays of loyalty to Chamberlain and affection for him. He had, at the outset, ensured that no evidence of intrigues or schemes on his part existed.

The campaign against Chamberlain: critics and criticisms

Although Churchill had no apparent connection with those whose interventions against Chamberlain had helped to bring him to power – he did not seem to lead them or their rebellion – he nonetheless appeared to command influence with them as well as having benefited from their actions. Nor did he dissociate from them; but, rather they received office or it was proposed to them; and they continued to demand that Chamberlain be removed from the government – a demand which Churchill did not meet, but did not prevent from being made. Churchill derived political advantage from the campaign against Chamberlain and, though he deprecated publicly attempts to find a scapegoat, he earned enormous personal benefit from the search. Moreover, he formulated his own interpretation of recent events and their cause in the terms of Chamberlain's critics: Chamberlain was held responsible for the war and the disasters: he had failed to stop Hitler or to prepare before or after the war. The attack on Chamberlain which helped to bring Churchill to power continued throughout May and June, from two loose groups with overlapping members: the tory rebels and labour party leaders on the one hand, and the Lloyd George group of pacifists, radicals and Welsh men on the other. It was articulated in the newspapers, particularly the *Daily Herald*. Although Churchill did not join the campaign, he could control it: when he intervened the campaign was stopped 'more suddenly than it began'. But he did not do so until it had had its effect, and opinion had shifted against Chamberlain.[1]

Chamberlain saw his critics as constituting loosely a group of glamour boys, labour party men who with others sometimes met under the leadership of Clement Davies – and a Lloyd George group. He identified the group responsible for 'building up a "hate"' against him as including a party which 'met every evening at the Reform under the chairmanship of Clement Davies ... [the] Welshman who [ratted] from the last government and worked his hardest to whip up opposition to it'.[2] The group included Amery, Macmillan and Boothby, among those now in the new government; and it had been attended by Attlee, Greenwood and Sinclair.[3] The rumours suggested that Davies and the 'labour men' were trying 'to whip up opinion' against him 'on the ground that [he] let down the BEF by underequipping them'.[4]

The critics and criticisms overlapped: Chamberlain's alleged failings both before and after the outbreak of war were seen to lead to and deserve the vote against him. Chamberlain was held responsible for not having 'stopped Hitler long ago ... introduced conscription [or] developed arms production'; and the outbreak of war not only was seen to vindicate such a judgement but the Norwegian disaster, followed as it was by the defeat in France, lent it further substance. The serving members who voted against Chamberlain during the Narvik debate were cited not merely by way of explanation for his fall but as evidence for his deserving to fall. Not only did they hold Chamberlain responsible for failure but they seemed entitled to do so by virtue of being in uniform. Churchill, though insisting there should be no scapegoats, that all were equally responsible, that they were 'all guilty' – nonetheless did not stop the critics; and his version of events came to coincide with theirs.

The discontent of the military after Narvik was seen to justify the political revolt, as well as to explain it. Dalton noted how Wise had 'come straight back from Namsos to vote against the government ... on behalf of [his] men'; they had been bombed by the Germans 'and had nothing with which to reply'; and when he returned to his mess after voting against the government 'everyone ... said "well done"'.[5] Nicolson claimed that 'the whole navy' was reported to be 'absolutely insistent' on Chamberlain's going and that in the army feeling was 'even worse'.[6] Hogg felt

---

[1] For Churchill, the critics and the criticisms see below, pp. 93–8. For the campaign suddenly stopping 'like turning off a tap' see Chamberlain to Ida, 8 June 1940, NC 18/1/1160; Chamberlain diary 7 June 1940.
[2] Chamberlain to Hilda, 1 June 1940, NC 18/1/1159.   [3] Ibid.
[4] Chamberlain diary, 4 June 1940.
[5] Dalton diary, 9 May 1940.   [6] Nicolson diary, 9 May 1940.

obliged to vote against the government to register his protest 'at the total failure of the war office to provide for [his battalion's] ... equipment or training'. He had tried to bring matters before Stanley but received an intimation that he was too busy to see him.[7] Macmillan considered that the young tories in uniform 'voted with us against the government because ... their loyalty to the king overcame their loyalty to the old man and Margesson [i.e. Chamberlain and the chief whip]'; and 'when they saw the mess in Norway, they made up their minds'.[8] If the vote against the government was to be explained and justified because of Chamberlain's failure to provide for the army, that view was perpetuated by the events in France and the evacuation of the British forces. The *Daily Herald* suggested for example that 'the glorious BEF was flung into the inferno "unarmoured" owing to the lethargy of the late government'. The *News Chronicle* and *Daily Mail* joined the *Daily Herald* on the 5th in producing 'passages ... which ... showed an intention to make [Chamberlain] responsible for the alleged shortcomings in the equipment of the BEF'.[9]

The hostility to Chamberlain evoked by the military unpreparedness for Narvik once again emerged during the battle of France and persisted after the return of the BEF. It was reflected in the demand for Chamberlain's removal even from the government and for removal of his close colleagues. There was, as Nicolson put it 'a growing feeling against ... "the old gang"'; and the men who returned from the front felt that 'Kingsley Wood and Inskip let them down and must go'. Chamberlain would also 'have to go'. Boothby thought 'the movement against Chamberlain, Simon and co.' did not originate in the Commons but reflected 'the wave of ... popular resentment arising out of the stories told by ... the BEF [now back] ... in a highly inflamed state of mind'. Boothby wished that those 'whose criminal negligence in the past [was] ... responsible for our present plight should now ... resign.'[10] According to Chamberlain, the *News Chronicle* reached 'a new pitch' by 6 June 'with articles naming [Chamberlain] and other conservatives as likely to resign'.[11] Chamberlain became increasingly aware that his position 'in the country, in the party and in his own town ha[d] deteriorated'; and there was, according to Moore-Brabazon, by early July 'a very definite feeling to get [him] and Kingsley Wood out'. Wood was thought to have run the

---

[7] Hailsham to Chamberlain, 10 May 1940, NC 7/11/33/73.
[8] Dalton diary, 10 May 1940.
[9] Chamberlain to Hilda, 1 June 1940, NC 18/1/1159; Chamberlain diary, 5 June 1940.
[10] Nicolson to Sackville-West, 6 June 1940, *Letters*, pp. 90–1; Boothby to Lloyd George, l0, 15 June 1940, LG G/3/13/22, LG G/3/13/23.
[11] Chamberlain diary, 6 June 1940.

air ministry badly and then to have been 'promoted by it which [got] everybody's goat good and proper'.[12] Halifax too must go – for either being too weak or too wrong, or both. Brabazon thought he had been 'wrong all along the line ... much too soft and does not really know how to deal with gangsters'. Lloyd George thought Halifax must go; otherwise Britain would not 'get the friendship of Russia and the United States in full measure'.[13] By 21 July there was what struck Channon as evidence that 'our reign is slowly ending' – an attack by Attlee on Halifax in *The Times*.[14]

Although it is not clear how strong or how general were the antipathies to Chamberlain, they did exist and continued to be articulated between May and July 1940 in the context of the disasters in which the country found itself between Narvik and the Battle of Britain. The critics blamed Chamberlain and the 'old gang' not only for the specific failure to prepare for war, but for the general deficiences of foreign policy – stretching back nine years to the formation of the national government in 1931 – a date convenient to the labour men. That was when the trouble started, certainly in Dalton's view; and subsequent years were characterised by British foreign policy 'being in a mess'.[15] Lloyd George, who still did not think things were right, blamed the foreign office – which 'had committed all the possible blunders ... [and was] making a muddle both in the East and in the Baltic' – and Halifax.[16] His supporters wanted him in government. Addison, his friend and former coalition minister, hoped he would 'join the government'; and Stokes thought he should combine with Churchill – 'who did his best to warn us of the peril ahead'.[17] Whereas for Lloyd George the general mistakes occurred since his own fall in 1922, with the foreign office being particularly to blame, his supporters looked more specifically to the 1930s when those responsible for the 'mess' began the fatal course of action (or inaction) which led to the war about which Churchill had warned. Although Lloyd George was said to have no personal animus against Chamberlain, he considered his continued presence in the cabinet 'a source of ... bewilderment and irritation to the working classes'; while Halifax's inclusion impeded relations with the United States and the Soviet Union.[18]

[12] Reith diary, 25 June 1940; Moore-Brabazon to Hoare, 6 July 1940, Templewood XIII:17.
[13] Moore-Brabazon to Beaverbrook, 17 July 1940, Brabazon, AC 71/3, Box 6, BBK file; Beaverbrook to Hoare, 29 July 1940, BBK C 308.
[14] Channon diary, 21 July 1940.   [15] Dalton diary, 16 May 1940.
[16] Beaverbrook to Hoare, 29 July 1940, BBK C/ 308; Lloyd George to Maisky, 1 Aug. 1940, LG G/14/1/15.
[17] Addison to Lloyd George, 19 June 1940, LG G/1/4/43; Stokes to Lloyd George, 19 June 1940, LG G/19/3/8.
[18] Boothby memorandum, 9 July 1940, BBK C/47.

Addison, who had held office under Lloyd George as a liberal, and then under MacDonald as a labour MP during 1930 and 1931, hoped Lloyd George would join the government and 'get rid of the duds who ... landed us into this mess'.[19] Boothby wanted Lloyd George in the government and to propose that those 'whose criminal negligence in the past [was] mainly responsible for our present plight' should resign. Lloyd George's inclusion would restore British 'prestige' in the Soviet Union. He wanted Lloyd George to form 'a dictatorial triumvirate ... [with] Winston ... [and] a representative of ... Labour ...'.[20] Richard Stokes, labour MP for Ipswich wanted Lloyd George to 'hurl into outer darkness' those who 'deliberately invited war instead of ... giving a revision of ... Versailles'.[21] Sir Richard Acland, labour MP since 1935 although he did not want Lloyd Georgian government hoped for an independent opposition to eliminate 'every trace of Chamberlainism'.[22]

For Lloyd George and his supporters Chamberlain and Chamberlainism were held responsible for the 'present plight'. For those whom Churchill had brought with him to power (or influence), though Chamberlain personified the cause, that, in turn, could be traced to the 1931 crisis and the formation of the national government. Lindemann for example, Churchill's scientific advisor and 'a great Winstonite' put the starting date in 1932: since then every decision in foreign policy had been 'wrong' and 'they would have done ... better if every time they had decided by tossing a coin', for they then would 'probably have been right half the time'.[23] The failures and the mistakes in foreign policy were now seen to have a particular culmination – the Munich agreement of 1938. Munich, 'Municheer', Munich spirit came to represent not merely the agreement with Hitler itself, but a foolish if not wrong one; and the variations on the word came to represent righteous dismissal and disparagement of the previous administration and its policies, by contrast with the present patriotic one. When Chamberlain fell Dalton recalled his own efforts and those of Macmillan 'now nearly two years ago to begin this sort of thing'.[24] Duff Cooper defended what Churchill judged an intemperate broadcast by maintaining that he stood out against 'the Munich spirit' which was 'not dead in this country'. This view of that spirit subsequently became the accepted interpretation of the foreign policy of

[19] Addison to Lloyd George, 19 June 1940, LG G/l/4/13.
[20] Boothby to Lloyd George, 15 June 1940, LG G/3/13/23. Boothby was 'struck by the astonishing vigour ... and ... fertility of ... his mind' and considered he would be 'a tower of strength ... if ... he could be brought in' Boothby to Bracken, 9 July 1940, BBK C/47.
[21] Stokes to Lloyd George, 19 July 1940, LG G/193/8.
[22] Acland to Lloyd George, 17 May 1940, LG G/1/3/4.
[23] Dalton diary, 22 July 1940.   [24] Ibid., 10 May 1940.

the Baldwin and Chamberlain administrations in the 1930s. The 'Munich spirit' Cooper held, at worst 'degenerates into treason' and at best was founded on the belief 'that you can defeat your enemy by kind words and courtesy and that it is unwise and impolitic to disturb them by insult and defiance'. Cooper insisted that he held 'the opposite view' and would 'continue to do so'.[25] The new men, the view implied, were patriotic, courageous, strong-minded, unlike the men of Munich who were at worst treacherous or at best weak. Such a line might be needed in wartime propaganda, when Britain was fighting, alone, Nazi Germany: but it excluded the similarities which existed between Churchill's appreciation of Britain's interests and those of his predecessors. Churchill himself did not draw any parallels. His standing with the new men depended on there not seeming to be any parallels, while his acceptance by the old men depended on his appearing less radical than his supporters expected.

Churchill and Lloyd George

Churchill's considered view of events prior to his coming to office was affected by the conflicting requirements of those on whose support he depended. In his own account – written after the war – he suggested that his predecessors of the 1930s were fools rather than knaves, and magnanimously maintained that all were in some part guilty. At the time he took care not to castigate Chamberlain or to cast himself as the hero of revisionist history. At no stage did he, by word or deed, join the Chamberlain antagonists. While his general line and the fact that he was not Chamberlain may have been what the new men wanted, Churchill did or said nothing which might have antagonised Chamberlain and his supporters.[26] Yet at the same time he promoted the heroic view of himself by continued analogy and implication and by tolerating the unfavourable comparisons with himself which were made by Chamberlain's critics.

Just as Churchill was not explicitly antagonistic to Chamberlain but rather implied criticism of him, so too his relations with Chamberlain's critics were close but not open, and their basis was unclear. What Chamberlain referred to as the 'hate' campaign certainly continued until Chamberlain made it clear to Churchill that unless it stopped he might, in

---

[25] Cooper to Churchill, 12 June 1940, PREM 4 83/1A.
[26] Churchill on 18 June referred in the Commons to those who wanted 'an inquest ... on the Government ... during the years which led up to this catastrophe. They seek to indict those who were responsible for the guidance of our affairs.' This, he warned, 'would be a foolish and pernicious process. There are too many in it. Let each man search his conscience and search his speeches. I frequently search mine.' House of Commons, 18 June 1940, *Into Battle*, pp. 225–34; see also Churchill, *Second World War*, I, pp. 3–34.

his own defence, have to attack members of the government. That campaign had been partly the work of some labour men, the Welsh radical Clement Davies, and partly the result of the personal enmity of Lloyd George, who with his supporters was determined to force Chamberlain's resignation.

Churchill had wanted, at the outset, to include Lloyd George in the government. Lloyd George might pose less danger inside the government than outside it – whether as a focus of discontent or the proponent of negotiated peace. Indirectly as a maligner of Chamberlain he may also have had his uses – though that would stop if he were included in the government. Churchill was said to have 'consulted' him two or three times and approached him through Beaverbrook with the result that Lloyd George considered by late May that 'he would be receiving ... a definite offer of a post in the cabinet'.[27] Churchill approached him personally on the 28th to ask whether he would be 'prepared to enter the war cabinet' – though he made it 'quite clear' that his doing so would depend on Chamberlain's acquiescence, without which Churchill would not 'proceed with the offer'.[28] Chamberlain had continued to object to the prospect and would have been willing to resign rather than serve with Lloyd George; but Churchill continued to press Chamberlain to concede, which he did on 6 June.[29] In the event Lloyd George did not respond. Chamberlain had insisted that agreeing to Lloyd George depended on Lloyd George's dropping 'his personal feud'; and 'that the campaign ... against [Chamberlain] ... by The Daily Herald, The News Chronicle and some members of Parliament shall be stopped' before any announcement was made.[30]

Churchill wanted Lloyd George back in the government for a number of reasons: not only to bring back the victor of the First World War and the leader rejected by those who 'threw away' the victory, but also to stop his becoming 'the focus for discontents'.[31] Inclusion of Lloyd George would 'take away the only possible spearhead of attack on the government' and satisfy that group – of odd labour MPs, Lloyd George liberals, glamour boys – which felt that he would save the country and was the only man who could make good the disasters brought about by Chamberlain.[32]

27 Liddell-Hart diary, 27 May 1940.
28 Lloyd George to Churchill, 29 May 1940, draft, LG G/4/5/47.
29 Chamberlain to Hilda, 1 June 1940, NC 18/1/1159; Chamberlain diary, 5, 6 June 1940 Chamberlain to Churchill, 6 June 1940, NC 7/9/87; Churchill to Chamberlain, 6 June 1940, NC 7/9/98; Halifax diary, 6 June 1940.
30 For Lloyd George's not responding, see p. 97; Chamberlain diary, 5 June 1940; Chamberlain to Churchill, 6 June 1940, NC 7/9/87.
31 Churchill to Chamberlain, 6 June 1940, NC 7/9/86.
32 Chamberlain diary, 5 June 1940.

Noel-Buxton (League of Nations supporter, labour MP disarmer) thought that 'all the thousands' who believed in Lloyd George were 'anxiously waiting to hear what ... [he would] have in the new government'.[33] Lloyd George's supporters from the last war and the coalition expected him to be called: Lee of Fareham felt he 'ought to be ... in the ... war cabinet' and that 'the call ... must come before long'; Sir William Sutherland who had held office during the coalition gave Lloyd George the credit for having 'knocked out Chamberlain's government' and thought he 'ought to have been in ... instead of Chamberlain'; for although Churchill had done 'so much' to warn of 'German armaments and warlike intentions', his new colleagues were a 'pedestrian ... lot' and the country might 'have to call on ... Lloyd George'; Addison wanted him to 'join the government' and to get rid of those 'who ... landed us into this mess'.[34] So too did the glamour boys and the labour MPs. Boothby wanted Lloyd George to make plain those 'responsible for our present plight' should resign, and to form a triumvirate with Churchill and a labour member as the 'only government ... capable of saving us'; Stokes, labour MP for Ipswich, wanted him to 'bring us safely through the stormy seas ahead' and combine with Churchill 'who did his best to warn us of the peril ahead' to 'save us from disaster'; Acland advocated an independent opposition given the failure to insist on the inclusion of 'gutsy' forces and to eliminate 'every trace of Chamberlainism'.[35]

Not only would Lloyd George's inclusion satisfy his supporters, remove a possible focus of opposition and seem to be directed against Chamberlain, but it would also stop the prospect of a negotiated peace. For as Beaverbrook put it, while there was one camp in the country which thought that Churchill 'should bring him in', there was another which thought that 'Hitler will put him in'.[36] Lloyd George would be at the centre of the peace which his supporters urged upon him, and for which the case was made on the grounds that there should be an agreement when the country was still strong or because military matters would hardly improve and would result in a stalemate. One exponent of such views was Tavistock. He thought Hitler's strength 'so great ... it is madness to suppose we can beat him by war on the continent' and that it was not possible to rid the world of 'undemocratic methods of government' by

[33] Noel Buxton to Lloyd George, 9 May 1940, LG G/1/14/10.
[34] Lee of Fareham to Lloyd George, 17 May 1940, LG G/11/9/12; Sutherland to Stevenson, 15 May 1940. LG G/19/7/12; Addison to Lloyd George, 19 June 1940, LG G/l/4/13.
[35] Boothby to Lloyd George, 15 June 1940, LG G/3/13/23; Stokes to Lloyd George, 19 June 1940, LG G/193/8; Acland to Lloyd George, 17 May 1940, LG G/1/3/4.
[36] Beaverbrook to Hoare, 14 Aug. 1940, Templewood XIII:17; Dalton diary, 31 July 1940; though Beaverbrook thought that view 'a great injustice', ibid.

'complete victory over Germany'. He therefore urged Lloyd George that peace should be made 'now rather than later ... [when] our strength is still very great'; he hoped Lloyd George would either bring this 'home to the government' or else bring his support for such a course 'to the notice of the German government'. Bedford looked to Lloyd George as the 'one statesman in this country who ... could deliver the world from its agony' and wanted a peace initiative: if the Germans 'received fair peace terms a dozen Hitlers could never start another war on an inadequate ... pretext'. Stokes conveyed to Lloyd George the wishes of a group of MPs which hoped in late June that Hitler's impending speech 'could form the start of negotiations' and that Lloyd George would prevent any intemperate remarks from English ministers until both houses had discussed the matter: Lloyd George should alert Churchill about this view – either as theirs or his own 'with the knowledge that some 30 MPs support you'. Stokes did not consider a 'military defeat' of Germany possible, while a 'starvation victory' would 'leave things worse than before' and his all party group of roughly thirty MPs and ten peers prepared to form 'a rallying ground of agreement' and a 'just peace with disarmament'. The government should state Britain's 'constructive aims for all the world to know and ... should seize the earliest opportunity ... to enter into negotiations for a peace within the framework of those aims'. Noel Buxton was 'very glad' to have heard Lloyd George 'raise the question of possible negotiations' in his speech to the Commons on 4 July; and he thought there was support for initiating talks 'without waiting for proposals from the other side, or for military events'.[37]

Lloyd George's following of malcontents who wanted him in the government and Chamberlain out of it may to some extent have tempted Churchill to follow their lead. But Churchill was also keen on his own account to have Lloyd George's help. He would be 'a valuable counsellor'. Churchill was sentimental about their old association and the first wartime coalition. Moreover, he was anxious both to remove 'the only possible spearhead of attack' and the focus of those who wanted a negotiated peace either because they thought Britain was now stronger than she would be or because they did not believe that she could win the war. It was not clear how far Lloyd George shared the views of his supporters and Churchill may have wanted him in government (and thereby no longer a threat) because he suspected that he must have done.

[37] Tavistock to Lloyd George, 15 May 1940, LG G/3/4/7; Bedford to Lloyd George, 2, 21 Sept. 1940, LG G/3/4/8, G/3/4/10; Stokes to Lloyd George, 19, 25 June, 17 July 1940, LG G/19/3/8, G/19/3/7, G/17/3/12; Noel Buxton to Lloyd George, 7 June, 9 July 1940, LG G/15/11/3, G/15/11/4.

Lloyd George himself did not make his position clear. On 7 June, he wanted to 'think over the offer' – though he had already refused the ministry of agriculture because it did not involve war work.[38] His attitude to negotiated peace seemed ambiguous. In the House of Commons on 10 May he had 'sought to justify Hitler on the grounds that we had broken faith with Germany' and seemed to separate himself from the government in a position from which he might be called to make the peace.[39] Churchill did not trust him 'not to be defeatist' and did not know 'where his mind was'. At one stage he had been 'certainly defeatist' thought lately 'seemed ... firmer'; but it was not clear whether his refusing to join any government with Chamberlain and Halifax had been a pretext to stay out and he would 'thus be left in a position to form an alternative government'.[40] He kept his views on the subject to himself; procrastinated on the offer and had, by 10 June given 'no sign of life', remained 'silent', did not speak in the secret session and had not replied by 21 June, the day of the armistice, by which time Churchill seemed to Chamberlain to be 'fed up with him' – and may have decided to proceed no further.[41]

Churchill and Chamberlain

Despite the advantages of bringing in Lloyd George, Churchill had to weigh them against the disadvantage of losing Chamberlain and its implications for his standing with the party. Therefore, although Churchill persisted at the outset with his approaches he seemed to make it clear to Lloyd George that it depended on Chamberlain's not vetoing the proposal. For Lloyd George it was 'not a firm offer' and 'until ... definite' he could not consider it. He maintained that he was 'no office seeker' but rather wanted to help his country which had been 'plunged' into disaster by the 'ineptitude of her rulers' of whom several remained in the government and two in the cabinet. Moreover Lloyd George made it clear that he would be unlikely to accept a post such as the ministry of agriculture where he would not be responsible for a department 'not vital to the most urgent problems with which ... they have to deal'.[42]

---

38 Chamberlain diary, 7 June 1940.
39 Chamberlain to Ida, 11 May 1940, NC 18/1/1155; Halifax diary, 6 June 1940.
40 Chamberlain diary, 31 May, 11 June 1940; Chamberlain to Hilda, 1 June 1940, NC 18/1/1155.
41 Chamberlain diary, 10, 15 June 1940; Chamberlain to Hilda, 15 June 1940, NC 18/1/1161; Chamberlain to Ida, 21 June 1940, NC 18/1/1164; Beaverbrook to Hoare, 29 July 1940, BBK C.308.
42 Lloyd George to Churchill, 29 May 1940, draft, LG G/4/5/47; Lloyd George to Churchill, 31 May 1940, 'not sent', LG G/4/5/49.

The difficulties posed by Lloyd George and the demands he made could have been surmounted had Churchill made clear that he was worth it. But he was not clear. And certainly not at the expense of Chamberlain. 'Feeling' in the party for Chamberlain might have 'broken out' had he been dropped (see pp. 40, 42); and Chamberlain was, or so Churchill claimed, 'far more help' to him than Lloyd George; there was 'no comparison' between them; and he himself did not 'trust' Lloyd George, did not 'know his mind' or whether 'he was not a defeatist'. The reasons for bringing him in also constituted reasons for not doing so.[43] Moreover in the course of reassuring Chamberlain, Churchill helped to convince himself of the advantages of not pressing for Lloyd George and simultaneously confirmed Chamberlain in his loyalty. By early June he was telling Chamberlain he would 'think no more of it', had 'only toyed with the idea'.[44] He had written to Lloyd George of the 'great deal of help [he had had] from Chamberlain'; that he had 'joined hands with him and must act with perfect loyalty'; and could ask Lloyd George to go no further than he had done.[45]

The need for Churchill to 'act with perfect loyalty' was not a new consideration but one which had been paramount in the circumstances of his replacing Chamberlain as prime minister. While the suspicions amongst conservatives at the time – of his having intrigued, been a hypocrite, pursued a 'spoils policy' and ousted the 'proper conservatives' – had not amounted to a sustained and articulated opposition, Churchill had anticipated and dealt with them by standing aside and seeming to be apart from the successful attack on Chamberlain. He may then have feared – as he later did – a split in the party, possibly on the lines of 1916, not to mention the prospect of the unflattering analogy being made between the sordid intrigues of Lloyd George and his own. Whatever the case may have been, Churchill did not seem to have any truck with the disreputable – before or after he ousted Chamberlain. As a result, though the differences about Churchill in the party remained, the divisions did not: and it was for the same considerations that Churchill took care not to favour or include Chamberlain's opponents at his expense, balancing his own exploitation of their criticism with meticulous displays of loyalty to Chamberlain. Just as at the outset of the political crisis, at the time of the Narvik debate, Churchill had seemed to avoid intrigue, association with the Chamberlain critics or thrusting himself forward, so too during his first months in office there was no *evidence* of his being anything but

[43] Chamberlain to Hilda, 1 June 1940, NC 18/1/1159; Chamberlain diary, 28 May 1940.
[44] Ibid.; Churchill to Chamberlain, 6 June 1940, NC 7/9/86.
[45] Churchill to Lloyd George, 29 May 1940, LG G/4/5/48.

loyal to his predecessor, though his position was, in fact, far more ambiguous.

Before Chamberlain had fallen, for example, Churchill had refused to co-operate with any plan to prolong his government and refused to agree to Halifax as prime minister. When, after the news of Hitler's attack in the west, Chamberlain had proposed 'to restore confidence in the government by having all parties in' Churchill had been doubtful; he did not 'approve of the delay' and 'was pressing for early changes in the government'.[46] When Kingsley Wood privately advised him how best to act, Churchill took the advice. Wood, it seems, had by 9 May abandoned Chamberlain in favour of Churchill. Having made it clear both to Churchill and Eden that Churchill 'should succeed', Wood advised that 'if asked he should make plain his willingness' but not to agree to Halifax [as prime minister] and not to 'say anything'.[47] However Churchill was not Chamberlain's preferred successor. Chamberlain, who considered the time had come for a national government (which he could not form), inclined towards Halifax who might also prove less contentious than Churchill for the labour party. Attlee, for example, was reported on the 9th as preferring Halifax to Churchill. But Halifax had reservations about his own succession 'to take it would create quite an impossible position' as he would be in the Lords with Churchill in the Commons running defence and would soon become 'a more or less honorary prime minister'.[48] When, therefore, Churchill met Chamberlain and Halifax to consider the succession, he could not count on automatic success and took care to pursue, discreetly, his own claims. Chamberlain's preference was for Halifax, though he did not express it. After Halifax had expressed objections to his own succes-

---

[46] Halifax diary, 9, 10 May 1940; Eden diary, 10 May 1940.

[47] Even if he had not abandoned Chamberlain, Wood was known to be 'very active with Winston'. Hoare notes, 'Thursday' (9 May), Templewood, XII:III; Eden diary, 9 May 1940.

[48] For Chamberlain's (and the labour party's) inclining towards Halifax rather than Churchill, see Halifax diary, 9 May 1940; Dalton diary, 9 May 1940; Chamberlain to Ida, 11 May 1940, NC 18/1/1155. Halifax's account of his discussion with Chamberlain on the morning of the 10th records that Chamberlain thought 'it was clearly Winston or myself ... if it were myself he might continue to serve in government' and 'did not think much' of Halifax's arguments against his own candidacy. Chamberlain on the 11th explained in a letter what had happened: his belief that he himself could not get a national government and that he 'sent for Attlee and Greenwood ... to ask ... whether the labour party would join a government under me or if not under someone else. I did not name the someone else ... but I had understood that they favoured Halifax, and I had him in mind. He declared ... he would find it too difficult being in the lords ... Later I heard that the labour party had changed their minds and were veering towards Winston and I agreed with him and Halifax that I would put Winston's name to the king.' Chamberlain to Ida, 11 May 1940, NC 18/1/1155. For Chamberlain's envisaging becoming prime minister after the war, see p. 104 below.

sion, Churchill accepted these with 'much less reluctance' (than Chamberlain). He 'could not but feel the force' of the objections; and so Halifax, instead of being persuaded that his objections should not prove to be obstacles, found himself eliminated. Only Churchill remained, and there was no contest.[49]

Yet Churchill had not openly intrigued but had followed the advice of Wood, now acting not as Chamberlain's friend but as the agent for Churchill's succession. He had not attacked the government before or during the debate; nor had he sided with its enemies. He alluded to his share of responsibility for the failings of the government during the debate; and he took care not to press his own claims, even with his associates: when he noted – to Eden – that Chamberlain 'would not be able to bring in labour and . . . a national government must be formed' he does not seem to have proposed himself specifically. Whatever the doubts about his hand in the events leading to his succession, there could be no certainty. He had not acted disloyally; was not obviously determined to replace Chamberlain; had not openly associated with the malcontents, office seekers, labour party or those vindictive to Chamberlain – though he was their choice. He had kept his silence and bidden his time until circumstances brought him to power. While his succession may not have been as natural as he subsequently made out, his discretion made it more inevitable, and his continuing care more lasting. While his relations with Chamberlain's critics may have been closer than he conceded, their nature remained ambiguous. And when, for example, he had to choose between displaying support for Chamberlain or for his critics, Churchill had no hesitation in backing Chamberlain. This happened not only on the general issue of Lloyd George – when Churchill was resolved to persuade Chamberlain to accept his inclusion rather than allow Chamberlain to resign – but on the specific matter of Chamberlain's terms. Churchill had been quick to co-operate with Chamberlain's request that Lloyd George should be asked to drop his feud and that the newspaper campaign be called off, as well as the attacks which persisted from all quarters.[50] He had promised Chamberlain – a propos the Amery, Lloyd, Macmillan, Boothby plan to supersede the cabinet with a committee of safety of three – that 'if there is any more of this nonsense they will go'. He had followed Chamberlain's suggestion in dealing with any attacks in the House that 'this was no time for raking up the past or . . . scapegoats' and 'we must all

[49] Chamberlain to Ida, 11 May 1940, NC 18/1/1155; Eden diary, 9 May 1940; Halifax diary, 9 May 1940; Cadogan diary, 9 May 1940.
[50] Eden diary, 9 May 1940; Chamberlain to Churchill, 6 June 1940, NC 7/9/87; Churchill to Chamberlain, 6 June 1940, NC 7/9/86; Chamberlain diary, 7 June 1940.

work together to defeat the enemy'. He had reassured Chamberlain that he would see Attlee and Greenwood 'to tell them to call off the *Daily Herald*' and the press generally to 'stop this campaign'; and he kept the cabinet back on 6 June 'in order to exhort Archie Sinclair and the Labour people on the subject of stopping the heresy hunt against members of the previous Government especially Neville and Kingsley Wood'.[51] Bound up with Churchill's reactions to the critics was his determination to keep Chamberlain himself and his loyalty.

So successful was Churchill in winning Chamberlain's loyalty and avoiding a division in the party that by late September he felt Chamberlain could now be dropped, that Halifax could be moved and that Eden, 'glamour' boy and friend, could come to the cabinet as foreign secretary, symbol of the anti-Municheers.

Even before he formally became prime minister, Churchill hoped Chamberlain 'would stay, would lead the House of Commons and continue as leader of the party'.[52] His first act after seeing the king was to write to Chamberlain to thank him for 'promising to stand by ... [him]' and also to Halifax, assuming that he could 'count on' his remaining foreign secretary and leader of the lords.[53] He wanted Chamberlain to keep the leadership of the conservatives, and maintained that with his 'help and counsel' and 'the support of the great party' which he led, he would succeed.[54] Not only was it better for Churchill 'not to undertake the leadership of any one ... party', given that his was a national government, but otherwise the 'criticism among those ... personally devoted ... [to Chamberlain] would ... have broken out'.[55]

Churchill's precautions in respect of Chamberlain, mattered enormously – given Chamberlain's suspicions of Churchill and the unpleasantness of the Narvik debate. Even before he fell, Chamberlain had considered Churchill's reputation 'inflated' and needing 'debunking'; that he had been 'virtually responsible' for Trondheim (and the Norway disaster) – having at first acccepted the sea lords' objections but then 'put it across the other service ministers'.[56] Chamberlain had found the debate

---

[51] Chamberlain to Ida, 21 June 1940, NC 18/1/1162; Chamberlain diary, 5, 6 June 1940; Halifax diary, 6 June 1940.
[52] Eden diary, 9 May 1940.
[53] Churchill to Chamberlain, 10 May 1940, NC 7/9/88; Churchill to Halifax, 10 May 1940, HFX MCF A4.410.19.1.
[54] Churchill to Chamberlain, 10 May 1940, NC 7/9/88.
[55] Churchill to Chamberlain, 16 May 1940, NC 7/9/84; Chamberlain to Hilda, 19 May 1940, NC 18/1/1156; Davidson to Baldwin, 14 May 1940, SB 174:275–7.
[56] Reith diary, 3, 7 May 1940.

'a very painful affair ... particularly for its exhibition of personal and party passion' and he would 'much rather have gone out altogether'.[57]

Churchill quickly overcame Chamberlain's reservations by his persistent attentions – both flattering and affectionate – facilitated by his not having had any open part in the attack. He hoped to follow Chamberlain's 'self-forgetting dignity and public spirit' and thought his success would depend on Chamberlain's 'help and counsel'. He was 'proud to have [his] friendship and ... confidence'; and was 'to a very great extent' in Chamberlain's hands.[58] He included Chamberlain in the news of his early discussions with the labour party and his thoughts on ministerial appointments.[59] He would be 'most grateful' if Chamberlain would lead the house as lord president of the council for the two 'must work so closely together' and he hoped Chamberlain would return to live at 11 Downing Street – his 'old quarters, which we both know so well', and asked that he and Halifax join him even before the cabinet met to 'look at the maps and talk things over'.[60] Even when the exploratory operation for cancer made Chamberlain's return seem unlikely, Churchill seemed to assume that he would come back, but begged him not to do so until he felt 'really fit'.[61] All were 'delighted', he wrote to Chamberlain at the end of August, 'to learn of [his] ... improved progress' and though Chamberlain must not 'hesitate to take another week', Churchill could not 'conceal ... that there [were] several topics ... on all of which [he would] ... welcome [Chamberlain's] counsel', quite apart from that on general policy.[62] He was, when Chamberlain returned in early September, 'very glad [he] was back. He felt lonely and would welcome [his] counsel.' Nor did he think they would differ, for they were in his view 'complementary'. Whereas 'he was up and down, [Chamberlain] was more steady [and] ... it was helpful to feel that his decisions were approved by [Chamberlain's] judgement'.[63] He continued to see to whatever practical arrangements he could to make Chamberlain's convalescent state easier, and if necessary Chamberlain should leave London during the heavy raids but he would be 'kept fully informed of all

57 Chamberlain to Ida, 11 May 1940, NC 18/1/1155; Chamberlain to Mary, 11 May 1940, NC 1/20/1/198.
58 Churchill to Chamberlain, 10 May 1940, NC 7/9/80.
59 Churchill to Chamberlain, 11 May 1940, NC 7/9/81.
60 Churchill to Chamberlain, 11 May 1940, NC 7/9/81 (but, see below note 65).
61 Churchill to Chamberlain, 21 Aug. 1940, NC 7/9/93. It was not thought by early August that he would return, or at least return soon. Dalton diary, 30 July 1940; Crookshank diary, 3 Aug. 1940; Beaverbrook to Hoare, 14 Aug. 1940, Templewood XIII: 17 [16].
62 Churchill to Chamberlain, 31 Aug. 1940, NC 7/9/94.
63 Chamberlain diary, 9 Sept. 1940.

business'.[64] Nor would he accept the resignation which Chamberlain, on account of his incapacities, decided on 22 September to put 'unreservedly in [Churchill's] hands'. Although privately he considered that illness would force Chamberlain 'to give up soon', he would hear nothing of resignation. He asked Chamberlain to 'continue at your post and give ... me your aid which I so greatly value' and urged that they both 'go on together through this storm'.[65]

Churchill succeeded in winning Chamberlain, not only because of his persistent attentions (all the more welcome, given the 'painful' nature of Chamberlain's fall) but because of Chamberlain's sense of duty and his feeling at the outset that the new arrangements would be temporary, for the duration of the war. He would have fallen in with Churchill's initial suggestion that he should 'lead the ... commons as lord president of the council'.[66] He felt it his 'duty to set an example of unity'; had promised that he would serve under either Halifax or Churchill; had even been willing to drop his objections to Lloyd George, for one couldn't deny Churchill that – given the burden he had to bear.[67] Under such hostile attack, he may have been all the more willing to be convinced that Churchill did rely on Halifax and himself; and he did not wish to doubt Churchill, who had been 'most handsome in his appreciation of [his] willingness to help and ... ability to do so'.[68] Rather, he identified the labour party as the principal source of objection. He would have been given the exchequer by Churchill had he wanted it, but he could not take it on account of labour: they would 'quickly' make his position 'untenable' and the 'only chance of letting their passions die down [was] to take a place which [did] ... not bring [him] ... into conflict with them'.[69] In a sense he tended to detach Churchill from that group and interpreted the bitterness of the debate as springing from 'personal and party passion' and 'the frustrations' of the office seekers, rather than his own mistakes or bad judgement.[70] He may have thought that by remaining in office he would vindicate himself, as well as best serve the need of unity. He may

---

[64] He had, for example instructed that the air-conditioning in Chamberlain's shelter be seen to and offered Chamberlain the use at night of the shelter at No. 10. Churchill to Chamberlain, 9 Sept. 1940, to Mrs Chamberlain, 20 Sept. 1940, NC 7/9/95, 7/9/96; Chamberlain diary, 14 Sept. 1940.

[65] Chamberlain to Churchill, 22 Sept. 1940, NC 7/9/97; Eden diary, 24 Sept. 1940; Churchill to Chamberlain, 24 Sept. 1940, NC 7/9/98.

[66] This was not the leadership of the House which Churchill himself would take, but the deputy leadership. In fact Chamberlain did not take the job, which went instead to Attlee as 'the Labour Party made trouble'. Chamberlain to Hilda, 17 May 1940 NC 18/1/1156; Churchill to Chamberlain, 11 May 1940, NC 7/9/81.

[67] Chamberlain to Mary, 11 May 1940, NC 1/20/1/198; Halifax diary, 9 May 1940. For dropping his objections to Lloyd George, see pp. 94, 100.

[68] Churchill to Ida, 11 May 1940, NC 18/1/1155.   [69] Ibid.   [70] Ibid.

also have thought that he could balance Churchill inside the government – just as he had hoped Stanley would do outside it at the dominions office: 'steady the boat in the House of Commons from the outside'.[71] In any case he did not, at the outset, consider the arrangement permanent but envisaged his returning to lead the government at the end of the war: the course which he would find far less harrowing. He had 'always thought [he] could not face the job of being prime minister in war' and he 'could not but feel relieved that the ... responsibility was off him'.[72] He came to describe Churchill as having 'behaved with the most unimpeachable loyalty'; and throughout his illness was struck by his help.[73] And he could not, by late September, thank him 'sufficiently for [his] sympathetic consideration of [his] difficulties at this time'.[74]

Churchill's success in keeping Chamberlain and (by assiduous attentions to his susceptibilities) winning his loyalty had prevented any division in the party. So much so that though he rejected Chamberlain's offer to resign on 24 September and insisted that Chamberlain must take what time he needed to regain his strength, he could now allow him to go. He had already begun to plan for his departure. Halifax would remain in the cabinet – but make way at the foreign office for Eden. Yet Churchill would do nothing for the moment; and it was not until the Dakar episode (added to other causes of complaint) provoked a restlessness amongst politicians and in the newspapers, that Churchill resolved on reconstruction.

Dakar and the public criticism of Churchill

Despite the growing admiration for Churchill by autumn 1940 as a war leader of courage and resolution, he was not free from criticism. The unsuccessful expedition to Dakar, in particular, made him the object of attack. But although at the outset he was keen on the expedition, he was willing to call it off once the Vichy French clearly intended to anticipate it.

The capture of Dakar by de Gaulle's Free French was designed to counter German influence spreading, with Vichy's connivance, in West

---

[71] Halifax diary, 13 May 1940.
[72] Ibid., 15 May 1940; Chamberlain diary, 9 Sept. 1940. He could not, he wrote, face the sending of men to 'misery and destruction'; and he found it 'too terrible' to write letters of condolence twice in a lifetime. 'Any ideas which may have been in [his] mind about ... further political activity and even ... another premiership after the war have gone. I know that is out of the question.'
[73] Chamberlain to Ida, 21 June 1940, NC 18/1/1162.
[74] Chamberlain to Churchill, 22 Sept. 1940, NC 7/9/97.

Africa. De Gaulle's expedition would have considerable British support; and plans were laid in London in August for the 'prize of Dakar' which seemed to have 'a reasonable prospect of success'. The expedition suffered delays. Vichy got wind of it and sent naval reinforcements in early September from the Mediterranean which reached Dakar first. The operations began on 23 September. But de Gaulle's first approach and landing went badly and the choice had to be made whether 'to continue the effort which would ... have turned into a major operation', or to cut the losses. The operation was duly abandoned.[75]

Although Churchill at first had been a 'warm advocate' of the operation, when the news arrived of the French reinforcements, he was of a mind – with Halifax and the cabinet – to stop it. But it seems that pressure from de Gaulle, and the admiral and general concerned, resulted in its going ahead.[76] The failure of de Gaulle to take Dakar, and the losses incurred, provoked in certain newspapers a series of criticisms which extended to a more general malaise about Churchill's administration, policy and men, and in which the left was thought to be implicated. Reaction amongst the politicians to Dakar was characterised by its scepticism of Churchill himself, his rashness, bad judgement and dubious nominees – all the complaints which the events of previous months and Churchill's reactions to them had done much to quieten. The episode was thought to have revealed Churchill 'to be as incautious as ever' and to have provoked 'much criticism'; feeling at the Carlton Club was said to be 'running high against him'.[77] Was this Churchill's 'Dardanelles of this war' – hardly surprising given his choice of men?[78] Indeed, since Spears was 'mixed up' with Dakar, it seemed 'no wonder' that 'it went wrong'.[79]

Churchill had to contend not only with other politicians, but also with newspapers such as the *Sunday Pictorial* and *Daily Mirror*. He took these attacks seriously. At the cabinet on the 7th he was 'frightfully excited' and 'holding forth about disgraceful articles in [the] "Mirror" and "Sunday Pictorial"'.[80] The *Sunday Pictorial* had 'characterised the Dakar affair as "another blunder" and had used language of an insulting character to the government'; an article by H. G. Wells in the same journal had contained a 'slashing attack' on generals Ironside and Gort – while its 'general tenor ... had been that until the army was better led, we stood no chance of

---

[75] Halifax to Hoare, 26 Sept. 1940, Templewood XIII:20 [41].

[76] Ibid. – a view supported by Butler who explained that whilst Churchill had the final say, he was not 'really in favour of' the ill-fated Dakar expedition.

[77] Channon diary, 26 Sept. 1940; Butler to Hoare, 27 Sept. 1940, Templewood XIII:17:232; Crookshank diary, 27 Sept. 1940.

[78] Crookshank diary, 27, 28 Sept. 1940.   [79] Ibid; Dalton diary, 26 Sept., 1 Oct. 1940.

[80] Halifax diary, 7 Oct. 1940; Cadogan diary, 7 Oct. 1940.

beating the Germans'.[81] There had also been a leading article which attacked several members of the government and in Churchill's view it 'obviously [sought] to undermine confidence in the government'. Much the same line had been taken in the leading article in that morning's *Mirror*.[82] Churchill saw in its tone 'clear evidence of fifth column activity' and he considered the 'immediate purpose of these articles seemed to be to affect the discipline of the army, to ... shake the stability of the government and to make trouble between the government and organised labour'.[83] These articles stood for something 'most dangerous and sinister, namely, an attempt to bring about a situation in which the country would be ready for a surrender peace'.[84] He continued to reiterate his view that the newspapers concerned 'were trying to "rock the boat" and shake the confidence of the country in ministers'; that the Wells article and the prominence accorded it 'must ... weaken discipline in the army' and that an attempt was being made to 'poison relations between members of the government'. He was 'determined to put a stop to these attacks' but, before the discussion was adjourned, agreed that Beaverbrook and Attlee should see representatives of the Newspaper Proprietors Association.[85]

Along with the specific criticisms of the Dakar incident, Churchill also had to contend with more general criticisms of his government in the newspapers (including allegations that there was inadequate provision of bomb-shelters in London). The criticisms over shelter, thought to be organised by the *Daily Worker* and the Communist party, had come to a head with the height of the air battle in mid-September when the shortage of deep shelter, particularly in the East End, became evident. The government was concerned not only 'at the daily trek from the East End to secure deep shelter in other parts of London' but with what seemed to be organised incidents (such as window-breaking) and the advocacy of the *Daily Worker* and Communist party for deep shelter.[86] Leaflets were being distributed suggesting that the West End had been provided with better shelters; and certain MPs were thought to have had some part in fostering the agitation.[87] But the criticisms extended into a general attack on the government's negligence and on that of Anderson (home secretary

---

[81] Cabinet, 7 Oct. 1940, WM(40)267, CAB 65/9.   [82] Ibid.
[83] Ibid; Halifax diary, 7 Oct. 1940.
[84] Cabinet, 7 Oct. 1940, WM(40)267, CAB 65/9.
[85] Cabinet, 7, 9 Oct. 1940, WM(40)267, WM(40)268, CAB 65/9; Cadogan diary, 7 Oct. 1940.
[86] Wallace recorded that the parties which had got into the Savoy and broken the windows of the Mayfair 'appear on the surface to be organised'. Wallace diary, 16 Sept. 1940.
[87] Ibid., 18 Sept. 1940.

and minister of home security) in particular. For instance, the campaign in the Scottish edition of the *Daily Worker* for deep shelter for Scotland was thought to be 'a well-organised communist conspiracy to dishearten the public by suggesting that the government ha[d] been foolish if not criminal – not only over ... shelter but in every other thing that they can think of'; there seemed to be accumulating evidence of 'cleverly conducted whispering campaigns of different kinds in the East End'.[88] Anderson was seen not only as wrong, but as ineffective; his appeal, for example, to the public on 18 September not to use the tubes had been neglected. But, more seriously, it was claimed that if the battle of London were lost, it would be as the result of 'civilian failures', and these would be due to the inadequate deep shelter and services for bombed-out populations – the 'responsibility' for which was Anderson's.[89]

Churchill was able to deal with the particular criticisms about Dakar by undermining the premise on which they were made – making little, if not light, of the operation. It was not really a British one; and certainly had not been intended to be long or serious; indeed, failure was better than a prolonged battle. He subsequently explained to the Commons (on 8 October) that it had been a 'primarily French' operation; that Britain, while ready to give 'a measure of support' was 'no more anxious than ... de Gaulle to get involved in a lengthy or sanguinary conflict with the Vichy French'; that the arrival of the Vichy fleet carrying Vichy partisans had transformed the position at Dakar – the result not of 'any infirmity of purpose on the part of the Government' but rather one of 'those mischances which often arise in war'. But in any case the tide, and 'not the mere eddies of events ... [would] dominate the French people'.[90] Not only did Churchill make little of the episode publicly, but the government reconstruction which followed Dakar ostensibly as a result of Chamberlain's resignation, would serve as a distraction.[91]

Churchill and the party leadership

Although on 24 September Churchill had rejected Chamberlain's offer of resignation and hoped he would 'continue at [his] post and give me [the]

---

[88] Ibid., 21 Sept. 1940.
[89] Brown to Beaverbrook, 19, 24 Sept. 1940, BBK C.68. See also Wallace diary, 1 Oct. 1940.
[90] House of Commons, 8 Oct. 1940, *Into Battle*, pp. 279–93.
[91] The next day, Churchill became leader of the conservative party. In discussing the intended changes with Chamberlain after Dakar, Kingsley Wood explained that Churchill was 'worried about the attacks ... on the government ... was looking for some means of distracting public opinion before parliament met on the 8th and was thinking of reconstructing his government', Chamberlain diary, 30 Sept. 1940. See pp. 107–10 below.

aid which I so greatly value', he had already begun to consider the changes which would follow Chamberlain's resignation.[92] The same day he spoke to Eden about Chamberlain's illness and explained that he 'would have to give up soon'; when he did, Churchill 'must bring another Tory into War Cabinet and [Eden] was [the] only one country would accept'; if Halifax became lord president, Churchill would like Eden to take the foreign office but if not to be lord president.[93] Churchill may or may not have been right about the country accepting no other tory but Eden in the cabinet; he may have been considering 'the country' in terms of the reaction against Chamberlain, 'Munich' and Narvik – and the newspaper campaign. Whether he was right to do so is not clear. But the outstanding consideration as far as the reconstruction went continued to be the party itself. When Dakar forced the pace and Churchill decided to reconstruct, Halifax stayed at the foreign office, and Eden remained out of the cabinet.

Whatever plans he had had of bringing Eden into the war cabinet as foreign secretary and moving Halifax to Chamberlain's post, Churchill abandoned them partly in deference to the conservatives. Chamberlain would be resigning not only from the cabinet but from the party leadership; and Churchill resolved to take that himself. Churchill wanted Chamberlain's resignation to be seen as the result of Chamberlain's own insistence on account of his illness (and not because Churchill had asked for it!). He also thought better of bringing in Eden at the expense of Halifax, who would remain at the foreign office, or even at the expense of the more useful conservative, John Anderson, who would become lord president.

On 29 September Chamberlain was approached – through Kingsley Wood – about going. Not that Churchill desired him to resign; indeed, he 'would like [him] to stay if there was any chance of ... getting back to work in a reasonable time'. Chamberlain could not say that – though he claimed he was 'quite ready to go at any moment'. But he did not seem to be. Nor did he think Churchill would be sensible to ask him to. Rather, it would be wiser to 'keep [him] as long as possible because if [he] did get well enough [he] could give ... more help personally and ensure ... more support politically, than anyone else'.[94] If he were 'dropppped' then Churchill 'might have to face a good deal of criticism from conservatives'.

Wood pressed Chamberlain to go by alluding to the impossible

---

[92] Churchill to Chamberlain, 24 Sept. 1940, NC 7/9/98. See pp. 103–4.
[93] Eden diary, 24 Sept. 1940.
[94] Chamberlain dates the account of Wood's visit as '30th' but as it seems to have been a Sunday, it was more likely the 29th, i.e. the day before Churchill's letter was sent down on the 30th. Chamberlain diary, 30 Sept. 1940; Chamberlain to Mary, 1 Oct. 1940.

physical conditions in London and holding out the prospect of Churchill's failing: 'it did not look ... as if the present administration would be
long-lived and an alternative [one] would be v. desirable'.[95] Though
Chamberlain did not move from his view, he conceded Churchill's
request, which reached him next day, 'to make room ... and on the whole
[would] ... welcome the release from responsibility'. Churchill wrote the
same day that he would no longer 'press' him to remain and that he
needed more help; he proposed 'to make a number of changes ... and to
accept the resignation ... which you have proffered.'[96] Chamberlain
'replied at once accepting the situation and proposing an exchange of
letters for publication', to which Churchill agreed.[97]

Churchill's intention was that Chamberlain's resignation should not
appear to be the result of his having been forced out. He hoped that
Chamberlain would resign without any reluctance and Wood had been
despatched to see how the land lay. But Chamberlain had some objection;
so Wood – in order to encourage him to co-operate – referred to the
likelihood of Churchill's going out soon and Chamberlain's being called
to serve in the next administration. Churchill's formal letter was not in the
form of a request, but rather of a concession – conceding that he,
reluctantly, had finally agreed no longer 'to press' Chamberlain to stay at
his post. But Chamberlain's reply for publication that he was going in
order 'to facilitate changes' upset his designs, and instead of publication
on the 2nd, Margesson arrived to change that letter – which he did not
'like'. On his advice Chamberlain rewrote it 'to make it appear that
[Chamberlain] was insisting on resignation, instead of being asked to
resign to facilitate changes'. Chamberlain complied, though he did think
his 'original version ... more correct' and he handed over both 'the new
letter and one resigning the leadership'.[98]

With Chamberlain's resignation properly arranged, Churchill proceeded with his reconstruction of the cabinet. But in the event he resolved
to keep Halifax at the foreign office, possibly, as Chamberlain suggested,
because to move Halifax from it 'would be taken to mean a change of
policy and a condemnation of my policy'; and because Eden had not, in
his view, 'been a good foreign secretary before or would be a good one
now'; and if this coincided with Chamberlain's being dropped, Churchill
might 'have to face a good deal of criticism from conservatives'.[99] He had
asked Eden on the 30th whether he would join the cabinet as lord

---

[95] Ibid.   [96] Churchill to Chamberlain, 29 Sept. 1940, NC 7/9/99.
[97] Chamberlain diary, 30 Sept. 1940; Churchill to Chamberlain, 30 Sept. 1940, NC 7/9/101.
The letters would be published on 'Wed.', 2 October. Chamberlain to Churchill, for
publication, 1 Oct. 1940, NC 7/9/103.
[98] Chamberlain diary, 2 Oct. 1940.   [99] Ibid., 30 Sept. 1940.

president or stay where he was and explained that, as Eden knew, he 'had hoped to be able to move [Halifax] to lord president' but feared that if he suggested it 'Edward would ask to go altogether, which Winston did not want at the moment Neville was leaving'. Eden inclined to stay where he was and Churchill 'seemed to agree'.[100] He had been 'divided in his mind' between putting Eden or John Anderson into the war cabinet; and though there were 'certain political advantages' about Eden, Anderson would 'be better at tying up endless cross problems that arise on the home front'. Halifax felt that Anderson would give him more help, wrote to Churchill to tell him so, and advised Eden to 'stop where he was'.[101] The changes were announced on 3 October and published on the 4th: Anderson instead of Chamberlain, Morrison (the Londoner) to home security (instead of Anderson), Bevin brought into the war cabinet – and Halifax unchanged. Five days later Churchill became leader of the conservative party. Chamberlain had also resigned from this post 'given that his health had made it necessary to resign from the cabinet' and that under these circumstances it was 'no longer appropriate . . . [to] retain the leadership of the party'.[102]

There were some grumblings. According to Crookshank 'a lot of chaps [were] annoyed at the proposal [that Churchill should lead] . . . all too much rushed'.[103] But the proceedings went according to design. Margesson had made the arrangements and discussed them with Churchill. The proceedings would be kept short: 'an omnibus resolution . . . from the chair thanking Neville for his services and proposing Winston as his successor'. Halifax, as leader of the party in the Lords should 'according to precedents . . . take the chair', thank Chamberlain for his services and propose Churchill as his successor, and Churchill hoped Halifax would do so.[104] The meeting went as arranged; but what 'touched [Halifax] very much was the evident personal feeling of real sorrow and regret and regard' for Chamberlain – that is quite apart from the 'common form' of the resolution of thanks and affection and its support.[105] Churchill's speech was 'clever'; not only did it have 'a humorous dig at his own past and a laudation of the great purposes and patriotism of the conservative party' but it included a reference to his close work with Chamberlain in

---

100 Eden diary, 30 Sept. 1940. When Wood told Chamberlain that Churchill was thinking of 'substituting Anthony Eden for Halifax', Chamberlain did not like the proposals, made not on merit 'but for political reasons'. Chamberlain diary, 30 Sept.1940
101 Halifax diary, 30 Sept. 1940.
102 Chamberlain to Halifax, 2 Oct. 1940, HFX MCF A4.410.1.5.
103 Crookshank diary, 8 Oct. 1940.
104 Margesson to Halifax, 4 Oct. 1940, HFX MCF A.4.410.5.
105 Halifax to Chamberlain, 9 Oct. 1940, NC 7/11/33/88.

the past thirteen months and how their friendship had grown.[106] He referred to the 'heavy and painful' loss which the party and he had suffered 'through the illness which ha[d] forced ... Chamberlain to withdraw'; to the 'personal regard ... respect and admiration for [his] courage and integrity'; to his own having seconded the nomination of Chamberlain as leader three years earlier, and to the last thirteen months when 'our friendship, which was to some extent on both sides inherited, was welded in the fires of war into a comradeship of mutual trust and close identity of view'.[107]

Churchill's coming to power and his remaining there owed less to the forces of destiny than it did to his handling of the antipathies he prompted and to his dominating the circumstances which surrounded Chamberlain's deposition. The doubts and reservations which he had long provoked persisted – with fresh emphasis – when he became prime minister: his judgement, choice of men, his dubious conservatism, and now his links with labour. Churchill's patient courtship of Chamberlain and determination to avoid giving any indication that he was part of the opposition may not have entirely won the Chamberlainites hearts, but it ensured their support (if reluctant); at the same time, Churchill did nothing to prevent the impression amongst Chamberlain's opponents that he was one of them.

But Churchill's shrewd manipulation of men might not have been sufficient in itself were it not for his reaction – by apparent contrast with that of his colleagues – to the war. Whereas for them the rapid and, it seemed, inexorable defeat of France, followed by Hitler's preparations to invade and the Battle of Britain were a source of dispiriment, for Churchill they prompted a series of defiant interventions. His initial visits to the French to rally them indicated what was to follow. Rousing, heartening speeches, which displayed what seemed to be Churchill's unique courage. In the course of first the battle of France and then that of Britain, Churchill won the hearts, if not the minds, of many critics and increased his stature amongst supporters.

---

[106] Halifax diary, 9 Oct. 1940.
[107] Ibid.; Speech delivered at Caxton Hall on election to leadership of conservative and unionist party, 9 Oct. 1940, *Into Battle*, pp. 292–4.

Part II

The Middle East, imperial defence and the Balkans (October to December 1940)

The P.M.'s secretary woke me at 5.30 to tell me that Mussolini was starting in on Greece. I was annoyed with him waking me because there was obviously nothing to be done about it, more than we are doing, and I dissuaded him from waking Winston ... I looked in to see Winston as I came away at 8.30 and found him very much annoyed after all with his Private Secretary who had woken him at 6.45. I told him that was a good deal better than 5.30.

Halifax diary, 28 October 1940

You have taken a very bold and wise decision. I hope to reinforce you as soon as possible

Churchill to Longmore, 1 November 1940

('I had sent a flight of Blenheims over to Athens to assist in their air defence immediately the Italian invasion started. I did not ask permission to do so'. Note made by Longmore on this cypher)

... political considerations for the sending of some token force had obviously become overwhelming; in fact I suspect the British minister at Athens had gone a long way beyond his brief in his endeavours to get the Greeks to oppose invasion ... it is important the Italians should not hold Crete ... On the other hand it is a definite commitment to hold it ourselves, one which will grow rapidly and already the cries for fighter defence are being heard ... In general the Middle East command bustles with problems ... [T]here are four offensive [fronts] (Western Desert, Sudan, Aden and Kenya) and seven defensive (the above four plus Alexandria, Malta and Haifa). If Greece and Crete are to be anything more than a passing commitment, the latter figure rises to nine on a stretch of 3,000 miles.

Longmore to Portal, 2 November 1940

My anxiety is lest by dividing our limited resources we risk failure in both theatres. We have always taken the line with the Greeks that we cannot help them on land or in the air. We are convinced that, however disagreeable, we should hold to that line and continue to assemble our forces here. I submit that ineffective help to the Greeks may have worse effect on Turks than to withhold help on grounds that we are collecting force here that will be really effective later.

Eden to Churchill, 3 November 1940.

5   Churchill and the Middle East

Operation 'Compass' and the events leading to it

The Middle East command included Egypt, Sudan, Palestine, Transjordan, Cyprus and – in time of war – British Somaliland, Aden and Iraq. Wavell, who had taken up command in August 1939, believed from the outset that Germany would seek to dominate eastern and south-eastern Europe and Italy through the Mediterranean and North Africa. The Middle East command should therefore not only defend Egypt and the Middle East, but take any possible offensive measure which would make for allied domination of the Mediterranean, and ultimately it should seek to take the counter-offensive against Germany in eastern and south-east Europe. This accorded with the general view of the intelligence services that the German threat to the Middle East would be via the Balkans. Wavell's first task, as he saw it, was to secure Egypt and the Canal, the base of the Allied effort in the war, through action by land, air, sea. On land, the western desert along the Egyptian frontier with Italian-ruled Libya must be defended by a bold forward policy. When Italy entered the war in June 1940, Wavell's forces numbered 86,000, of whom 36,000 were in Egypt. His first task then, in his view, was to secure the frontier with Egypt. This led to small operations in the western desert, on and inside the Libyan frontier, in Cyrenaica and in defence of Egypt against Italian advances ordered in September. As Wavell began to plan an offensive for later in the year so that his armies could advance across Cyrenaica to Tobruk and possibly further, in London reports had suggested by early August that the Italian strength on the Egyptian frontier was sufficient to permit invasion at any time. From early September reports suggested that the Italians were preparing a Greek campaign, possibly in late October. Such was the background against which plans were being made in London for the reinforcement of the Middle East once the danger of invasion receded.[1]

[1] See Connell, *Wavell*, pp. 210–12, 234–8, 269–73, for a full discussion with a summary and reproduction of documents. For a discussion of the intelligence reports, see F.H. Hinsley,

The background: May–September 1940

For Churchill there was no question throughout the summer of 1940 of the demands of the Middle East upstaging, in any way, the home theatre and the prospect of invasion. That is not to say that Churchill belittled the importance of Egypt; but rather, while he acknowledged its significance, he also deferred considering it as an active theatre. If reinforcements were needed, they could be found not in a steady stream from home, but from the outlying theatres to the Middle East, from occasional convoys, and from more efficient deployment of existing resources. Until the Middle East became a fighting theatre, Churchill's immediate object was that Egypt, the canal and the route to the East must remain secure, the troops safe, and the attitude of Greece and Turkey benign. It could become the next theatre of war only once Britain was secure. Not until the danger at home diminished, would he countenance that, subject to the home theatre commanding first priority, the 'essential point' was to make Egypt secure – whether through redeployment from outlying theatres, transfers, or partially trained troops.[2] Fresh reinforcements could only be sent from home provided they were despatched by the fastest possible route – the Mediterranean, and *not* the Cape.[3]

Churchill's intention was that the Fleet in Alexandria should serve to uphold the position (and he opposed its transfer) – influencing the dominions, Turkey, Greece and the position of the Middle East as a whole.[4] A Middle East committee would be set up at home 'to keep under review ... the conduct of the war in the Middle East' and 'to lift our affairs in the East and Middle East out of the catalepsy by which they are smitten'.[5]

The Mediterranean and the Middle East should be 'vigorously handled'

British Intelligence in the Second World War: Its Influence on Strategy and Operations (with E.E. Thomas, C.F.G. Ransom, and R.C. Knight), London, HMSO, 1979, pp. 199–205, 215–18, 251–5, 259–61.

[2] Cabinet, 13 Aug. 1940, CA to WM(40)255, CAB 65/14; Pound to Cunningham, No. 2, 14 Aug. 1940, BL Add. MS 52561; during the battle of France, Churchill contemplated making good withdrawals from Palestine by sending Indian troops to Palestine and Egypt, see Churchill to Ismay (and others), 29 May 1940 and Churchill to Eden, 6 June 1940, Churchill, *Second World War*, II, pp. 112, 145–6.

[3] He pressed in August that the armoured brigade proposed for Egypt (fifty infantry tanks) should go through the Mediterranean, and was prepared to risk them. See cabinet 13, 15 Aug. 1940, WM(40)225, 228, CAB 65/14; also Churchill to Ismay for chiefs, 11 Aug. 1940, in Connell, *Wavell* pp. 259–60; Churchill to first lord and first sea lord, *Second World War*, II, pp. 396–71.

[4] Note of conversation between prime minister, first lord, first sea lord, vice-chief of naval staff, 17 June 1940, AVAR 5/4/26.

[5] Churchill to Eden, 6 June 1940, *Second World War*, II, pp. 145–6; cabinet, 16 July 1940, WM(40)205, CAB 65/8.

– for the war would eventually move there. Hitler, once he failed here, would 'probably recoil eastwards ... even without trying invasion, to find employment for his army' and the Germans would have a 'great need' to press and aid the Italians 'to the attack of Egypt'. By late August he was 'anxious as regards the defence of Egypt' and he warned that 'a major invasion of Egypt from Libya must be expected at any time now' and the 'largest possible army' must be assembled towards the western frontier.[6] A big army must be formed in the Delta and 'the Middle East [would] absorb all our surplus for a long time to come' once 'battle at home die[d] down'. All political and administrative considerations must be set in proper subordination to this – that is, preparations to resist the invasion of Egypt.[7] There had already been a 'continuous stream of convoys with reinforcements to the Middle East' and they must 'expect heavy fighting ... before very long'.[8] Churchill considered that they must attack the Italians right away 'this autumn', given that the Germans would be 'more likely to lay strong hands on [the] Italian war machine and then the picture will be very different'. Cunningham should lay plans with the army and airforce for 'an operation against Italian communications in Libya' designed to hamper any large scale offensive against Egypt.[9] Although the escalation of the Battle of Britain in the third week of September made him more hesitant – he resisted sending 'anything more' and ruled that ten cruiser tranks proposed in convoy WS3 be held back; nonetheless he did not appear to differ from Eden, whose idea it was to 'gather the strongest army in the Middle East possible in the next few months'. On 27 September he recommended that the balance of argument there 'was in favour of despatching ... [to] the Middle East the aircraft ... awaiting despatch during the rest of September and ... October.'[10]

6 General directive for commander-in-chief Middle East, 23 Aug. 1940, PREM 3/309/l; the document is dated 16 Aug. by Churchill in his *Second World War*, II pp. 379–82, though the directive was not finalised before 21 Aug., when the defence committee considered Churchill's original version and an amended version by the vice-chiefs of staff. The directive was approved at the meeting subject to further amendments and approved at the cabinet on 23 August. Defence committee, 21 Aug. 1940, DO(40)28, CAB 69/l; Cabinet, 23 Aug.1940, WM(40)233, CAB 65/14; Churchill to Smuts, 27 June 1940, *Second World War*, II, pp. 200–l; cabinet, 16 July 1940, WM(40)205 CAB 65/8; prime minister to first lord and first sea lord, 13 Aug. 1940, *Second World War*, II, pp. 396–7.
7 Cabinet, 23 Aug. 1940, WM(40)233, CAB 65/14; general directive for CinCME, 23 Aug. 1940, PREM 3/309/1; Amery to Linlithgow, 2 Sept 1940, IOL MS. Eur. F 125/9.
8 House of Commons, 5 Sept. 1940, *Into Battle*, pp. 263–71.
9 Churchill to Cunningham, 9 Sept 1940, BL Add. MS 52566.
10 Eden diary and extracts, 16–24 Sept 1940, Avon, *The Reckoning*, pp. 137–8; DMO to CIGS, 19 Sept. 1940, WO 106/2035; Cabinet, 27 Sept. 1940, WM(40)260, CAB 65/9; Churchill to Eden, 24 Sept. 1940, *Second World War*, II, pp. 442–3.

October–December 1940

By mid-October, Churchill thought it no longer 'unlikely that Germany [would] advance south eastwards through the Balkans in the immediate future'; and he urged that should October pass without invasion, they 'should begin the reinforcement of the Middle East ... to the utmost ... shipping permits'.[11] He had, from early October, thought it 'right to make preparations' for the sailing of specific convoys; and had told the House on the 8th that despite the 'imminent threat of invasion ... [they] had] not failed to reinforce ... the Middle East'. Though 'it would be premature' to discount the prospect of an invasion attempt, none the less they would 'have to consider in the near future the extent to which [they] could afford to reinforce the Middle East at the expense of this country'.[12] He therefore proposed that should October pass without invasion, reinforcements via the Cape should begin – men, armoured units, fighters and bombers, not to mention a programme for reinforcing the Mediterranean fleet.[13] Churchill planned in the short term to attack the Italian position and in the long term to build up the army to deal with a German descent.

Churchill hoped there would be action in the Middle East in the form of a 'forestalling offensive' in view of the danger of the Italians building up concentrations; for it would not, in his view, 'be sound strategy to await the concentration and deployment of overwhelming forces'; and what would happen if the enemy did not venture to move 'until the Germans arrive[d] in strength'?[14] He hoped that it would be possible to reform the army in the Middle East and 'secure the largest proportion of fighting men and fighting units' for he 'fear[ed] that the proportion of fighting compared to ration strength [was] worse [there] than anywhere else'.[15]

Churchill had not expected that the countries immediately in the German path – should Germany decide on an eastward thrust – could 'do more than greatly delay her progress'; but that delay could be exploited

---

[11] Defence committee, 15 Oct. 1940, DO(40)34, CAB 69/1 ; prime minister to Ismay for chiefs of staff, 15 Oct. 1940, circulated as WP(40)421, CAB 66/13; (Churchill published what was most probably an earlier version, dated 13 October in *Second World War*, II pp. 443–6).

[12] Defence committee, 3 Oct. 1940, DO(40)33, CAB 69/1; House of Commons, 8 Oct. 1940; cabinet, 10 Oct. 1940, WM(40)269, CAB 65/7.

[13] Prime minister to Ismay for chiefs of staff, 15 Oct 1940, circulated as WP(40)421, CAB 66/13. But the immediate reinforcements, such as the second armoured division, already agreed on, should, in his view, use the Mediterranean to avoid being out of action for too long. Defence committee, 3 Oct. 1940, DO(40)33, CAB 69/1.

[14] Churchill to Eden, 26 Oct. 1940, PREM 3/308.   [15] Ibid.

'to develop our army in the Middle East'.[16] Nor did he intend to intervene in the event of an Italian attack on Greece for, in his scheme, British armies would meet both Italians and Germans in the Middle East, for which reinforcements were planned and an offensive anticipated. As a result, when Italy attacked Greece on 28 October there was no reason to change his intentions. He reiterated that the reinforcement of the Middle East would continue; to the 72,000 troops already sent, another 53,000 should be added by the end of the year; more than 'half our best tanks had been sent' and 'we were ... re-equipping and then increasing our air forces overseas'.[17] In 1941 the German army could 'move where it pleased ... and ... help Italy with men and munitions'; and though Britain 'could not expect to undertake decisive operations' they were aiming at a total of 55 divisions, 25 to 30 of which would be in the Middle East 'to be reinforced at the rate of one division per month, or faster if shipping was available'.[18]

Since Crete – considered vital as a base – must be secured, there was no case for modifying the existing plans of concentrating all on the Middle East. Just after news of the attack reached London Churchill told his colleagues that 'nothing which was available at short notice would be likely to affect the immediate situation'.[19] The defence comittee which he had summoned that evening agreed, rather, on the importance of Crete: 'every effort should be made to assist the Greeks to defend Crete against an Italian attack' and thus secure 'for ourselves the use of Suda Bay for our naval forces and of an advanced aerodrome'.[20] Churchill wired Eden of the need to make an effort 'to establish ourselves in Crete and that risks must be run for this valuable prize' and reminded him of the importance of Suda Bay as a base. Crete was vital to the security of Egypt, its successful defence 'invaluable ... to defence of Egypt [its] loss to Italians [would lead to] grievous aggravation [of] all Mediterranean difficulties'. Churchill urged that 'so great a prize [was] worth the risk and almost equal to [a] successful offensive in Libya'.[21]

For Churchill, Crete mattered in the context of the security of Egypt; Greece did not; and he reminded his colleagues on the 29th that while 'certain military measures in support of Greece/were in preparation' none the less the cabinet ought to be 'under no illusion as to the extent of the assistance [they] ... could give'; they were 'severely limited by the size of [their] forces in the Middle Eastern Theatre'.[22] He reiterated for the

16 Cabinet, 9 Oct. 1940, WM(40) 268, CAB 65/9.
17 Defence committee, 31 Oct. 1940, DO(40)39, CAB 69/8.
18 Ibid.   19 Cabinet, 28 Oct. 1940, CAB 65/9.
20 Defence committee, 28 Oct. 1940, DO(40)37, CAB 69/1.
21 Churchill to Eden, 29 Oct. 1940, PREM 3/308.
22 Cabinet, 29 Oct. 1940, CA to WM(40)279, CAB 65/15.

benefit of Attlee and Halifax (see p. 148) two days later that while they were 'doing all [they] could to help Greece ... it would be wrong and foolish to make them promises which we could not fulfil'.[23] Turkey also mattered; for Churchill anticipated that in 1941 the German army 'could move where it pleased', would have 'ample forces for simultaneous campaigns in Spain and against Turkey and Russia' as well as helping Italy with men and munitions. The Germans 'would inevitably turn ... to the Caspian and ... the Baku oilfields' – in which event, Russia would have to fight for 'without oil for her agriculture, her people would starve'. But if Turkey resisted 'she might greatly delay the German advance to the Suez Canal; and we should therefore back her up with all we could send'.[24] He had, even before the attack, hoped that during his visit to the Middle East (see pp. 137–41) Eden would meet the Turkish mission which had, 'probably' the object of 'assessing our strength in that part of the world'; and after the attack that the Turks would 'undertake to neutralise Bulgaria' – particularly given the reports from Turkey that she intended to 'make her position vis-a-vis [sic] Bulgaria perfectly clear' and that the Turks would fight if attacked.[25]

Churchill therefore, before and after the Italian attack on Greece, had been concerned with preparations for the steady reinforcement of the Middle East, although he could not yet entirely discount invasion. In public and in private he alluded to his making good the deficiencies in the Middle East to which he expected Hitler soon to turn. He did not intend to abandon that course and was not deflected from it by the attack on Greece. Instead, he determined that Crete be secured because, in his view, it was vital to the security of Egypt; he hoped that Turkey could be prevailed upon to hold out against the Germans, for that would delay a Hitlerian *drang* directed at Egypt. But he did not expect the countries in Hitler's path to do more than delay and he may, therefore, have seen no reason to divert resources except to Turkey – where to delay Hitler in his advance on Egypt would give time to build resources in the Middle East. If he balanced resources carefully between the home and the Middle East theatres, and if Britain could hold off invasion until October, the resources needed for meeting the Germans could be despatched. Meanwhile, Eden should go out to Cairo and the visit would be 'of great value

[23] Note of a meeting between prime minister, lord privy seal and secretary of state for foreign affairs, 12.30 p.m, 31 Oct. 1940, CAB 127/14. It was agreed that the draft telegram to Palairet in Athens might be modified by Halifax 'in order that the telegram might not be too discouraging to Sir Michael Palairet'.
[24] Defence committee, 31 Oct. 1940, CA to DO(40)39, CAB 69/1.
[25] Cabinet, 9 Oct. 1940, WM(40)268, CAB 65/15; meeting between prime minister, lord privy seal and secretary of state for foreign affairs, 31 Oct. 1940, CAB 127/14.

especially as a Turkish mission was shortly arriving', and there would just be the time to build up the armies to exploit the delay afforded by the resistance of those countries in Hitler's path.[26] Moreover, Wavell should launch a forestalling offensive to destroy the prospect of the Italians building up strength; and the large tail of the desert army should be done away with. It did not occur to Churchill to modify this plan when the Italians attacked Greece on 28 October. He had in any case anticipated the fall of these countries, if not to Italy then to Hitler when he chose to turn south, as he inevitably would. No; he would stick to his plans to meet the Germans in the Middle East and continue to build up the concentrations there. Crete, of course, must be taken and Turkish resistance encouraged – to delay the German march sufficiently to give time to build up their armies in the Middle East.

Within days of the attack and his first reaction that there was nothing they could do which could help Greece, Churchill seemed to change. He began to advocate assistance to the Greeks. He urged both direct help, particularly the despatch of aircraft, and indirect help in the form of attacking Italy elsewhere, despite objections from the Middle East where Eden and the commanders wanted all their resources for Wavell's proposed offensive. Although Churchill's change had been partly prompted by political considerations – the sympathy for the Greeks at home, considerations of American sentiment towards Greece, the need not to seem to abandon the Greeks to their fate – he also alluded to the military arguments. From having at the outset considered Greece to be insignificant in the grand scheme of imperial defence, he now suggested that it no longer was. But it did not yet matter in itself absolutely, but rather on account of the importance of the Greek islands (as well as Crete) for Mediterranean security; and on account of the impact which helping Greece – and Greece in turn resisting – would have on the Turks, thought to hold the key to the Middle East.

In pressing the case for Greece against military advice and that of Eden, Churchill began the process which led to the commitment just over four months later, to aid Greece against Germany, and the bargain with Stalin just four years later to secure influence over Greece, even if it meant abandoning to the Soviets most of Eastern Europe. In each of those cases Churchill had, through his military arguments for Greek intervention – based as they were on the need to influence Turkey – come to be convinced that Greece in itself was strategically important; almost as much as Turkey had been; and that given Turkish refusal to co-operate, Greece could and must now play the role in the Mediterranean tradi-

[26] Cabinet, 9 Oct. 1940, WM(40)268, CAB 65/15.

tionally accorded by Britain to the Turks: that of guaranteeing the key to Britain's imperial position. Within three days of the attack, Churchill had become a protagonist of helping the Greeks – both directly and indirectly. On the one hand he urged assistance, particularly aircraft, financial help and the setting up of a committee to see what could be done; and on the other, he urged that Greece could also be helped indirectly by British attacks on Italy or Italian bases. As for the direct help, he made it clear on the 1st that he admired the action taken by Air Marshal Longmore in the Middle East, whose own reaction to the attack had been to despatch a Blenheim squadron – 'a very bold and wise decision'. He hoped to reinforce him 'as soon as possible';[27] and resolved that further air reinforcements should be sent to Greece from the Middle East, given that it would be impossible for anything to arrive from the United Kingdom in time. 'Immediate arrangements' should be made to send four heavy bomber and four Hurricane fighter squadrons to the Middle East, and Eden should 'send at once to Greece one Gladiator squadron, two more Blenheims ... three in all ... and at earliest one more Gladiator squadron' with anti-aircraft guns to precede the squadrons.[28] Immediate British air reinforcements to Greece 'would thus amount to four squadrons in all', to be followed by a second Gladiator squadron once the arrival of Hurricane reinforcements in Egypt 'made this possible'. Churchill, for his part, continued 'trying every day to speed up the arrivals ... of Hurricanes ...' in Longmore's command and proposed that the defence committee consider 'what more we could do ... to help the Greeks'.[29] Not only would there be aircraft for the Greeks, but a committee would be set up to consider help and to co-ordinate shipping. By the 18th the committee on assistance to Greece was sitting and as a result of first recommendations (accepted by the chiefs of staff with certain modifications) 'four shiploads of munitions were about to be sent to Greece'.[30] In addition, the financial help about which the Cabinet heard on the 18th was more than the Greeks had asked for; the first advance would be £5,000,000 'unaccompanied by

[27] Churchill to Longmore, 1 Nov. 1940, Longmore, DC 74/102/15.
[28] Cabinet, 4 Nov. 1940, CA to WM(40)282, CAB 65/16; Churchill to Ismay, for CAS and COS, 1 Nov. 1940, Portal:1:1940; Churchill to Eden, 4 Nov. 1940, PREM 3/308.
[29] Cabinet, 4, 13 Nov. 1940, WM(40)282, WM(40)288, CAB 65/16, CAB 65/10, Churchill to Longmore, 13 Nov. 1940, PREM 3/309/1. The intention, by 4 November, was to send to Greece, as soon as properly defended aerodromes were ready, three Blenheim squadrons (including the one already sent) to be followed by a second Gladiator, together with essential personnel, transport, equipment and ancillary services. To compensate for these withdrawals, reinforcements (34 Hurricanes and 32 Wellingtons) would be despatched to Egypt arriving early December. COS to CsinCME, appended to cabinet 4 November, WM(40)282, CAB 65/16.
[30] Cabinet, 18 Nov. 1940, WM(40)290, CAB 65/10.

any request for the payment of interest or the repayment of instalments of principal'.[31]

Churchill's advocacy of the Greeks seemed to be at the expense of the Middle East theatre and all the more strong given his deprecatory attitude to the talk of an offensive there. He seemed to suggest that it was an unlikely event given that 'everyone [was] fixed on idea of set-piece battle of Mersa Matruh' which would 'for that v. reason [make it] unlikely [to] ... occur'. He referred to difficulties of 'attacking across the desert' and implied there might not be a 'major offensive ... in Libya possible during [the] next two months' – as a result of which risks should be run to stimulate Greek resistance; and he thought of the proposals from the Middle East as 'various minor offensives ... plus major defences at Mersa Matruh'.[32]

As for indirect help – Churchill's plans for harassing Italy involved direct attacks on Italy itself, on the fleet at Taranto 'and generally against southern Italy'.[33] Bases in Greece would be used; and it was also intended to increase the weight of attack from Malta, while the continued action of the Mediterranean fleet would undermine Italian communications with their armies.[34] The successful attack on the Italian fleet at Taranto on 11 November in his view 'brought home the importance of hitting the Italians as hard as we could' and if the Greeks could maintain themselves against Italy throughout the winter 'the situation in this quarter might develop greatly in our favour'.[35]

Churchill's change of heart about helping the Greeks may have been more apparent than real. But his change of attitude to Greece was not. It had been prompted by overlapping and confused considerations, ranging from the sentimental case for helping the Greeks to the military impact which such help might have on Turkey. Churchill did not think that the Greeks could be abandoned in view of the political repercussions: 'No one [would] thank us for sitting tight in Egypt with ever growing forces while Greek situation and all that hangs on it is cast away'; and 'our public opinion was most anxious for British intervention in Greece' If Greece were overwhelmed it would be said that 'in spite of our guarantee

[31] Cabinet, 18 Nov. 1940, WM(40)290, CAB 65/10.
[32] Churchill to Eden, 3 Nov. 1940, PREM 3/308.
[33] Cabinet, 4 Nov. 1940, WM(40)282, CAB 65/16; Churchill to Portal, 2 Nov. 1940, Portal:1:1940:11a.
[34] Churchill to Portal, 2 Nov. 1940, Portal:1:1940:11a. Using Malta went 'against ... previous policy not to use Malta as an offensive base so as to avoid Italian retaliation there', but the governor agreed with the new course. Dill to Eden, 2 Nov. 1940, WO 193/963.
[35] Cabinet, 13 Nov. 1940, WM(40)288, CAB 65/10.

we had allowed one more small ally to be swallowed up'.[36] And he reminded the House that despite 'all the blows ... and ... burdens ... we have not abandoned one jot ... any of our obligations ... towards the captive and enslaved countries of Europe or towards any of those countries which still act with us', the latest of which was Greece, whose action in resisting 'unmitigated brigandage' constituted the 'valiant, sudden uprising of the Greek nation'. By 21 November, they had 'already almost entirely purged their soil of the conscript invaders'.[37] Militarily too the case for intervention could be made. Greece, her islands and Athens, could be seen as strategically vital in themselves. If the Italians secured the Greek islands 'they would be in a position to dominate the Black Sea approaches with their airforce, and to interfere more effectively with our shipping in the Mediterranean'. Strategically, the loss of Athens would be 'as serious a blow to us as the loss of Khartoum and a more irreparable one.[38] Moreover, there was a 'reasonable prospect that a Greek front against Italy could be built up'; and that with aid and vigorous resistance Greece 'might check [the] invaders'.[39] They were 'probably as good as Italians' and the Germans were 'not yet on the spot'. But Churchill also came to see Greece as a means of influencing Turkey; aid to Greece 'must be attentively studied lest whole Turkish position is lost through proof that England never tries to keep her guarantees'. The collapse of Greece 'without any effort by us [would] have deadly effect on Turkey and future of war'.[40] They could not, in Churchill's view 'hope to preserve the Turkish alliance if our reinforcements to Greece were on a smaller scale than now proposed'.[41] In addition, there was the chance to take bold action. If they were to miss a 'great opportunity ... we shall have to pay heavily hereafter for it'. 'Safety first is the road to ruin in war.'[42]

Churchill insisted that the Greeks must he helped and continued to do so despite the objections of Eden and the Middle East command who 'thought that we should not send more air reinforcements than the one composite Blenheim squadron'. The 'turn' taken by events 'made it

[36] Churchill to Eden, 3 Nov. 1940, PREM 3/308; cabinet, 4 Nov. 1940, WM(40)282, CAB 65/16.
[37] House of Commons, 9, November, *Into Battle*, pp. 310–13; 21 Nov. 1940, *Unrelenting Struggle*, pp. 5–10.
[38] Cabinet, 4 Nov. 1940, WM(40)282, CAB 65/16.
[39] Churchill to Eden, 3 Nov. 1940, PREM 3/308; cabinet, 4 Nov. 1940, CA to WM(40)282, CAB 65/16.
[40] Churchill to Eden, 2 Nov. 1940, PREM 3/308.
[41] Cabinet, 4 Nov. 1940, CA to WM(40)282, CAB 65/16.
[42] Churchill to Eden, 3 Nov. 1940, PREM 3/308; Churchill to Portal, 2 Nov. 1940, M.258, Portal:1:1940:11a.

necessary to accept a risk in the Middle East' – 'of a temporary nature'.[43]
It was 'only natural' that the commanders on the spot would feel they
were being 'unduly weakened by the despatch of air forces to Greece and
... should lodge a protest'; but there could be no countermanding the
despatch of No. 80 squadron due to leave for Crete on 14 November –
though Longmore could make representations about the second Gladiator squadron if he still felt after the arrival of the Hurricanes that 'he was
... too weak in fighter[s] to spare [it]'.[44]

Churchill's resolute advocacy may have been partly designed to
countermand the objections of Eden and the commanders and somewhat
provoked by it. They in turn may have misinterpreted the fervour of his
intention on account of their fears of the weakness of Egypt. But Churchill in fact had no intention of despatching air support beyond what had
been decided at the outset; though this, he also implied was not the result
of a decision in principle, but rather the result of practical problems.
Though a larger contingent had been considered (of four squadrons each
of Hurricanes and Wellingtons) it had been rejected for there was 'no
prospect of improvising aerodromes to operate so many squadrons'.[45] He
continued to maintain, in the face of further 'urgent' requests for aircaft
to counteract Italian action, that 'we could not increase our air reinforcement beyond what we had already arranged to send'.[46] But he continued
to emphasise what had been sent and imply that further despatches were
impeded not by any lack of goodwill on his part, but by the practical
obstructions which existed – partly on account of the Greeks themselves.
He emphasised to his colleagues on 18 November the amount being done
– the despatch of Gladiator and Blenheim squadrons – and explained that
such impediments as existed were the result of the failures of the Greeks
themselves. As he wired Palairet, it was 'useless to talk about Hurricanes
as immediate reinforcements since they cannot land at Crete en route';
and to fit extra tanks in place of guns and then re-assemble for operations
'would be a long business'. Moreover, it was not clear whether Greek
personnel could either service or operate Hurricanes 'without special
training'.[47] And when he told the cabinet on the 19th of the defence
committee's decision to 'stick to the promises ... made to send five

---

[43] Cabinet, 4 Nov. 1940, WM(40)282, CAB 65/16.
[44] Defence committee, 11 Nov. 1940, DO(40)41, CAB 69/1.
[45] Cabinet, 4 Nov. 1940, WM(40)282, CAB 65/16.
[46] Cabinet, 18 Nov. 1940, WM(40)290, CAB 65/10. He added that he had seen a report that
    the landing grounds in Albania were already so congested that the arrival of German air
    reinforcements on this front seemed improbable.
[47] Defence committee, 18 Nov. 1940, DO(41)44, CAB 69/1 and Churchill to Palairet
    appended.

squadrons but no more', he implied that it was a case of the requests themselves being 'impossible and unreasonable' rather than the British response.[48] The practical difficulties in moving aircraft from one country to another were not 'quite realised by the lay mind and evidently ... not ... in Greece'; and the air attaché in Athens should acquaint Palairet with them 'and thus prevent impossible and unreasonable requests being put forward'.[49]

Although within days of the Italian attack Churchill had changed from holding that there was nothing 'we could do', to maintaining that the Greeks must be supported, his schemes were in fact measured and contained. They were provoked by the political case for intervention of 'the small but famous and immortal Greek nation'; by the fight of king, government and country 'for life and honour, and lest the world should be too easily led in chains' and, not least, by the guarantee given (albeit with the French) to Greece to come to her aid 'if she were the victim of unprovoked agression'.[50] But he had also made the military case – not only of the strategic importance of Greece and her islands for the Middle East and Mediterranean but of the attitude of the Turks whose importance to the Middle East position was acknowledged by all.

Churchill's advocacy for helping the Greeks initially emerged from the political argument and was presented in terms of it; but it quickly came to involve the military case. Such a case may have been necessary to overcome the objections in the Middle East and to convince both himself and others that Greece was not an unnecessary and hopeless gamble. But the advocacy was tempered by restraint; no more than first agreed upon would be sent to Greece; and reinforcements to Greece should not interfere with plans for the Middle East.

Churchill continued to be concerned about the reinforcements to the Middle East; and after Eden's return, though he still seemed to be a protagonist of Greece this was because nothing was expected to happen in the Middle East. But once Wavell's campaign began on 7 December, Churchill became increasingly preoccupied with the Middle East; delighted with the Libyan success, but exhorting Wavell to more and more. He was determined to exploit the success. It was a matter of time before Hitler marched south, particularly as he could not leave his 'flagging ally' for long. Though it was not clear which route the Germans would take, certain preparations could be made in addition to clearing the Italian menace from the desert. Aerodromes could be built in Greece and

[48] Cabinet, 19 Nov. 1940, WM(40)29, CAB 65/16.   [49] Ibid.
[50] House of Commons, 5 Nov. 1940, Into Battle, pp. 301–8.

a huge force collected in the Middle East on land and sea, which would affect the Middle East in general and would influence the Turks in particular.

Even while advocating support for the Greeks, Churchill continued to consider it in the context of the Middle East – that is, beyond the arguments which involved the strategic importance of the islands or of Turkey. He continued to allude to the weakness of the Middle East, particularly in the air; to acknowledge the risk which diversions to Greece caused and to maintain that they were exceptional or of an emergency nature; they were only 'temporary'. He saw no reason that Portal's plans for reinforcing Egypt by 1 February should not 'go forward quite independently of the emergency action ... to aid Greece'.[51] He persisted throughout the Greek demands that 'the urgent need during the coming months was to build up our strength in the Middle East' and the limitations of shipping must not 'interfere with the urgent military necessity of concentrating such forces as we required in the Middle East'.[52] Though the decision to divert aircraft from Egypt to Greece would reduce by half the air strength in Egypt – where 'the air was already our weakest point', the risk was only 'of a temporary nature ... since large air reinforcements ... were on the way to Egypt by various routes' and should arrive by early December; and he maintained that he would not have 'favoured' such a course were it not for the prospect of 'immediately ... mak[ing] good'.[53] He continued to press for the exact timetables of despatches and that Wavell would act.[54]

Churchill therefore maintained that he would not have gone ahead in supporting the Greeks – even in the limited way in which he did – had he not been in a position to make good the deficiencies, or had the risk posed been not merely of a temporary nature, or if plans for continued reinforcing of the Middle East had not been persisting. He had pressed Eden initially for those reasons and because it was unlikely that they could count on a 'set-piece battle of Mersa Matruh', given that the enemy would await both the completion of the pipe-line and the development of larger forces. Eden 'should run risks to stimulate Greek resistance' with no major offensive of their own possible in the next two months.[55] But nor

---

[51] Churchill to Portal, 2 Nov. 1940, Portal:1:1940:11a.
[52] Defence committee, 14 Nov. 1940, DO(40)43, CAB 69/1.
[53] Cabinet, 4, 12 Nov. 1940, WM(40)282, WM(40)287, CAB 65/16.
[54] Churchill to Ismay for chiefs of staff, 18 Nov. 1940, PREM 3/2881; to secretary of state for war and CIGS, 22 Nov. 1940, PREM 3/288/1; to Wavell, 22 Nov. 1940, PREM 3/309/1.
[55] Churchill to Eden, 3 Nov. 1940, PREM 3/308.

should Eden abandon the 'special plan' (a desert offensive) 'though perhaps some postponement may be necessary'.[56]

When Eden returned from the Middle East Churchill, though he continued to advocate aid for Greece, seemed less to do so at the expense of the Middle East. Eden brought more detailed news of Wavell's plans for an offensive and Churchill began to press for early action. He was 'very sorry that European events ha[d] forced [him] to complicate them' and promised Wavell 'full support at all times in any offensive action'. Unremitting efforts would be made to remount the air force on the latest machines at the earliest moment and Churchill hoped that Wavell would soon 'be far better off than before'.[57] There should be no delay. Wavell must let him know either that the aircraft reinforcements were insufficient or that he would act when they arrived. But it was 'not clear' that Wavell had made up his mind; and Churchill feared that 'every day's delay endanger[ed] secrecy in Egypt'.[58] He urged Wavell to take advantage of recent events: the 'Italian check on Greek front and the British naval successes at Taranto, the 'poor showing [of] Italian air men ... over here ... [and] reports ... of low morale in Italy'. 'Above all' the general political situation made it 'very desirable' for Wavell to undertake his proposed operation.[59] In his view 'the moment had come to run risks in order to increase the pressure on the Italians before the Germans could come to their assistance'; and given that the Greeks might be able to hold the front against the Italians for a long time, that would give 'an opportunity to strike the Italians in the western desert of Egypt'.[60] The operation was all the more urgent on account of the prospect of German intervention; for Churchill thought it 'unlikely that Germany will leave her flagging ally unsupported indefinitely'; that it was not clear 'how long [it] would ... be before the Germans could strike at Greece through Bulgaria'; that she might be contemplating not only a strike 'through Bulgaria to Salonika' but also 'persuading Turkey ... to stand aside'.[61] Wavell's operation was important for the 'whole Middle East position,

---

[56] Churchill to Eden, 4 Nov. 1940, PREM 3/308.
[57] Churchill to Wavell, 11 Nov. 1940, PREM 3/309/1. A draft in Eden's hand promised to sustain Wavell 'whether the outcome be well or ill', prime minister to CsinC, in Eden's hand, undated, PREM 3/288/1.
[58] Churchill to Wavell, 22 Nov. 1940, PREM 3/309/1; Churchill to Eden and Dill, 22 Nov. 1940, PREM 3/288/1.
[59] Churchill to Wavell, appended to defence committee, 13 Nov. 1940, DO(40)42, CAB 69/8.
[60] Defence committee, 13 Nov. 1940, DO(40)42, CAB 69/8.
[61] Churchill to Wavell, 13 Nov. 1940, appended to DO(40)42, CAB 69/8; to Eden and commander-in-chief general staff, 22 Nov. 1940, PREM 3/288/1; cabinet, 25 Nov. 1940, WM(40)295, CAB 65/16.

including Balkans and Turkey ... [and] French attitude in North Africa, Spanish attitude ... Italy ... and generally ... the whole war'.[62]

Churchill also urged the Libyan operation in order to influence Turkey, as the Turks would probably reply to a call 'to come in' by demanding 'immediate assistance' or by refusing. 'A British victory in Libya would probably turn the scale, and then we could shift our forces to the new theatre ... There might just be time for Wavell to act in Libya before the pressure becomes too decisive.'[63] Given the danger of Germany attacking Greece through Bulgaria, they would be 'bound to urge Turkey to the utmost to enter the war'. Indeed, it might be that Wavell's operation 'would in itself determine [the] action of Yugoslavia and Turkey' and 'anyhow, in event of success, we should be able to give Turkey far greater assurances of early support than it has been in our power to do so far'.[64] By the 26th it had been agreed that 'we want Turkey to come into the war as soon as possible'; that though not being pressed to take 'special steps to help the Greeks', they would like a Turkish warning to declare war in the event of a German move through Bulgaria to Greece: it was 'vital that Turkey should fight there and then'; if not, she would be alone and 'the Balkans will have been eaten up one by one and it will be beyond our power to help her'.[65]

Churchill continued to look to events – to Wavell's campaign and its political and strategic implications for Mussolini – in the context of anticipating Hitler's next move. In one sense, Wavell's success would precipitate such a move for Hitler was 'bound' to come to the aid of his flagging ally. Churchill did not know when or where he would do so but that should make no difference to Wavell's plans. For Hitler would most likely march southwards – possibly exploiting the fears of the Balkan countries and Turkey to gain unopposed access; whatever the route, Egypt would be the object; and to secure Egypt, the Libyan frontier and the Mediterranean coast, it was urgent for Wavell to act quickly and dramatically against the Italians to prevent their concentrating forces or attacking before the Germans arrived.

Churchill became impatient at what seemed the small scope of the operation, and the delay in launching it, and in pursuing the enemy once it started on 7 December. He was anxious lest Wavell was 'only playing

---

[62] Churchill to Wavell, 26 Nov. 1940, PREM 3/288/1.
[63] Churchill to Eden and Dill, 22 Nov. 1940, PREM 3/288/1.
[64] Churchill to Wavell, 22 Nov. 1940, PREM 3/309/1 and 26 Nov. 1940, PREM 3/288/1.
[65] He asked the defence committee to consider whether 'it would be to our advantage to bring Turkey into the war at this stage', cabinet, 25 Nov. 1940, WM(40)295, CAB 65/16; Churchill to Eden for ambassador, 26 Nov. 1940, Churchill, *Second World War*, II, p. 486.

small and ... not hurling on (*sic*) his whole available force ... fail[ing] to rise to the height of circumstances'.[66] He complained to Eden on 12 December that 'we were not pursuing the enemy and had much to say about missed opportunities'; he spoke to Halifax two days afterwards about 'the necessity of developing any success (i.e., in Egypt).[67] Pursuit would 'naturally ... hold the first place in [Wavell's] thoughts' and 'nothing would shake Mussolini more than a disaster in Libya itself'. Wavell's 'first objective' after the initial advance 'must be to maul the Italian Army and rip them off the African shore'; while 'very glad' to learn of Wavell's plans for Bardia and Tobruk and of the capture of Sollum and Capuzzo, Churchill urged that 'only after' he could 'get no farther' would he 'relinquish the main hope in favour of secondary action in the Soudan or Dodecanese'.[68] He pressed Wavell, reminded him of the efforts made to send 'strong reinforcements to Egypt' – notwithstanding the risk of invasion at home and the great handicaps from the outset 'the French defection ... the risk of invasion ... the depletion of our air forces in Egypt ... to support the Greeks' and their replacement from home – and promised 'that if he cared to run the risk of undertaking offensive operations he would be supported by those at home even if the operation was unsuccessful'.[69]

His impatience may have been exaggerated by the operation's success. It was a 'case of satisfaction that we had been able to carry out these movements without any hindrance from the enemy'. At the outset Halifax found him on the 10th 'in good heart about the news coming in from Egypt'; and as a result of a telephone call from him, Halifax wired Cairo to ask 'whether [the] military situation [which looked very good] did not afford [an] opportunity of pushing Egypt into war'.[70] Publicly he was optimistic: he told the House of the operations on the 10th; how the advance began on the 7th 'in a single bound across 75 miles of desert ... successfully accomplished'; and of the attacks on the 9th on the Italian position in the Sidi Barrani, Buq Buq and coastal areas 'the preliminary phase [of which] ha[d] been successful';[71] and on the 12th how Sidi Barrani had been captured 'and the whole coastal region with the exception of one or two points ... is in the hands of the British and Imperial troops. Seven thousand prisoners ha[d] already reached Mersa Matruh.'

---

66 Churchill to Dill, 7 Dec. 1940, PREM 3/288/1.
67 Eden diary, 12 Dec. 1940; Halifax diary, 14 Dec. 1940.
68 Churchill to Wavell, 13 Dec. 1940, Connell, *Wavell*, pp. 296–7; to Wavell, 17 Dec. 1940, PREM 3/309/1.
69 Cabinet, 9 Dec. 1940, WM(40)302, CAB 65/10.
70 Ibid.; Halifax diary, 10 Dec. 1940.
71 Cadogan diary, 10 Dec. 1940.

Though too soon 'to measure the scale of these operations ... they constitute[d] a victory ... in this African theatre of war ... of the first order', removing those acute anxieties for the defence of Egypt.[72] His reaction became less measured with further success. He told the cabinet on the 16th in respect of the news that Halfaya had been cleared though Solum and Fort Capuzzo were still held by the enemy that 'these operations constituted an event of first class importance', the results of which had been 'more than we dared to hope'. He told the House of the operation against Bardia and the 'formidable' risk run in the attack.[73] He was, next day, 'in great form because of the outcome of the battle in the western desert'; he spoke to the ministers' meeting 'joyfully of victory in Africa'; announced that 'in Wavell we have got a winner' and Wilson had 'also done wonderfully well'; recalled the 'cautious ... forecasts' of the generals who at first had spoken 'only ... of a "raid"' and had not known what to expect at Sidi Barrani; explained the lack of hard resistance by the Italians whose air force was 'astonishingly ineffective'; concluded that though the battle was 'by no means over yet ... it ha[d] removed the threat to Egypt and will make repercussions all round the Mediterranean through the whole Middle East and as far as Moscow'.[74]

But the successful operations against the Italians in Libya were not to obscure the matter of Germany's next move: indeed, they might precipitate it. Churchill continued to be preoccupied with what Hitler would do and considered his 'next move ... a matter of speculation'; it looked as if 'he did not mean to make any effort in the Balkans', that he might 'take charge of Italy, but that would not be a victory for him'. Perhaps within three weeks 'and certainly within three months, he must make some violent counter stroke'. Would it be an attempt 'to invade us' or to launch 'a gas attack on us on an immense scale'? Perhaps 'a blow through Spain' or Italy or to the Mediterranean through France; perhaps through Bulgaria to Salonika – 'the easiest one of all' – though perhaps Hitler did not want to 'get wrong with both the Russians and the Turks'.[75] He thought in mid-December that 'the most menacing outlook was in Spain' and Hitler might 'move in that direction with the object ... of occupying the North African coast'.[76] If Germany did that then Britain would 'have to take some action ... in Spain or in North Africa'.[77] Although they had 'no

---

[72] House of Commons, 10, 12 Dec. 1940, *Unrelenting Struggle*, pp. 11-13, 14-15.
[73] Cabinet, 16 Dec. 1940, WM(40)306, CAB 65/10; House of Commons, 19 Dec. 1940, *Unrelenting Struggle*, pp. 18–26.
[74] Eden diary, 17 Dec. 1940; Dalton diary, 17 Dec. 1940.
[75] Cabinet, 16 Dec. 1940, WM(40) 306, CAB 65/16; Dalton diary, 17 Dec. 1940.
[76] Cabinet, 16 Dec. 1940, WM(40)306, CAB 65/16
[77] Defence committee, 16 Dec. 1940, DO(40)50, CAB 69/1.

wish to draw Germany down on Greece' he had been pressing for the construction of aerodromes in Greece and considered that 'German intervention in the Balkans was to be anticipated in the long run'. He wanted the development 'on a large scale' of aerodromes which could take both fighters and heavy bombers and suggested they be constructed south of the Olympus–Aerta line.[78] These would also serve for bombing the Romanian oilfields – though he promised that there could be 'no question' of that 'without first having obtained the permission of the Greek government'.[79] Moreover, aerodromes 'of proper size' would be constructed 'from which we could aid the Turkish defence if attacked'. In general, they were planning 'a very large army . . . and ample sea-power in the Middle East' which would 'face a German lurch that way'.[80]

Summary

Churchill intended to secure the Middle East by an early forestalling offensive against the Italians and by despatching steady reinforcements to hold the position for the future against the Germans. Though he continued to maintain that the planned reinforcements of the Middle East would not be at the cost of the home theatre, by mid-September he envisaged large scale operations in the Middle East. In this scheme the Balkans in general, or Greece in particular, were of no importance, except in so far as they mattered to the security of Egypt. Therefore, when Italy attacked Greece on 28 October, Churchill had no reason to be deflected from his general scheme; he reminded his colleagues that they must be under 'no illusion' that there was anything which they could do which would be of immediate value to Greece. Crete alone mattered as a base vital to the security of Egypt; and Turkey could play a dominant part in delaying a Hitlerian march southwards.

But within days of the attack Churchill became a protagonist of support for the Greeks – and he urged that air assistance should be sent and other means of helping examined. His reasons for doing so tended to emerge from overlapping political and military considerations: politically the cause of Greece had evoked much sentiment, and in any case Britain was, in some measure, committed by the guarantee of 1939; militarily Greece fitted into the scheme of imperial defence whereby not only Crete but the Aegean islands and Athens could all be seen as vital to the

---

[78] Cabinet, 27 Dec. 1940, WM(40)310, CAB 65/16; Churchill to Portal, 15 Dec. 1940, Portal:1:1941:1 ; 22 Dec. 1940, Portal:1:1940:36.
[79] Ibid.
[80] Churchill to Portal, 22 Dec. 1940, Portal:1:1940:36; to prime minister of Australia, 13 Dec. 1940, Churchill, *Second World War*, II, p. 541.

Mediterranean position and the defence of Egypt. Furthermore, the military case for helping Greece could be made in terms of its affecting the Turks, thought to hold the key to Britain's imperial position. The strength of Churchill's protagonism may have been designed to counteract the objections of Eden and the Middle East command, who in turn, may have misinterpreted its degree. Despite his strong words, Churchill's intentions *vis à vis* Greece were strictly limited and at no stage superseded his plans to build huge forces in the Middle East, to attack the Italians, and to prepare to resist a German 'lurch'. This became increasingly clear once Wavell's campaign began on 7 December. Churchill's impatience to extend it and exploit the successes became all the more marked given that it would have some bearing on precipitating a Hitlerian attack. Churchill expected it – though he knew not from where – if not immediately, then within three months and set about preparing aerodromes in Greece, building up his forces in Libya and maintaining a strong fleet in the Mediterranean.

6   Eden and the Middle East

The background: May–September 1940

Throughout the summer, Eden appeared to be a strong protagonist of making good the deficiencies in the Middle East. The exigencies of the Battle of Britain did not deter him from making Wavell's case; or from despatching – and stating that he was doing so – parcels of reinforcement: additional supplies of ammunition in late July (when he also had plans for armoured cars and spares).[1]

Wavell's visit and his tales of woe encouraged Eden to feel righteous. The deficiencies were, he thought, 'shocking', and they would 'have to make him a parcel ... and send it out soon'. Equipment shortages must be made good, the despatch of convoys and armoured reinforcements hastened. Wavell, he minuted Churchill, lacked 'all the weapons which ... ma[d]e up a modern fighting force' – from ... anti-tank and anti-aircraft weapons to guns and Brens.[2] He pressed for plans to proceed for the despatch of the three armoured units and the 'considerable consignment of equipment, especially guns' which should follow 'as quickly as practicable'; and for preparations for a September convoy of Australian and New Zealand forces, 'or further armoured units' or both.[3]

Eden's position, therefore, was that of a persistent, continual advocate of more to the Middle East – whether specific parcels (named equipment, numbered troops), or reinforcements in general. 'We must not let up on that continuous stream, however great our preoccupations here at home', he wrote on 19 September. He pressed in late September for air replacements for the Middle East, which would have 'an effect ... out of all proportion' to the loss to the United Kingdom; and urged on the 27th

---

[1] Cabinet, 31 July 1940, CA to WM(40)216, CAB 65/14.
[2] Eden diary, 8 Aug. 1940; Eden to Churchill, 13 Aug. 1940, Avon, *The Reckoning*, pp. 129, 131–3.
[3] Eden to Churchill, 21 Aug. 1940, ibid., p. 133.

that a programme should be drawn up of the forces it was 'proposed to send to the Middle East month by month'.[4]

But Eden was not as stout-hearted as his interventions – or subsequent account – might indicate. Whereas his rhetoric and his views seemed to be distinct from Churchill's, the distinction was not of substance. Eden, as Churchill, advocated strengthening the Middle East at the expense of endangering the home front, and on this account he was willing to countenance both withdrawals and modifications of strategy. For example, he acquiesced in Wavell's withdrawal from Sollum and announced in late July for it was 'impossible . . . to spare any considerable reinforcement in the way of tanks', though there might be something in a few weeks.[5] The reinforcements announced in August – armoured units, equipment, the Antipodean troops, regular convoys from September onwards – 'would depend on how the Battle of Britain developed in the next few days' (i.e., after 21 August); and in September the decision 'could not be dissociated from the likelihood of invasion of these islands being attempted this autumn'.[6] He made it clear, even in late September, that apropos the programme of reinforcements which he wanted to see drawn up, it would be necessary to consider the position month by month to decide whether it 'permitted of the despatch of forces and equipment on the basis of the programme'.[7]

Though loyal to Wavell to the extent of claiming with Dill that neither knew of any other 'better qualified to fill this very difficult post at this critical time',[8] Eden also seemed unsure. During a discussion with Churchill he had not, he thought, enough 'evidence to compel a change' – though when asked about a possible successor, he proposed Auchinleck. Indeed, he may already have accepted the prospect of change during Wavell's visit to London – and pressed Churchill that Wavell should not be kept there indefinitely: he should 'either return, or be replaced'.[9]

Moreover, Eden's apparent differences with Churchill at the time and in retrospect may have been designed to show that he could and would 'stand up' to Churchill or to mark himself out as being responsible for and preoccupied with the great issues of imperial defence. As far as Churchill went, such a stand was hypothetical: there was no substantive difference,

[4] Eden to Hankey, 19 Sept. 1940, Hankey 11/14; Eden memo, 'Despatch of Aircraft to the Middle East', 26 Sept. 1940, WP(40)387, CAB 66/12; cabinet, 27 Sept. 1940, WM(40)260, CAB 65/9. For the discussion on shipping arrangements for a convoy in late September, cabinet 2 Sept. 1940, WM(40)239, CAB 65/9; WP(40)239, CAB 65/9.
[5] Cabinet, 31 July. 1940, WM(40)216, CAB 65/14.
[6] Eden to Churchill, 21 Aug. 1940, Avon, *The Reckoning*, p. 135.
[7] Cabinet, 27 Sept. 1940, WM(40)260, CAB 65/9.
[8] Eden to Churchill, 13 Aug. 1940, Avon, *The Reckoning*, pp. 131–2.
[9] Ibid; Eden diary, 15 Aug. 1940, ibid, p. 133.

though there were disagreements about the timetable and route for the despatch of reinforcements. Eden may have gained some advantage by stressing such disagreements, appearing as a result to be more of a protagonist of the Middle East than Churchill, who refused to concede any suggestion of conflicting demands. In championing Wavell, apparently in defiance of Churchill, Eden may have gained Wavell's uncritical support – with ultimate implications for the independence of Wavell's advice throughout the following spring, when Eden, as foreign secretary resolved on a course of British military intervention in Greece.

October–December 1940

By October Eden thought that the risks in the Middle East were such that the Middle East should be reinforced; and he urged air and armoured reinforcements. By October he had begun to advocate substantial and specific reinforcements to the Middle East without the proviso that they could not be at the expense of the home theatre. Though still a matter of balancing risks between the home and the Middle East, Eden implied that those of the Middle East were greater and particularly urged air and armoured reinforcements. He pressed for further air reinforcements (for the British air force in Egypt and Sudan was 'even at present heavily outnumbered') and he urged that aircraft were central to desert conditions – they would 'prove even more important in fighting [there]' than in the French battle.[10] Eden thought the risk as far as the air went was greater in the Middle East than at home – where the position would become 'stronger ... with bad weather ... production and American help'. By contrast, in the Middle East 'flying conditions [would] be as good as they [would] be bad over England in the next few months'. Already the air forces in the Middle East were 'inferior to the Italian forces'; and in the event of strong German air reinforcement 'the whole of our position in the Middle East' would be threatened.[11] He also pressed for specific armoured reinforcements; for the remainder of the second armoured division, which included two cruisers and two light tank regiments and he also pressed for the despatch of armoured reinforcements in November – which would mean their withdrawal from battle now; conceded that they must 'weigh the balance of risk' but concluded that 'on balance ... it [was] right'. Although they would, as a result, have to rely

---

[10] For Eden's proposals for future convoys see WP(40)406, 5 Oct. 1940, CAB 66/12 ; Eden to Sinclair, 4 Oct. 1940, Avon, *The Reckoning*, p. 142.
[11] Eden published extracts from his to Churchill, *c.* 7 Oct. 1940 and his memorandum for the cabinet, *c.* 8 Oct. 1940, Avon, *The Reckoning*, p. 143.

on 'I' tanks in the event of invasion, there was 'accumulating evidence of German assistance to Italians in Libya' and should that 'eventuate' within the next two months the presence of these armoured forces might 'just turn the scales in Egypt'.[12] On 11 October Eden left for Cairo.

Before leaving for Cairo Eden had come to consider the risks in the Middle East greater than at home and had pressed for air and armoured reinforcements. Once there, his advocacy became more marked as he was struck by the deficiencies, particularly in the air. The matter was urgent, given not only the Italian danger but also the hazards which would accompany a German arrival as well as the general prospect of launching any offensive. He may have been affected particularly by the case of the commanders: Longmore who had greatly 'impressed me with his grasp and vigour in no way exaggerate[d] ... present weakness'.[13] And he had also made it clear that he was 'not at present in a position to give the army effective support if serious military operations developed'.[14] It was 'essential' for successful defence, let alone any offensive military operations in the near future, 'that air reinforcements should ... keep pace with those on land'. He had 'no doubt that air reinforcement [was] the essential'. Longmore had 'frequently represented to [the] air ministry that determined Italian [air] offensive, more particularly if carried out with German support, would entirely overwhelm his three forward fighter squadrons'.[15]

Eden proposed more specifically that they might be given authority 'to raise three complete new squadrons'; that one company of tanks would be added to the November convoy, which Wavell wished to offload at Port Sudan 'and use ... in ... projected offensive against Kassala'; that there were 'urgent requirements of small stores for the armoured division'; that the 'I' tanks could 'play a much more important role in the fighting in this theatre than [had been] thought'; and that Wavell would like a battalion of 'I' tanks and a brigade recovery section.[16] He hoped that some of the sailing dates of convoys might be brought forward or that additional convoys might be added to the programme; that if the interim October convoy were abandoned, then the slow November convoy could be advanced to leave on the 1st rather than the 7th; that the fast convoy should sail on 17 November as arranged (the armoured division reaching

[12] WP(40)406, 5 Oct. 1940, CAB 66/12.
[13] Eden to Churchill, 17 Oct. 1940, PREM 3/308. He added that the number of Italian fighters seen in one patrol now 'often exceeds our total strength available in these forward squadrons'.
[14] Eden to Dill, 26 Oct. 1940, PREM 3/308.
[15] Ibid.; Eden to Churchill, 17 Oct. 1940, PREM 3/308 .
[16] Eden to Dill and Churchill, 15, 24, Oct. 1940, PREM 3/308; Eden to Dill 26 Oct. 1940, PREM 3/308.

Suez on 14 December and liners a few days later); and wondered whether two ships containing two cruiser tank regiments for Egypt might be taken through the Mediterranean. He thought an additional convoy could sail towards the end of November to supplement those already advised – especially as none was due to leave before 1 November.[17]

The attack on Greece did not change Eden's views. Nothing could be done for Greece, though Crete should be secured. They must, rather, concentrate on military success in the Middle East. The reinforcement of the Middle East was for Eden and the command all the more urgent, given the danger of an Italian move and all the more necessary given Wavell's plan for an offensive – about which Eden hinted in his wire of the 17th. 'Politically' he claimed that the 'whole situation would be immeasurably improved if we were able to gain some military success'; and though Italy might 'by some offensive of her own upset any plans we make ... this must not prevent us laying our own plans'; perhaps the 'most hopeful field' for military success might be the Sudan'.[18]

The Italian attack on Greece on the 28th changed nothing – and did not deflect Eden from the Middle East. On the contrary, Eden insisted at the outset that nothing could be done for Greece. Whereas before he had left London he had proposed support in the air as well as by sea in the event of an enemy attack, after the attack he maintained they were 'not in a position to give effective help by land or air' and 'another guaranteed nation look[ed] like falling to the axis'.[19] Crete, however, was another matter; and all concerned were 'equally anxious to make sure of Crete'.[20] He also considered with the command other means of affecting Turkish opinion – such as an attack on the Dodecanese (it being claimed that 'the effect on the Turks of a successful action ... would be very great') or the despatch of a military mission to Turkey to deal with technical matters and help 'in the maintenance of ... equipment and ... training with it'.[21]

Eden's first reaction to the Italian attack on Greece – that there was 'nothing they could do' – became all the more determined when it seemed that in London plans had changed and Greece was 'now to dominate the

---

[17] Eden memo, 5 Oct. 1940, WP(40)406, CAB 66/12; note of conference at GHQ Cairo, 16 Oct. 1940, WO 193/963; Eden to Dill and Churchill, 26 Oct. 1940, PREM 3/308. He thought the use of the Mediterranean for the armoured reinforcements would save three to four weeks.

[18] Eden to Churchill, 17 Oct. 1940, PREM 3/308.

[19] Eden diary, 28 Oct. 1940; memorandum for cabinet, c. 8 Oct. 1940, Avon, *The Reckoning*, p. 143.

[20] Eden to Churchill, 29 Oct. 1940, PREM 3/308.

[21] Minutes of a conference at GHQ Cairo, 16 Oct. 1940, WO 193/963; Eden to Dill and Churchill, 16 Oct. 1940, PREM 3/308. Eden also implied that the Turks were won over;

scene'. That was 'strategic folly'. Egypt was 'more important than Greece' and Eden resolved to return to London, alert them of 'certain projects' and 'above all try to stop folly of diverting men, aeroplanes and materials from here to Greece'. The best way to help Greece was 'by striking at Italy, and we can do that most effectively from areas where our strength has been developed and where our plans are laid'.[22] Eden reiterated for Churchill's benefit that British policy to Greece 'had been clearly laid down on several occasions and communicated to the Greek government'; and it had been made plain, particularly on 22 September, that 'any assistance ... to Greece [could] not be given until German Italian threat to Egypt [was] finally liquidated, the security of Egypt being vital to our strategy and incidentally to the future of Greece'.[23] He warned that by dividing their limited resources they would 'risk failure in both theatres'. The line with the Greeks had always been that they could not help them on land or in the air; and 'however disagreeable we should hold to that'; besides, ineffective help to the Greeks might 'have worse effect on Turks than to withhold.'[24] Moreover, Eden and the command were concerned at the impression 'being given by statements from London that air support [was] being given and British troops ha[d] landed'; for the extent to which they could help was 'very limited' and indeed the air was 'limited to one squadron on its way' and the troops to 'one battalion in Crete'. With the Middle East command he hoped that instructions would be given 'not to raise hopes which cannot be realised'.[25]

Eden opposed diverting to Greece not only because that had been British policy and there was in any case nothing which could be given, but because of the paramountcy of Egypt – all the more so given the plans for an offensive there. The defence of Egypt was, he maintained, 'of paramount importance to our whole position in the Middle East'; Egypt was the 'most urgent commitment ... and must take precedence ... [over] Greece ... also essential if [they were] to retain the support of Turkey'.[26] Moreover, he wired about Wavell's plan 'to strike a blow against Italians in Western Desert at the earliest possible moment, probably this month';

that theirs had been a 'most friendly attitude'; that they had expressed themselves as favourably impressed by the number of troops and organisation of defence in Egypt.
22 Eden to Churchill, 1 Nov. 1940, WO 193/963; Eden comments on Churchill wire, 1 Nov. 1940, Avon, II, p. 168; Eden diary, 2 Nov. 1940.
23 Eden to Churchill, 3 Nov. 1940, WO 193/963.
24 Eden to Dill and for Churchill, 3 Nov. 1940 (d. 1955), PREM 3/309/1.
25 Eden to Dill and for Churchill, 3 Nov. 1940, PREM 3/309/1. Eden added that they 'much hope[d] ... instructions can be given [to the] BBC and others ... not to raise hopes which cannot be realised'. Churchill omitted this extract from his account, whereas Eden reproduced it. Churchill, *Second World War*, II pp. 478–9; Avon, *The Reckoning*, p. 170.
26 Eden to Churchill, 3 Nov. 1940, PREM 3/308.

the plan involved certain risks and required all trained and fully equipped troops in the western desert and reserve in Egypt; the margin was small 'and any withdrawal of troops or equipment would mean cancelling plan and remaining on the defensive'.[27] They could not from existing Middle East forces 'send sufficient ... to have any decisive influence upon ... fighting in Greece' and to do so would not only 'imperil our whole position in the Middle East' but it would 'jeopardise plans for ... offensive operation'.[28] (Even as far as Crete went, air reinforcements would be at the expense of the western desert where the force was at present 'too weak to allow [Longmore to] give support to the army should a major battle develop'.[29]) Though Crete was to be secured, it was not at the expense of the western desert, nor indeed need it be. But Eden implied there was no need for Cretan defence to be at the expense of the desert; and the preliminary steps involved the despatch of a battalion and a further force of brigade headquarters and another battalion, anti-aircraft batteries, some sappers and other units, while a squadron of fighters and bombers would be sent 'as soon as aerodrome facilities were available'. It was unnecessary to keep 'any large British military garrison in Crete' for once the Cretans organised 'one battalion together with AA defence would suffice'; and given that the fleet served as the first line of defence and that the Italians were unlikely to attack while it was in the Mediterranean until Greece itself was overrun there seemed to be no case for doing more.[30] In any case there would be difficulties in using aircraft for Crete possessed 'only one aerodrome which [could] be made serviceable' which was 'very vulnerable to air attack' and Longmore was reluctant to 'add any more ... to the Greek commitment in present conditions ... [which] would lead to a large wastage of ... aircraft'; and even though Crete was valuable 'as a means of securing Eastern Mediterranean' the fleet could not be based at Suda Bay for more than a few hours at a time 'owing to lack of anti-submarine protection'. Moreover, the very weapons which the Greeks needed 'AA guns, anti-tank guns and rifles' were those which were 'precisely ... our most serious shortage here'; no trained equipped formation larger than a brigade could be sent; and that would deprive the western desert of its only reserve.[31]

Despite opposition to diverting, Eden agreed with Longmore and Wavell to divert, for political reasons. In principle, his position continued to be that he opposed the diversion of resources from the Middle East to

27 Ibid.   28 Churchill to Eden, 1 Nov. 1940, WO 193/963.
29 Eden to Churchill, 1 Nov. 1940, WO 193/963.
30 Eden to Churchill, ibid.; 3 Nov. 1940, PREM 3/309/1.
31 Ibid.; Eden to Dill and Churchill, 3 Nov. 1940, PREM 3/309/1.

the Balkans; that the policy already laid down for Greece should be stuck to; that Egypt should take pre-eminence over Greece, particularly given the weakness of the Middle East and the impending operations there; that that was the best way of helping the Greeks for whom there could be very little other assistance – particularly given that what the Greeks needed was what was in short supply at home. Though Eden objected to the cries to divert to Greece as 'folly', though he deprecated the 'weakness of our policy ... that we never adhere to the plan ... ma[d]e' and that if it had been intended 'to help Greece ... we should long since have laid our plans accordingly' instead of which the 'deliberate decision' not to do so 'was gone back on', he did not refuse absolutely to divert or threaten to resign, but conceded reluctantly.[32] Yet he did so against his own judgement; and with Wavell and Longmore he agreed to the risks 'in view of political commitments to aid Greece' despite feeling that the withdrawal of one of our three fighter squadrons from the western desert or 'a third of our fighter force [was] a very drastic cut and unless we can improve upon present plans cannot be replaced for some weeks'; and he did so despite Longmore's warning that they were 'too weak now to give effective support to the army in battle should a major engagement develop' and his hypothesis that Italy's attack on Greece had been designed 'to induce us to weaken ourselves in the vital theatre of Egypt'.[33]

When he returned to London Eden continued to object to diversions to Greece and to press for resources to be kept in the Middle East – though at no stage did he refuse outright. He explained the position in the Middle East, stressing the weakness in the air and warning of the German danger. He recalled Wavell's own summing up of strategy in three parts – 'to ensure the security of Egypt by the defeat of the Italian forces ... threatening it', 'to foster rebellion in Abyssinia and by raids and local offensives from Sudan and Kenya, ... to liquidate the Italian forces in East Africa' and 'to build up forces to assist Greece, Turkey and other Middle East countries' – and he warned of the dangers should the Germans attack and not the Italians.[34]

Eden warned that though very little traffic between Italy and North Africa had been detected, the more serious danger came from the Germans. If they began to send reinforcements to Libya 'it would become a matter of great importance to interrupt their communications'; and he anticipated that the position would be 'completely altered if German

---

[32] Eden diary, 3 Nov. 1940.
[33] Ibid. 4 Nov. 1940, p. 171 Eden wrote that the demands were heavy but had 'no doubt been modified by our own strong warnings'; Eden to Dill and Churchill, 5 Nov. 1940, WO 193/963; 6 Nov. 1940, PREM 3/308.
[34] Cabinet, 12 Nov. 1940, WM(40)287, CA CAB 65/16; Avon, *The Reckoning*, pp. 174–5.

forces on a considerable scale, with large number of tanks, arrived to take part in the Western Desert battle'.[35] He continued to press for air reinforcements for the Middle East: there would be a total fighter strength of three fighter squadrons in Egypt – two in the western desert and one in Alexandria and Cairo – and that was unlikely to change, given that as soon as enough machines had arrived to form a new squadron, a second Gladiator squadron must go to Greece. He wished the move would not be automatic and that it would be decided 'in the light of events ... whether it should go to Greece or stay in Egypt'.[36] The British weakness was, he warned, in the air; and for some time after the withdrawal of the five squadrons to Greece, not only would there be merely three fighter squadrons available and a 'serious shortage of anti-aircraft guns', but they must 'bear in mind the possibility of German air forces operating against our line of communications, which would create a most dangerous situation'.[37]

He warned that 'one must not place too high hopes on "Compass" ... at present a limited operation' though he did concede that it might influence the Turks and the Greeks and had begun by late November to consider where the army should be deployed if Compass went 'reasonably well'. They must 'continue to hammer the Italians, in Africa or Europe or both'. The army could not be left 'inactive' in Africa and Eden – who wondered whether the Greeks should now be reinforced, and if so where – proposed that he should pay another visit.[38]

Although cautious about Wavell's operation before the attack was launched and delighted afterwards, Eden began to entertain higher hopes of what might be the next stage. At first he continued to impress his colleagues with the difficulties of the desert operation and to support Wavell against Churchill – maintaining that matters should be left to Wavell. He explained to the cabinet that 'the main purpose of the operation ... [was to] attack the 2nd Libyan division which occupied a position south of Sidi Barrani' and if successful 'to exploit the situation by a sweep towards the coast'; 'we might hope to inflict a decisive defeat on the 1st and 2nd Libya divisions' but 'the difficulties of communications were ... very great, and might well operate to prevent any very large advance'.[39] According to his own account he continued to protect and support Wavell against interference by Churchill. Before the attack he 'made it plain' to Churchill, who wanted news of 'Compass' and showed

35 Cabinet, 12 Nov. 1940, WM(40)287, CAB 65/16.
36 Eden minute, 9 Nov. 1940, Avon, *The Reckoning*, pp. 173–4.
37 Cabinet, 12 Nov. 1940, WM(40)287, CAB 65/16.   38 Eden diary, 25 Dec. 1940.
39 Cabinet, 9 Dec. 1940, WM(40)302, CAB 65/16.

indignation that Eden had not asked the date, that he 'did not believe in fussing Wavell with questions'; that he 'knew his plan'; that Wavell 'knew our view [and] had best be left to get on with it'.[40] After the attack had begun – well – Eden delivered, on the 12th, an 'angry riposte' to Churchill who telephoned complaining 'that we were not pursuing the enemy' and further suggested that all of this showed 'we should have held Somaliland', which Eden considered 'most ungenerous' particularly as 'we had not a gun there.'[41] He replied to Wavell's 'excellent appreciation of his plans' which arrived on the 17th by sending 'a telegram of approval at once, before argument could confuse it'.[42]

Eden seems to have been taken by surprise at the initial success; he thought after the news of the capture of Sidi Barrani on the 11th that it all seemed 'too good to be true'; at first he thought only of that 'then began to think of the capture of Sollum ... [and then] of the conquest of Libya'.[43] But he had already begun to look beyond Compass and the deployment of the army should it go 'reasonably well'. They must 'continue to hammer [the] Italians either in Africa, or Europe or both'; and given that the army could not be left inactive in Africa, Eden wondered whether the Greeks should be reinforced, and if so where. He had already considered another visit to the Middle East and talks with the Greeks and the Turks.[44] And when Churchill replaced Halifax with Eden as foreign secretary on 20 December, Eden became an eager protagonist of Balkan intervention – by contrast with his opposition to such a course as secretary of state for war.[45]

By October Eden had become less ambiguous about the Middle East. Although he still thought that risks must be balanced, he maintained that the risks in the Middle East were greater. He left for Cairo in early October and once there his advocacy became more marked, affected as he was by the deficiencies which he found, particularly in the air, and the urgency of the position in view of Wavell's plans for an offensive. Moreover, the danger of a German descent persisted. Eden was still in Cairo when the Italians attacked Greece on 28 October; but the attack served to strengthen, not modify, his resolve. There was nothing to be

---

[40] Eden diary, 4 Dec. 1940.   [41] Ibid., 12 Dec. 1940.
[42] Avon, *The Reckoning*, pp. 181–2.
[43] Eden diary, 11 Dec. 1940; Nicolson diary, 12 Dec. 1940.
[44] Eden diary, 25 Nov. 1940.
[45] A note written to Beaverbrook about aircraft from Greece (30 fighters promised in response to Metaxas' appeal to Roosevelt) referred to 'the delay in reaching a solution ... causing an unfortunate impression in both Greece and the USA' and suggests some reasons why Eden's views of what mattered changed. He hoped the Greeks could be provided with aircraft 'at small sacrifice to ourselves'; Eden to Beaverbrook, 24 Dec. 1940, BBK D. 338.

spared for the Greeks; nothing could be done. It had not been British policy to intervene and there was no sense in substituting a series of ineffective expedients for the policy laid down and agreed. The best way to help Greece would be to strengthen the Middle East. This, in any case, would have good repercussions for the Turkish attitude – with which Eden had concerned himself throughout his visit. And although it had been agreed as a matter of policy to secure Crete, the amounts to be employed there were limited.

Eden continued to argue when in the Middle East and after his return to London that Egypt was paramount and should take pre-eminence over Greece. The prospect of Wavell's offensive should serve to modify any decision to divert. After his return he outlined Wavell's general strategy and explained, in cautious terms, his proposals for an offensive. Eden's caution may have been designed to temper the hopes of his colleagues in London and protect and support Wavell. He had confidence in him, or so he claimed, and thought he ought to be left to get on with matters. Or Eden may not have entertained many hopes himself. Once the victories began, he seemed overwhelmed and suggested they exceeded all his hopes. Even then Eden had already begun to reflect on what might be tackled next and, by contrast with his first reaction to the Italian attack on Greece, had now begun to consider moving the armies to the Balkans – a process which was encouraged by his leaving the war office and becoming foreign secretary.

The background: May–September 1940

Halifax anticipated some trouble, some time, in the Balkans – where Greece should be bolstered -- and in the Middle East, where the Germans would pose the serious threat.

In the Balkans, the Greeks should be stiffened against an Italian attack – with promises of financial support and of bombing raids on Italy. Halifax did not think, by early September, such an attack would necessarily be immediate. Although Metaxas – who seemed to be 'taking a firm attitude' – could not be further pressed 'to intensify ... precautionary defence measures', Halifax thought some promises might be made. The minister in Athens suggested military and financial help and Halifax thought they should promise 'more intensive bombing of military targets in Italy ... [and] should be ready to consider financial help' – to which the cabinet agreed, as it also did to investigate operating bombers from Greek aerodromes.[1] As to the Middle East, the impression Halifax had from Wavell was that 'provided the Italian forces were engaged, he was not too unhappy about the position' – but would regard German armoured reinforcements as constituting a 'serious' position.[2] Indeed, if invasion were 'off', it was thought by Cadogan that Hitler would 'have a winter campaign in North Africa and send a couple of thousand planes to help the Italians' – though Halifax maintained that Germany and Italy 'seemed to want to keep out of the war as long as they can'.[3]

By September Halifax could not 'at all exclude the possibility that Hitler [was] deliberately scaring us with invasion in order to check reinforcements to Egypt where the main blow was to be delivered'. In his view, they ought to keep up 'a small steady stream' of reinforcements; and

[1] Halifax diary, 30 Aug. 1940.; cabinet, 21 Aug. 1940, WM(40)231 CAB 65/8; 26 Aug. 1940, WM(40)234 CAB 65/8. Halifax on 30 August thought Italian–Greek tension 'seem[ed] to be lessening and I still don't think the gangsters want to see trouble in the Balkans'.
[2] Cabinet, 23 Aug. 1940, WM(40)233, CAB 65/14; Halifax diary, 9 Aug. 1940.
[3] Cadogan diary, 21, 31 Aug. 1940; Halifax diary, 22 June 1940.

he thought that it would be wrong to stop the flow of modern aircraft for the consequences of a setback in the Middle East 'might be very serious'.[4]

October–December 1940

By October Halifax did not think there would be an invasion, but considered that Hitler would postpone an attempt until the spring. The point of contact would, rather, be the Middle East; though when and how Hitler would attack there was perplexing. The route by the Balkans, Syria, Palestine to the Gulf and the canal was long – though the reports suggested it might be used. In that scheme Turkey was vital. Halifax continued to be concerned with the Turks – whether approaches should be made – and with the implications of the Soviet attitude on the Turks. After the attack on Greece he did not want either the Greeks or Palairet discouraged, though there was, he thought, 'nothing more' to be done for the Greeks. Yet Greece's holding out came to matter to Halifax on account of its impact on the other Balkan countries and on Turkey.

Halifax's evidence, by 10 October, was that 'an attempt to invade this country [had] been postponed until the spring of 1941'. Hitler would 'keep it all ready in order to prevent us feeling as free as we should like to help the Middle East'. By the 24th 'it really seem[ed] as if the invasion of England ha[d] been postponed for the present'.[5] Instead, Hitler would look to the Middle East 'the next point of big contact'.[6] But how precisely that would happen was not clear. Did Hitler intend to invade Egypt via Syria, or 'to walk into the Suez Canal through Anatolia and Syria?' Though 'a longish way to go', Halifax did not 'put it past him'.[7] The Germans were reported to have been studying 'the possibility of action in Greece and Yugoslavia'; and there was 'much talk of Hitler going down through the Balkans, Turkey and Syria to Palestine and the Canal'.[8] Hitler's moves were unclear and even late in November in London they were 'more or less in the dark' about his intentions in the Mediterranean. On the likelihood of 'an immediate advance' through the Balkans, 'some ... military pundits ... [thought] Hitler ha[d] left it a bit late ... this year';

---

4 Halifax to Hoare, 26 Sept. 1940, Templewood XIII:20.
5 Cabinet, 10 Oct. 1940, WM(40)269, CAB 65/9; Halifax to Linlithgow, 12 Oct. 1940, IOL MSS. Eur. F 125/152 (b)/50; Halifax to Hoare, 24 Oct. 1940, Templewood XIII:20:[53]; Halifax thought it had been planned for 15 or 16 September, 'when they made their biggest attack by air and lost 185'.
6 Halifax to Linlithgow, 12 Oct. 1940, IOL MSS. Eur. F 125/152 (b)/50.
7 Cadogan diary, 9 Oct. 1940; Halifax diary, 9 Oct. 1940; cabinet, 9 Oct. 1940, WM(40)268, CAB 65/9; Halifax to Linlithgow, 12 Oct. 1940, IOL MSS. EUR F 125/152 (b)/50.
8 Cabinet, 10 Oct. 1940, WM(40)269, CAB 65/9; Halifax to Linlithgow, 12 Oct. 1940, IOL MSS. Eur. F 125/152 (b)/50; Halifax to Hoare, 24 Oct. 1940, Templewood XIII:20:53.

and the possibility also existed of Germany 'sending reinforcements for the Italian troops in Libya, through Italy itself'. The only certainty was uncertainty and it was 'too early yet to be at all definite about German intentions'.[9]

Whatever his uncertainty about Hitler's intentions, Halifax was clear about the importance of Turkey; about the attitude to be taken to her; and the need, also, to consider the Turkish position in view of the imponderable attitude of the Soviets. In this scheme, German plans vis-à-vis the Turks would need to be anticipated. Was the German action in making aerodromes in Romania and developing anti-aircraft defences in the oilfields designed 'to intimidate the Turks'?[10] Given the prospect of a German campaign directed towards 'the Persian Gulf or the Suez Canal' should British approaches to the Turks be made? Almost certainly the Turks in that event would 'be sure to ask what help we could give them in the way of equipment'. It was also likely that the Russians would help indirectly, for the Turkish position, already 'uncomfortable ... would be more so if Russia, either from fear of Germany or from cupidity, lent herself to German plans'.[11] Halifax thought 'some play' should be made for the benefit of the Turks 'with the measures proposed to strengthen our position in the Middle East'.[12] By mid-October it did look 'as if the Germans intend[ed] to consolidate their position first in Roumania and then in Bulgaria with a view to bringing pressure to bear on Turkey ... on Yugoslavia and Greece'. If Hitler intended to threaten Turkey, he must then make use of the Yugoslav rail communications, otherwise he would not be able 'to concentrate and maintain a sufficiently large force in that part of the world'.[13]

Before the attack on Greece, Halifax had been concerned, principally, with the Turks – given the possibility of Hitler's moving on Egypt or the Persian Gulf through the Balkans, Syria, Palestine – and the role the Turks would play in such an event. The Turks for their part were reassuring. They maintained that it was 'impossible for the Germans either to cross the Straits or even if they [did] ... to drive across Anatolia'. They continued to give 'an encouraging account' of the government's attitude which would be to make the position vis-à-vis Bulgaria 'perfectly clear'; and also make clear that 'the Turks would fight if attacked'.[14] As

---

[9] Halifax to Hoare, 24 Oct. 1940, Templewood XIII:20:53.
[10] Cabinet, 9 Oct. 1940, WM(40)268, CAB 65/15; Halifax to Linlithgow, 12 Oct. 1940, IOL MSS. Eur. F 125/152 (b)/50.
[11] Ibid.   [12] Cabinet, 16 Oct. 1940, WM(40)272, CAB 65/9.
[13] Halifax to Hoare, 24 Oct. 1940, Templewood XIII:20:53
[14] Halifax diary, 30 Oct. 1940; note of a meeting of prime minister, lord privy seal and secretary of state for foreign affairs, 31 Oct. 1940, CAB 127/14.

for Greece, though she did not matter to Halifax in the same way, his view was that the Greeks should be reassured at the outset about help. Once they began to hold out, their military success had implications wider than those arising out of defeating Italy, for it would affect Germany too in the context of the Balkans, Turkey and the Middle East.

Just after the attack Halifax maintained that 'there was obviously nothing to be done about it more than we are doing', But he was reluctant to discourage Palairet or the Greeks; and while agreeing with Churchill's first message to the effect that there was nothing, given that 'it would not be right to discourage ... Palairet too much ... [he] asked whether it would not be possible for us to put a few aeroplanes in Greece itself at once'.[15] But, in addition to a desire not to discourage the Greeks (by offering 'a few' aeroplanes and by toning down the wire to Palairet), Halifax came to look upon Greece as in itself militarily significant on account of the effect of its resistance on the other Balkan countries, Turkey and the general Middle Eastern position – whether threatened by the Italians or by Hitler himself.

The first feeling that they should do what they could – that they should not discourage the Greeks – quickly turned to stronger feelings of a case for support. For example, Cadogan's first reaction, that they should 'concentrate on Italy ... [as] the only thing to do', became much firmer within days. He was glad, 'thank heaven', of the decision to do all they could in the air. But this would have to be kept secret – the difficulty being 'to find a way of heartening the Greeks without disclosing ... weakness in the Middle East'. The king and Metaxas should be told 'in strict confidence the number of squadrons being sent'.[16] Besides, the Greeks unexpectedly holding was encouraging; Halifax very quickly thought Greek resistance would affect not only Italy, but Germany. Cadogan continued to be impressed by the Greeks' holding out, though was sure it could not last.[17] Halifax was struck at the outset by the Italians seeming 'to be hesitant'; and by both Germany and Italy being 'equally surprised at the effective Greek resistance' and by Germany's prospective timetable having been 'disarranged'. Germany did 'not like to be too anxious to go through either Bulgaria or Yugoslavia or to help Mussolini'.[18]

Greece very quickly came to matter for Halifax on account of its effect elsewhere. Within days of the attack he was justifying the despatch to Greece on the grounds of its impact on the other Balkan countries. For 'to

[15] Halifax diary, 28 Oct. 1940; note of meeting of prime minister, lord privy seal and secretary of state for foreign affairs, 31 Oct. 1940, CAB 127/14.
[16] Cabinet, 4 Nov. 1940, WM(40)282, CAB 65/16.   [17] Cadogan diary, 21 Nov. 1940.
[18] Halifax diary, 4 Nov. 1940; cabinet, 25 Nov. 1940, WM(40)295, CAB 65/16; Halifax diary, 4 Nov. 1940; Halifax to Hoare, 29 Nov. 1940; Templewood XIII:20:[62].

have sent no help to Greece would have undermined the will to resist of the other Balkan countries'.[19] Their attitudes and alignments, and those of Turkey, continued to concern Halifax – given their impact on the German march southward whether through the Aegean, Bulgaria, Yugoslavia or Turkey and Syria. Yugoslavia, for instance, Halifax thought would 'probably' resist if Germany decided to intervene in the Balkans; and he hoped the Yugoslavs would join the Turks in a joint declaration that 'they would make war [on Bulgaria] if she allowed the Germans to enter her territory'. It became unlikely that the declaration would materialise as Yugoslavia 'was afraid to commit herself so openly', though they would be encouraged to think that 'we shall help them to resist'.[20] Bulgaria was the more difficult of the two. Her borders with Greece and Turkey and her likely response to a German move had made her attitude central to the question of a German advance. If Germany decided to intervene in the Balkans, more probably she would go through Bulgaria – 'unlikely to resist' – than through Yugoslavia 'which would probably do so'.[21] Despite repeated representations the Bulgars had not given Greece any assurance that they would not attack 'thus enabling Greek forces on the Thracian frontier to be transferred to the Albanian front'; and there were, moreover, reports of King Boris having been to Berlin (and having brought his foreign minister with him) in a German aeroplane. They were reported to have been pressed by Hitler and Ribbentrop to join the Axis; and assured that they had 'nothing to fear from Turkey ... [who] would now ... gradually align herself with the axis powers'.[22]

The Turkish position did not become clear – nor was it clear what was the best line to be adopted with the Turks. Halifax thought the Molotov visit to Berlin might mean that 'an anti-Turkish policy was under consideration'; Germany and the Soviet Union might join 'in some attempt to overawe Turkey'; but though Halifax did consider warning the Soviets of a breach should they try to intimidate the Turks, he did not do so 'lest that embarrass Turkey'.[23] Nor was Halifax certain that they should try to bring Turkey into the war at this stage. By contrast with the chiefs, who on balance favoured doing so ('on the ground that the sooner she committed herself openly the better. If she postponed a decision she might find reasons for not standing by the Allies'), Halifax was against 'putting

---

[19] Cabinet, 4 Nov. 1940, WM(40)282, CAB 65/16.
[20] Cabinet, 22, 25 Nov. 1940, WM(40)294, WM(40)295, CAB 65/10, CAB 65/16; Cadogan diary, 24 Nov. 1940.
[21] Cabinet, 25 Nov. 1940, WM(40)295, CAB 65/16.
[22] Cabinet, 6, 22 Nov. 1940, WM(40)283, WM(40)294, CAB 65/10.
[23] Cabinet, 11, 13, 15 Nov. 1940, WM(40)286, 288, 289, CAB 65/10.

any strong pressure on Turkey at the present time'. The Turks would react 'surely' by asking 'for large additional consignments of munitions – a request which we should not be in a position to meet'. Moreover, if Turkey came into the war now that would 'almost certainly bring down a German attack on the Aegean'; and was that 'in our interest ... if ... it might be postponed until we had time to make fuller preparations'? Furthermore, Halifax doubted whether there was 'anything we could do which would persuade Turkey to come into the war, unless and until Germany atacked, or marched through Bulgaria or Yugoslavia'. Given that there were two routes to the Aegean open to Germany – through Yugoslavia or Bulgaria – a 'tripartite understanding between Turkey, Yugoslavia and Bulgaria would block both'.[24] But Halifax did hope for a Turkish public declaration of intention 'in the event of Bulgaria falling into German hands' or of the Germans attacking, possibly as an alternative to pressing the Turks now (lest that led to demands) and with a view to strengthening their neighbours; and he continued to maintain that, if helped, the Turks would fight not only if Germany attacked Bulgaria, but also if she attacked Yugoslavia. Though it is not clear on what grounds, he had come to think by the end of November that the Turks seemed 'pretty steady' and all the reports went to show that 'the Molotov visit did not amount to much'.[25] By early December the feeling was that they had probably done all they could and Hugessen was rightly 'against pressing the Turks too much to pronounce what they [would] do in every hypothesis'.[26]

Although by late December the Greeks were reluctant to allow the preparation of aerodromes by Britain in northern Greece for fear of provoking Germany, they were about to open discussions with the Turks about the future of the Dodecanese.[27] But the long-term future of the Balkans was a complicated matter. Cadogan thought that 'even to talk about reinstating these small countries [was] rather absurd' – the past twenty years having shown 'they can't stand by themselves and must [not] be taken too seriously'.[28]

By early December attention was concentrated on success in the western desert – and the question of terms, should the Italians seek them, and how, more generally, success should be developed.[29]

For Halifax Germany, not Italy, posed the threat to the Middle East; and a German descent on Egypt through the Balkans, Syria and Palestine

[24] Cabinet, 22, 25 Nov. 1940, WM(40)294, CAB 65/10, WM(40)295, CAB 25/16.
[25] Cabinet, 22, 25 Nov. 1940, WM(40)294, WM(40)295, CAB 65/16; Halifax to Hoare, 29 Nov. 1940; Templewood XIII:20:62.
[26] Cadogan diary, 2 Dec. 1940.   [27] Cabinet, 27 Dec. 1940, WM(40)310, CAB 65/10.
[28] Cadogan diary, 4 Dec. 1940.   [29] Halifax diary, 9, 10, 12, 13, 14 Dec. 1940.

should be anticipated. In such a scheme, Turkey (and by geographic association Greece) were vital and both must be strengthened. While something should be done to encourage the Greeks in face of Italian attack – such as holding out the prospect of intensive bombing of military targets in Italy or of giving financial help – Greece mattered more on account of its impact on Turkey. Halifax's concern, after the Italian attack, that the Greeks should not be discouraged, quickly came to merge with the view that Greek resistance mattered for Turkey and the other Balkan countries. However the Turkish position was unclear and Halifax did not think strong pressure should be put on the Turks to join the war for the present. Either they would make impossible demands for munitions, or Turkey's coming in would bring a German attack on the Aegean too soon to allow for adequate preparation. Nothing could, he thought, persuade the Turks to come into the war until Germany marched through Bulgaria or Yugoslavia. In such circumstances sustaining Greek resistance might be seen as one of the most practical ways of stiffening the Turks.

The views of other politicians

From the outset there was, amongst the wider circle of politicians (on the front and back benches), no conflict about priority between the home and Middle East theatres. The expectation was that the Middle East would be reinforced, and even at the height of the battle in the west, reinforcements were not to be cancelled, though they might be held up.[30] Speculation about Hitler's next move continued – and commonly concluded that it would be Egypt and the Middle East, though there was no certainty about the route. Chamberlain continued to anticipate a Hitlerian descent on Egypt – through Turkey, Palestine and Syria, or Spain and North Africa – which might be difficult to stop without endangering the home front. An attack on Egypt would be 'set off' against a failure of invasion.[31] Beaverbrook expected a German move on the Middle East though opposed reinforcing that theatre even long after the danger of invasion had diminished.[32] Amery at the India Office thought by late August that the

---

[30] Cabinet, 27 May 1940, WM(40)141, CAB 65/7; Cabinet, 23 Aug. 1940, CA to WM(40)233, CAB 65/14; Cabinet, 26 Aug. 1940, WM(40)234, CAB 65/14; Cabinet, 2, 27 Sept., WM(40)239, WM(40)260 CAB 65/9.

[31] Chamberlain diary, 1 June 1940; Chamberlain to Ida, 8 June 1940, NC 18/1/1160; Chamberlain to Ida, 7 July 1940, NC 18/1/1164; Chamberlain to Hilda, 14 July 1940, NC 18/1/165; Chamberlain to Ida, 20 July 1940, NC 18/1/1166; Chamberlain to Halifax, 11 Oct. 1940, NC 7/11/33/89.

[32] Chamberlain to Ida, 7 July 1940, NC 18/1/1164; Halifax to Hoare, 26 Sept. 1940; Templewood XIII:20; Beaverbrook memo, 24 Sept. 1940, WP(40)386, CAB 66/12. When

'main anxiety [was] really Egypt' and feared it would be a race against time to reinforce. By late November he thought the Germans would want to consolidate in the Balkans over winter 'and then be in a position to walk through Turkey to Syria and Iraq in the spring'.[33] Amongst the service ministers, forecasts reflected the individual responsibilities. Alexander's concern was with the Mediterranean and the need to anticipate the enemy there by seizing bases. He came to the view, by December, that they should concentrate on beating Italy and Germany and leave Japan to the United States.[34] Sinclair at the air ministry wondered about future policy towards Greece and wondered whether they should continue to build the air force there, given the danger of the Greeks not holding out.[35] Outside the government Lloyd George was gloomy about prospects in the Middle East. By late October he entertained rumours of an 'impending disaster in Egypt' where British forces were inadequate, the Germans were providing bombers and mechanical divisions, the navy was unable to intercept reinforcements and Greece would fall to the Axis.[36]

the cabinet agreed to the despatch of aircraft, Beaverbrook wanted his dissent recorded, Cabinet, 27 Sept. 1940, WM(40)260, CAB 65/9; Dalton diary, 28 Sept. 1940; for his draft intimating resignation, see Beaverbrook to Churchill, 30 Sept. 1940, BBK D/414; Cadogan diary, 12 Nov. 1940; Cabinet, 12 Nov. 1940, WM(40)287, CAB 65/10, CAB 65/16.

33 Amery to Linlithgow, 20, 30 May 1940, 17 June 1940 (in letter begun 13 June), 9 July 1940 (in letter begun 4 July); MS. Eur. F 125/9. He thought on 30 May that the Germans might attempt invasion but was 'confident that will fail'; Amery to Linlithgow, 27 Aug. 1940, MS. Eur. F 125/9; Amery to Hankey, 5 Sept. 1940, Hankey 11/14; cabinet, 12 Nov. 1940, WM(40)287, CAB 65/16; Amery to Linlithgow, 25 Nov., 3 Dec. 1940, MS. Eur. F 125/9.
34 Note of meeting between Alexander, Paul, VCNS, 19 May 1940, AVAR 5/4/4; Alexander to Cadogan, 17 Sept. 1940, AVAR 5/4/43; Alexander to Halifax, 2 Dec. 1940, annex to COS, 2 Dec. 1940, COS(40)411, CAB 79/8.
35 Sinclair to Eden, 25 Dec. 1940, Avon FO 954/11, Gr/40/6.
36 Lloyd George to Stevenson, 21 Nov., 22 Oct., A.J.P. Taylor, *My Darling Pussy. The Letters of Lloyd George and Frances Stevenson, 1913–41*, London, 1975, pp. 247–8, 243–6.

8 The Military and the Middle East

London

For the chiefs of staff in London, the first priority was the security of the home theatre, the next that of the Middle East. Although, from the outset, the deficiencies of the Middle East were considered dangerous, it was nonetheless accepted throughout the summer that few reinforcements could be spared until the threat of invasion at home decreased. Pound, chief of naval staff did not see, in May, how, despite the deficiencies in the Mediterranean, reinforcements could be spared – troops, aircraft, submarines. Subsequently specific reinforcements became possible and by mid-October the admiralty was 'extremely anxious to reinforce the Mediterranean' on the lines proposed by Churchill and hoped for a programme of reinforcements after the end of the year.[1] Dill, chief of the imperial general staff, though supportive of Wavell and his needs, was initially uncertain that anything could be done and did not see that the British army would be 'ready to carry out any offensive operation for a long time to come on a large scale'. By October he was anxious to reinforce the Middle East, particularly in the air.[2] Newall, chief of air staff before Portal, opposed the despatch of reinforcements at the expense of the home defence, though by late September he was prepared to concede certain limited parcels. By mid-October his plans (approved by the chiefs of staff) for reinforcing the Middle East involved the equipping, bringing

---

[1] Chiefs of staff, 25, 27 May 1940, COS(40) 149, 153, CAB 79/4; Pound to Cunningham, 20 May, 14 Aug. 1940, BL Add. MSS. 52560, 52561; Pound to Cunningham, 6 June, 20 July, 14 Aug. 1940, BL Add. MSS., 52560, 52561; cabinet, 27 Sept. 1940, WM(40)260, CAB 65/9; defence committee, 15 Oct. 1940, DO(40)34, CAB 69/1; Defence committee, 3 Oct. 1940, DO(40)33, CAB 69/1; chiefs of staff, 26, 27 Oct. 1940, COS(40) 360, 361, CAB 79/7.
[2] Dill to Wavell, 27 May, 13 June 1940, Connell, *Wavell*, pp. 231, 239; Headlam diary, 7 Aug. 1940; Reith diary, 16 Aug. 1940; chiefs of staff, 27 May 1940, COS(40)153, CAB 79/4; Dill to Wavell, 6, 13 June 1940; Connell, *Wavell*, pp. 233, 239; Eden diary, 13 Aug. 1940; Dill to Eden, 10 Oct. 1940, enclosing memo for Eden's approval, as from Eden, 10 Oct. 1940, WO 193/960; Dill to Eden, 21 Oct. 1940, WO 193/963.

up to strength and expansion of first line strength of existing squadrons in the Middle East, rather than sending new units.[3]

The chiefs, therefore, in their overall scheme for the Middle East, looked to the reinforcement of that theatre once the threat of invasion diminished and also resisted the withdrawal of forces. Bases, such as Crete, in the eastern Mediterranean must be taken in order to anticipate attack by either Italy or Germany; entangling promises to Greece or Yugoslavia should be avoided; Turkey should be kept in the scheme of things, encouraged and assisted to develop 'administrative facilities in Thrace and Anatolia'.[4] By mid-October after invasion became less likely, preparations began to send to the Middle East a steady stream of reinforcements in the manner proposed by Churchill's minute of 15 October, though with individual reservations entertained by the chiefs.[5] Dill who pressed for urgent, particularly air reinforcements, considered the constraints of shipping would govern what could be sent. Pound opposed using the Mediterranean route and supported Cunningham's preference for the Cape.[6]

With regard to Greece and Turkey the chiefs did not dissent from the general position that although Turkey might have to be encouraged, there was nothing to spare for Greece (despite reports of a likely attack and despite uncertainty about whether the German advance would be through the Balkans or Libya).[7] Given Longmore's reports of the shortage of

[3] Chiefs of staff, 25, 27 May 1940, COS(40)149, 153, CAB 79/4; cabinet, 27 Sept. 1940, WM(40) 260, CAB 65/9; 'Air Reinforcements for the Middle East', memorandum by the CAS, WP(40)419, 14 Oct. 1940, CAB 66/12; Dill to Eden, 21 Oct. 1940, WO 193/963.

[4] Chiefs of staff, 24 May 1940, COS(40)146, 30 May 1940, COS(40)159, CAB 79/4; the seizure of Crete was considered in the event of Italian hostility, chiefs of staff, 13 May 1940, COS(40)129, CAB 79/4; chiefs of staff, 10 June 1940, COS(40)175, CAB 79/4; Chiefs of staff, 6 Sept. 1940, COS(40)298, CAB 79/6.

[5] Defence committee, 15 Oct. 1940, DO(40)34, CAB 69/1; Churchill to Ismay for chiefs of staff, 15 Oct.1940, WP(40)421, CAB 66/13; Dill to Eden, 21 Oct. 1940, WO 193/963. The decision on 4 October to prepare for the despatch of convoys leaving on 1 and 17 November had been taken in the context of keeping all the options open as long as possible given the prospect of an invasion attempt during October, cabinet, 4 Oct. 1940, WM(40)266, CAB 65/15.

[6] Dill to Eden, 10 Oct. 1940, enclosing memo for Eden's approval, as from Eden, 10 Oct. 1940, WO 193/960; defence committee, 15 Oct. 1940, DO(40)34, CAB 69/1; Dill to Wavell, 22 Oct. 1940, WO 193/956; Dill to Eden, 17 Oct. 1940, PREM 3/308, 21 Oct. 1940, WO 193/963; Dill to Wavell, 22 Oct. 1940, WO 193/956; Pound to Churchill and first lord, 23 July 1940, in Churchill, Second World War, II, p. 395; defence committee, 12 Aug. 1940, DO(40)25, CAB 69/1; cabinet, 23 Aug. 1940, WM(40) 233, CAB 65/14, CAB 65/18; Pound to Cunningham, 20 Sept., BL Add. MS. 52561; defence committee, 3 Oct. 1940, DO(40)33, CAB 69/1.

[7] Cabinet, 7 Oct. 1940,WM(40) 267, CAB 65/9; cabinet, 9 Oct. 1940, WM(40)268, CAB 65/9, CAB 65/16; defence committee, 15 Oct. 1940, DO(40)34, CAB 69/1; cabinet, 25 Oct. 1940, WM(40)277, CAB 65/9.

aircraft in Egypt, it was out of the question to send any to Greece although Crete might be helped by aircraft based in Egypt.[8] Greece might be given the kind of encouragement to enable her resist Axis pressure but the chiefs had no illusions as to her resisting attack. 'Greek resistance would crumble' and in any case the 'front line defences in Egypt did not lie in Greece'. Any direct military assistance would be confined to sending a small force to Crete.[9] Turkey, by contrast, did matter and the chiefs hoped to draw the Turks into their schemes for Middle East defence. The Turks should have 'all the material aid we could possibly spare' in addition to the war material supplied under the treaty programmes; and any future requests for air, anti-aircraft, or anti-tank units should be discussed during Dorman-Smith's visit to Ankara. And the commanders should consider the scale of help they might offer the Turks, now or in the spring.[10]

The attack on Greece did not initially prompt a change of heart. The chiefs did not concede Greek requests for help by sea to defend Crete and by air to defend Athens. Instead of direct help, counter-measures – such as bombing raids – would be taken against Italy and fresh bases would be needed in the Mediterranean.[11] For the cabinet on the 28th the same position was also taken: no promises had been made to the Greeks, who had for some time been asking for help and 'we had been extremely guarded in our replies'. Any help to Greece would mean the diversion of forces 'urgently required elsewhere'. However there would be counter measures: bombing Italy itself, the fleet's preventing Italian troops landing in Crete and a battalion's leaving for the islands. The line in public would be that all 'in our power to help the Greek government' was being done.[12]

Within days the position *vis-à-vis* helping the Greeks had begun to soften as the tone of the chiefs matched the change of heart of the politicians in favour of some measure of support. The chiefs considered that there might be limited air assistance to Crete by aircraft based in Egypt; the defence committee maintained that Crete must be defended, Suda Bay secured as a base and that some field and anti-aircraft guns should be despatched to Crete. A Greek bureau in London might be set

[8] Chiefs of staff, 28 Oct. 1940, COS(40)362, CAB 79/7.
[9] Chiefs of staff, 21 Oct. 1940, COS(40)355, CAB 79/7; chiefs of staff to CsinCME, No. 19, 22 Oct. 1940, CAB 79/7.
[10] Chiefs of staff, 8 Oct. 1940, COS(40)340, CAB 79/7; Chiefs of staff, 21 Oct. 1940, COS(40)355, CAB 79/7; chiefs of staff to CsinCME, 22 Oct. 1940, COS(40)356, CAB 79/7.
[11] Chiefs of staff, 28 Oct. 1940, COS(40)362, CAB 79/7.
[12] Cabinet, 28 Oct. 1940, WM(40)268, CAB 65/15.

up and a naval, military and air mission despatched to Athens.[13] A squadron of Blenheims would also be sent to Athens to afford the Greeks 'tangible proof of our assistance'.[14] The feeling on the 1st at the cabinet was that 'if ... the Greeks put up good resistance we should have ... to take some risks ... to send them help'. On the 3rd, the chiefs of staff, who had a minute before them from Churchill, agreed on 'the outline of a plan for assisting the Greeks' – involving the preparation of aerodromes, the establishment of anti-aircraft protection, and the despatch of three Blenheim and one Gladiator squadron with personnel, transport and equipment. They told the commanders that it was 'necessary to give Greece the greatest possible material and moral support at the earliest moment', though any diversions would be made good by early replacements from home.[15]

Not only did a change of heart occur in the first days after the attack, but allusion was increasingly made to the military (as well as political) grounds for help, partly on account of Portal's strategy of establishing bases in Greece and Turkey – to counter a German march south or south-east and from which to bomb Romanian oil. On 15 November, it was considered that the despatch of anti-aircraft guns to Greece 'might prove well worthwhile on military grounds'. Portal, on the 19th, warned Longmore 'of the danger of serious Greek reverse owing to lack of help from us, especially fighters' which must 'outweigh danger of temporarily weakening fighters in Egypt'.[16] None the less the commitment was contained: if things went badly, a decision about final withdrawal would be taken in London, but Longmore should have the authority to withdraw

---

[13] Chiefs of staff, 28 Oct. 1940, COS(40)362, CAB 79/7; defence committee, 28 Oct. 1940, DO(40)37, CAB 69/1. The proposal was for bombing military objectives in Rome; chiefs of staff, 31 Oct. 1940, COS(40)367, CAB 79/7.

[14] Defence committee, 31 Oct. 1940, DO(40)39, CAB 69/1. Although 'the Greek air force was weak ... there were many aerodromes on the mainland'.

[15] Cabinet, 1 Nov. 1940, WM(40)281, CAB 65/16; Churchill's proposal was for the despatch of four additional heavy bomber squadrons to the Middle East – to fly to Greece or Crete via Malta – and four Hurricane fighter squadrons, Churchill to Portal, 1 Nov and 2 Nov. 1940, Portal:1:1940 11 and 11a and Portal to Churchill, 1 Nov. 1940, Portal:1:1940:11b; chiefs of staff, 3 Nov. 1940, COS(40)371, CAB 79/7; chiefs of staff, 3 Nov. 1940, COS(40)371, CAB 79/7; CsinCME, No. 22, 4 Nov. 1940, WO 193/963, (the same wire appended to cabinet minute on the 9th is under 23, WM(40)282, CAB 65/15); CsinCME, No. 22, 4 Nov. 1940, WO 193/963. The chiefs of staff instructed that aerodromes be prepared for three Blenheim and two fighter squadrons; chiefs of staff to CsinCME, attached to chiefs of staff, 4 Nov. 1940, COS(40)372, CAB 79/7.

[16] Chiefs of staff, 15 Nov. 1940, COS(40)390, CAB 79/7; Cabinet, 20 Nov. 1940, WM(40)292, CAB 65/10; Portal to Longmore, 20 Nov. 1940, PREM 3/309/1; Portal to Longmore, 19 Nov. 1940, attached to DO(40)45, CAB 69/1.

the British air force in Greece if he though it was 'in serious jeopardy'.[17] By early December Portal's scheme was to send bomber squadrons to the Middle East 'ready to meet any situation that develope[d]'. Longmore should prepare the aerodromes in Greece; and aerodrome facilities would serve 'as a means of assisting Turkey ... and also to enable us to hit Germany in the Romanian oilfields' and would be 'of considerable value if the Germans attempted to move south eastwards'. He also planned for the operation in the Balkans of a 'high proportion of the air forces now in Egypt ... [those] now in Greece' and reinforcements from the home theatre. And by late December as well as pressing on with the aerodromes in Turkey, the Greek islands and the mainland, Longmore was to prepare 'for basing a large air force in Greece'.[18]

Events in Greece and the reaction which they prompted were to have implications for policy – and assistance – to Turkey whose role in the event of a German advance through the Balkans and Syria to the Middle East was central. The chiefs considered that the most likely course of a German advance would be through the Balkans and Syria to the Middle East via Turkish Thrace, Anatolia into Syria, and then southwards to Palestine and Egypt. Turkish resistance was 'the main bar to German progress to the south eastward'. The chiefs thought that everything should be done to strengthen the Turkish will and ability to resist Axis pressure. Direct assistance now or in the spring and the establishment of a mission ready to move to Turkey should she join the war were considered; while the importance of Russia's not 'aligning herself against us in the near or Middle East ... should take first place in all our dealings with the Soviet government'.[19]

The problem was how far to encourage the Turks to resist German demands, given that the 'amount of help which we could give Turkey was strictly limited by our general shortage of material'? The Turks themselves seemed to envisage something 'more substantial' than the technical equipment asked for prior to the attack on Greece.[20] While plans might be prepared for giving assistance and a mission formed in the Middle East 'ready to move into Turkey ... [if she became] involved in the

[17] Ibid; Chiefs of staff, 7, 11 Nov. 1940, COS(40)378, 385, CAB 79/7.
[18] Portal to Peirse, 5 Dec. 1940, Portal:9:1940:7a. Portal to Churchill, 18, 23 Dec. 1940, Portal:1:1941:1a, Portal:1:1941:1d; chiefs of staff, 20 Dec. 1940, COS(40)434, CAB 79/8; chiefs of staff, 20 Dec. 1940, COS(40)434, CAB 79/8; chiefs of staff, 6 Dec. 1940, COS(40) 417, CAB 79/8; chiefs of staff, 20 Dec. 1940. COS(40)434, CAB 79/8; Portal to prime minister, 23 Dec. 1940, Portal:1:1941:1d.
[19] Chiefs of staff, 30 Oct. 1940, COS(40)366, CAB 79/7; 'An advance by the enemy through the Balkans and Syria to the Middle East', report by the chiefs of staff, 1 Nov. 1940, WP(40)431, CAB 66/13.
[20] Chiefs of staff, 30 Oct. 1940, COS(40)366, CAB 79/7.

war', none the less the Turks, if pressed to join the war now, would ask for large consignments of munitions, a request which could not be met. Moreover Turkey might be exposed to German bombing.[21]

Dill had doubts about pressing Turkey to enter the war in support of Greece lest that 'alienate her sympathies'. The Turkish attitude he thought 'must ultimately depend on Russia'. Turkey was presently 'performing a useful role in preventing Bulgarian aggression against Greece' whereas entry into the war now 'might expose her to ... German air bombardment throughout the winter' reducing her eventual powers of resistance to a German advance when it took place. Dill did envisage the possibility of British troops going to Turkey, arranged through the mission under Marshall Cornwall, the senior general who would 'ultimately ... command such forces as it may be found necessary to employ in support of the Turkish army'.[22]

The chiefs continued to be concerned that Turkey should resist any encroachment and fight back. It was 'an essential part of [British] strategy, that Turkey should resist by arms' any attack or infringement. This would involve fighting on the frontiers, holding the Straits, continuing in Anatolia, or holding an Anglo-Turkish line to stop an advance on Suez or on the Iraqi or Iranian oilfields. In such circumstances British policy was 'to support Turkey by all possible means including the despatch to Turkish territory of such forces as may be necessary ... preceded by ... staff conversations'.[23] Difficulties, however, remained. On the one hand no specific commitment could be made to the Turks. It was 'impossible to state ... in advance' the forces to be employed in Asia Minor. Much depended on the Italian situation and the Middle East reinforcement programme. Nothing was to be promised which was 'beyond our ability to provide with reasonable certainty'.[24] On the other hand the Turks did not want a mission. In November they suggested a 'staff conference' to consider the amount and form of help, having been

[21] Defence committee, 5 Nov. 1940, DO(40)40, CAB 69/1; cabinet, 28 Oct. 1940, WM(40)278,CAB 65/15; defence committee, 5 Nov. 1940, DO(40)40, CAB 69/1; cabinet, 25 Nov. 1940, WM(40)295, CAB 65/10; defence committee, 25 Nov. 1940, DO(40)46, CAB 69/1; cabinet, 22 Nov. 1940, WM(40)294, CAB 65/10; cabinet, 25 Nov. 1940, WM(40)295, CAB 65/10; chiefs of staff, 9, 13 Nov. 1940, COS(40)384, 387, CAB 79/7.
[22] Dill to Eden enclosing memo for Eden's approval, 10 Oct. 1940, WO 193/960; Dill to Eden, 21 Oct. 1940, WO 193/963; chiefs of staff, 9 Nov. 1940, COS(40)384, CAB 79/7; Dill to Wavell, 19 Nov. 1940, WO 106/212; chiefs of staff, 23 Nov. 1940, COS(40) 394, CAB 79/7.
[23] Draft telegram to Kelly, attached to chiefs of staff, 4 Dec. 1940, COS(40) 415, CAB 79/8.
[24] Chiefs of staff, 11 Dec. 1940, COS(40)423, CAB 79/8; chiefs of staff, 21 Dec. 1940, COS(40)435, Annex COS to CsinCME, CAB 79/8; chiefs of staff, 4 Dec. 1940, COS(40) 415, annex draft to Kelly, CAB 79/8.

'taken aback' at the idea of a mission. The chiefs accepted, hoping that eventually representatives of the three services would be attached to the Turkish command. They wanted 'the whole question of assistance ... cleared up ... by the resumption of staff conversations' to discuss the stage at which the Turks would enter the war, their plans, British support and combined action regarding Syria.[25]

The offer to the Turks, the proposed mission and the preparation or seizure of bases in Greece, Turkey and the Aegean were all for the longer term. The chiefs considered that operations in the western desert must 'have absolute priority'. None the less, the attack on Greece complicated matters. On the one hand, the chiefs continued to regard the Middle East, the desert campaign, the securing of Egypt's Libyan frontiers and the reinforcement of the Middle East as predominant. On the other they continued to think that the Turks should be drawn in, and they had also begun to consider assistance to Greece on its own – military – terms. Moreover Turkey, Turkish resistance and support to the Turks began to be thought of partly in the terms of the influence which help to Greece would bring to bear. Thus Greece, which was not for the chiefs at the outset the first line of Egypt's defences, gradually came with Turkey to be seen as central to the Middle East position – the 'single strategical theatre of war' where the deployment of resources would be for the Middle East command, subject to such instructions as might be necessary 'to meet political and wider strategical needs'.[26]

The Middle East command

Throughout the summer the Middle East commanders were concerned about the deficiencies in the command and pressed for its reinforcement. Egypt and its security was the overriding concern; and persistent requests for reinforcements affected relations with Churchill and the chiefs in London throughout the entire period. There was less ostensible cause for difference during the Battle of Britain and before the attack on Greece. But in the immediate aftermath of the Italian attack apparent differences opened when politicians and chiefs of staff in London appeared determined to divert to Greece.

[25] Chiefs of staff, 11 Dec. 1940, COS(40) 423, CAB 79/8; chiefs of staff, 21 Dec. 1940, COS(40) 435, CAB 79/8; chiefs of staff, 21 Dec. 1940, COS(40)435, Annex COS to CsinC, CAB 79/8.

[26] Chiefs of staff to prime minister, annex to chiefs of staff, 31 Dec. 1940, COS(40)444, CAB 79/8; chiefs of staff to CsinCME, annex to COS, 21 Dec. 1940, COS(40)435, CAB 79/8. For the seizure and preparation of bases: chiefs of staff, 20 Dec. 1940, COS(40)434, CAB 79/8; chiefs of staff, 6 Dec. 1940, COS(40)417, CAB 79/7; chiefs of staff, 20 Dec. 1940,

In Cairo Wavell's general plan was defensive. He intended to hold what was necessary and let the rest go, to have a small force available for despatch to Crete or elsewhere at short notice. He was confident he could hold the position unless the Germans 'put up a full dress attack on Egypt'. He urged that Middle East requirements of equipment and ammunition be met, and during his visit to London in August reiterated his needs. In October he anticipated that the main strategic problems in the Middle East over the next six months would be the defence of Egypt, the liquidation of Italian East Africa and support of Turkey and Greece – of which 'the defence of Egypt against attack from Libya is the main problem'.[27] Admiral Cunningham thought the position in the Middle East depended 'almost entirely on the fleet' and felt that if they could 'hold on for the next two or three months' (from August) and if the other services were 'properly reinforced' they would 'pull through all right'. Cunningham also pressed for reinforcements throughout the summer and did not consider his difficulties were 'realised at home'.[28] Air Marshal Longmore continued to warn of the dangerous air deficiencies, and of the danger to his squadrons of an Italian, or joint Italian–German offensive. Before the attack on Greece he wired Palairet that because of the shortages of 'modern aircraft in Egypt' it was 'out of the question to send any aeroplanes to the Greeks'. He impressed Eden who believed he 'in no way exaggerated[d] his present weakness' and was not in a position to give the army effective support if serious military operations developed. Longmore urged that air reinforcements 'should at least keep pace with those on land' even for 'successful defence, let alone ... offensive military operations'.[29]

COS(40)434, CAB 79/8; chiefs of staff to CsinCME, 21 Dec. 1940, WO 106/2144; chiefs of staff to CsinCME, annex to chiefs of staff, 30 Dec. 1940, COS(40)439, CAB 79/8.
27 Cabinet, 11 July 1940, WM(40)200, CAB 65/14; Wavell to Cunningham, 15 May 1940, BL Add. MS. 52569; Wavell to Dill, 31 May 1940, Connell, *Wavell*, p. 233; cabinet, 11 July 1940, WM(40)200, CAB 65/14; cabinet, 31 July 1940, WM(40)216, CAB 65/14; Wavell, notes on situation for CinC India, 11 July 1940, IOL Eur. MSS. F 125/153; Avon, *The Reckoning*, p. 130; cabinet, 11, 31 July 1940, WM(40)200, WM(40)216, CAB 65/14; defence committee, 12 Aug. 1940, DO(40)25, CAB 69/1; Pound to Cunningham, 14 Aug. 1940, BL Add. MS. 52561; Wavell, note on strategy in the Middle East in the winter of 1940/41, 24 Oct. 1940, WO 193/963.
28 Cunningham to Pound, 13 July, 3 Aug. 1940, BL Add. MSS. 52560, 52561; Cunningham to Pound, 27 June 1940, BL Add. MS. 52560; Cunningham to Pound, 13 July 1940, BL Add. MS. 52560; Cunningham to Pound, 3 Aug. 1940, BL Add. MS. 52561; Cunningham to admiralty, 10 Sept., BL Add. MS. 52566; Cunningham to Pound, 22 Sept. 1940, BL Add. MS. 52561; Cunningham to Pound, 22 Sept. 1940, BL Add. MS. 52561.
29 Notes of a conference at GHQ Cairo, 16 Oct. 1940, WO 193/963; Eden to Churchill, 17 Oct. 1940, PREM 3/308; Eden to Churchill, 17 Oct. 1940, PREM 3/308; Eden to Dill, 26 Oct. 1940, PREM 3/308; Eden to Dill, 26 Oct. 1940, PREM 3/308; chiefs of staff, 28 Oct. 1940, COS(40) 362, CAB 79/7.

After the attack on Greece, priorities were more complicated. Even though Longmore initially despatched air support to the Greeks, he did not envisage sending much further help. Whereas previously adamant that he could spare nothing for Greece or the Dodecanese, after the attack he resolved to divert to Greece. It had become 'politically . . . essential to send token force to Greece' even at the expense of forces in the Middle East, and he had despatched the Blenheims without 'ask[ing] permission to do so'. But that was a 'token force'. Longmore warned against Greece and Crete becoming 'more than a passing commitment', and was reluctant to add further squadrons for that would lead to wastage. Although with Wavell and Eden he conceded more on the instructions of the chiefs he warned not only of the risks posed to the desert, but of the practical difficulties: shipping and the different weather conditions.[30]

Wavell, whose plans for a desert offensive to secure Egypt were under way, feared that developments in Greece might result in his having to send reinforcements from Egypt. The long term plan had been not to reinforce Greece but to secure Crete by sending an infantry brigade with anti-aircraft units to help the Greeks hold the island; and Wavell, with Eden, reacted to the attack with apprehension 'lest the cries from Greece should result in our being asked to divert any part of our very small resources from here'. Though with Longmore and Eden he agreed to the reinforcements laid down by the chiefs of staff 'given the political commitments to aid Greece', these would increase the risk in the western desert. Moreover any increase in commitment or attempt to hasten rate of despatch to Greece would 'mean serious risk to our position in Egypt'. The best way to help Greece would be through a successful desert operation.[31] Longmore took up the implications for the offensive, of reduced air support. He warned that they were 'too weak now to give effective support to the army in battle should a major engagement develop', there having been 'consternation' at the outset over the removal of a 'large portion of the air force in Egypt'. He feared there would be a strong British army in the western desert waiting to do something, with 'quite inadequate air force to support them for next two months' and warned of the risks being run by denuding the western desert and Alexandria of fighter protection – all

[30] Longmore to Portal, 31 Oct. 1940, CAB 127/14; note by Longmore at foot of Churchill to Longmore, X 286, 1 Nov. 1940, Longmore DC 74/102/15; Longmore to Portal, 2 Nov. 1940, Portal:12:HQRAFME; Longmore to Portal, 2 Nov. 1940, Portal:12:HQRAFME; Eden to Churchill, 3 Nov. 1940, WO 193/963; Longmore to Churchill, 15 Nov. 1940, PREM 3/309/1.

[31] Eden diary, 1 Nov. 1940, Avon, *The Reckoning*, pp. 166–7; Eden to Dill and Churchill, 5 Nov. 1940, WO 193/963; Wavell to Wilson, 2 Nov. 1940, Connell, *Wavell*, pp. 279–80; minutes of conference at GHQ Cairo, 16 Oct. 1940, WO 193/963; Wavell to war office, 28 Oct. 1940, WO 193/856; Eden to Churchill, 3 Nov. 1940, WO 193/963.

of which was exacerbated by the uncertainty over the arrival of air reinforcements – particularly the date.[32]

For Admiral Cunningham, who doubted that the Greeks could hold the Italians if they 'meant business', the attack on Greece might eventually lead to advantage – that of working 'from Greek ports and ... aerodromes'. He did not expect an early attack on Crete, 'unless and until Greece is overrun'. Nor did he think a large British garrison would be needed in Crete: 'once the Cretans are organised, one battalion together with AA defences would suffice'.[33]

For the commanders, at least initially, the attack on Greece did not alter strategy in the Middle East. British policy laid down that no assistance to Greece could be given 'until German–Italian threat to Egypt is finally liquidated, the security of Egypt being vital to our strategy and incidentally to the future of Greece'. And given the limited extent to which Greece could be helped the commanders were 'greatly perturbed' at the impression being conveyed from London 'that air support is being given and British troops have landed'.[34]

That the Greeks did better than expected did not simplify things for the commanders preparing for the desert offensive, at odds, it seemed, with the sentiments of and instructions emanating from London. This was not just a matter of the inadequacy of reinforcements, or the apparent determination to divert scarce supplies to Greece. Wavell, for example, who maintained that the operation planned against the Italians for early December was more of a raid, deprecated the tendency by Churchill to make too much of it or to raise premature hopes.[35]

What of the future? The commanders expected the war to move southeast in the spring, considered the importance of Salonika and the need to open conversation with the Turks as soon as possible. The Dodecanese should be captured in order to control supply lines to Greece and Turkey and to forestall the prospect of their being surrendered to the Turks by

---

[32] Longmore to Portal, 5 Nov. 1940, Portal:12:HQRAFME:2a; Eden to Dill and Churchill, 6 Nov. 1940, PREM 3/368; Longmore to Air Ministry, 19 Nov. 1940, appended to DO(40)45, CAB 69/1; Eden to Dill and Churchill, 5 Nov. 1940, WO 193/963; Longmore to Portal, 5 Nov. 1940, Portal:12:HQRAFME:2a; Longmore to Churchill, 15 Nov. 1940, PREM 3/309/1; Longmore to Air Ministry, 15 Nov. 1940, appended to DO(40)45, CAB 69/1; Wavell and Longmore to chiefs of staff, 30 Nov. 1940, WO 106/2127.

[33] Cunningham to his aunt, 5 Nov. 1940, BL Add. MS. 52588; Eden to Churchill, 3 Nov. 1940, WO 193/963.

[34] Eden to Churchill, 3 Nov. 1940, WO 193/963. Parry to Dill and Wavell, 2 Nov. 1940, PREM 3/308; Eden to Dill and Churchill, 5 Nov. 1940, WO 193/963; Cabinet, 12 Nov. 1940, WM(40) 287, CAB 65/16.

[35] Wavell to Dill, 6 Dec. 1940 (2 signals), Connell, *Wavell*, pp. 288–9; Wavell to Dill, 10 Dec. 1940, Connell, *Wavell*, p. 293; Wavell to Dill, 12 Dec. 1940, 14 Dec. 1940, WO 106/2144.

Italy under German pressure or as a bribe to remain neutral.[36] Wavell would, 'if possible', have prepared 'a force for the assistance of Greece ... at any rate ... a brigade group ... [for] Crete' for the spring, but nonetheless thought Turkey mattered more. He had hoped to hold out the prospect of 'substantial help in the spring' to both Greece and Turkey, but if both could not be helped, then assistance 'should go to Turkey' and a force prepared to assist the Turks if attacked in the spring.[37] Not so Longmore, at least in late November. He not only resisted despatching support to Greece, but did not see that there could be anything for Turkey. Assistance to the Turks would only be 'at the expense of Greece' and immediate air assistance with fighter aircraft to Turkey was 'out of the question, except at the expense of Greece'. And for a land battle the Turks would want air assistance, particularly fighters and the technical equipment and additional artillery, all of which 'we lack ourselves'.[38] Cunningham anticipated that in the spring of 1941 they might well 'be faced with a drive south east by Germany'. He looked at operations against the Dodecanese in the context of ensuring that the line to Greece, Turkey and the Dardanelles was not menaced by enemy ports and aerodromes.[39]

General conclusions

Preoccupation with the security of Egypt, the Mediterranean and the Middle East continued, therefore, even at the height of the Battle of Britain. Reinforcements for the Middle East, though sometimes delayed, were not cancelled. Churchill set the tone: there was no conflict of interests between the home and Middle East theatres, both of which commanded equal priority. Although there seemed to be some disgruntlement on Wavell's part – supported by Eden – on the whole Churchill's lead was followed and no conflict of interests was seen to exist. However, although once the danger of invasion passed attention focused on the Middle East, the question of priority was complicated in the aftermath of the Italian attack on Greece.

Before the attack there had been no question of military, or air,

---

[36] Commanders in chief to chiefs of staff, 28 Dec. 1940, WO 106/2144; chiefs of staff to CsinCME, 16 Dec. 1940, WO 106/2122.
[37] Minutes of conference at GHQ Cairo, 16 Oct. 1940, WO 193/963; Wavell to war office, 28 Oct. 1940, WO 193/856; Eden to Churchill, 3 Nov. 1940, WO 193/963; Wavell, note on strategy, 24 Oct. 1940, WO 193/963.
[38] Wavell and Longmore to chiefs of staff, 30 Nov. 1940, WO 106/2127.
[39] Cunningham to Churchill, 12 Dec. 1940, BL Add. MS. 52567; cf. minutes of a conference held at GHQ Cairo, 14.30, 16 Oct. 1940, WO 193/963.

assistance for Greece, though Crete would be held; after the attack the matter was not so clear. Air Marshal Longmore in the Middle East took the decision to divert some air squadrons to Greece; and in London although Churchill, Halifax, and the chiefs of staff initially intended to stand by the existing plan, their resolve faltered for a variety of reasons. Political considerations and those of honour, a desire not to discourage the Greeks, a feeling that there might be some impact on Turkey: all of these prompted a rhetoric of greater help for Greece, though not at the expense of the long-term commitment to Turkey. In the Middle East it was another matter, for Wavell was planning a desert operation, and he and Eden feared that demands from Greece would result in instructions to divert, which they opposed. However, Churchill's change of heart was more apparent than real. Eden and Wavell mistook the rhetorical promises as being stronger than they were. In fact Churchill supported whole-heartedly the proposed desert offensive, although his sympathetic reaction to Greece may have suggested otherwise. What change there was, on the part of Churchill, Halifax or the chiefs, was a gradual change of perspective over November and December – in talking about Greece and Greek resistance in military terms, though on account of the impact on Turkey, which was important given the prospect of a Hitlerian swoop through the Balkans and Syria onto Egypt.

Part 3

The Greek decision (January to March 1941)

Our conclusion is that the hazards of the enterprise have considerably increased. Nonetheless, despite our misgivings and our recognition of a worsening of the general situation we are not as yet in a position to question the military advice of those on the spot who in their latest telegram describe the enterprise as not by any means hopeless
Commentary by chiefs of staff in Churchill to Eden, 5 March 1941

[Eden] commenting on the Prime Minister's message, remarked that the real alternative for Greece was whether she should stand up and fight Germany or allow herself to become a victim of German seduction like Roumania ... [Eden] and the three commanders-in-chief in turn expressed the view that in spite of the heavy risks involved, it was necessary that we should go ahead in Greece. [Eden] pointed out that if we now withdrew we should have lost once and for all all hope of bringing Yugoslavia into the war and that the effect on the Turkish position might be incalculable ...

[Dill] said that the situation was grimmer than we thought. None the less, he saw no alternative but to go ahead with our plans ...

Admiral Cunningham and Air Chief Marshal Longmore pointed out that there was a risk of losing most of the convoy ships and most of our air forces in Greece ... General Wavell remained of the opinion that provided we could get our forces into Greece there was a good prospect of a successful encounter with the Germans. The results of success would be incalculable and might alter the whole aspect of the war ...

[Eden] summed up the discussion by saying that all agreed that we must go ahead ... an interim reply should be sent to the prime minister to the effect that ... we were unanimously agreed that, in spite of the heavy commitments and grave risks undoubtedly involved, especially in view of our limited naval and air resources, the right decision was taken in Athens.
Record of Meeting held at GHQ Middle East, 5 p.m., 6 March 1941

What a thankless task you have. After working night and day here to get an arrangement on which we can at least fight, you are met on arrival in Egypt by the suggestion that it would be better for us to leave Greece to her fate. I felt quite sick with horror when I read the PMs telegram to you. But, thank God, it now looks as if you and the three commanders in chief had averted this appalling prospect. I don't think I could have gone to the king of Greece with a message on those lines.

Palairet (at the British legation, Athens) to Eden, 7 March 1941

Mr Menzies said ... it was curious that, while the decision was being taken in virtue of the trust we reposed in the judgement of our advisers in the Middle East – the foreign secretary, the chief of the imperial general staff and the three commaders in chief – the arguments with which they had supplied us told against, rather than in favour of, their advice.

The prime minister said that a considered military appreciation was on the way home from Cairo that would supply the detailed arguments; but we knew the conclusions already. The time had now come for taking a decision. In his view it was our duty to go forward, making the necessary communications to the Dominions whose forces were to take part in the campaign.

The War Cabinet ... confirmed the decision to give military assistance to Greece, and agreed that all the arrangements to this end should proceed.

Cabinet, noon, 7 March 1941

9   The Greek decision: the background

Greece and the threat of a German attack

Although the Italian attack on Greece and sustained Greek resistance had led to a modification of British policy to Greece, none the less the sudden preoccupation with Greece was, by December, superseded by Wavell's desert offensive. With the success of that offensive by January, and the prospect of German intervention in Greece (possibly as part of a Hitlerian *Drang nach Osten*), attention returned to Greece. Although the Greeks had managed to sustain resistance to Italy, they could not stand up to the Germans. Should Britain try to prevent such a collapse by aid or, indeed, military intervention? Britain was bound to Greece by the declaration of 1939: that in the event of Greek (or Romanian) independence being threatened by action which the government(s) thought it vital to resist 'His Majesty's Government would feel themselves bound at once to lend the Greek or Roumanian Government . . . all the support in their power.' Moreover, failure to help, or to prolong Greek resistance, would have repercussions on the other Balkan countries and Turkey. If it were decided to strengthen Greece, to what extent should full-scale military intervention be planned? Wavell's armies would soon be in a position to halt their triumphant campaign and stand by ready for diversion to the Balkans.

Since October intelligence reports had suggested that Hitler might be planning to march on Greece. By January reports suggested that a German attack on Greece might be imminent, although it was also possible that the German activity was designed to intimidate Greece, Yugoslavia and Bulgaria before advancing to Turkey; or that German action in Bulgaria might stop there. Whatever the differences about Hitler's timetable, it was decided, first to offer help to the Greeks and, when they initially refused, to offer help to Turkey. By early February the Greeks had somewhat rescinded their refusal and the Turks seemed open to some kind of help. It was therefore decided that Eden, accompanied by

Dill, should visit the Middle East to see how best to succour Greece. They left on 10 February.[1]

In London Churchill and the chiefs of staff became increasingly dubious about military intervention and intimated to Eden, in the Middle East, that he need not force help on the Greeks. He, however, had found a Middle East command which appeared no longer to oppose intervention in Greece – the course which he and Dill favoured for a variety of reasons. Discussions with the Greeks led, on 22 February, to a plan for British and Greek forces to stand on the Aliakmon Line; and, on 4 March, Eden signed a formal agreement under circumstances less auspicious than those of 22 February. Despite serious misgivings, the agreement was ratified by the cabinet on 7 March.

Part 3 considers the different views of the different groups during the period leading up to this commitment. After noting the positions of the Greeks and the Yugoslavs, as perceived by the British, it discusses the evolving views and interventions of those concerned on the British side in the Middle East and in London. Before all this, however, the views of some recent historians about the Greek decision will be examined.

Historians on the Greek decision

John Connell bases his account of the Greek decision on what he believes to be the difference in perspective between General Wavell, the subject of his biography, and Churchill. According to Connell, 'Wavell's vision was fixed firmly on what he could do in his own Command, with the troops and the equipment he possessed ... He wanted finally and totally to defeat the Italians in Africa before ... other ventures.' His initial reluctance to abandon the desert campaign was not to be taken as opposition to intervention in Greece. On the contrary, he did not need persuading. 'The problem, as he saw it, was that of finding the means to implement the choice he had already made.'[2] Churchill thought in terms of the wider stage; the impact of intervention (or non-intervention) on the Balkans and Turkey; and the prospect 'of Constantinople replacing Cairo as the centre of gravity'.[3]

Elisabeth Barker argues that the Balkan campaign was seen from the start 'as a military gamble, justifiable only in so far as it enabled Britain to keep or win Allies on the Continent of Europe' and that the decision to

---

[1] For the British and French guarantee to Greece and Romania of 13 April 1939, see *Grand Strategy*, vol. I, N. H. Gibbs, *Rearmament Policy*, London, HMSO, 1976, pp. 707–14. For a discussion of the intelligence background, see Hinsley, *British Intelligence*, vol I, pp. 249, 251–61, 347–60.

[2] Connell, *Wavell*, pp. 286–7, 335–6.   [3] Ibid., pp. 285–6, 330–1.

intervene was also influenced by the desire for a foothold on the continent from which to attack Germany. Although no decision was taken before Eden and Dill left for the Middle East, it was, in her view, clear where Churchill's (and Eden's) heart lay. And she argues that these wider political and long term strategic factors influenced, not only Churchill and Eden, but the chiefs of staff.[4]

In his biography of Anthony Eden, David Carlton emphasises – by contrast with Barker – the difference in views between Eden and Churchill.[5] His view is that Churchill and Eden reversed roles on the Greek question. From having been something of an enthusiast for intervention just after the Italians attacked in 1940, Churchill became by the following March more cautious and circumspect. Eden, on the other hand, who at the outset was reluctant to divert any forces to Greece from Egypt, where Wavell was about to launch a campaign, became by March an enthusiast for military intervention. Carlton considers that Eden's interest sprang from his desire to bring Turkey into the war and to form a Balkan front. Greece must hold out against Hitler as the means to the end of drawing Yugoslavia and Turkey into collective resistance. Such hopes, based on an unrealistic assessment of Turkey and wishful thinking about wider aims, prevented Eden from challenging the military advice. Even after the Greeks failed to move their troops in good time to the Aliakmon position and the Turks failed to join in, Carlton points out that Eden still maintained that a 'fair chance' existed and ignored the hints from London to call off the operation. Carlton emphasises the misplaced optimism that the enterprise might turn out to be sound, on which the decision in Cairo was based. He considers Eden to have been 'the moving force behind the policy' – a prisoner of his public reputation. Carlton leaves it to the reader to decide whether this was a matter of seeing policy in the wider context of Turkey and a Balkan front designed to keep Hitler out of Asia Minor, or whether it was a matter of feeling honour-bound to Greece, or whether both of these considerations weighed on Eden.

The Greeks

The Greeks' line, until late February, continued to be that Hitler would not attack their country. Although they would not provoke such an attack by receiving full-scale British help, they did want specific equipment, and to know precisely what they could expect. Against the background of continued British expectation of German intervention, against offers of help and preparations for support, the Greeks none the less

---

[4] Barker, *British Policy*, pp. 96–103.   [5] Carlton, *Eden*, pp. 167–80.

maintained until February that it would not be in German interests for the war to spread to the Balkans; any preparations to anticipate an attack would serve merely to provoke it.

For example, in late December, Papagos thought that the Germans would try to get what they wanted without fighting – possibly by occupying Bulgaria. He did not believe (or claimed he did not), that 'it was in the interests of Germany to spread the war to the Balkans'. As late as early February he still 'did not believe they would attack Turkey or Greece'. Germany, he maintained, 'wanted a peaceful Balkans', and 'by occupying Bulgaria she would be in a position to strike swiftly at Turkey, Greece, or Yugoslavia [so] that she could achieve her object without fighting'.[6] Moreover the conditions in early 1941 made a German advance now 'most unlikely and in fact almost impossible owing to condition of roads and bridges'. Whether the Greeks really believed that the Germans did not intend to attack, unless provoked, is not clear. But they stuck to the line until late February when the Germans made it impossible to continue to do so. They explained away the German concentrations as designed 'to warn both ourselves and Russians off Balkans and as preparatory steps in case they are ... forced to intervene'.[7] A German offensive in Salonika was 'unlikely to take place unless [Britain] provoke[d] it'. Palairet could not 'shake the conviction' that 'the despatch of British forces to Salonika would immediately precipitate German attack' which would not happen 'until they saw signs of our establishing base there', when they would do so 'to frustrate our plans at the earliest possible moment'. By 7 February Papagos still held that the German army would not 'increase its glory by over-running small nations like Greece' and, therefore, that it would not do so 'unless provoked by the arrival of British forces intended for operations against Germany'.[8] Any British reinforcement before the Germans crossed the Greek frontier 'would only provoke ... immediate action'.[9]

Papagos had considered the prospect of building a Balkan front – to eliminate the Bulgarian danger – 'in conjunction with Yugoslavia, Turkey

[6] Heywood to Wavell and Dill, c. 31 Dec 1940, received 1 Jan. 1941, also to Wavell and Dill after conversation with Papagos, 3 Jan. 1941, Avon FO 954/11, Gr/41/1; Heywood to Dill and Wavell, 7 Feb. 1941, PREM 3/309/1.

[7] Wavell to Dill, 0/34761, 10 Jan. 1941, annex to Chiefs of staff, 11 Jan. 1941, COS(41)15, CAB 79/8.

[8] Palairet to foreign office, no. 58 of 26 Dec 1940, received 11 Jan. 1941, Avon FO 954/11, Gr/40/7; Palairet to foreign office, 20 Jan. 1941, FO 954/11, Gr/41/9; Heywood to Dill and Wavell, 7 Feb. 1941, PREM 3/309/1.

[9] Heywood to Dill and Wavell, 7 Feb. 1941, PREM 3/309/1.

and perhaps Bulgaria' in order 'to be ready for all contingencies'.[10] The first step should be to 'clear up ... Bulgaria' – which 'should not ... remain neutral and mobilised'. She must join the allies or else demobilise: 'Failing that a preventative war should be made upon Bulgaria.'[11] Given the dispositions of the other Balkan countries, the omens for such a course seemed good. The Yugoslav Nish and Skorse armies were mobilised and reinforced; the Turks had strong forces in Thrace; and the Greek army had more than four divisions on the Bulgarian frontier (with a fifth formation in that area). This was a 'sufficient force to settle Bulgaria in two months' and it was not possible for Germany to intervene within that time.[12] That aspiration of late December may have been modified by the failure of the Turks or the Yugoslavs to commit themselves and the likelihood, by early February, that the Germans 'would enter Bulgaria very soon'. But even then Papagos did not appear to believe they would attack Turkey or Greece. They wanted 'a peaceful Balkans' and could achieve their object without fighting given that 'by occupying Bulgaria ... [they] would be in a position to strike so swiftly at Turkey, Greece, or Yugoslavia'.[13]

At the same time as refusing British forces – unless and until the Germans crossed their frontier, the Greeks none the less demanded other support. They also wanted to know what precisely they could expect, and urged a plan to be prepared. From the outset they had wanted other support (other, that is, than troops). Their holding out against the Italians would depend on this. The king, on 8 January, was 'quite convinced of victory – if only we would send him more arms'; mechanical transport, anti-aircraft artillery, some anti-tank guns and perhaps some light tanks or carriers were needed immediately, and further units would be needed by early spring.[14] Even after refusing units in mid-January, the great need was still for equipment. They wanted to know precisely how much the British could supply, not only in order to hold out against the Italians, but to withstand a German attack. Although by 17 January they had refused RAF squadrons for northern aerodromes (agreeing only to reconnaissance), they wanted to know what else could be sent. How many squadrons over and above the four already here and the three due 'could be allotted

---

[10] Heywood to Wavell and Dill, *c*. 31 Dec 1940, received 1 Jan. 1941, also after conversation with Papagos, 3 Jan. 1941, both in Avon FO 954/11, Gr/41/1.

[11] Ibid.

[12] Ibid. Papagos thought the Germans had only between 35 and 40,000 men in Romania and there were no signs of preparations on a large scale for German intervention in the Balkans.

[13] Heywood to Dill and Wavell, 7 Feb. 1941, PREM 3/309/1.

[14] Ibid.; Channon diary, 8 Jan. 1941; Wavell to Dill, 10 Jan. 1941, appended to chiefs of staff, COS(41)15, CAB 79/8.

from Egypt and by what date? If ... agreed they could use Salonika aerodromes.' Papagos was also anxious to appreciate 'what defence would be available for Salonika area'.[15] By 4 February the situation was thought in Greece to be 'desperate'; the shortage of material, particularly guns, made the finish of the Albanian campaign difficult, and in two months there would be no artillery ammunition left. 'Unless England could send such material and substantial reinforcements rapidly, it would be difficult for long to resist a German attack.'[16] Greece 'would fight to the end' but the end was not according to the (new) prime minister 'very far distant'.[17] By the 7th, although he gave the impression that he was 'gambling on his belief that Germany will not interfere in a purely Italian Greek war in Albania', Papagos none the less intended to offer such resistance as he could 'for reasons of policy and honour' if the Germans did attack Greece before the Albanian campaign was over. Such resistance could not be protracted 'unless ... substantial assistance from the outside' were received.[18]

By this date the Greeks had all but abandoned the certainty that the Germans would not intervene; and, determined to fight on, they no longer put up resistance to British intervention in advance of air attack on Greece. Papagos mentioned that Metaxas's death stiffened morale; if Germany did attack Greece, she would resist, but Greek resistance would be more of a political than an effective military operation 'given that Turkey and Yugoslavia would not help and Britain was unable to do so'. On 8 February Papagos confirmed Metaxas's earlier statement – to the effect that he would appeal for British help when the Germans crossed the Danube or Dobruja frontier. When Papagos had implied earlier that he would not seek help until the Germans crossed the Greek frontier, he had in fact been unaware of Metaxas's statement. But now he confirmed the position it took in a note to Palairet. Once the Germans had crossed the Romanian and Bulgarian frontier, it would be for the British government to decide whether British reinforcements should be sent to Greece and, if so, when.[19] It was time to prepare a plan 'for the Aliakmon position based on the minimum force which could be brought there'. The plan would be amended as and when the possibility of additional forces occurred. But Papagos did not want reconnaissance of the Aliakmon position; that would be 'useless until we knew what kind of British forces could be sent to assist holding the position'. They would leave it to the British to decide

---

15 Longmore to Portal, 17 Jan. 1941, PREM 3/309/1.
16 Heywood to Wavell and Dill, 4 Feb. 1941, PREM 3/309/1.
17 Ibid.   18 Heywood to Wavell and Dill, 7 Feb. 1941; PREM 3/309/1.
19 Heywood to Dill and Wavell, 7 Feb. 1941, PREM 3/309/1; British military mission Athens to Wavell, repeated to war office, 9 Feb. 1941, PREM 3/309/1.

'whether British reinforcements should be sent to Greece and if so when'. If Britain intended such a course, 'it was essential to start building up stocks, supplies and ammunition at once'.[20] Urgent requests for aircraft material for the army – without which there might be 'very serious consequences' – were also made. So too were demands for 'the utmost help from the RAF in Greece, both in fighters and bombers' for the large-scale operations in Albania due to start in mid-February (and expected to last about twenty days).[21]

The Greek decision to allow the British in before Hitler crossed the Greek frontier provided the occasion for the decision in London, by the cabinet, to concentrate on Greece (see below, pp. 176–205); and it also coincided with the refusal of the Turks to admit British forces. Against the proposal for a plan 'for the Aliakmon position based on the minimum force that [initially] could be brought there', Eden and Dill left for the Middle East, to see how best to succour Greece.[22] Eden intended to visit Athens first and thought the affairs of Greece 'perhaps even more urgent than those of Turkey'. The Greeks, for their part, were – or claimed to be – 'delighted and honoured' by the visit but would prefer Eden to go to Angora first, given that the attitude of Turkey 'on which so much depend[ed] [was] still uncertain', whereas that of Greece was 'well known'.[23] The Greek decision to admit the British in advance of the Germans followed their failure to form a Balkan front – which would render Bulgaria harmless – and the abandonment of the view that the Germans would steer clear of a war in the Balkans. It coincided with their demand both for more supplies and to know what they could expect; and it was anticipated by the decision to extend the war against the Italians. To what extent the Greeks had, all along, feared a German attack is unclear. But they could no longer ignore its prospect – particularly as failure to form a front made them powerless to resist. They intended to leave British military intervention to the British; they proposed that there should be a plan, probably based on the Aliakmon position. They had claimed that they would fight the Germans – even if such resistance would quickly come to an end, but did not state their intention expressly to do so

[20] British military mission in Athens to Wavell, repeated to war office, 9 Feb. 1941 (reporting talk with Papagos late 8 Feb. 1941), PREM 3/309/1.
[21] Eden to Palairet, 8 Feb. 1941, enclosing Coryzis to Greek minister of 28 Jan. 1941, Avon FO 954/11, Gr/41/13. The Greeks maintained that they had repeatedly drawn the attention of the military mission in Athens; Cadogan minute, 12 Feb. 1941, sent by Churchill to Portal with note 'Please report what can be done', Portal:1:1941:24.
[22] For initial discussions and developments see pp. 176–205; Heywood to Wavell and Dill, 7 Feb. 1941, PREM 3/309/1.
[23] Palairet to Eden, 12 Feb. 1941, Avon, FO 954/11 Gr/41/15; Eden to Palairet, 12 Feb. 1941, FO 954/11, Gr/41/16.

on 7 February. It may be that they intended their apparent resolve to resist to indicate that this was their intention; but it may also be that what they would do would depend on the amount of support they expected from Britain – to be resolved by the Eden–Dill visit and the attitude of the Turks.[24]

The arrival of Eden coincided with the end of all doubt about whether the Germans did intend to attack. Demands would be made, which if not met would lead to war. To resist the Germans, help would be needed. Greece would, it was expected, shortly be asked 'to terminate war with Italy and to return to her old frontier' – though she would not be expected to pay Italy. It might also 'be necessary for Germany to occupy Salonika'.[25] The Greeks maintained they would not concede and would continue to fight 'until Italy [was] driven out of Albania and ... German approach to Salonika would be met with all available Greek resistance'. But the Greeks had only three divisions available in that area; and unless help were forthcoming 'from either Turkey, Yugoslavia or ourselves, Greece could not be expected to hold out for long'.[26]

By 20 February, therefore, the game was up and the Greeks had resolved to resist. But the uncertain attitude of Yugoslavia made it very difficult for Papagos to decide upon a fixed line of defence. If the Yugoslavs collaborated with the Greeks, the Germans would not make serious efforts down the Struma Valley; but if Yugoslavia remained neutral, Salonika would have to be abandoned.[27] The Germans had announced their intention to present an ultimatum which the Greeks would resist. The Greeks had initially hoped there would be no such ultimatum – and that a Balkan front would stop Hitler from getting a foothold, without fighting, from Bulgaria; when that possibility faded, they were prepared to watch him go into Bulgaria – and hoped he would leave it at that. But even before the German notice of an ultimatum was given, the Greeks acknowledged that they could not count on Hitler and invited the British to come in, in advance of an attack. The Germans were unlikely to attack down the Struma valley if the Yugoslavs collaborated with the Greeks, owing to the vulnerability of this line to attack from Yugoslavia.

---

[24] The government suggested that they meet nobody 'except the king, President of the Council and commander in chief'. Palairet to foreign office, 12 Feb. 1941, Avon FO 954/11, Gr/41/15.
[25] Palairet to foreign office, 19 Feb. 1941, PREM 3/309/2.   [26] Ibid.
[27] Salisbury Jones to Wavell and CIGS, 20 Feb. 1941, PREM 3/309/1.

The Yugoslavs

The Yugoslav attitude had (like that of the Greeks), seemed a simple one: in theory, pro-British; in practice determined *not* to encourage or provoke a German attack and therefore antagonistic to any measures (such as British help to Greece) which might do so.

From early January Campbell's reports suggested that while Prince Paul would 'find means of never letting his country "do us a bad turn"', he would not allow his affection for Britain, or his conviction about 'the essential and general importance of our cause' to prevent him acting 'in what he decides are the best interests of Yugoslavia'.[28] Prince Paul was said to fear Britain's provoking a German attack – either by intervening in Greece or by making a Balkan front. He was said to be 'playing for time' until Britain was more powerful. He did not want British troops sent to Greece for that would 'bring the Germans southwards' and the proclamation of a Balkan front would 'be a direct challenge to Germany and ... she would invade Yugoslavia at once'. Prince Paul was reported to wish to preserve peace, at least until the following September when he would hand over to Peter.[29] He was, by mid-January, 'alarmed at our proposal to send increased military assistance to Greece and to build up a Salonika front' – which he thought would provoke a German attack on Salonika.[30]

[28] Campbell to Eden, 14 Jan. 1941, Avon FO 954/33, Yu/41/2.
[29] Ibid.; Channon diary, 12 Jan. 1941.
[30] Cabinet, 14 Jan. 1941, WM(41)6, CAB 65/21.

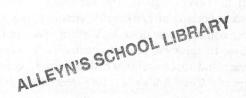

10 Churchill, Eden and the Greek decision: January to 10 February 1941

Churchill: the case for supporting Greece

Churchill's stand for the Greeks seemed, by early December, to be somewhat superseded by his advocacy of Wavell's desert campaign. His exhortations to Wavell to press on and his delight in the early victories made it seem that enthusiasm for Greece had given way to priority for Libya. But in the aftermath of the Libyan victories, Churchill's attention once more switched to Greece. Prompted by the prospect of Hitler's turning on the Balkans and a German descent on Salonika via Greece, by the need to stop Hitler and prevent the Greeks making a separate peace, by the implications of Greek resistance for Turkey and for the other Balkan countries, he began to advocate that the Libyan campaign should now take second place. He pressed for preparations to prevent a German move on Salonika; and warned of the dangerous implications not only for Greece, but for other Balkan countries, Turkey, and the whole Middle East position.

On 6 January Churchill raised the prospect of reinforcements for the Greeks – four or five more squadrons and possibly part of the 2nd armoured division.[1] He anticipated that Longmore's airmen, who must be remounted upon the best machines, 'might soon have to operate in Greece and in Turkey against the Germans'.[2] Eden's warning of a German descent coming after Wavell's victories may have led to the feeling that more could now be done in Albania, if not in Greece and Turkey, than in Libya; to the view that the campaign in Libya 'must now take second place'; and to Churchill's instructions to consider 'further assistance to Greece'.[3] Churchill's plans for Greece had two new characteristics – they

---

[1] Eden had warned of an imminent German descent and suggested a quick despatch of the 'I' tanks. Churchill to Ismay for chiefs of staff, 6 Jan. 1941, Portal:1:1941:1A; Churchill to Longmore, 7 Jan. 1941, PREM 3/309/1.

[2] Churchill to Alexander and Pound, 6 Jan. 1941, Portal:1:1941:8.

[3] Cabinet, 7 Jan. 1941, WM(41)3, CAB 65/17; Cadogan diary, 7 Jan. 1941; defence committee, 8 Jan. 1941, DO(41)1, CAB 69/2.

involved more than the mere preparation of bases, and they were characterised by a sense of urgency about a German advance. Supporting Greece must, he held, 'have priority ... the western flank ... of Egypt has been made secure'.[4]

Churchill expected a German descent on Salonika, via Bulgaria – with fatal consequences for the Greek resistance in Albania and implications for neighbouring countries. By 8 January 'all information pointed to an early advance by the German army, which was massing in Roumania, with the object of invading Greece, via Bulgaria'. It 'might start about 20th January'.[5] The Bulgarians would connive at the German action and there would follow 'the rapid advance of a comparative small force of deadly quality on Salonika'. Unless this force were stopped 'all the Greek divisions in Albania would be fatally affected'. Britain must, therefore, 'do [the] utmost to assist the Greeks on their North East frontier by affording them help with aircraft, armoured fighting vehicles, artillery, anti-tank and anti-aircraft guns, even at the expense of a further advance into Libya'.[6]

Churchill continued to insist that the German advance would soon start and anticipated, or dismissed, objections. Already the Germans were massing in Romania; the Bulgars would connive; and Greece, already 'fully engaged in Albania, would find itself in a hopeless position'.[7] Even though the weather at this time of year did not favour an advance through Bulgaria, 'the Norwegian campaign had shown that Germany was not deterred by snow'. Indeed, the Germans were more likely to act now given that 'we hoped [they] ... would put [it] off until the spring'.[8] Nor should there be doubt about Germany's intentions. Hitler was not bluffing. His concentrations in Romania, far from being 'merely a "move in a war of nerves" or a "bluff ..."' were part of a continual troop movement and sustained operations, prior to the 'early establishment of armoured force and strong air force in Bulgaria followed by a rapid advance aiming at Salonika' – not by a large force but by one 'of deadly quality'.[9]

Churchill wanted the Germans' advance stopped and Greece prevented from making a separate peace. Otherwise 'exactly the same part [might be played] in Greece as the ... break through on the Meuse played in France'; and all Greek divisions in Albania would be 'fatally affected'. In addition, the 'destruction of Greece would eclipse victories ... in Libya

[4] Churchill to Portal, 6 Jan. 1941, Portal:1:1941:8; defence committee, 8 Jan. 1941, DO(41)1, CAB 69/2; Churchill to Ismay for chiefs of staff, 7 Jan. 1941, PREM 3/186/7.
[5] Defence committee, 8 Jan. 1941, DO(41)1, CAB 69/2.
[6] Ibid.; defence committee, 10 Jan. 1941, DO(41)3, CAB 69/8.
[7] Defence committee, 8 Jan. 1941, DO(41)1, CAB 69/2.   [8] Ibid.
[9] Churchill to Wavell and Longmore, 11 Jan. 1941, PREM 3/309/1.

and might affect decisively Turkish attitude, especially if we had shown ourselves callous of [the] fate of allies'. They must now conform plans 'to large[r] interests at stake'. While nothing should hamper the capture of Tobruk 'all operations in Libya are thereafter subordinated to aiding Greece'.[10] The position was becoming increasingly urgent. The Germans were, by 26 January, 'already establishing themselves upon the Bulgarian aerodromes and making every preparation for action against Greece'; and, preparatory to such infiltration, the German army and air force were being established in Romania.[11] The Greeks must not make a separate peace – and Churchill continued to allude to the need to keep them in the field. He maintained that 'sustaining of [the] Greek battle, thus keeping in the field their quite large army [becomes] an objective of prime importance'; and that 'the massive importance of taking Valona and keeping the Greek front in being must weigh hourly with us'. He did not think it 'right' for the sake of Benghazi to lose the chance of the Greeks' 'taking Valona, and thus to dispirit and anger them, and perhaps make them in the mood for a separate peace with Italy'. Wavell must now 'conform [his] plans to larger interests at stake' given that 'the destruction of Greece would eclipse victories ... in Libya and might affect decisively [the] Turkish attitude'.[12]

Churchill was, in addition, concerned by the impact of continued Greek resistance on her neighbours – Turkey, Yugoslavia and Russia. Yugoslavia's atttitude might be determined by the support for, and fortunes of, the Greeks. The Germans might not in any case attack Yugoslavia, but 'push on through Roumania to the Black Sea and ... down through ... Bulgaria to Salonika, rather than force [their] way through Yugoslavia'.[13] The Turks too might be affected. Support for Greece would show them 'that we stood by our friends'; and Turkish resistance would depend 'on the manner in which we could support the Greeks. They would be likely to see whether yet again one of our friends was to be trampled down without our being able to prevent their fate'.[14] The Russians too would be influenced, particularly given how 'obnox-

[10] Ibid.; chiefs of staff, 11 Jan. 1941, COS(41)15, CAB 79/8.

[11] Churchill to Wavell, 26 Jan. 1941, WO 216/2; Churchill to Roosevelt, 28 Jan. 1941, Churchill, *Second World War*, I, pp. 23–4.

[12] Churchill to Longmore, 7 Jan. 1941, PREM 3/309/1; Churchill to Ismay for chiefs of staff, 6 Jan. 1941, Portal:1:1941:9a and PM M 8/1, 7 Jan. 1941, PREM 3/186A/7 (dated 6 Jan. in Churchill, *Second World War*, III, pp. 5–10); Churchill to Wavell and Longmore, 10 Jan. 1941, PREM 3/309/1 and chiefs of staff, 11 Jan. 1941, COS(41)15, CAB 79/8.

[13] Prince Paul had warned the Greeks that if they allowed British land forces to enter Greece, then his government 'would allow the Germans to attack Greece through Yugoslavia'. Cabinet, 20 Jan. 1941, WM(41)8, CAB 65/7.

[14] Defence committee, 8 and 10 Jan. 1941, DO(41)1, DO(41)3, CAB 69/2, CAB 69/8.

ious' a German advance to the Black Sea would be to them. If, when the Germans entered Bulgaria, Turkey came into the war, and Yugoslavia stood firm; if the Greeks took Valona and maintained themselves in Albania and if Turkey were an active ally then 'the attitude of Russia may be affected favourably'.[15] Though the Russian attitude was unknown, 'a German advance ... the ultimate objective [of which] would be the oil at Baku' was against her interests. Russia 'would be much encouraged by Turkish resistance to Germany'; and the Russians who would have 'much to fear from a Germany on the Black Sea' might 'be ready to move', their actions regulated by fear – though fear would also restrain the Russians from war.[16]

On top of the diplomatic and military implications, there were political ones. For even if support had no military effect, it was, 'from the political point of view ... imperative to help the Greeks against the Germans'. They must 'show the world and our own people that we were helping Greece' and Turkey that 'we stood by our friends'.[17] But Churchill did not hold out much hope of military results. They 'might find it impossible to hold the Germans in Greece'; they should 'face the possibility of German infiltration into Italy', of 'German control of Sicily and Pantellaria'. But they would, in any case, still hold Africa where their position was 'far better than had seemed possible three or four months ago'.[18]

Churchill was not, therefore, necessarily sanguine about military success. While 'there was no other course open to us but to make certain that we had spared no effort to help the Greeks who had shown themselves so worthy', none the less they might not save them: 'It might be that the help which we could bring to the Greeks in the time available would not be enough to save them'.[19] Churchill did not seem to contemporaries to be confident and he gave the impression that he thought 'Greece [was] lost'; that Hitler would permit Mussolini 'to go only so far down hill – and [was] now preparing for the attack which must bring its inevitable results'; that that would be 'a blow to British prestige' and he appeared to be 'considering ways and means of preparing the British public for it'.[20] At

---

[15] Churchill to Ismay for chiefs of staff, 7 Jan. 1941, PREM 3/186A/7. Churchill acknowledged that his appreciation of the Russian position was speculative when he told the defence committee on Jan. 1941 that 'the Russian attitude was unknown', DO(41)1, CAB 69/2.
[16] Defence committee, 8 and 12 Jan. 1941, DO(41)1 and DO(41)3, CAB 69/2, CAB 69/8.
[17] Ibid.
[18] Defence committee, 12 Jan. 1941, DO(41)3, CAB 69/8. He also wired Smuts that they could not 'guarantee success'. Churchill to Smuts, 12 Jan. 1941, Churchill, *Second World War*, III, p. 19.
[19] Defence committee, 8 Jan. 1941, DO(41)1, CAB 69/2.
[20] Sherwood, *Hopkins*, I, p. 240.

the same time a Greek debacle would be offset by the African campaign; by the defeat of the Italians in Africa, Britain would 'control the Mediterranean and the Suez [sic] against Germany'. Although he spoke 'with no great assurance' it was clear that he intended 'to hold Africa, clean out the Italians and co-operate with Weygand if the opportunity permitted'.[21]

Churchill intended that the Libyan victory would make possible operations elsewhere. After Benghazi, Libya would take second place. The destruction of the Italian armed forces in north-east Africa 'must be our prime major overseas objective in the opening months of 1941'. Once the Italian army in Cyrenaica was destroyed, then 'the Army of the Nile becomes free for other tasks' and with the capture of Benghazi 'this phase of the Libyan campaign would be ended'. He could not 'look beyond Benghazi at the present time' and if Tobruk were taken there would be very few Italian troops 'and by no means their best east of Benghazi'.[22] Although he would extend no further than Benghazi it may be that it might have to stop with Tobruk, 'which would provide us with a good harbour on which to base our western flank in the Middle East'. After that 'when the western flank of Egypt has been made secure' supporting Greece 'must have priority'. While Wavell's plans for advancing to Benghazi were approved, he should prepare a force for the Dodecanese and 'begin immediately to build up in the Delta a strategic reserve to be used in Greece or Turkey as occasion may require'.[23]

Churchill: Greece and Turkey

Before early February, Churchill made little distinction between Greece and Turkey in terms of British interests. 'Priority for Greece' covered the diversions both to Greece and to Turkey. Thus, at first, he had anticipated the establishment of bases in Greece and Turkey. He did not consider that the two countries were in competition with each other. Their respective roles were complementary. Turkey must co-operate in defeating German moves and provide facilities for British aircraft. The Turks should 'realise the danger arising from the German infiltration of Bulgaria and ... must grant us the same facilities in their own country, as the Germans were receiving in Bulgaria'. The president of Turkey would be asked to agree to advance parties, stores and other facilities 'so that our air forces could

[21] Ibid.; Hopkins to Roosevelt, in Sherwood, Hopkins, I, p. 243.
[22] Churchill to Ismay for chiefs of staff, 6 Jan. 1941, Portal:1:1941:1A, and 7 Jan. 1941, PREM 3/186A/7.
[23] Churchill to Ismay for chiefs of staff, 7 Jan. 1941, PREM 3/186A; defence committee, 8 Jan. 1941, DO(41)1, CAB 69/2; Churchill to Ismay, 21 Jan. 1941; annex to DO(41)61, CAB 69/2.

operate without delay when the emergency arose'.[24] They would like to send, as soon as facilities could be provided 'at least ten squadrons of fighter and bomber aircraft apart from the five now in action in Greece which [we] intend[ed] to maintain to help her in the fight'. They would, moreover, 'fight the air war from Turkish bases with ever increasing air forces of the highest quality ... [and] give the Turkish army the additional air support which they need to sustain their famous military qualities' and place Turkey in a position to bomb the Romanian oilfields 'if any German advance is made into Bulgaria'. British bomber forces in Turkey would, moreover, serve to 'restrain Russia from aiding Germany'; and Turkey, 'once defended by air power, would have the means perhaps of deterring Germany from overrunning Bulgaria and quelling Greece' and of counterbalancing the Russian fear of the German armies. There was not, Churchill urged, 'an hour to lose' and the Libyan victories would enable Britain 'to give a far more direct and immediate measure of aid to Turkey in the event of our two countries being allied in war'.[25]

In early February, however, Churchill began to distinguish the roles of Greece and Turkey – to each of which changing emphasis was now given. He was, possibly, prompted by Portal's proposal to send ten squadrons to Turkey, having already asked the Greeks to prepare for fourteen squadrons; by the predicament they would face if the Turks did accept and then 'Greece demand[ed] further aid beyond the five squadrons allotted'; and by the case which could be, and had since November been, made for Greece. While 'in it with [Portal] up to the neck ... [had] [they] not in fact promised to sell the same pig to two customers?'.[26] Churchill came down in favour of Greece. It would be wrong, he thought, to abandon the Greeks 'so that we could later help Turkey'. The Greeks were 'putting up a magnificent fight and ... prepared to fight the Germans' whereas Turkey was 'shirking her responsibilities and taking no action to prevent the Germans establishing themselves in a threatening position in Bulgaria'.[27] 'We were not bound to the Turks. They had not accepted our offer.' But the Greeks could not be blamed if they 'bowed to the superior force of the Germans, if we refused them help'. Not only did Churchill choose the Greeks because they were fighting, but he suggested there were indirect military advantages *vis-à-vis* the Turks – 'it would suit us to have a genuinely neutral Turkey blocking our right flank'. Moreover, there was a chance of delaying the Germans, possibly for 'long enough to encourage

---

[24] Chiefs of staff, 29 Jan. 1941, COS(41)35, CAB 79/8.
[25] Ibid.; Churchill to President Ismet Inonu, 31 Jan. 1941, PREM 3/309/1.
[26] Churchill to Portal, 6 Feb. 1941, Portal:C:1:1.
[27] Defence committee, 10 Feb. 1941, DO(41)7, CAB 69/2; Cadogan diary, 10 Feb. 1941.

the Turks, and possibly the Yugoslavs to join the battle'.[28] All in all, Greece superseded Turkey – not only because she was fighting, but also because of the indirect consequences for Turkey. 'Greece was fighting and Turkey ... doing nothing but evade ... obligations' and we ought to 'do all we can to help Greece. That may encourage Turkey'.[29]

It was in the context of thinking about possible Turkish intervention that Churchill proposed for the first time that a fighting chance of holding the Germans in Greece existed; and that plans should be put in motion for doing so. Hitherto the military case had been made in terms of the effect support would have on Greek morale, of the danger of Greece abandoning the struggle against the Italians in Albania, of the implications for the other Balkan countries and Turkey. Churchill now claimed that 'it was [not] impossible for the Greeks and ourselves to hold the Germans ... advancing down the Struma Valley'.[30] If the German advance was held up 'for some months' then the chances of Turkish intervention would be favoured. They should 'offer the Greeks the transfer to Greece of the fighting portion of the army which has hitherto defended Egypt and make every plan for sending and reinforcing it to the limit with men and material'.[31] Although they did 'not know what Greece [would] say to a great offer of this kind ... [or] what [were] her means of resisting an invasion from Bulgaria by German forces ... [he thought it] ... reasonable to assume they ha[d] a plan'. If it were good, 'it would be worth our while to back it with all our strength, and fight the Germans in Greece hoping thereby to draw in both Turkey and the Yugoslavs'. Wavell should begin his plans and preparatory moves for shipping; and Eden and Dill would leave on a mission, the object of which was 'the sending of speedy succour to Greece against an attack by Germany'.[32] They would help concert 'all possible measures both diplomatic and military against the Germans in the Balkans' and would visit Athens and Angora. At least four divisions (including one armoured) 'and whatever additional air forces the Greek air fields [were] ready for' and all available munitions might be offered 'in the best possible way and in the shortest time'.[33]

While there was to be a 'slowing down if necessary in all African and

[28] Defence committee, 10 Feb. 1941, DO(41)7, CAB 69/2.
[29] Cadogan diary, 10 Feb. 1941.
[30] Churchill to Wavell, 11 Feb. 1941, annex to DO(41)8, CAB 69/2; defence committee, 10 Feb. 1941, DO(41)7, CAB 69/2. He alluded to the dangerous results of Greece, if she were 'trampled down or forced to make a separate peace with Italy, yielding also air and naval strategic ports against us to Germany, effect on Turkey will be v. bad'.
[31] Churchill to Wavell, 11 Feb. 1941, DO(41)8, CAB 69/2.
[32] Ibid.; Churchill note for Eden, 12 Feb. 1941 in 'Report of Mission ... ', Avon FO 954/33, Yu/41/21.
[33] Churchill to Wavell, 11 Feb. 1941, annex to DO(41)8, CAB 69/2.

Mediterranean theatres' (except for Eritrea and the Dodecanese) and the strongest and best-equipped force should be formed in the Delta for despatch to Greece, none the less some ambiguity remained about Turkey. Wavell must be 'content with ... a safe flank for Egypt at Tobruk'. He must now make himself 'secure at Benghazi and concentrate all ... forces in the Delta in preparation for movement to Europe'; 'thereafter Greece and/or Turkey must have priority'; his 'major effort must now be to aid Greece and/or Turkey'.[34] Turkey was not, then, excluded; and if it proved impossible 'to reach any good agreement with the Greeks and work out ... a ... military plan' then they must save what they could from the wreck (definitely Crete and whatever Greek islands they could as air bases) and reconsider the advance on Tripoli – though these would 'only be consolation prizes after the classic race ha[d] been lost. There [would] of course always remain the support of Turkey'.[35]

The emphasis was similar in the note of instructions which Churchill gave to Eden about the trip to the Middle East command, Angora and Athens which he began on 10 February. He urged that 'while it was our duty to fight, and if need be, suffer with Greece, the interests of Turkey in the second stage were no less important to us than those of Greece'.[36] Eden should aim at the formation in the Delta 'of the strongest and best equipped force ... which could be despatched to Greece at the earliest moment ... to be provided out of the existing armies and air forces in the Middle East'. Churchill's instructions about priority for Greece seemed clear; but they none the less allowed that Turkish interests 'were no less important ... than those of Greece'.[37]

In the weeks preceding Eden's mission to Greece, Turkey and the Middle East Churchill had, then, advocated giving military support to Greece against German intervention. But along with this advocacy went a recognition that the prospects of achieving victory were small: the justification for helping Greece lay rather in the effect on morale, its political implications and the longer-term military advantages of such a course, than in hope of immediate success on the battlefield. However, early in February, Churchill did, for the first time, entertain the idea that the German advance might be held. Once he distinguished between the case for supporting Greece and that for supporting Turkey, Churchill gave Greece priority; but he was careful to stress that this was not incompatible – and indeed in certain ways strengthened – his support for Turkey.

[34] Ibid.; Churchill for Eden, 'Report of Mission ... ', 12 Feb. 1941, Avon FO 954/33, Yu/41/21.
[35] Churchill to Wavell, 11 Feb. 1941, annex to DO(41)8, CAB 69/2.
[36] Churchill for Eden, 12 Feb. 1941, 'Report of Mission ... ', Avon FO 954/33, Yu/41/21.
[37] Ibid.

Eden

Eden's appointment as foreign secretary in December 1940 coincided with his abandoning protagonism of the Middle East and Wavell's Libyan campaign over and above all other calls. Reports of Hitler's descent through the Balkans – probably via Greece – and Eden's view that he could and should be stopped, provided a new task for Wavell's victorious armies which could now wind up their campaign in North Africa, and prepare to move to Greece. The case for helping the Greeks rested on the political obligation to do so and the impact on Turkey (seen by Eden as 'the key to the Middle East'), on the other Balkan countries and on the Soviet Union.

During early January, Eden's attention was diverted to the threat to the Balkans. All the signs pointed to imminent German action. The mass of information tended to show 'that Germany is pressing forward her preparations in the Balkans with a view to an ultimate descent upon Greece'. The date mentioned was the beginning of March, though Eden believed they intended 'to antedate their move'.[38] Germany would 'seek to intervene by force to prevent complete Italian defeat in Albania'. The increased enemy air forces operating against the Greeks, which were slowing down Papagos's advance, were, Eden thought, an omen: for the Germans tended 'to establish superiority in the air before making any move on land'.[39] Hitler was more likely to attack the Greeks through Italy, than to move through Bulgaria, precipitating a fight from the Turks.[40] The attitude of Bulgaria caused Eden 'grave disquiet'; there were, by 6 January, a number of indications 'that Bulgaria was under strong pressure from Germany' and the government seemed to have 'little control of events' – their press 'now little else but the mouthpiece of Axis propaganda'.[41] Eden, as a result, wanted to move as a matter of urgency. It was, he thought, 'a race' as to whether the Italians could be defeated in Libya 'before Germans loose their attack on Greeks'.[42] On 7 January he urged that there was 'more to be done, now in Albania than in Libya'; and he proposed to tell the Greeks that 'we ... would do what we could to help them'.[43] Once he had decided on that, nothing deflected him, not even a Greek refusal; and plans were laid for a visit to the Middle East, possibly

---

[38] Eden to Churchill, 6 Jan. 1941, Avon FO 954/1, Bul/41/1.
[39] Ibid. He did not know whether military operations through Bulgaria against Salonika were possible at that time of year.
[40] Avon, *The Reckoning*, p. 253; Sherwood, *Hopkins*, I, p. 238.
[41] Cabinet, 6 Jan. 1941, WM(41)2, CAB 65/17; Eden to Churchill, 6 Jan. 1941, Avon FO 954/1, Bul/41/1.
[42] Eden diary, 4 Jan. 1941.
[43] Cadogan diary, 7 Jan. 1941, Cabinet, 7 Jan. 1941, WM(41)3, CAB 65/17.

by Eden, although he would not force help on the Greeks. It was for them to say 'whether they wanted ... Wavell to visit Athens and to be the judges of German reactions'.[44] He did not accept Greek fears that Hitler would necessarily react to help by intervention; and refused to 'believe in the cry that ... this or that action ... [could] "provoke" Hitler into ... action which he would otherwise not take'. Palairet should 'disabuse the Greek government of this idea which ... [was] of course the object of German propaganda'.[45] There would be a visit to the Middle East; and the idea mooted by 23 January had taken more shape by the 29th. There was 'much rough weather [ahead] in Central Mediterranean ... [and] Turkey [was] the key'; and the feeling was that Eden should go out to Turkey.[46]

At the outset Eden wanted to encourage the Greeks to keep up their fight and to influence Turkey. Their morale, he thought, 'showed signs of sagging now that their advance had slowed down'; they were 'a temperamental race' and were 'in a flap'; and 'we must do something to maintain their morale'.[47] British help to Greece would also affect Turkey, thought by Eden to be the 'key' to the Middle East. Though he maintained the Turks would resist a German move through Bulgaria, he continued to be anxious on that score. Such a move, 'possibly at first by the same methods as had been used in Roumania without directly infringing the neutrality of Yugoslavia and Turkey' was for Eden 'the main danger'; warnings had been issued 'as to the consequences of allowing these tactics to succeed' and 'the danger of a German infiltration into Bulgaria'.[48]

Turkey remained an uncertain quantity – but one to which Eden and his colleagues prepared to turn directly when the Greeks, in late January, refused all help in men. The Turks had continued to give little away. By 14 January they would not, for example, concede that they would 'resist infiltration though they would "resist an attack"'.[49] The government's subsequent statement 'to the effect that [they] were on the alert for any threat' and that all precautions might be taken, struck Eden as marking

---

44 Cabinet, 14 Jan. 1941, CA to WM(41)6, CAB 65/12.
45 Eden to Palairet, 18 Jan. 1941, Avon FO 954/11, Gr/41/8. After the Greek refusal, Cadogan thought they'd 'better go on in North Africa'. Metaxas had refused all aid in men, and guns 'if accompanied by crews'; while they could not 'force assistance down Metaxas' throat' Cadogan none the less thought 'these Balkan states are probably wrong. But they are all terrified. And it may be the Germans are hoping to lure a small British force into the Balkans, to destroy it.' Cadogan diary, 16, 20 Jan. 1941.
46 Eden diary, 23 Jan. 1941; 29 Jan. 1941. Portal was keen, as was Churchill, who was anxious also that he see Wavell who, he felt, was 'insufficiently aware of Balkan dangers'.
47 Defence committee, 8 Jan. 1941, DO(41)1, CAB 69/2; Cadogan diary, 7 Jan. 1941.
48 Cabinet, 13 Jan. 1941, WM(41)5, CAB 65/17; 23 Jan. 1941, WM(41)9, CAB 65/17.
49 Cadogan diary, 14 Jan. 1941, i.e., resist as the Yugoslavs would.

'some advance on any recent public expression of the Turkish government's attitude'.[50] Eden may have wanted to encourage the changes; and in view of the Greek refusal (of all aid in men) followed by Metaxas's death, he may have thought that they should concentrate directly on Turkey (for the Greeks, in any case, had been offered help partly to stiffen the Turks). All anticipated much 'rough weather ahead in [the] Central Mediterranean and Balkans'. Turkey was 'the key' and they must 'intensify ... efforts' there. Eden would go to Turkey and the Turks would be offered ten squadrons. By 31 January it was 'more or less settled that [Eden would] ... go out' and a draft to the Turkish president was being prepared.[51]

Eden prepared to leave for Turkey with the idea that an offer would be made but that his initial task was to bolster Turkey and then bolster Greece. And the means of bolstering Turkey continued to be seen as varying between concentrating on Greece, or concentrating on Turkey itself. The Greek refusal and Metaxas's death need not necessarily augur ill provided the Turks were more pliant. But at the same time Eden should not appear to be abandoning the Greeks. He should avoid 'the appearance' that they were 'deserting Greece and falling back on a backward Turkish defence line'.[52]

How the Turks would react to the British offer and how far they would commit themselves continued to be a matter for speculation. The Turks would make no commitment and it was impossible to discover whether they would be influenced by generous offers of help. The first intimation of their reaction to the offer of air help left Cadogan with the view that they had 'given ... no concrete proof that they had any back bone at all'. It was 'in the same sort of timorous sticky terms employed by the Greeks'.[53] But by the end of the first week in February the Turks seemed more positive, according to reports from Angora. Moreover their preliminary reply by 8 February was 'not too discouraging' and they even seemed to contemplate Eden's visiting Angora.[54] If they had more coming to them, they seemed to imply that then they would be firmer. In Angora Campbell was 'convinced of [the] extreme importance of increasing military supplies to Turkey without delay'. The president had urged that 'if Turkey had had all that we promised we might have had a different

---

[50] Cadogan diary, 21 Jan. 1941; cabinet, 23 Jan. 1941, WM(41)9, CAB 65/17. By the 21st they did not seem 'very convincing in the role' (i.e., of being 'all right').

[51] Cadogan diary, 31 Jan. 1941; Eden diary, 29 Jan. 1941.

[52] Cadogan diary, 29 Jan. 1941.

[53] Ibid., 3 Feb. 1941.

[54] Cabinet, 6 Feb. 1941, WM(41)14, CAB 65/17. Eden told the cabinet that a message from Angora suggested that Colonel Donovan had been 'impressed by the attitude of Turkey towards the alliance', Cadogan diary, 8 Feb. 1941.

answer'; Campbell thought that 'the Turkish government [felt] that their present state of inadequate preparations exclude[d] the possibility of any action likely to be provocative'. They maintained that British air or artillery in Turkey would mean Turkish entry into the war and would prejudice Turkish and British interests.[55] As for Yugoslavia and Russia, Eden was not sanguine, particularly if Britain persisted in helping Greece.

Eden feared the implications of a German move into Bulgaria 'by the same methods as ... used in Roumania without directly infringing the neutrality of Yugoslavia or Turkey'. The Yugoslavs would not commit themselves to resisting such a move, should Britain persist in helping the Greeks or Salonika. Rather, they would comply with German moves through Yugoslavia itself. Although 'the consequences of allowing these [German] tactics to succeed' were put to the Yugoslavs, the Yugoslavs, in turn, could not be got to say they would resist an attack.[56] The Regent was said to have 'lost his head and his nerve'; to be 'alarmed' at the British offer to Greece and the intention 'to build up a Salonika front ... [which] would provoke the Germans into making a strong attack on Salonika'.[57]

Nor did Eden expect the Soviets to resist any German moves. Should Hitler move, either through Bulgaria, or 'more likely ... through Italy to attack the Greeks ... Russia was frightened and would keep out'. According to Cadogan, Eden was 'alive to uselessness of expecting anything from these cynical blood-stained murderers'.[58] He saw their policy as one which 'would continue to be dominated by fear'. For Eden 'the great question mark [was] the attitude of the Soviet Government towards the ... German military occupation of Roumania and German intentions ... in the Balkans'. But Russia, they must assume, would take 'no overt action to prevent the Germans carrying out their schemes'. He did not know, by 17 January, whether Hitler had (helped by German troop concentrations in Romania), extracted from Stalin 'an undertaking that he [would] not interfere with or hamper Germany's plans in Bulgaria and [would] restrain Turkey from doing so either'.[59]

He wanted the Soviets warned of 'the danger to their ultimate interests ... [of] allowing the Germans a free hand in the Balkans now'. The Russians must 'know this ... even [though] they hardly dare admit it

---

[55] Campbell to foreign office, 7 Feb. 1941, PREM 3/309/1.
[56] Cabinet, 13 Jan. 1941, WM(41)5, CAB 65/17; Cadogan diary, 14 Jan. 1941.
[57] Cadogan diary, 15 Jan. 1941. Eden continued to maintain that 'our views are unaltered' and the force was intended not for offence, but 'to defend Greece against German attack through Bulgaria'.
[58] Cadogan diary, 6 Jan. 1941; Sherwood, *Hopkins*, I, p. 238; cabinet, 13 Jan. 1941, WM(41)5, CAB 65/17.
[59] Cabinet, 13 Jan. 1941, WM(41)5, CAB 65/12; Eden to Cripps, 17 Jan. 1941, FO 954/24, SU/41/1.

themselves'.[60] There was nothing very much he could envisage doing *vis-à-vis* the Soviet Union; and he did not advocate 'further political or economic offers to the Soviet Government' and did not think much would be gained by fresh attempts to 'reach a settlement of the various outstanding Baltic questions' – patience must be employed until military success 'inspired in the Soviet Government some fear of the Germans'.[61]

Thus, in the run up to Eden's departure for the Middle East, a series of overlapping considerations had marked his views of the nature of his task: the need to help Greece, for a variety of reasons, including that of its effect on Turkey; the importance of Turkey to Britain's role in the Middle East; the refusal by the Greeks of troops; the ambiguous attitude of the Turks; and the refusal of Soviets and Yugoslavs to play a part in stopping Hitler. Eden, therefore, had a somewhat unsettled view about which country should be accorded priority by Britain. Greece had initially been offered help, for many reasons – including the prospect of influencing Turkey. The Greeks had turned down aid in men, and the Turks had been offered help. The Turks had responded to this offer, by suggesting that they would not accept British air or artillery units but possibly would accept materials and other aid proposed. To Eden, Turkey had been the key. He had thought the best way to get the Turks to fight would be to help Greece. Yet the claims of the Greeks themselves were, none the less, not to be superseded. (Throughout the course of Eden's visit it would become less and less clear whether help to Greece should be seen as a consideration which constituted an end in itself, or merely as a means to bolster Turkey. This was one factor in the failure to decide on priority as between Greece and Turkey.)

When he left Britain on 10 February, Eden left behind the refusal of Churchill to accept that 'our first obligation is to Turkey' – an opinion with which the foreign office agreed: for 'Greece was fighting and Turkey was doing nothing but evade rather plain obligations.' They should do 'all we can to help Greece' and that might 'encourage Turkey'.[62] Abandonment of Greece would confirm Turkey in its 'equivocal attitude'. The object of Eden's mission, as relayed to Wavell, did not clarify the problem: 'to give the best chance to concerting all possible measures, both diplomatic and military, against the Germans in the Balkans'.[63] Eden still

---

[60] Eden to Cripps, ibid.; He took the opportunity to emphasise the danger of a German infiltration into Bulgaria during discussion with a Soviet representative (as well as a Greek, Yugoslav and a Turk). Cabinet, 23 Jan. 1941, WM(41)9, CAB 65/17.

[61] Eden to Cripps, 17 Jan. 1941, FO 954/24, SU/41/1.

[62] Cadogan diary, 10 Feb. 1941. Dill had held that the first obligation was to Turkey.

[63] Ibid.; Churchill to Wavell, 11 Feb. 1941, annex to defence committee, 11 Feb. 1941, DO(41)8, CAB 69/2.

held that the best way of ensuring that the Turks would fight was to give effective help to the Greeks. The Greeks 'were anxious to know what we were prepared to do, so that they could make their plan'. If they could be told that specific forces would be provided then they could discuss how best to use them 'and agree upon our joint action'. On the other hand, if Britain 'held back and allowed the Greeks to be [crushed], it was almost certain that the Turks would not fight'.[64] Eden had Turkey in mind. But he may, in addition, have been struck by the recent claims by Coryzis, the new Greek prime minister, that the British had failed to provide adequate help, and by his fears for the future. If 'the necessary measures [were] not taken for the urgent and indispensable reinforcement of our air force, the situation [might] become critical'. Coryzis specifically asked that the 'immediate' assignment of thirty Mohawks should be made; that the assurance be given that a small monthly quota of American production be granted; that munitions and raw materials be supplied; and that Churchill himself should be warned of the prospective tragedy should the 'supreme efforts of the Greek Army, of the whole Greek nation ... stumble and falter' because of 'material deficiencies rendering impossible the effective continuation of the war' as well as shortages of guns and equipment.[65]

Eden had warned that 'the best way of ensuring that Turkey would fight would be to give effective help to the Greeks'. If they failed, then they would lose 'all hope of facing Germans with the Balkan front ... [and] probably ... our safe communications with Turkey and ... Yugoslavia'. If they held back and allowed the Greeks to be crushed 'it was almost certain that the Turks would not fight'.[66] On making the case for putting the Greeks first, Eden also referred to other factors: to the 'general obligation under the guarantee of 1939 and the appeal of the new Greek president of the Council'; and to his mission, the principal stated object of which was 'the sending of speedy succour to Greece against an attack by Germany' and 'to make both the Yugoslavs and the Turks fight at the same time'.[67] While Eden recalled that he and Dill ought to bear in mind 'our duty to fight, and, if need be, suffer with Greece' they should remember that 'the interests of Turkey in the second stage were no less important to us than those of Greece'.[68] Moreover, the journey to Cairo had as one of its principal objects that of 'visiting Angora, to consult with

[64] Defence committee, 10 Feb. 1941, DO(41)7, CAB 69/2.
[65] Eden to Palairet, 8 Feb. 1941, enclosing Coryzis to Greek minister of 28 Jan. 1941 with schedules, Avon FO 954/11, Gr/41/13.
[66] Defence committee, 10 Feb. 1941, DO(41)7, CAB 69/2.
[67] 'Report on the mission of the Secretary of State for Foreign Affairs to the Eastern Mediterranean, Feb.–April 1941'; Avon FO 954/33, Yu/41/21.
[68] Ibid.

the Turkish government'; and the difficulty remained of what, precisely, constituted the second stage; and to what extent fighting and suffering with the Greeks was principally to be seen as a way of influencing Turkey.[69]

[69] Ibid.; Eden to Palairet, 11 Feb. 1941, FO 954/11, Gr/41/14.

11 The chiefs of staff at home and the Greek decision: January to February 1941

Collective views

For the chiefs of staff, intervention in Greece was from the outset seen to be a decision of high political and strategic importance to be taken by Churchill. It was also a course, they were told, about which there was no choice, even thought it might fail.

When the chiefs considered, in early January, the question of establishing air bases in Salonika, they thought this involved issues 'of the highest political and military importance' which must be referred to Churchill.[1] He, in turn, persisted in asking the chiefs to consider 'whether we could now afford some further assistance to Greece ... particularly by reinforcing our air detachment in that country'.[2] And he set out the position for them (and his colleagues) at the defence committee on the 8th of a likely 'early advance by the German army ... [now] massing in Roumania, with the object of invading Greece via Bulgaria'.[3]

At the defence committee on the 8th chaired by Churchill which they, the service chiefs and Eden attended, it was agreed to send early and full support to Greece.[4] Given the 'probability of an early German advance into Greece through Bulgaria', 'it was ... from the political view [of the first importance to] ... do everything possible, by hook or by crook to send at once ... the fullest support within our power' to Greece. The form and extent would be decided within the next forty-eight hours; and the chiefs of staff would, in the light of these, recommend the instructions to

---

[1] Chiefs of staff, 2, 3, Jan. 1941, COS(41)3, COS(41)6, CAB 79/8. When later the chiefs of staff were urged by the foreign office to send a token supply of armaments to Yugoslavia (and suggesting Bren gun carriers) the chiefs, who thought that any surplus of Bren gun carriers would be needed 'to meet our own deficiencies and ... supply ... our allies who were fighting for us', decided that the foreign office, when recommending the supply of arms to foreign countries, should indicate the order of priority. Chiefs of staff, 12 Feb. 1941, COS(41)50, CAB 79/9.
[2] Cabinet, 6, 7 Jan. 1941, WM(41)2, 3, CAB 65/17.
[3] Defence committee, 8 Jan. 1941, DO(41)1, CAB 69/2.
[4] Ibid.

be sent to the Middle East command to be considered next day by the defence committee. Churchill pointed out that such help as might be given could not save the Greeks 'the help which we could bring ... would not be enough to save them' but none the less 'there was no other course open to us but to make certain that we had spared no effort to help the Greeks who had shown themselves so worthy'.[5]

The chiefs therefore were acting on the assumption that the decision ('of highest political and military importance') had been taken to offer immediate and full support to the Greeks; and their instructions for the Middle East command were ready by 9 January. The German advance through Bulgaria to attack Greece was unlikely to be resisted by the Bulgarians; and the decision had therefore been taken by the government 'to afford the Greeks the maximum possible assistance ... [to ensure] they resist German demands by force'. Turkey was a central consideration. The 'extent and effectiveness of ... aid to the Greeks will be a determining factor in the attitude of Turkey and [would] influence the USA and Russia'.[6] Help to the Greeks would 'almost entirely' in the first instance come from the Middle East and so once Tobruk was taken 'assistance to Greece must take priority over all operations in the Middle East'. The Turks should be told 'in general terms that we were disposed to give considerable assistance to the Greeks in the event of a German attack ... that their support would be of great value and would have a favourable effect on Russia'; while they should also exert influence 'to stimulate the Yugoslavs to adopt a firm attitude in the face of German threats'.[7] Speed would be of the greatest importance; and the necessary preparations would be set on foot while discussions proceeded with Metaxas. The Greek theatre would be the responsibility of the Middle East command; and assistance would probably take the form of specialist and mechanised units as well as air forces to support the Greek divisions.[8]

The chiefs, therefore, did not resist the decision. They expected the German descent, saw the importance politically and militarily of the issues involved and recognised that Wavell's Libyan armies would soon need new tasks (by 9 January they were reported to be thirty miles west of Tobruk). They also realised that support to the Greeks would matter for the Turks and would affect the other Balkan countries and Turkey, and

[5] Ibid.
[6] Defence committee, 9 Jan. 1941, DO(41)2, CAB 69/2; chiefs of staff to CsinCME. 10 Jan. 1941, PREM 3/309/1.
[7] Ibid.
[8] Chiefs of staff to CsinCME, 10 Jan. 1941, PREM 3/309/1; defence committee, 9 Jan. 1941, DO(41)2, CAB 69/2.

accordingly they had their instructions ready by 9 January.[9] If by any chance the Germans were bluffing, any assistance sent to the Greeks 'would be of great value to them in their campaign in Albania'.[10]

The chiefs of staff, then, had prepared to divert to Greece as a result of political instructions. When the Greeks refused, they were inclined to accept the refusal and to seek fresh instructions and other priorities. The Greeks turned down both units and RAF squadrons for the northern aerodromes, but agreed to reconnaissance. Dill would seek further instructions for Wavell at the cabinet – though their own inclination was now to concentrate on Turkey.

The Greek refusal, they implied, should be taken at face value. In their view, the Greeks 'must be the judge of what should be done to help them. We could not force ourselves upon them'; they must be made aware of British information, though not its source; and they 'must realise that we are not trying to form a "Salonika front" but are trying to support them with technical arms'.[11] For the chiefs of staff, the Greeks had settled the matter; and given their refusal, they should not be forced against their will. So long as the offer had been clearly made and the information in British hands made known to them, there was nothing more to be done. There was no question of sending the kind of forces suggested by Metaxas for possible offensive action. Troops 'in sufficient numbers to act offensively as well as defensively' were 'out of the question' and if the special forces suggested instead on 10 January were not sent now, but waited until the German advance, 'these ... could not arrive in time to be effective'. In any case, in the event of such an advance it might be necessary 'to send out forces to Turkey instead of to Greece'. There was 'no question of ... forcing ... aid'. If the Greeks 'with full knowledge of our information' had refused, then they must 'submit to their judgement'.[12] Until the cabinet considered the new situation, no arrangements should be made 'which would commit us to sending an expeditionary

---

[9] Churchill explained the next day, the 10th, to the defence committee, that they had taken this course 'to show the world and our own people that we were helping Greece and to show Turkey that we stood by our friends. We wanted Turkey to come into the war and ... hoped that Yugoslavia might also join. Russia might then be ready to move.' Defence committee 10 Jan. 1941, DO(41)3, CAB 69/2, CAB 69/8; cabinet 6, 9, Jan. 1941, WM(41)2, 4, CAB 65/17.

[10] Chiefs of staff, 11 Jan. 1941, COS(41)15, CAB 79/8.

[11] Defence committee, 16 Jan. 1941, DO(41)5, CAB 69/2. The draft they had prepared for the defence committee followed a report from the Middle East on conversations with the Greeks and a telephone call from Churchill conveying his views; chiefs of staff, 16 Jan. 1941, COS(41)21, CAB 79/8. The two new factors were the refusal itself and the reports of German aircraft in the Mediterranean.

[12] Defence committee, 16 Jan. 1941, DO(41)5, CAB 69/2; chiefs of staff to commanders in chief, 17 Jan. 1941, PREM 3/309/1.

force to Salonika'.[13] Preparations at Salonika and neighbouring points 'should ... be confined to making ready to receive those units ... required to maintain the squadrons which might operate in that area'. And the Greek refusal, together with the arrival of German aircraft in the Mediterranean, would mean that the decision to give priority to helping Greece after the capture of Tobruk, would now have to be modified.[14]

Initially, the chiefs of staff had stood aside from a decision about Greece, leaving the responsibility to Churchill. Once the Greeks refused help, their attitude became one of unwillingness to press them. In view of the refusal, the appearance of German aircraft in the Mediterranean and Churchill's views, the chiefs considered that the forces might be sent instead to the Turks. Even before the Greeks refused the chiefs had wanted to impress upon the Turks that 'sooner or later ... they [the Turks] would have to deal with the German invasion of the Balkans'. They should, therefore, 'lay their plans and conduct their foreign policy on this assumption'.[15] After the Greek refusal it was thought that 'it would be better to send [the troops] to Turkey' than to Salonika, for which they would be too late if they did not go now. The feeling that they might have to 'render assistance to Turkey as well as to Greece', that after Tobruk they should 'be entitled to revise [the] decision [of] ... first priority ... [for] Greece', became rather a feeling that they should offer substantial assistance to the Turks.[16] The Middle East commanders were warned – on the 21st – that after Benghazi they must create a strategic reserve for 'rendering assistance to Turkey or Greece within the next two months';[17] and matters were brought to a head by the death of Metaxas and the continued German infiltration of Bulgaria.

On 29 January the position, Churchill told the cabinet, was 'an anxious one' and must be 'carefully watched'. It was, the chiefs of staff agreed, 'now essential to bring the Turks to realise the danger arising from the German infiltration of Bulgaria'; and to counter this danger 'they must grant us the same facilities in their own countries as the Germans were receiving in Bulgaria'.[18] Churchill would draft a telegram to the Turkish president 'setting out our view of the situation' and calling on him 'to receive immediately advance parties together with stores and other facilities so that our air force could operate without delay when the emergency

---

13 Chiefs of staff to CsinCME, 17 Jan. 1941, PREM 3/309/1.   14 Ibid.
15 Chiefs of staff, 11 Jan. 1941, COS(41)15, CAB 79/8.
16 Defence committee, 16 Jan. 1941, DO(41)5, CAB 69/2; cabinet, 20 Jan. 1941, WM(41)8, CAB 65/21.
17 Chiefs of staff, no. 49, to CsinCME, 21 Jan. 1941, WO 216/2.
18 Cabinet, 29 Jan. 1941, WM(41)11, CAB 65/17; chiefs of staff, 29 Jan. 1941, COS(41)35, CAB 79/8.

arose'. The draft was ready by the 30th and an explanation for the Middle East command of 'our view of the Balkan situation and the action which we proposed to take in Turkey' was ready by the 31st: 'German infiltration into Bulgaria ha[d] led the prime minister with the agreement of the chiefs of staff' to wire Inonu with an offer. A 'different emphasis on the various objectives' to that given in theirs of the 21st was now necessary. 'The Graeco-Turkish situation predominates and should have first place in your thoughts.' Steps to counter German infiltration into Bulgaria must have the highest priority. The advantage of going on to Benghazi 'and thus securing Egypt and the fleet base' though fully realised, must not 'prejudice ... European interests'.[19]

The decision to make an offer to Turkey did not exclude continued discussion about what should happen to Wavell's forces after Benghazi. Tobruk had fallen by 23 January – opening the way for the next priority of 'assistance to Greece' agreed on 9 January; Churchill hoped Yugoslavia would join in such a course and Russia would move. But even if the Germans could not be held, 'we would still hold Africa where our position was far better than had seemed possible 3 or 4 months ago'. With regard to Hitler's other possible moves, Ismay did not think he would try invasion. A move through Spain, possibly into North Africa, seemed less likely than in the past. Spanish opinion had swung 'towards us in the last six months'. The difficulty 'from our point of view [was] that the initiative must rest with Hitler, and ... since we can do nothing until and unless he moves, he must get a good start'. The most likely course, 'a move through Bulgaria into Greece' would be 'much more difficult to cope with'. The whole of the Greek army was deployed in Albania, and 'the remnants in Greece could scarcely delay, much less stop, the German advance on Salonika'. If the Greeks allowed Britain to establish an expeditionary force in advance of a German move it might be 'a different story'. But the Greeks would not do so 'on the grounds that any attempt on our part to establish a front in the Balkans would precipitate the German advance'.[20]

In North Africa, Wavell's victories continued to provide the changing circumstances against which any decision would be taken. On 10 February it was expected that Benghazi would be reached 'in a day or two'. In 'what way should our forces in the Middle East now be employed'?[21] The chiefs considered that the possession of Tripoli would be 'of some strategic value'. It would 'increase our ability to strike by air at Metropolitan

[19] Chiefs of staff, 29, 30 Jan. 1941, COS(41)35, 36, CAB 79/8; chiefs of staff to Cs in C, no. 53, 31 Jan. 1941, PREM 3/309/1.

[20] Defence committee, 9, 10, Jan. 1941, DO(41)2, 3, CAB 69/2, CAB 69/8. Ismay to Brooke-Popham, 9 Feb. 1941, BP V/1/6.

[21] Cabinet, 6, 10 Feb. 1941, WM(41)14, 15, CAB 65/17.

Italy and Sardinia ... deny the enemy a base from which to ... attack ...
Egypt ... encourage ... Weygand to resist a German occupation of
Tunisia'. They were not sure that it would diminish Axis domination of
the Sicilian narrows; and acknowledged that the capture of Benghazi
removed 'the air threat to Egypt from the west'. And by 'limiting our
advance to the Benghazi area we shall be able the sooner to release men
and equipment to assist Greece and Turkey and to build up our strategic
reserve in the Middle East'.[22]

Although there would be advantages to taking Tripoli, none the less the
command had been told that 'after ... Tobruk the European situation
must take priority'; and the uncertainties of the Balkans 'made it very
desirable that the army of the Nile should concentrate' and the chiefs
would prepare instructions on the basis that 'no serious operation should
be undertaken beyond Benghazi'.[23]

Dill, the war office and the generals

For Dill, before he left with Eden for the Middle East, Turkey, not
Greece, was the key to the Middle East. He did not think that Wavell
should divert to Greece, thereby exposing the Middle East and endangering the troops; and the feeling at the war office inclined against
entanglements or commitments in Greece which could not be sustained.
The Greek refusal in mid-January served, therefore, to encourage the
soldiers' favoured view that they should concentrate on Turkey. It is not
clear how far they either pressed this course with the politicians, or simply
acquiesced in what they regarded as the decisions about high political and
strategic matters which were, quite properly, a matter for the politicians.

At the outset there was a wariness even with regard to establishing an
air base at Salonika – for that might lead to 'a land commitment we
should not have the power to sustain'. A 'full appreciation of our strategic
policy in that theatre of war' would be necessary before deciding on the
despatch of bombers to Salonika.[24]

Nonetheless Dill acquiesced, as did the other chiefs, in the decision to
give Greece priority and he set about wiring Wavell to prepare him for the
diversion from the Middle East to the Balkans. Dill may not have
envisaged a very large diversion; indeed, he may have been reconciled to
the prospect by the numbers being left to Wavell's discretion. He may
have wished to encourage Wavell to resist by implying that the final

[22] Chiefs of staff, 10 Feb. 1941, COS(41)41, CAB 79/9.
[23] Defence committee, 10 Feb. 1941, DO(41)7, CAB 69/2.
[24] Haining's view, chiefs of staff, 3 Jan. 1941, COS(41)6, CAB 79/8.

decision would depend on his own discussions with the Greeks. He wired Wavell on 8 January that the Greek situation was 'causing ... anxiety [and] help [could] only come from [Wavell] or Longmore'; and on the 11th that the policy, as Wavell would see from Churchill's wire, was 'quite clear'. 'The troops and air forces [which could] ... be usefully employed in assisting the Greeks must depend on [his] conversations with Metaxas.'[25] It is not clear whether Dill may have been being deliberately ambiguous. He may have wished Wavell's own discussions to be the decisive factor. For without the commanders' support, the decision might not be taken, or might involve merely token assistance.

Once the Greeks refused assistance, Dill looked to the opportunities in North Africa and to the prospects of helping Turkey. He considered Wavell and his soldiers were 'doing wonders'; saw the capture of Benghazi as being of the greatest importance and wanted 'urgently' the date (i.e., proposed for its capture) 'in connection with assistance it may be necessary to give Turkey'.[26] Once the offer to the Turks was made, Dill tended to put them first; though this did not necessarily involve excluding either Africa or Greece.

As for North Africa, Wavell had 'done marvels' though Dill expected 'a very difficult year ahead'. As to Greece, he wondered what could be done 'from here to help the Greeks' and contemplated 'the chances of Italian collapse in Albania and of Greeks continuing to fight'. But if forces were sent, they were, he thought, 'certain to be annihilated or driven out again'; and diversion would both expose Egypt and leave nothing in reserve for Turkey.[27]

The Greek refusal; the dangers posed to Benghazi, and to the troops themselves, by diverting; the difficulty of finding troops, all of whom were already 'fully employed'; the practical impossibilities of diverting: all these factors encouraged Dill, just before leaving on his mission, to be more resolute for Turkey than for Greece – though how far he pressed the politicians is unclear.

He told the chiefs on the 10th that the Greeks 'had refused our offer of assistance in Macedonia and it was unlikely that we could now spare any

[25] Dill to Wavell, 8 Jan. 1941, Connell, *Wavell*, p. 309; Dill to Wavell, 11 Jan. 1941, PREM 3/309/1.
[26] Dill to Montgomery Massingberd, 19 Jan. 1941, MM 160/15; Dill to Wavell, 29 Jan. 1941, PREM 3/309/1. Dill had also been concerned to stop enemy reinforcements from Italy to North Africa and wanted 'high priority ... to any measures calculated to stop or interfere', chiefs of staff, 2 Jan. 1941, COS(41)4, CAB 79/8. Simultaneously he planned for the steady despatch of troops, Dill memo 'convoys', COS(41)5, CAB 79/8.
[27] Dill to Montgomery Massingberd, 12 Feb. 1941, MM 160/16; Dill to Heywood, 6 Feb. 1941, PREM 3/309/1; Dill to Wavell, 7 Feb. 1941, WO 106/2144.

troops to help them'. Assistance to Turkey was 'of greater importance'.[28] In face of the feeling in favour of priority for Greece at the defence committee which agreed on his and Eden's mission, Dill was 'inclined to say our first obligation is to Turkey'.[29] Moreover he continued to allude to the practical difficulties of finding forces not already 'fully employed'. It would, he claimed when discussing the size of the force which could be found from Egypt for Greece, be 'difficult for ... Wavell to find four divisions in the immediate future to send to Greece'. Except for three divisions – the 2nd armoured, the New Zealand and the 6th British, all Wavell's trained and equipped formations 'were already engaged in operations'. In his view, 'all the troops in the Middle East [were] fully employed, and ... none [were] available for Greece'.[30] What was, or was likely to be, available would, Wavell now warned, depend on 'arrival of equipment and troops ... [in] passage and ... progress of operations in East Africa' – while the 'limiting factor in sending force to Greece [was] likely to be shipping and escort'.[31] Whether he held out amongst the politicians is unclear. Certainly at the war office, he seemed vehemently opposed. He regarded the policy as 'unsound', thought the government was 'trying to force an unsound policy down Wavell's throat, and down the throats of the Greeks and Turks' and that 'it would be playing into [German] hands ... to send our forces to the European side of the Mediterranean at this stage of the war', that they were 'certain to be annihilated or driven out again'. Moreover, the dispersion of forces 'would leave the vital centres of Egypt and Palestine unduly exposed to attack'. Though it had been argued that British prestige would suffer in America if they did not go to the rescue of Greece, 'it would suffer still more in the end when we failed as we were convinced we would do'.[32] Dill did not want to go to the Middle East, and before leaving gave it as his view that 'all the troops in the Middle East [were] fully employed, and that none [were] available for Greece'.[33] But in any case he wired Wavell on the 11th that the 'general feeling' was that assistance to Greece and/or Turkey must come first. No serious operations beyond Benghazi should

[28] Chiefs of staff, 10 Feb. 1941, COS(41)47, CAB 79/9.
[29] Cadogan diary, 10 Feb. 1941.
[30] Defence committee, 11 Feb. 1941, DO(41)8, CAB 69/2; Kennedy, *Business of War*, 11 Feb. 1941, pp. 74–5.
[31] Wavell to Dill, 11 Feb. 1941, WO 106/2144.
[32] Kennedy, *Business of War*, pp. 75–6; Kennedy's account of the substance of a talk with Dill on the day of his departure in which Kennedy associates himself with Dill's views. These tally, even as far as the same words being used, with the wire to Wavell of 7 Feb., where Dill referred to the danger of exposing Egypt, leaving nothing for Turkey and being annihilated and driven out. Dill to Wavell, 7 Feb. 1941, WO 106/2144.
[33] As reported to Kennedy, Kennedy, *Business of War*, pp. 74–5.

be undertaken; and the commanders must prepare 'to send the largest possible land and air forces from Africa to the European continent ... to assist the Greeks against a ... German attack'.[34]

After Dill left for the Middle East, Haining acted in his place.[35] Rather than come down in favour of Greece, or Turkey, Haining's intention was to uphold the status quo as far as existing supplies and equipment went, pending the discussions. Of the 50 per cent of equipment sent to overseas theatres, mainly the Middle East, some 5 per cent found its way to Turkey.[36]

It may be that at the war office after Dill's departure, the view continued to be that the lead should be taken from the politicians (modified as this might be by the advice of Eden and Dill), despite the war office's inclination to concentrate on Turkey. Thus the general staff, according to Kennedy, considered by 16 February that they ought not to waste efforts on Greece; that a political front in the Balkans was 'no use unless ... backed up by an effective military front' which was impossible because Balkan countries were so ill equipped and Britain had not 'sufficient forces'; that the 'real bastion' of our position there was Turkey; that 'nothing we can do can make the Greek business a sound military proposition'. And yet, despite this, the war office was resigned to acquiesce in the consensus. Once Dill and Wavell wired in favour of going ahead the chiefs advised on 24 February that 'on balance ... the enterprise should go forward'.[37] How far Kennedy (who thought this wrong) pressed his case is not clear. Kennedy maintained, at least in retrospect, that the cabinet 'had never asked for or received a purely military view from either the chiefs or Wavell'. All the service advice on the problem had been coloured by political considerations.[38] It is not clear whether

---

[34] Dill to Wavell, 11 Feb. 1941 in Connell, *Wavell*, p. 327; chiefs of staff to CsinCME, no. 56, 12 Feb. 1941, PREM 3/309/2.

[35] In Brooke's view, Haining was a 'poor substitute' for Dill; might 'make some mistakes'; and would 'want watching', Brooke diary, 17 Feb. 1941.

[36] Chiefs of staff, 15 Feb. 1941, COS(41)56, CAB 79/9. Of the equipment output, 40 per cent was retained at home; 10 per cent went to India, 50 per cent went to the overseas theatres, mainly the Middle East – of which 5 per cent found its way to Turkey.

[37] After staying at Dytchley on 15/16 February when he reviewed the situation for Churchill, Kennedy dictated a long note of the 'gist of [his] talk' with the prime minister, explaining that it represented 'the views of the General Staff at this time'. Kennedy, *Business of War*, pp. 81–5. Cabinet, 24 Feb. 1941, WM(41)20, CAB 65/21. The chiefs' view was reported to the cabinet, their report on policy in the Middle East having been agreed that morning for circulation to the cabinet. Chiefs of staff, 24 Feb. 1941, COS(41)67, CAB 79/9.

[38] Kennedy, *Business of War*, p. 85. The discussion amongst the chiefs beginning at 4.45 p.m. on 23 February, which broke to consider preparation of the report for the cabinet, itself may have been influenced by Churchill's views. The minutes record that during the discussion 'instructions were received by telephone from the prime minister', chiefs of staff, 23 Feb. 1941, COS(41)66, CAB 79/9.

such a point was made explicitly during any of the discussions. Indeed, had it been made at the outset, it would not have been thought to matter. The chiefs had been told by Churchill in early January that it would fail, but there was no choice but to go in. Greece was, and was seen to be, a hopeless venture. None the less something, it was thought, ought to be done for political reasons. In time, however, for a variety of reasons the chiefs and professionals, no less than the politicians, came to regard Greece as militarily a hopeful prospect (see below, pp. 219–56) and the military considerations tended to overlap with the political exigencies.

Pound

Pound's concern was for the lines of communication between Egypt, Greece and Turkey, which were endangered by the German presence in the Mediterranean. He wanted to secure Benghazi and the Dodecanese in order to safeguard Alexandria. The advent of the German air force had, by late January, 'altered the picture very considerably' and would make Cunningham's task 'a much more difficult one'.[39] It was 'essential ... to get Benghazi and the Dodecanese ... [to safeguard] position at Alexandria ... and also so that lines of communication from Egypt to either Greece or Turkey [were] cleared'.[40]

Pound was not clear what Hitler's next move would be 'as regards Spain, Vichy and the Balkans'.[41] With Portal, he seemed to favour the Greek project, the implications of which, for the navy, were unambiguous. The chiefs' instruction to the Middle East command (of 12 February) to give priority to diverting to Greece would involve plans for 'the collection of the necessary shipping for the move of the maximum forces to Greece at the earliest possible moment'.[42] Pound continued to support the Greek operation though he also made play (as he did on 7 March) of the 'new facts' and fresh difficulties since 24 February. 'Our shipping difficulties had increased'; in particular the Suez Canal was being 'put out of action for considerable periods by mining from the air' and they must also expect 'mining at Pyraeus and Vol which would increase the difficulties of disembarkation and of maintaining supply'.[43] But he did not speak

[39] Pound to Cunningham, 27 Jan. 1941; BL Add. MS. 52561.   [40] Ibid.
[41] He thought the situation was 'most involved in many directions as we do not know what Hitler's intentions are'. Pound to Cunningham, 8 Feb. 1941, BL Add. MS. 52561.
[42] Kennedy, *Business of War*, pp. 75–6; chiefs of staff to CsinCME, 12 Feb. 1941, PREM 3/309/2.
[43] Cabinet, 7 Mar. 1941, WM(41)26, CAB 65/22. Alexander, on 5 March, had thought that Hitler's message was significant; that he was waiting until he knew what the Turkish action would be if the Germans moved into Greece; and as soon as he was certain an ultimatum would be delivered to Greece. Cabinet, 5 Mar. 1941, WM(41)24, CAB 65/22.

out against the diversions and saw the Mediterranean as a problem of communication lines to be kept open by the navy.[44]

Portal

Portal began by urging support for the Greeks. In early January, German forces were being assembled in Romania and Portal warned Longmore that 'an early advance on Thrace through Bulgaria [did] not seem improbable'. The 'most probable immediate development' would be the passage of armoured and air forces into Bulgaria, and from there a rapid drive on Salonika supported by dive bombers 'blast[ing] ... through Greek defences unless we helped'.[45] He insisted on help for the endangered Greeks. An imminent German advance through Bulgaria – and the Italian success in Albania – made the danger more urgent. Longmore must divert substantially from North Africa. Portal 'fully appreciate[d]' Longmore's reluctance 'to interrupt successful chase of Italians in Libya and other operations in Africa, but for political reasons priority must now be given to helping Greece' – over whom hung the immediate 'threat of German invasion via Bulgaria, besides the future menace of Italian counter-attack in Albania'.[46] The effect of standing by would be serious – not only on Greece, but on Turkey, and on opinion. The 'absence of British help might put Greece out of the war, keep Turkey out and cause most serious political consequences both here and in America'.[47] Whether a 'major threat' to Greece developed or not, Portal maintained that success in that theatre would 'far exceed in value anything that can be done against Italy in Africa after capture of Tobruk'.[48] Even if the Germans were late and the advance was not 'as early as ... hitherto ... suggested'; or even if they did not come and 'were bluffing', none the less 'any assistance which we sent to the Greeks would be of great value to them in their campaign in Albania'.[49]

Portal pressed, at the outset, not for small parcels, but for substantial help for which Longmore must make the necessary arrangements. He doubted that the despatch of merely two Gladiator squadrons would 'do

---

[44] Pound to Cunningham, 8 Feb. 1941, BL Add. MS. 52561. Pound thought the capture of Benghazi 'most satisfactory' although it would increase the naval commitment 'as regards maintaining [it] by sea', but it did remove 'a considerable part of the air menace from Alexandria'.

[45] Portal to Longmore, 8 Jan., 9 Jan. 1941, PREM 3/309/1.   [46] Ibid.   [47] Ibid.

[48] Portal to Longmore, 11 Jan. 1941, PREM 3/309/1.

[49] Chiefs of staff, 11 Jan. 1941, COS(41)15, CAB 79/8. Portal explained to the chiefs of staff that reports had come indicating that JU88 and long range fighters were to be removed to Romania in the near future. 'This supported the view that an advance through Bulgaria was contemplated, but not as early as had hitherto been suggested.'

any good'. Longmore should consider instead 'two or three squadrons Hurricanes and one or two squadrons Blenheim IV'.[50] He would be 'glad' to know the 'broad proposals after forthcoming discussions with Greeks' and Longmore should 'proceed with aerodrome preparations, immediately, if Greeks ... agree'.[51] By the 16th there were four squadrons operating in Greece, two more on their way from Egypt and a further one due to leave once weather permitted. Metaxas had been pressed as to the need for aerodromes capable of receiving a maximum of fourteen squadrons south and west of Mount Olympus. The Salonika area would be used by the Greek air force.[52] Though he acknowledged that operations in Africa might as a result be 'limited, or even stopped' diversions were of 'extreme importance and urgency' and he urged 'the need for making plans at once'.[53]

In pressing for Greece, Portal anticipated the preparation of Balkan bases which would not only serve to hamper a German advance, but could be used to bomb Romanian oil. Therefore, when in late January it was decided to offer support to Turkey, Portal quite logically changed his priorities. He saw the infiltration of Turkish air as his priority after Libya – a means of threatening Romanian oil, defending Constantinople and Smyrna and supporting Turkish military operations in Thrace against southward advance by Hitler. The Turks might 'allow us [to] infiltrate air forces into Turkey forthwith' (as the Germans were doing in Bulgaria) to the extent of ten or fifteen squadrons. Despatch, which would be subject to 'stabilised situation in Libya' would take priority over operations against East Africa, Abyssinia, Sicily and over 'further assistance to Greece'.[54] If the Turks accepted the proposal, Portal wanted preparations to proceed 'as quickly as possible'.[55] He emphasised for Longmore's benefit that when Cyrenaica was secure, 'the despatch of air forces to Turkey [was] of greater importance than anything except Malta and Mandibles'. The question was not of impressing the Turks, but 'of trying to deter Germany by fear of bombing Roumania, from absorbing Bulgaria, Greece and Turkey without firing a shot' and then 'dominating the Eastern Mediterranean and Aegean'. If that could be prevented or

50 Portal to Longmore, 9 Jan. 1941, PREM 3/309/1.
51 Portal to Longmore, 11 Jan. 1941, PREM 3/309/1.
52 Portal to prime minister, 17 Jan. 1941, Portal:1:1941:1.
53 Portal to Longmore, 9 Jan. 1941, PREM 3/309/1.
54 Of the 10 to 15 fighter squadrons Portal envisaged, there would be 3 fighters, 4 Blenheims, 3 Wellingtons at first, possibly followed later by 2 more fighters and 3 more Blenheim squadrons from Greece. Portal to Longmore, 30 Jan. 1941, PREM 3/309/1.
55 Ibid.

delayed then the squadrons in Turkey would have 'far more weight than in helping to beat Italians in Africa'.[56]

In addition to wanting to fight the Germans, rather than the Italians, there were practical reasons for concentrating on Turkey and for not trying to help, simultaneously, both Greece and Turkey. The case for Turkey rather than Greece was made in terms of meeting the Germans rather than the Italians. 'So long as Germany [did] not invade Greece' then the operation of squadrons there would merely be against the Italians; squadrons in Turkey, however, 'will be preparing against move by Germans'.[57] The Turks had been promised ten squadrons and they 'must prepare to send all ten'. Greece had been promised only one more; and Longmore must 'carefully avoid any further commitment'. Otherwise it would be difficult for one headquarters to keep 'closely enough in touch with both Greek and Turkish authorities'. It was not evident that the Greeks could hold out against the Germans 'either Thracian frontier or Olympus–Arta line' and the 'very early withdrawal of [Longmore's] units in Greece [would] be essential either to Turkey ... or ... to area south of Lamia-Lepanto line' that is, if Longmore believed the Greeks could hold out against the Germans.[58] If the deterrent succeeded and the Germans did not advance into Macedonia, then the 'question of sending units across from Turkey to help Greece against Italy might arise', but that would be dealt with at the time.[59]

But Portal did not remain set on the Turks, because he could not count on them. If they were to accept after seeing Eden, well and good; but they might not. Their replies had been non-committal – and time was running out. By 10 February he returned to the prospect of Greece. It was 'important ... [to] know what the Greeks intended to do if the Germans advance into Greece and what they expected of us'. The Greeks 'apparently thought that strong British reinforcements would arrive at the critical moment'. Aerodromes in Greece were being improved; but they might be of use to the Germans and 'our six squadrons might be in some jeopardy' in the case of a German advance.[60] By the 12th he seemed (to Dill) to have settled for Greece, arguing that the air force should be given a platform in Greece from which to bomb the Germans in Romania and Italy.[61] The same day, with Dill and Pound, he sent the formal instructions to the Middle East. The only way of making sure 'that the Turks do fight is to give sufficient support to the Greeks to ensure that they fight'.

[56] Portal to Longmore, 31 Jan. 1941, PREM 3/309/1.
[57] Portal to Longmore, 8 Feb. 1941, PREM 3/309/1.
[58] Portal to Longmore, 8 Feb. 1941, PREM 3/309/1.   [59] Ibid.
[60] Chiefs of staff, 10 Feb. 1941, COS(41)47, CAB 79/7.
[61] Kennedy, *Business of War*, p. 76.

As regards the size of forces from Egypt, no more could be said at this stage 'than [that] they should be as strong as possible, and that the ten squadrons RAF ... originally earmarked for Turkey, [could] be drawn upon'.[62]

Once he came down again in favour of Greece, he wanted immediate help for them. He referred Longmore to the appeal from the Greeks 'for immediate air assistance ... in their battle in Albania'. And despite his having deprecated using the air force against the Italians (in Albania or north Africa) he now suggested that Longmore should do what he could; he would render 'such immediate help as [he was] able'. Portal would be 'glad to hear ... what immediate help [Longmore could] send'.[63] He was reluctant to accede to a Turkish request for anti-aircraft equipment and stores of bombs and aircraft spares, pending the discussions 'due ... in the near future', for if the equipment were despatched without personnel, 'the Turks would tend to regard it as due under existing arrangements and might claim it as their own'.[64]

Portal's calculations of the air position in Greece may have prompted him to throw his weight behind proceeding – especially as nothing could be done with the Turks. He may by then have abandoned all hope of getting the Turks to co-operate in time; and may have calculated that, given the German delay in transporting aircraft, they might well take the chance. Already in Greece they had seven squadrons and Longmore hoped to raise this to fourteen (possibly sixteen) during March.[65] By 6 March there were a total of ten-and-a-half fighter squadrons in the Middle East, of which three were in Greece and one flight in Crete. 'We had five bomber squadrons in Greece.'[66] Further reinforcements to Greece would depend on other operations. By the end of the month, if not sooner, Longmore hoped to form two new fighter squadrons. Germany, it was thought on 24 February, would take some time to develop the full weight of her air effort from Bulgaria; and though the total strength of the German air force in Romania was between 400 and 500, 120 of these were co-operational aircraft and 'we should have about 250 machines'.[67] By

62 Chiefs of staff to Wavell, 12 Feb. 1941, PREM 3/309/2.
63 Portal to Longmore, 13 Feb. 1941, PREM 3/309/2. Portal thought that this might possibly include the despatch of No. 33 squadron previously promised and use of Wellingtons from aerodromes near Athens against Italian aerodromes and Port of Valona.
64 Chiefs of staff, 15 Feb. 1941, COS(41)56, CAB 79/9.
65 Cabinet, 24 Feb. 1941, WM(41)20, CAB 65/21.
66 Cabinet, 6 Mar. 1941, WM(41)25, CAB 65/22.
67 Ibid.; Cabinet, 24 Feb. 1941, WM(41)20, CAB 65/21.

6 March the Germans had a total of 475 aircraft in Romania (of which 160 were fighters and 160 bombers).[68]

Had Portal thought these margins dangerous, he might not have gone ahead, despite his desire at the outset for bases to deter the German advance. He may have thought there was nothing else to be done – and may have been prompted by the Axis pact. By 6 March the Bulgarians had definitely signed – thereby opening the way for a bloodless German domination from which to threaten Greece and Turkey. Given that the Turks had done nothing and that the Greeks, despite all, were still fighting, willing to fight and to co-operate, Greece offered the only chance. By 24 February (and more certainly by 6 March) intervention in Greece seemed to offer the only way of continuing with the preparation and establishment of the Balkan bases. If the Greeks were abandoned, or gave up without a fight, they would not withstand the Germans; the air force could not operate from Greece; and the Turks were less likely than *ever* to co-operate. Portal's message to Longmore to do what he could for the Greeks in Albania had in the same sense modified the earlier view that the air force should fight the Germans not the Italians. For only if the Greeks succeeded in holding out against the Italians could Portal secure the bases he wanted against the Germans. There was no sign that the Turks would co-operate and there was no time to wait for them to do so. The bases were needed urgently and preparations should be made. Portal's scheme for bases came, *faute de mieux*, to depend on Greece; and once this was so, Portal was prepared to lend whatever support he could to intervention in Greece. He may have succeeded because he had a view on the object of intervention – when others differed about political, diplomatic, military aims – and because Churchill regarded him as the 'real strategist' – a man with 'diplomatic as well as strategical insight'.[69]

---

[68] Cabinet, 6 Mar. 1941, WM(41)25, CAB 65/22.
[69] Kennedy, *Business of War*, pp. 75–6; Brooke diary, 4 Feb. 1941; Dalton diary, 4 Feb. 1941.

12 The Middle East command and the Greek decision

Wavell

Wavell's plans were for the desert, not the Balkans or Turkey. He hoped to exploit his success now that the Italians were on the run. He wanted to extend operations to Tobruk and perhaps on to Benghazi. He might go as far as Tripoli, though that would tie up his forces in North Africa to the exclusion of their fighting elsewhere. At first, he was filled with dismay about the instructions to divert to Greece, which would neither help the Greeks nor stop the Germans, if they came, which in any case they might not. He did not, however, refuse to divert, though he thought a Greek refusal should be accepted; and he intended to warn the Greeks that if they refused there might be nothing for them later. As for Turkey, he did not think she would accept the offer, which would seem a mere drop in the ocean. Once Eden and Dill arrived he abandoned what remained of his opposition to diverting.

Wavell intended to extend his operations to Tobruk, and perhaps Benghazi; and, while the Italians were on the run, to exploit his success. In early January he planned 'to move on to Tobruk' as soon as Bardia had been 'mopped up' and investigate an advance from Tobruk towards Benghazi.[1] Reluctant to curtail his successful Libyan advance (or abandon his Sudan offensive) he thought they must 'continue . . . advance in Cyrenaica while [they had] the Italians on the run'.[2] An advance to Benghazi would help both the navy and air force 'by driving back enemy air bases and by giving ports and air bases for our own use'.[3]

Wavell, therefore, was 'fill[ed] . . . with dismay' by the instructions on 10 January that operations in Libya must be 'subordinated to aiding

---

[1] Wavell to Smith, 5 Jan. 1941, Connell, *Wavell*, pp. 302–3; Cunningham to Pound, 5 Jan. 1941, BL Add. MS. 52561.
[2] Longmore to Portal, 9 Jan. 1941, PREM 3/309/1; Wavell to Dill, 9 Jan. 1941, Connell, *Wavell*, pp. 309–10.
[3] Wavell to Dill, 18 Jan. 1941, PREM 3/309/1.

Greece'.[4] This would have a dangerous effect on Libya, but without stopping the Germans – if they came. The German concentrations were designed, he thought, to help Italy by inducing Britain 'to disperse ... in Middle East and ... stop ... advance in Libya'. He was, as a result, 'desperately anxious lest we play the enemy's game and expose ourselves to defeat'.[5] The shortages in the Middle East were already at a dangerous level; convoys had been cut and instead of rapid and progressive increases to his forces, the drafts and units 'essential to keep even present force in being' were being cut.[6] Anti-aircraft and fighter shortages were 'the most serious factor' in the Middle East and if 'still further dispersed by [the] Salonika commitment [they would] be weak everywhere, with none of [our] ports, bases and other vulnerable points properly protected'.[7] Further demands would render Wavell's desert advance impossible and weaken his offensive capacity. The situation for forward troops was 'becoming most dangerous and any further advance impossible'.[8]

Apart from the implications they would pose for Libya, diversions to Greece would not help Greece. Rather, the advance in Cyrenaica would indirectly 'help ... more than sending small additional amount of transport'. Intervention in Salonika would halt the Libyan advance, give the Italians time to recover; and it would lead to further demands, or else 'retreat or defeat'.[9]

Either the help would make little difference to the Greeks or it would be wasted if the Germans did not come, for 'Nothing' could be done from the Middle East 'in time to stop German advance if really intended'.[10] The number of troops would not enable 'the equivalent of three Greek divisions to hold Salonika if the Germans [were] really determined to advance on it'.[11] What was proposed amounted to no more than 'a dangerous half measure'. Nor was Wavell convinced that the Germans would come – in which case the troops would be locked up to no avail. The Germans might hesitate to enter Bulgaria lest 'by doing away with Bulgarian neutrality ... Roumanian oilfields [were exposed] to bombing

[4] Wavell to Dill, 10 Jan. 1941, PREM 3/309/1. Churchill to Wavell and Longmore, 11 Jan. 1941, appended to COS(41)15, CAB 79/8. Wavell, who suggested Longmore shared his views ('It fills us with dismay'), was commenting on Portal to Longmore(X 744) of January 9th: 'for political reasons priority must now be given to helping Greece ... ', which preceded formal instructions from the chiefs of staff. Portal to Longmore, 9 Jan. 1941, PREM 3/309/1.
[5] Wavell to Dill, 10 Jan. 1941, PREM 3/309/1.
[6] Wavell to Dill, 18 Jan. 1941, PREM 3/309/1.
[7] Ibid.   [8] ibid.
[9] Wavell to Dill, 9 Jan. 1941, Connell, *Wavell*, pp. 309–10; Wavell to Dill, 18 Jan. 1941, PREM 3/309/1.
[10] Wavell to Dill, 10 Jan. 1941, PREM 3/309/1.
[11] Wavell to Dill, 18 Jan. 1941, PREM 3/309/1.

attack'; 'Germany's fears in this respect may deter her'.[12] The Greeks themselves considered (by 10 January) that 'a German advance now most unlikely' and 'almost impossible owing to the condition of the roads', that German concentrations were designed 'to warn both ourselves and Russians off', and they might be seen as preparatory steps 'in case they [were] forced to intervene but not as showing any immediate intention of doing so'.[13] If it turned out that this was so and the Germans did not come, then the troops sent to Salonika would be 'locked up to no purpose' and it would be physically impossible 'to employ them to assist Greeks in Albania and then transfer them to Salonika in time'.[14]

However, in spite of all these considerations, at no stage did Wavell refuse to help Greece, or exclude the prospect of doing so; though if the Greeks turned help down, he would leave it at that. He was, for example, willing to ship captured Italian equipment, transport, guns and ammunition to Greece as early as possible and would 'increase such assistance as far as we can'. Despite Wavell's being 'urgently in need of' much the same things as the Greeks, he promised to do 'all we can to help [the] Greeks'.[15] He would co-operate with the instructions to despatch to Greece and if the Greeks accepted the proposed units would send the 'utmost available'. However, they should 'accept' Greek refusal and make all necessary reconnaissance and preparations of the Salonika front 'without giving any promise to send troops at future date'.[16] Wavell explained to the king that the British government 'did not propose to press the Greek government', though he warned him (the king of Greece) that Britain, which considered a German attack on Salonika more imminent than did the Greeks, did not understand the refusal of help. Help 'could not and would not be provided in a hurried manner'; and if, in an emergency, the Greeks asked for help, the units offered now 'might not be available later'.[17]

Along with the other commanders, Wavell expected that 'demands for air assistance ... [were] bound to follow' simultaneously with the Middle East position's becoming more dangerous. Whereas 'risks ha[d] been

12 Wavell to Dill, 18 Jan. 1941, PREM 3/309/1.
13 Wavell to Dill, 10 Jan. 1941, PREM 3/309/1.
14 Wavell to Dill, 18 Jan. 1941, PREM 3/309/1.
15 Wavell to Dill, 9 Jan. 1941, Connell, *Wavell*, pp. 309–10; Wavell to Dill, 10 Jan. 1941, PREM 3/309/1.
16 Wavell to Dill, 18 Jan. 1941 (0/36206 of 18/1), PREM 3/309/1.
17 Wavell to Dill, 18 Jan. 1941 (0/36091 of 17/1), PREM 3/309/1. When the king inquired what units were available, Wavell indicated he could supply two regiments of field artillery, one or two regiments of medium artillery, one regiment cruiser tanks and probably not more than one or two batteries of anti-aircraft artillery. When he asked whether any infantry formations would be sent, Wavell said he had 'no authority for any'.

justifiable against an unenterprising enemy' that would change 'when dealing with German forces'.[18] Not only did the commanders feel that the capture of Benghazi and the reduction of the Dodecanese was of 'utmost importance', they also considered that if Greece abandoned the war with Italy 'under threat from Germany', then 'immediate action to safeguard our interests in the Aegean' should be taken and the policy of holding Crete 'should still hold good'.[19] In spite of the Greek refusal and his own reluctance to press them, Wavell could not rule out the prospect of having to divert to the Balkans. Although he thought Tripoli might be possible after Benghazi and might 'yield to small force if despatched without undue delay', he hesitated to advance further 'in view of [the] Balkan situation'.[20]

By 10 February, Wavell probably expected that there would be some diversion, even though the Greeks had refused help and the Turks had not committed themselves. His 'available reserves' for Greece or Turkey would be one armoured and two other brigades now and further brigades in mid-March and April.[21] They would depend on the arrival of equipment and troops and might be modified by the progress of operations in East Africa. There would be 'sufficient' administrative and base units but not anti-aircraft units – only enough 'to give a low scale protection to our forces in Greece even if no such units are sent to Turkey'.[22] The limiting factor in sending force to Greece was likely to be 'shipping and escort' and that would also affect 'building up reserve of supplies and ammunition at Piraeus and Volos'.[23]

Nonetheless, by the time Eden and Dill left London, Wavell, who would prefer to proceed to Tripoli, expected that the Balkan situation would precipitate another course. Though the Greeks had refused land forces and the Turks would not commit themselves, Wavell assumed there would be a diversion. He had, from the first instruction to give Greece priority, made his objections clear; he had warned of the consequences for Libya and the futility for Greece of diverting. But he had in the end acquiesced; begun to consider what he could afford to send; and had been to Athens to discuss plans with the Greeks. Even after they had turned

[18] Wavell to war office with CsinCME to chiefs of staff, 27 Jan. 1941 (0/37843 of 27/1), WO 216/2.
[19] Ibid.; Wavell to war office, 27 Jan. 1941 (0/37842 of 27/1), PREM 3/309/1.
[20] Wavell to Dill, 10 Feb. 1941, PREM 3/309/1. Wavell's hopes were due to the extent of the Italian defeat at Benghazi.
[21] Wavell to Dill, 11 Feb. 1941, WO 106/2144. One armoured brigade group, New Zealand division, two brigades now; mid-March another armoured brigade group, New Zealand division, complete and Australian division of two brigades only, probably complete by mid-April. Another Australian division would be available at the end of April.
[22] Wavell to Dill, 11 Feb. 1941, WO 106/2144.   [23] Ibid.

down help, he knew that was not the end of it. By 11 February – by which time the Turks had been made an offer and had not taken it, and the Greeks had indicated that after all they would take help before the Germans actually crossed their frontiers – Wavell's calculations as to what he could send to Greece and or Turkey may have had something of resignation about them. The news from Ankara by mid-February was that the Turks recognised the 'inevitability of entering the war on our side sooner or later'. They preferred later owing to their present lack of equipment. Wavell considered that the Turkish general staff believed the squadrons, agreed by Churchill, were 'a drop in the ocean' compared with what they thought necessary 'to stem a German air attack on Thrace and on their communications across the straits to Anatolia'. The Germans could deploy 1,500 aircraft against them from Romania and Bulgaria and 1,300 aircraft would be necessary to repel and counter-attack.[24]

Benghazi was now safe and Wavell did not really think he could continue to Tripoli, given the 'Balkan situation'. Not a lot would be sent at the outset – only one armoured brigade group and less than one (New Zealand) division; and in mid-March a further armoured brigade group, the remainder of the New Zealand division and some of the Australian division – to be completed in mid-April, and a further Australian division at the end of April. There could only be limited anti-aircraft units – which would give low-scale protection to forces in Greece – even if nothing went to Turkey. Wavell had, since the first instruction, maintained that nothing they could send in time could stop a German advance in Greece. He did not subsequently retract that claim. The forces he could send and the low level of protection they would have did not suggest that his appreciation had changed. Nonetheless he proposed to instruct the British military mission to examine the problem with the Greek staff on that general basis – if Dill concurred.[25]

Not only did Wavell acquiesce, but he seemed to wish to reassure Churchill of his stout-heartedness. He claimed they had 'been considering problem of assistance to Greece and Turkey for some time'; that he hoped he might be 'able to improve' on the estimate (of reserves) wired on the 11th, particularly if the Australians gave him 'certain latitude as regards use of their troops'. He implied that matters had improved since his visit to Athens when 'Greek plans for defence against Germany were decidedly

---

24 Wavell to war office, 17 Feb. 1941, written 16 Feb. 1941, PREM 3/309/2. They particularly lacked mechanical transport and aircraft and armoured fighting vehicles. The Turks were willing to co-operate in accelerating the aerodrome construction programme and would allow the British to establish and improve base accommodation at Izmir and elsewhere.
25 Wavell to Dill, 11 Feb. 1941, WO 106/2144.

sketchy': for he thought 'they ha[d] been considering them since'. 'We will do our best to frustrate German plans in the Balkans.' He did warn that 'Greek and Turkish hesitations and Yugoslav timidity ha[d] made our task very difficult'. The shipping and ports situation would be 'bound' to make their arrival 'somewhat piecemeal'.[26] But all in all, by the time that Eden set off on his mission to succour Greece, Wavell had abandoned his opposition to helping Greece against Germany.

Cunningham

Like Wavell, Cunningham initially thought the British should concentrate on the Libyan offensive. He had hoped that it would not be interrupted; that the army 'won't stop as they fairly ha[d] them [Italians] on the run'; and that 'the war in this part of the world [should be cleared up] by next summer'. But the demands on the navy were immense. Convoys were being sent through the Sicilian narrows, and to Greece to help against Italian communications. In addition the demands of the Libyan campaign were, by 18 January, 'grow[ing] daily'; though Cunningham hoped they would reach a peak with the fall of Tobruk. Everything was 'going by sea including ... practically all the personnel'; and the strain on destroyers and small auxiliary craft was 'tremendous'. It was 'very difficult to find the right type of shipping for the job'. Small coastal carriers were required 'but there just aren't any'.[27] In addition, convoys were to be run through the Sicilian narrows east and to pass back empty mechanical transport ships; Cunningham also wanted to help the Greeks to 'get a grip on the Italian communication with Tripoli and Benghazi and there were always the convoys to Greece ... [and] ... local escorts for troop ships'.[28]

Despite his own inclination to persist with Libya, Cunningham did not oppose the instructions to divert to Greece – but he did not underestimate the difficulties, particularly for the navy. Cunningham was at sea when the first instructions to divert to Greece arrived and could not, therefore, be consulted 'on shipping question', which was expected to become

---

[26] Wavell to Churchill, 12 Feb. 1941, 0/41285 of 12/2, WO 106/2144. Note Wavell's view by 19 February that sending a force to the Balkans involved considerable risks; although a 'difficult choice ... I think we are more likely to be playing the enemy's game by remaining inactive than by taking action in the Balkans. Provided that conversations with the Greeks show that there is a good chance of establishing a front against the Germans with our assistance I think we should take it.' Wavell note, 19 Feb. 1941, Connell, *Wavell*, pp. 335–6.

[27] Cunningham to his aunt, 5 Jan. 1941, BL Add. MS. 52558; Cunningham to Pound, 18 Jan. 1941, BL Add. MS. 52561.

[28] Cunningham to Pound, 5 Jan. 1941, BL Add. MS. 52561.

'serious ... with [the] appearance [of] German air force in Mediterranean'.[29] He had, by early February, continued to be stretched by the
Libyan campaign (the disadvantages of which to the navy he noted) and
he was under no illusion about the fresh demands which the navy would
face – with Benghazi, the Dodecanese, Turkey, Greece.[30] A 'lot of nonsense [had been] talked about the advantage of Benghazi to the Navy'; the
only one he saw was that they had two hundred miles less of enemy coast.
But it was 'a commitment ... [and] two hundred miles nearer the Italian
bases than ours'.[31] There was, for Cunningham, a limit to what could be
done and the Dodecanese would make for further demands. It would not
be possible for the navy to take on a 'sea line of communication ...
comparable to ... [the distance] between John O'Groats and Lands End'
whilst engaged at the same time in covering Aegean traffic, Malta convoys
and active operations. With the light craft and escort vessels available
there could be no guarantee against interruption. Already the traffic
between Cyprus, Palestine and Egypt had to run unescorted for lack of
escorting vessels.[32] The prospect of diverting aircraft to Turkey would
also affect the navy.[33]

Cunningham agreed on 14 February to give Greece priority, although
he continued to warn of the difficulties. As far as Greece went, he warned
of the 'two obstacles to [its] execution'. If the Germans operated their
air-force from Bulgaria, then shipping in the North Aegean would be
'gravely threatened by bombing and in ports such as Salonika and their
approaches by aircraft mine laying'.[34] Fighter protection – of troop and
store convoys – was also a problem 'to provide and organise ... from
Greece, which ha[d] few developed landing grounds and where scale of
attack [would] be high'. He would do his best to get the convoys through;
but they 'must be prepared for casualties to ships and troops'. The 'more
serious' difficulties – of the magnetic and acoustic mine threat – also
struck Cunningham. He considered that it would be 'illusory' to embark
on this undertaking 'without facing facts that mine risks are considerable

29 Wavell to Dill, 13 Jan. 1941, PREM 3/309/1.
30 Cunningham to Pound, 6, 10 Feb. 1941, BL Add. MS. 52561. He had had doubts about
   the turn the Libyan campaign had taken; and the inferiority of British tanks, tank tactics
   and the absence of fighting spirit. He pressed Wavell to hold a line 'as far forward as
   possible'; thought Benghazi a 'magnificent piece of work' by the army, though the navy
   had been 'stretched to the limit and past it' in keeping them supplied.
31 Cunningham to Pound, 10 Feb. 1941, BL Add. MS. 52561.
32 Whereas reinforcements and equipment expected over the next month would help the
   army meet the commitments of the capture of Benghazi and the reduction of the
   Dodecanese, that would not apply to the navy or the air force. Commanders in chief to
   commanding officer, conveyed in Wavell to war office, 27 Jan. 1941, WO 216/2.
33 Longmore to Portal, 31 Jan. 1941, PREM 3/309/1.
34 Cunningham to admiralty, 14 Feb. 1941, PREM 3/309/2.

and that my reserves for combating them are extremely slender'.[35] Whilst Cunningham recognised jointly with the commanders that the Greek situation and steps to counter German infiltration into Bulgaria now had 'highest priority', from the naval point of view 'the new policy create[d] a heavy commitment in safeguarding the line of supply through Aegean'. It would entail 'establishing bases in Greek islands and Turkey'. They were, they claimed (recalling Cunningham's wire of 7 February) 'already completely extended in so far as ... present resources [were] concerned in covering the long lines of sea communication on Libyan coasts and in dealing with protection of Libya' – in addition to Mediterranean bases. If the Balkan situation developed 'the present acute shortage in light craft escorts, local defence units and personnel for shore bases [would] become critical' unless resources continued to be built up as rapidly as possible.[36]

Longmore

Although in the autumn Longmore had taken the initiative to send token air support to Greece when the Italians attacked, this had not meant that he supported 'priority' for Greece. On the contrary. In principle he recognised that Greece should have help, but in practice he thought the air force should support the army campaign against the Italians in North Africa. He was dismayed by the instructions to give priority to Greece, and then by those for Turkey. He did not think they should count on there being a German advance on the Balkans and Greece; and in any case they could not stop it if it came. Not only would diversion be futile for Greece, but it would have grave consequences for Libya. Yet Longmore, like Wavell, did not refuse outright; and having made his objections known, he acquiesced in the plans and preparations.

Longmore's concern in early January, like Wavell's, was for North Africa, not the Balkans or Turkey. He thought, on 10 January, priority for Greece was 'a most dangerous proposal' – given the air forces 'actually at [his] disposal' and the two fighter squadrons he would form 'when sufficient reinforcements arrive[d]'.[37] Next, he was (at the end of January) 'astounded' by the prospect of diverting ten to fifteen squadrons to infiltrate air forces in Turkey.[38] The squadrons would be out of use at a

---

[35] Ibid.
[36] Commanders in chief to chiefs of staff, 14 Feb. 1941, in reply to COS no. 53, PREM 3/309/2.
[37] Wavell to Dill, 10 Jan. 1941, PREM 3/309/1; Longmore to Portal, 10 Jan. 1941, PREM 3/309/1.
[38] Portal to Longmore, 30 Jan. 1941, PREM 3/309/1; Longmore to Portal, 31 Jan. 1941, PREM 3/309/1.

time when they were most needed. Portal could not have 'fully appreciate[d] the present situation in Middle East in which Libyan drive in full
career' – and the Sudan offensive (into Eritrea) was 'progressing satisfactorily'. Neither operation showed signs of 'immediate stabilisation'.[39]
Diversion would leave the army without supporting air force – especially
grave given that reinforcements did not match casualties – and the
advance rendered impossible. The Italians could take their chance to
reinforce and reorganize.

Although he 'fully realise[d]' the need for 'further assistance to [th]e
Greeks' he did not concede that they could 'further denude the air force
... supporting the British army round Tobruk'. They were still 'chas[ing]
the Italian Air Force in Libya'.[40] Moreover, he was reluctant to commit
himself to a programme for later, and the withdrawal of squadrons from
Libya would endanger the position of the forward troops and make
'further advance impossible'; it would also bring 'army operations in
Libya to a standstill' and 'far more dangerous, ... give time for [the]
Italians to ... reinforce their air forces in Libya'.[41] By the end of January,
neither the Libyan drive nor the Sudan offensive into Eritrea showed
signs of immediate stabilisation. Cunningham was emphasising the need
for 'defeat of German air forces in Mediterranean as first consideration.
Moreover, Longmore was unhappy about the pace of reinforcement – the
number of aircraft arriving in the Middle East was 'hardly keeping pace
with casualties'.[42] The danger that Italian resistance in Libya might be
stiffened as a result of German or Italian reinforcement existed; and the
presence of German aircraft made Longmore 'unwilling to denude completely ... the naval base ... at Alexandria and Delta area' of fighter
defence. He proposed therefore to delay the departure for Greece of the
No. 33 Hurricane squadron 'until the situation in Greece and Libya ha[d]
further clarified'.[43]

Longmore did not think the air force should be sent to Turkey for a
hypothetical event. No matter how strong the political advantages might
be 'of impressing the Turks', could they 'really afford to lock up the
squadrons ... propose[d] in Turkey' where they might remain inoperative
for some time – even against the Dodecanese – 'until the Turks declare[d]
their hand'? Would that not be 'foreaking the substance for the shadow'?

[39]   Longmore to Portal, 31 Jan. 1941, PREM 3/309/1.
[40]   Longmore to Churchill, 9 Jan. 1941, PREM 3/309/1.
[41]   Wavell to Dill, 10 Jan. 1941, PREM 3/309/1; Longmore to Portal, 9 Jan. 1941, PREM
       3/309/1; Longmore to Portal, 10 Jan. 1941, PREM 3/309/1.
[42]   Longmore to Portal, 31 Jan. 1941, PREM 3/309/1.
[43]   Longmore to Churchill, 9 Jan. 1941, PREM 3/309/1. Longmore to Portal, 19 Jan. 1941,
       PREM 3/309/1. The presence of German aircraft was confirmed on 19 January 'though
       numbers [were] yet unknown'.

(Besides the squadrons being needed elsewhere, Longmore had 'not sufficient personnel or stocks of bombs to disperse them in Turkey'.) Like Wavell, he did not at first concede that the Germans did intend to attack Greece. The concentrations were a 'move in [a] war of nerves' designed to induce the British to disperse 'and stop our advance in Libya'.[44] A German attack was 'considered here [to be] ... unlikely to arise during the winter'. These reports of an imminent German drive through the Balkans to Greece may have been inspired 'for the very purpose of relieving our pressure on the Italians in Libya as well as to compromise the Greek offensive in Albania'.[45] Diversions, which would have dangerous consequences for Libya, might be unnecessary (as an attack was unlikely during the winter) and foolish (British dispersal might be precisely the object of the enemy). Even if the Germans were to come, the diversions would be wasted for there was 'nothing' they could do from there 'to stop German advance if really intended'. 'If and when' the attack came, it 'would require very much more than a few Hurricanes or Blenheims to stop it'.[46]

Longmore also opposed diverting to Turkey. He deprecated the plans (at the end of January) to offer ten to fifteen squadrons which would serve to lock up the air forces and result in their probably remaining inoperative – 'foresaking the substance for the shadow'.[47]

In addition to the immediate military and strategic possibilities, long-term political considerations mattered for Longmore. Withdrawal would 'denude the imperial forces ... of air protection'. It would 'very probably lead to a subsequent withdrawal, possibly after very high casualties from air attack'. There would be 'political repercussions ... throughout the world particularly in Australia and in Egypt itself'.[48]

Despite his objections, Longmore did not refuse outright – but he would not commit himself to specific promises for the Greeks. He did not wish, in general, to extend his lines of communication and was conscious of Wavell's reluctance to abandon the Sudan or curtail Libya. But although he did instruct that one fighter and one bomber squadron should proceed to Greece with whatever Gladiators and Blenheim 1s could be made available, his position was one of honouring the letter, rather than the spirit of his instructions and of avoiding specific commit-

---

[44] Wavell to Dill, 10 Jan. 1941, PREM 3/309/1; Longmore to Portal, 31 Jan. 1941, PREM 3/309/1.

[45] Longmore to Portal, 10 Jan. 1941, PREM 3/309/1.

[46] Wavell to Dill, 10 Jan. 1941, PREM 3/309/1; Longmore to Portal, 10 Jan. 1941, PREM 3/309/1.

[47] Longmore to Portal, 31 Jan. 1941, PREM 3/309/1.

[48] Longmore to Portal, 10 Jan. 1941, PREM 3/309/1. The imperial forces included the Australians.

ments.[49] On 12 January he prepared to go to Athens having completed preparations 'for the ... redistribution of my squadrons to meet PM's ruling at earliest possible date'.[50] He was, however, 'reluctant to commit [him]self' to a 'further programme of more squadrons to Greece later on'. That would depend on the 'situation ... by that time ... on the Libyan front', on the air support needed in Abyssinia in the East African operations and on the number of squadrons which could be moved from Sudan to Egypt or Greece. In Athens he did not commit himself to specific numbers, even when pressed by Papagos on the 17th. He refused to be tied by Papagos's enquiry as to 'how many squadrons in addition to the four already [there] plus the three shortly due could be allotted from Egypt and by what date'. He 'could not commit [him]self to any definite figure or date ... it depended on [a] variety of uncertain factors'. He also thought they should refrain from basing squadrons in Salonika 'until sufficient number of squadrons and defence forces are available'.[51]

Longmore, therefore, though having opposed diversion at the outset – whether to Greece or Turkey – came to concede, and gradually to acquiesce in, such a course. He none the less anticipated difficulties. Despite his first reaction to the Turkish proposal (that it would be wrong to lock up the air forces in Turkey), within days he and the other commanders claimed they 'fully recognised' the 'soundness of high policy air infiltration to Turkey' (though the Dodecanese operations were an 'essential preliminary'). His 'only difficulty [was] to implement [the] proposal if Turk president should accept ... PM's offer early date'. It was 'impossible to withdraw large measure air [of] support to army whilst enemy in full retreat Libya and Eritrea'.[52] Time might be needed to make good existing deficiencies. Some respite would be needed 'for squadron maintenance repairs and replacement aircraft'. They were still awaiting spares and were behind programme in Blenheims; Mohawks had an engineering defect; and the Tomahawks were an 'unknown quantity'. Longmore would find it difficult to export in the quantity visualised – 'with hardly sufficient straw for bricks to meet minimum local requirements' – but by 6 February assured Portal that 'all preliminary preparations [were] now in hand'.[53] On 7 February Benghazi was occupied and Longmore began preparations for the withdrawal of squadrons which he

[49] Channon diary, 3 Jan. 1941; Longmore to Portal, 9 Jan. 1941, PREM 3/309/1.
[50] Longmore to Portal, 12 Jan. 1941, PREM 3/309/1.
[51] Longmore to Portal, 9 Jan. 1941, PREM 3/309/1; Longmore to Portal, 17 Jan. 1941, PREM 3/309/1. The first essential was 'to get on with the work of preparing the aerodromes'; though he had at the outset thought that if desired, one of the Blenheim squadrons, now in Greece, might be stationed in the Salonika area. Longmore to Portal, 10 Jan. 1941, PREM 3/309/1.
[52] Longmore to Portal, 6 Feb. 1941, PREM 3/309/1.   [53] Ibid.

proposed as 'Balkan reserve'. He also hoped that within three weeks the Eritrean situation might allow withdrawal from the Sudan. He was 'thinking in terms of Mandibles and Balkans'.[54]

For Longmore the objection had been to diverting away from the operations in North Africa, undermining their success, denuding at a time when reinforcements were scarce, and locking up the air force when needed elsewhere. The decision taken in London to offer Greece priority involved dropping an objection to diverting, not a distinction as between Greece and Turkey. With the other commanders he was prepared to drop that objection, and on 14 February wired that they fully realised that the Greek situation 'and steps to counter German infiltration into Bulgaria now have highest priority'. They also recognised the 'soundness of major policy of our own air infiltration into Turkey'.[55] Assuming the offer to Turkey was accepted, Longmore considered that operations against Germans should be co-ordinated by a senior air officer from a joint headquarters. It might be 'more convenient to operate the majority of squadrons either from Greece or Turkey'. This would 'avoid the impression of allotting so many ... to Greece and so many to Turkey'. It was 'probably best to consider the whole air force for that region inter-changeable between Greece and Turkey'.[56] Benghazi was now in British hands and the early capture of the Dodecanese was a 'key measure'.

There would be difficulty particularly if the Turks accepted the offer at an early date. From the naval point of view, the new course created 'a heavy commitment in safeguarding the line of supply through [the] Aegean' and would entail establishing bases in the Greek islands and Turkey – though they were already 'completely extended ... in covering the long lines of sea communication on Libyan coasts'.[57] If the Balkan situation developed without the continued building up of forces, then the present 'acute shortage in light craft escorts, local defence units and personnel for shore bases' would become critical and a considerable air defence commitment on Egypt and the lines from Beghazi to Tripoli and Sicily would remain.[58] It would be difficult 'fully to implement promises made to Turks ... if offer is accepted at early date' especially before the Dodecanese were taken.[59] Moreover, if the provision of anti-aircraft equipment to Turks was on anything like the scale envisaged, that would 'seriously aggravate air defence difficulties in Cyrenaica, Egypt, and Crete unless major proportion forthcoming from home'.[60]

[54] Longmore to Portal, 8 Feb. 1941, PREM 3/309/1.
[55] Commanders in chief to chiefs of staff, 14 Feb. 1941, PREM 3/309/2.
[56] Longmore to Portal, 8 Feb. 1941, PREM 3/309/1.
[57] Commanders in chief to chiefs of staff, 14 Feb. 1941, PREM 3/309/2.
[58] Ibid.   [59] Ibid.   [60] Ibid.

Despite the difficulties and shortages he envisaged if the Balkan situation developed, despite his earlier objections to diverting either to Greece or Turkey, Longmore had come to accept such a course. With the other commanders, he did see such a decision as being a matter of highest policy to be taken by the cabinet. He may have been influenced by the unambiguous nature of the instructions from London to divert, or be ready to do so, which suggested that the course was inevitable. He may have been encouraged by the fact that, at least in the case of Greece, no specific amounts were mentioned, and he would decide what was possible. His own objections had been partly based on what he saw as the conflicting needs of the Libyan theatre; taking Benghazi may have eased the air commitments in Africa and made the prospect of diverting possible. But none of these developments countered the specific reservations he had had at the outset: that there was not enough to stop the Germans in the Balkans; that the shortage of anti-aircraft cover would be critical; that the political repercussions, especially in view of the deployment of Australian troops, would be serious. Even before Eden reached the Middle East, commanders 'fully realise[d]' that Greece and the steps to counter German infiltration into Bulgaria now had highest priority, though they did anticipate shortages and difficulties.[61] Longmore too had come to such a view. As a result, when Eden arrived he found the commanders acquiescent.

[61] Ibid.

13　The Greek decision: 10th February to early March 1941

Eden, Dill and the Middle East command

When Eden and Dill reached Cairo the earlier reluctance of the command to divert to Greece had, then, become acquiescence – partly because such a course appeared inevitable. The commanders by then believed that help to Greece had been settled; and that it was their duty to make the best possible arrangements.[1] Eden, who himself was clear on the question of priority to Greece, was to report that he found considerable unanimity. Such unanimity did not, however, reflect the absence of doubts or reservations. But it may have been helped by Eden's not underestimating the professional difficulties – and by his having been privy to the early first objection of the command to diverting the previous November, after the Italian attack. Within two days of Eden's arrival, a clear plan, agreed with the Greeks, was reached. It was resolved, in Athens on 22 February, that the British and Greeks would stand, jointly, on the Aliakmon line.

Eden had arrived, therefore, in Cairo determined to succour the Greeks and somewhat relieved to find the commanders preparing to do so. But he quickly came to see Greece as an end in itself, accepting the prospect of defeat and the possibility that intervention might not necessarily have the desired effect on the Turks. Although clear that the Greeks should come first, the aim, or object, was less clear and the view of Greece as a means to bolster Turkey came to give way to the view of Greece as an end in itself.

Eden had set off on his mission to the Middle East with the objects of helping the Greeks and bolstering the Turks. There seemed to be no conflict between these aims, either in Churchill's instructions or in Eden's understanding of his task. If Greece were to yield to Germany without fighting, then 'Turkey's ability and will to fight would be gravely reduced' or she would 'only fight to resist attack upon her territory'. The Middle

---

[1] By the 21st, Wavell was preparing Wilson for his being appointed to command the force which, it was probable, would be sent to Greece. Wavell to Wilson, 21 Feb. 1941, Connell, *Wavell*, p. 338. For the rough timetable, see para 2 of Wavell to prime minister, 28 Feb. 1941, PREM 3/309/2.

East command should prepare for the move 'of the maximum forces to Greece';[2] and Eden would visit Athens before Angora, given that the 'affairs of Greece are perhaps even more urgent than those of Turkey'.[3] The 'gist of' his instructions, as he understood them, was 'first to send speedy succour to Greece against a German attack, second to make both Turks and Yugs (sic) fight or do the best they could. Third to provide for necessary help to Turkey in case Germany attack[ed] her.'[4] The assistance to be provided to Greece and the plan for Anglo-Greek action would depend on Greek plans for forming a front and on the size and composition of the forces diverted to Greece from the Middle East. That would be governed by the 'degree to which other commitments [were] to be pressed' while the needs of Turkey, in case of a German attack, 'must be born in mind'.[5] As to the form joint operations might take, Eden anticipated that they should establish 'a defensive front' with a 'reasonable chance' of withstanding or at least checking the German attack. The ideal line would be one covering Salonika, and this would also be a 'powerful inducement to Yugoslavia and Turkey to fight'. But it was 'impossible to judge' on existing information whether such a front could be formed; and an alternative way of helping Greece might be by means of Anglo-Turkish operations in Thrace directed against the 'left flank of German advance against Greece'.[6]

Eden was relieved on arrival to find that Wavell had already begun to prepare to divert; and he was keen to note the 'agreement' at the outset between himself, Dill and the command 'upon utmost help to Greece at earliest moment'.[7] The commanders, amongst whom he reported he found unanimity, may have been influenced by the single-mindedness of purpose with which he arrived; by his suggesting they had no choice in the matter; by his indicating that he was well aware of the risks; and by failure with the Turks. And, at a meeting with the commanders, there was agreement on 'utmost help' to the Greeks at the earliest moment. Despite the grave risk, 'to stand idly by and see Germany win a victory over Greece, probably a bloodless one at that, seem[ed] the worst of all courses'. It was better to fight even if they should fail; 'better to suffer

[2] See Eden's comments on chiefs of staff draft to CsinC, 11 Feb. 1941, Avon FO 954/1, Gr/41/15/A.
[3] Palairet had asked that Eden come to Athens after Turkey. Although Eden was inclined not to, he would take no final decision until he reached Cairo. At that stage Churchill considered that they should see the Greeks first. Palairet to foreign office, 1 Feb. 1941, Avon FO 954/11, Gr/41/15; Eden to Palairet, 12 Feb. 1941, Avon FO 954/11, Gr/41/16; Churchill to Eden 21 Feb. 1941, PREM 3/309/2.
[4] Eden to Wavell, 18 Feb. 1941, PREM 3/309/2.   [5] Ibid.
[6] Eden to Wavell, 18 Feb. 1941, PREM 3/309/2.
[7] Eden diary, 20 Feb. 1941.

with the Greeks than to make no attempt to help them', though 'a gamble to send forces to the mainland of Europe to fight Germans at this time'.[8]

When Eden conveyed the feeling in Cairo, he did not explain whether or to what extent he influenced the commanders. For example, in recognising that risks existed in diverting to Greece, Eden implied that the risks had both long been accepted, and lay behind the decision at the outset, and that acceptance of the dangers legitimised the decision. 'No one' could 'guarantee ... success.' But Eden had recalled, for the command, that when they had discussed the matter in London, they had been 'prepared to run the risk of failure thinking it better to suffer with the Greeks than make no attempt to help them'.[9] The unanimity behind supporting the Greeks, which Eden purported to have found in Cairo, may have been encouraged by his suggesting that the criterion in London for going ahead was acknowledged to be not success, but the desire to appear to do something even though military success was unlikely. Failure to act would have repercussions on Turkey and Yugoslavia: if they failed to help the Greeks, there was 'no hope of action by Yugoslavia, and the future of Turkey may easily be compromised'.[10] Concentration on Greece would, in practice, exclude the prospect of help to Turkey. The 'limitation of ... resources ... especially in the air, will not allow of help being given to Turkey at the same time if Greece is to be supported on an effective scale'.[11] Eden, Dill and the command decided 'unanimously' that 'it would be fatal ... to divide our effort and that we must for the present concentrate on giving assistance to Greece'. The Turks should be told 'frankly that we were determined to go to the assistance of Greece and that this was the best way of helping all concerned, including the Turks'. All possible aid should be offered to Greece 'at the earliest date', which would mean 'there would be little or nothing to spare for the Turks'. As to where the stand in Greece should be made, given the 'limited air forces available' it was, in Eden's view, 'doubtful whether we can hold a line covering Salonika' which Wavell was prepared to contemplate and Cunningham to supply.[12] No final decision on where

---

[8] Ibid.; Eden to Churchill, 21 Feb. 1941 ,PREM 3/309/2. At a meeting at the embassy that evening, Eden explained that 'the principle had been accepted ... [that] morning of offering the Greek Government to send all possible aid to Greece at the earliest date', meeting, HM Embassy, Cairo, 6 p.m., 20 Feb. 1941, FO Report, Avon MS., FO 954/33 Yu/4l/21.

[9] Eden to Churchill, 21 Feb. 1941, PREM 3/309/2.   [10] Ibid.

[11] Ibid.; see also record of a meeting at HM Embassy, Cairo, 6 p.m., 20 Feb. 1941, FO Report Avon MS 954/33 Yu/41/21.

[12] Eden to Churchill, 21 Feb. 1941, PREM 3/309/2; meeting at HM Embassy, Cairo, 6 p.m., 20 Feb. 1941, FO Report, Avon MS FO 954/33, Yu/41/21.

to stand, or on what to say to the Turks, would be taken until after discussions with the Greeks. Contact would be established with the Greek government and the Greeks would be invited to hold a secret meeting in Athens on 22 February.[13]

For his part, before leaving the United Kingdom Dill had rated Turkey strategically above Greece – though he also thought that Wavell might prepare estimates of diversions for Greece, the general feeling being that aid 'to Greece and/or Turkey must come first'.[14] How far he may have been influenced during the journey by Eden's views is not clear. Eden certainly put succour to Greece before that to Turkey, but was divided in his own mind as to whether this was to be a means of bolstering Turkey or of helping Greece for its own sake to withstand, or check, a German attack. Dill arrived in Cairo (according to himself) still of the view that 'we should concentrate on ... Turkey' and that forces sent to Greece would inevitably be lost.[15] But according to himself, the three commanders, Marshall-Cornwall and Heywood prompted him to change his mind. They 'made [it] clear' to him that Turkey would not fight 'at our bidding' though she might if 'by helping Greece we can stem a German advance'; that there was 'a fair military chance of ... holding a line in northern Greece if we act at once'; that Yugoslavia would not fight unless Turkey did, and the converse was true. But Dill now looked to saving the Balkans, rather than preserving the Turks and urged that 'our only chance of preventing the Balkans being devoured piecemeal is to go to Greece with all that we can find as soon as it can be done'.[16] When Eden met the commanders the 'general feeling' was that 'the best line would be to tell the Turks frankly that we were determined to go to the assistance of Greece and that this was the best way of helping all concerned including the Turks'. Limited resources, especially in the air, would 'not allow of help being given to Turkey at the [same] time if Greece is to be supported on an effective scale'. Without help to Greece 'the future of Turkey may easily be compromised'.[17]

Concentrating on Turkey could not now, as a course, be justified – given the dubious attitude of the Turks. Eden 'frankly ... did not know

---

[13] Ibid.; also annex 1, meeting at GHQME, Cairo, 11.45 a.m., 21 Feb. 1941, FO Report, Avon MS .954/33, Yu/41/21.
[14] Avon, *The Reckoning*, p. 193; Dill to Wavell, 7 Feb. 1941, WO 106/2144; Dill to Wavell, 11 Feb. 1941, Connell, *Wavell*, p. 327.
[15] Eden to Wavell, 18 Feb. 1941, PREM 3/309/2; Dill to Haining, 21 Feb. 1941, Avon, *The Reckoning*, pp. 197–8.
[16] Dill to Haining, 21 Feb. 1941, Avon, *The Reckoning*, pp. 197–8.
[17] Meeting at HM Embassy, Cairo, 6 p.m., 20 Feb. 1941, FO Report, Avon FO 954/33 Yu/41/21; Eden to Churchill, 21 Feb. 1941, PREM 3/309/2.

what they were likely to do'. In any case, Britain and Greece should, in his view, take their decisions 'independently of the attitude of Turkey and Yugoslavia'.[18] In view of the uncertainty of the attitude of Yugoslavia, Eden, Dill and the Middle East command agreed that 'the only sound plan from the military point of view was to stand on the Aliakmon line'.[19] Moreover the Turks were not reported to be near a state of readiness, did not know how to use technical arms, and had a low state of air operational efficiency. Wavell took the view (though Dill did not share it) that the Turks would be 'more a liability than an asset'.[20] They would be told that the British plan was to help Greece 'to the utmost of our capacity and as soon as possible'; that this would mean that there would be little to spare for Turkey but that it would be pointed out 'that to help Greece was to help Turkey'. Some assistance would be offered – both air and army material.[21]

At the time much was made by Eden (as it later was by Churchill, the politicians and professionals in London) of the degree of implied professional 'unanimity' about helping the Greeks which existed in Cairo. While there did appear to be 'agreement upon utmost help to Greece at [the] earliest moment', there was, however, scarcely unanimity on the factors behind such apparent agreement or on the professional case. Wavell and Dill, for example, disagreed about the Turks – Wavell made it clear that he had his doubts about their effectiveness, but Dill did not agree.[22] Longmore was dubious about the assumptions made of the air strength. He thought Eden and Dill had 'underestimated the air commitment left from capture of Benghazi' and that 'their information on extent of possible reinforcements to Greece appeared unduly optimistic'.[23]

Eden acknowledged that difficulties were thought to exist, but he did not allow that they would affect the decision or that the commanders thought they might. His 'own impression' about the air – on which there was 'gravest anxiety'- was that Longmore's squadrons were 'not quite up to standard of their counterpart at home'. But Longmore and Cunningham did not disagree with Eden's conclusion that the Greeks must 'in

---

[18] First discussions with Greek Government and First Anglo-Greek Plenary Meeting, 22 Feb. 1941, Avon, FO 954 Yu/41/21.
[19] First discussions with Greek government and informal meeting of British representatives, 22 Feb. 1941, FO Report, Avon MS. FO 954 Yu/41/21.
[20] Eden diary, 20 Feb. 1941.
[21] Meeting at HM Embassy, Cairo 8.45 p.m. 24 Feb. 1941, Annex 4, FO Report, Avon FO 954, Yu/41/21.
[22] Eden diary, 20 Feb. 1941, PREM 3/309/2.
[23] Longmore to Portal, 20 Feb. 1941, PREM 3/309/2.

the immediate future ... have first call on resources'. They wanted to avoid a line defending Salonika.[24]

In addition to the alleged unanimity, which strengthened the case for intervention, there was also the hope of military success. Such a hope had initially been held out to the Greeks in order to counter their reservations. But plans also came to be considered in terms of success – bizarre, given that they were going in with their eyes open to the prospect of failure. For at the same time, the prospect of success was now implied: Greece was not necessarily a forlorn hope and the Greeks (who feared that the premature despatch of resources would be regarded by the Germans as provocation) might be convinced that they had 'fair chances of checking and holding a German attack' by the size and quality of the forces ready for them. If troops were to be sent, then they should be sent 'at once'. It was 'vital that [the] British forces should be established before weather enable[d] the Germans to move. Our object is to forestall, not to precipitate, a German attack.'[25] If the Greeks accepted, then there was 'a fair chance of halting a German advance and preventing Greece from being overrun'. They were not 'without hope' that though 'a daring venture ... it might succeed to the extent of halting the Germans before they overrun all Greece'.[26]

The Greeks declared their determination to continue the war until final victory (and to resist a German invasion if necessary alone). They were agreeable to help 'provided ... a sound military plan could be agreed by [both] ... authorities' under which there would be 'a reasonable prospect of holding a line against a German attack'.[27] The prospect of military success in one way did not matter, yet in another was paramount. During the discussion with the Greeks on 22 February it was agreed that given 'the dubious attitude of Yugoslavia and Turkey, the only safe line to hold was the ... Aliakmon ... a strong and short natural line, which there appeared to be a good prospect of holding with the forces which we could send and those which the Greeks stated they were prepared to withdraw from Eastern Macedonia and Albania'. The 'only sound plan from the military point of view was to stand on the Aliakmon line'. Steps should be taken to withdraw British forces from the Middle East and Greek advanced troops in Thrace and Macedonia 'to the line which we should

[24] Eden to Churchill, 21 Feb. 1941, PREM 3/309/2.
[25] Note on approach to Greeks, 21 Feb. 1941, FO Report, Avon FO 954, Yu/41/21.
[26] Eden to Churchill, 21 Feb. 1941, PREM 3/309/2.
[27] First discussions with the Greek government, 22 Feb. 1941, III, Annex 2, annex 3 (Record No. 1), FO Report, Avon FO 954, Yu/41/21.

be obliged to hold if the Yugoslavs did not come in' (i.e., the Aliakmon line).[28]

The uncertainty about Yugoslavia strengthened the case for the Aliakmon position. Eden, Dill and Wavell made it clear then that 'it would not be safe to count on Yugoslavia'.[29] Eden maintained that they simply 'did not know what [Yugoslavia and Turkey] were likely to do'; that the decision should be taken 'independently' of their respective attitudes 'since if we waited to find out what [they] ... would do, it might be too late to organise effective resistance to a German attack on Greece'. Not only should they not count on Yugoslavia and Turkey, but unless they went ahead they could hardly hope for a change in the future; there was 'no hope of action by Yugoslavia and the future of Turkey may be compromised' if they failed to help the Greeks.[30]

But the Yugoslavs made it plain by the 27th that while Yugoslavia would defend herself against aggression and would not permit the passage of foreign troops across her territory, she would not 'in present circumstances ... decide precisely on the attitude that she would adopt in the event of a German move across Bulgaria'.[31] Although Eden continued to press the Yugoslavs, urged the view that German actions in the Balkans were encouraged by the absence of co-operation between Turkey, Yugoslavia and Greece, and pressed that Yugoslavia join with Britain and Greece to withstand Germany (rather than have her independence, like that of Romania 'bit by bit ... choked out of her and then Italy ... take her pound of flesh from the helpless victim'), he had resolved that what Yugoslavia did should not affect going ahead with Greece.[32]

On the basis, therefore, of a 'good chance' of success, the decision to stand on the Aliakmon line was reached by British and Greeks at Tatoi on 22 February. (Had the Yugoslavs been likely to come in, they might have considered defending Salonika.) The plan, drawn up with the Greeks on the basis of a 'good chance', had not been adopted without reference to the wider difficulties. Indeed, Eden's acknowledgement of these difficulties had made the case for going ahead all the stronger. Before the final decision, it was a matter of doing so in the full knowledge of the difficulties; and indeed, given the likelihood of failure. Though failure tended by then to be played down, its likelihood was never ignored (least of all after the decision as a result of which Eden was covered). For Eden,

---

[28] First discussions with the Greek government, 22 Feb. 1941, III, annex 3 Records No. 3 and 4, FO Report, Avon FO 954, Yu/41/21.

[29] Ibid.   [30] Ibid.; Eden to prime minister, 21 Feb. 1941, PREM 3/309/2.

[31] Attitude of Yugoslavia, 22–27 February, 1941, V, FO Report, Avon FO 954, Yu/41/21.

[32] FO Report, Attitude of Yugoslavia, 22–27 February, 1941 and Annex 8 and Eden to Prince Regent, 3 Mar. 1941, Annex 10, FO Report, Avon FO 954, Yu/41/21.

success had not been the only issue – rather, something, he thought, must be done as a matter of urgency and action must be taken at once, 'or it would be too late to send effective assistance'.[33] In that frame of mind he had found the Greek attitude 'from first to last ... entirely resolute'; their only doubt being 'whether to accept ... British troops now ... or to await German attack'. Given what Eden saw as determination to resist to the utmost, Britain had 'no alternative but to back them whatever the ultimate consequences'.[34]

Eden had, therefore, all along appeared to take into account the prospect of failure in Greece itself; to imply, at the same time, that there was a fair chance. Such a chance partly depended on the role of Turkey and of Yugoslavia. And Eden set about extracting expressions of intent from the Turks, of commitment from the Yugoslavs. In Athens and in Cairo the line to be taken with the Turks was to tell them 'frankly that we were determined to go to the assistance of Greece, and that this was the best way of helping all concerned, including the Turks'.[35] Discussions in Angora followed those at Athens; and the Turks welcomed the decision to help Greece, though they considered that Germany would attack Turkey rather than Greece. Turkey, according to the Turks, was bound to enter the war 'sooner or later'. They were reluctant to precipitate a German attack, but Turkey would fight if attacked and she remained loyal to Great Britain – but given that she had no offensive power, she would be more of a liability than an asset if she entered the war before she was prepared. While the Turks recognised the need to send support to Greece, it was – in their view – equally necessary to send support to Turkey, also threatened by Germany.[36] For their part, the Turks were probably relieved that there was no plan for them and very little support. Eden, however, concluded from the harmonious exchanges – possibly as the result of wishful thinking – that Turkey would enter the war at some stage, or immediately, if attacked; that 'the frank and realistic outlook of the Turks' had been impressive. All had left 'with the feeling that they are genuinely loyal and determined to play their part'.[37]

Eden had failed to get anything out of the Turks who made no

---

[33] Note on approach to Greeks, 21 Feb. 1941, First discussions with the Greek Government, 22 Feb. 1941, III, Annex 3 Record no. 1, FO Report, Avon FO 954, Yu/41/21. Eden reminded Churchill on the 21st that when the matter was discussed in London 'we were prepared to run the risk of failure'. Eden to Churchill, 21 Feb. 1941, PREM 3/309/2.

[34] Eden diary, 22 Feb. 1941; Eden to Churchill, 22 Feb. 1941, PREM 3/309/2.

[35] Assistance for Greece, record of meeting held at HM Embassy Cairo, 6 p.m., 20 Feb. 1941, Annex 1 FO Report, Avon FO 954, Yu/41/21.

[36] First discussions with the Turkish Government, 26–28 Feb. 1941, FO Report, Avon FO 954, Yu/41/21.

[37] Eden to Churchill, 28 Feb. 1941, PREM 3/309/2.

promises, but had avoided making ill-feeling by maintaining they would some time enter the war. They had refused to commit themselves on whether they would look on a German advance through Bulgaria and across the Greek frontier as a *casus belli*.[38] Though they made sympathetic noises about Britain helping Greece, which they balanced with ritual demands for support, they did nothing to indicate that their actions would be as Britain wanted, or that they were prepared, practically and in principle, to take the necessary steps to prevent German domination of the Middle East. The Turks would, most probably, have turned down full-scale assistance, and probably were determined not to provoke the Germans. Eden and the command were probably relieved that they had not made trouble and had made the right noises. This led them to believe they had not failed with the Turks. Yet one of the reasons given for intervention in Greece had been the good effect it would have on bolstering the Turks; such an aim was subsequently lost sight of. Instead of persisting with the Turks, Eden stopped with the first stage of his policy – help to the Greeks; and he hoped the Turks would not take too dim a view about it. This anxiety obscured his demanding from the Turks a clear statement of intent; and when, in Angora, Eden and his colleagues, having changed course, did not meet trouble from the Turks over the Greek decision, they considered that a success in itself.

As for the Yugoslavs, Eden continued to press them, but there was little indication of commitment. While Yugoslavia would defend itself against aggression – and would not permit the passage of foreign troops across her territory – she would not commit herself in advance on a German move against Bulgaria. Although Eden warned that the failure of Turkey, Yugoslavia and Greece to co-operate encouraged 'German activities in the Balkans', and although he pressed the Yugoslavs to assume a definite attitude, he had little success.[39] They refused to commit themselves. And despite the fact that plans with the Greeks had been made on the basis that they could not count on the Yugoslavs, none the less without them the prospects of successfully defending Salonika were slim. The force contemplated would be deployed in a covering position west of Salonika; Salonika itself would be covered by the Greek army in Macedonia. But the prospects of a successful defence of Salonika 'must largely depend on the attitude of Yugoslavia'. Prince Paul must know that the British held out 'good hopes of holding a line in Greece'.[40] Eden warned that Yugo-

---

[38] Anglo-Greek conversations, 2 Mar. 1941, FO Report, Avon FO 954, Yu/41/21.

[39] Attitude of Yugoslavia, 22–27 February 1941, record of conversation between the secretary of state and the Yugoslav ambassador ... 27 February 1941, FO Report, Avon 954, Yu/41/21.

[40] Ibid.; Eden to Churchill, 5 Mar. 1941, PREM 3/309/2.

slavia would be at Germany's mercy if the Germans subdued Greece and immobilised Turkey, and in the course of doing so 'occupy Salonica and dominate the Straits'. He had no doubt that Turkey and Greece, if attacked, would resist by force; and he urged the regent to resist the German evil and 'join with us and Greece in an attempt to withstand it'.[41] In the face of increasing doubts and difficulties, Eden became more and more resolute about intervention himself and more determined that they stand with the Greeks on its Aliakmon line.

Failure to bring in the Yugoslavs or Turks confirmed him in his feeling. And he continued in it despite the persistent warnings of Churchill to 'retain power to liberate Greeks from any bargain and ... liberate ourselves' should Eden feel 'not even a reasonable hope'. Even the discovery, one week after the decision taken with the Greeks to stand on the Aliakmon line, that the Greeks had not removed their advanced Greek troops in Thrace and Macedonia to the new line, did not alter Eden's intention.[42] Although Papagos was 'unwilling to give the order for withdrawal ... from Macedonia' and held that 'it was now too late to start', that withdrawal would 'alarm the Greek population in Macedonia', Eden was determined that the Greeks should proceed as agreed and move their forces. Militarily, according to Dill, it would be 'unsound to attempt to hold any line other than the Aliakmon' or to hold that with 'less than eight divisions (plus one ... in reserve) ... the necessary minimum (as agreed) during the Tatoi conversations'. Eden insisted that the Greeks be told that it was 'essential to get the minimum requisite troops ... to the Aliakmon line at once'. If sufficient could not be withdrawn from Thrace and Macedonia, then they must be brought from Albania.[43] Moreover, he refused to reopen discussions on the military prospects with the Greeks, on the question of offering effective resistance, and on the 'great disappointment' of the negative attitude of Turkey and Yugoslavia and Greece fighting alone. Eden insisted that 'this very question' had already been examined the previous week; that both Papagos and Wavell had thought there were good chances of Anglo-Greek forces holding the Aliakmon line; and that the decision to hold that line had been taken 'on the basis that the Turks and Yugoslavs would not come in'.[44] Not one of

---

[41] Eden to Prince Paul, 3 Mar. 1941, FO 954/33, Yu/41/21.
[42] Churchill to Eden, 1 Mar. 1941, Churchill, *Second World War*, 111, p. 86; record of Anglo-Greek conversations held at Athens, 2–4 March 1941, record of Meeting at H.M. Legation at Athens on 2 March (British representatives), FO Report, Avon 954, Yu/41/21.
[43] Ibid. (record).
[44] Record of meetings held at the Presidency of the Council, Athens ... from 10.45 p.m. on 2 March to 12.45 a.m. on 3 March, Meeting (A) Political aspects of Anglo-Greek Co-operation, FO Report, Avon 954, Yu/41/21.

these constituted a new factor. There was, he insisted, 'no change in the situation and we were at a loss to understand the disappointment which the Greeks now expressed at the attitude of the Turks and Yugoslavs'. But he also stressed that he thought prospects were not 'so black' and that 'our military experts thought the line on which we agreed had good chances of being held and a German attack on it checked'.[45]

It is not clear whether Eden believed his own proposition that things were not so black; or whether he was intent on reassuring the Greeks in order to keep them in the scheme. What is clear is that he was determined to go ahead; would brook no opposition from the Greeks; and was prepared to suggest that matters were no worse than they had been when the decision to stand on the Aliakmon line had been taken with them, one week earlier. In a sense that was true – none of the external factors had changed. But it was also true that even then there had been as much of a feeling that one was going ahead for political reasons and irrespective of the prospect of success – if not *on* that account. That had not changed. But the Greeks had failed to fulfil one presupposition – that they would remove the troops essential to holding the line – and this now rendered matters blacker than they had seemed one week earlier. The military experts, whom Eden maintained were confident, had in fact less reason now for confidence. In Dill's view they were 'now faced with a set of conditions different from those in which we had agreed the plan made at Tatoi'. Then they had been 'happy' to send their forces to co-operate with the Greeks in holding the Aliakmon line as 'proposed by ... Papagos himself'.[46]

Instead of opposing the scheme, with the conditions so different to those assumed and agreed at Tatoi, Dill prepared to meet the 'new conditions' and offered a revised scheme – though with poorer prospects than the earlier one, and reluctant co-operation from the Greeks. If Papagos 'could put adequate forces on the Aliakmon line to secure the position in co-operation with ourselves, we would hold that line with the full intention of operating forward of it, especially with armoured forces if the situation later made this possible'. Papagos would not concede. He had 'no more forces to put there' and it was 'no longer possible to withdraw the Greek forces from East Macedonia to the Aliakmon line'.[47] No Greek divisions 'at all were available'. This meant, as Dill pointed out, that there were 'insufficient troops to hold the line on which it had been intended to give battle'; and though his next proposals would mean a

---

[45] Ibid.
[46] Record of a meeting held at the British Legation, Athens, at 18.30 hours on 3 March 1941, FO Report, Avon FO 954, Yu/41/21.
[47] Ibid.

force of only seven or eight battalions (as against the old plan under which thirty-five Greek battalions would be made available) 'too small ... to allow our regarding [it] ... as a sound military proposition', a fresh proposal was patched up by the afternoon of 4 March.[48]

Papagos was reluctant to concentrate on the Aliakmon line; but the British insisted. Dill set out the terms and Eden who agreed, put them to Papagos.[49] The Greeks would concentrate on the Aliakmon line the 28th division from Florina; the 12th division from Western Thrace; the 19th motorised division from Larissa; the seven battalions from Thrace. By the night of the 4th a draft agreement was ready, for signature the next day, the terms of which were less favourable than those settled at the outset.[50] Three Greek divisions would be accepted for the Aliakmon line – the equivalent of about sixteen to twenty-three battalions – instead of the thirty-five they were originally led to expect – an option accepted according to Dill and Eden 'after some misgivings'.[51] Despite the 'misgivings', it was not considered 'by any means a hopeless proposition to check and hold the German advance on this line which is naturally strong with few approaches'. At worst 'it should always be possible to make fighting withdrawal from this line through country eminently suitable for rearguard action'.[52] Yet, although Eden and Dill claimed that they were 'all sure that ... [they had] arrived at correct decision', none the less 'the hard fact remain[ed] that our forces, including Dominion contingents, will be engaged in an operation more hazardous than it seemed a week ago'.[53]

Once tied by the decision, Eden began to stress that they had no choice but to proceed – a view shared by Palairet, Smuts and Dill. Whereas Eden had reached the decision because it was not a 'folorn hope' and because a reasonable chance existed, after the agreement was signed he increasingly stressed the risks, adding that, despite these, it had been 'necessary' to go ahead and 'the right decision was taken in Athens'. The 'real alternative' for Greece as he saw it, was 'whether she should stand up and fight Germany or allow herself to become a victim of German seduction like Roumania'.[54] In the face of Churchill's message to liberate 'the Greeks

[48] Ibid.; record of a meeting held at the British Legation, Athens, at 11.00 4 Mar. 1941; 17.45 hours 4 Mar. 1941, FO Report, Avon 954, Yu/41/21.
[49] Record of a meeting ... British Legation, 17.45 hours 4 Mar. 1941, FO Report, Avon 954, Yu/41/21.
[50] Ibid.; Record of a meeting ... British Legation, Athens, at 22.00 hours 4 Mar. 1941, FO Report, Avon 954, Yu/41/21.
[51] Eden and Dill to Churchill, 5 Mar. 1941 (written 4 March), PREM 3/309/2.
[52] Ibid.
[53] Ibid.
[54] Record of a meeting held at GHQ, Middle East, 6 Mar. 1941, at 5 p.m., FO Report, Avon 954, Yu/41/21; Eden to Churchill, 6 Mar. 1941, WO 201/1996.

from feeling bound to reject the ultimatum', Eden alluded to the views both of Palairet and Smuts – who were protagonists of standing by the Greeks. Palairet, for example, did not see how they could 'possibly abandon the King of Greece', given the assurance they had given him 'as to reasonable chances of success'; they would be 'pilloried by the Greeks and the world in general as going back on our word'.[55] Smuts held that they could not 'now back out'. The arrangement with the Greeks was already in train; and, in any event, were they to abandon them, they would be 'held up to public ignominy'. It might be said that a German victory in the Balkans would result in a great setback to our cause, but the setback 'would probably be greater if we stood aside and did not help'.[56] 'We should not leave Greece alone at this grave juncture', he wired Churchill on the 7th; and 'the consequences of such a step now might be worse in their effects in the Balkans and on our cause generally than even a possible set-back in action'. He did not discount the chance of holding out, and if the position on the Aliakmon line did not break in the next few weeks, 'we have reasonable chance to build up a stable front in Greece and immediate danger will pass'.[57]

For his part, Dill considered 'the situation was grimmer than we thought'. Yet he too saw 'no alternative but to go ahead with our plans'. There was a 'reasonable chance that we would get there in time', and if so, then there was 'a good chance of holding them'. If the Germans got there first, it should be possible to withdraw the majority of our forces without great loss.[58] Wavell, on the other hand, was less circumspect – though not so Cunningham – and therefore, with their respective cases put in response to Churchill's eleventh hour wire on the 6th, Wavell entertained higher hopes of the operation than the other commanders. Wavell 'remained of the opinion that provided we could get our forces into Greece, there was a prospect of a successful encounter with the Germans. The results of success would be incalculable and might alter the whole aspect of the war.' Wavell pointed out that the Germans were taking grave risks with 'a long and indifferent line of communications through

---

[55] Palairet to Eden, 6 Mar. 1941; PREM 3/309/2; 7 Mar. 1941, Avon FO 954/11, Gr/41/21. Palairet had been horrified at the prospect that they would not be fighting in Greece and felt 'quite sick with horror when [he] read the PM's telegram to [Eden] but thank God it now looks as if you and the 3 Cs in C had averted the appalling prospect. I don't think I could have gone to the king of Greece with a message on those lines.'

[56] Record of meeting at HM Embassy, Cairo, at 10.15 p.m., 6 Mar. 1941, FO Report, Avon 954, Yu/41/21.

[57] Smuts to Churchill, 7 Mar. 1941, Avon FO 954/11, Gr/41/22.

[58] Record of meeting held at GHQ Middle East, 6 Mar. 1941, 5 p.m. and ... at H.M. Embassy, Cairo, at 10.15 p.m., 6 Mar. 1941, FO Report, Avon 954, Yu/41/21.

countries not well disposed to [them]'.[59] Moreover, he had seen General Freyberg and General Blamey, had told them of the change in the situation 'and the greater risk involved'. Both, according to Wavell, 'appeared to be prepared to face these risks and had shown no signs of wanting to back out'.[60]

Cunningham and Longmore, by contrast, were less confident: their agreement with the decision in Athens was not the result of professional judgement. It may have been the 'only possible one', but had been taken against a rapidly deteriorating position – one worse than when initially considered.

Cunningham had emphasised the risk involved in the move of the army and the RAF to Greece. The risks and difficulties were many, the position having deteriorated since the original decision in Athens. If the Germans started an air offensive from Bulgaria against convoys and ports of disembarkation 'loss must be expected as [the] scale of anti-aircraft and fighter defence available will be very weak for some time to come'.[61] Moreover, surface action against convoys by the Italian fleet could not be excluded and this would exacerbate the effect of shortages. The move of British units to Greece would involve 'continual personnel, motor transport and stores convoy for next two months'. Escort and cover for these would 'absorb the whole activity of the Fleet'; destroyers would be very heavily worked and other offensive operations would have to be deferred.[62] Cunningham's resources were 'taxed to the limit and ... by normal security standards [his] commitments exceed[ed] available resources'.[63] Although 'the decision taken at Athens was the only possible one', none the less the naval situation had 'deteriorated' since the discussion in Cairo ten days previously. Cunningham was confident that he could protect the convoys to Greece (unless subjected to air attack) but he was 'not happy about what might happen in the event of air attacks on the convoys and at the ports of disembarkation'. He hoped to keep the Suez Canal open, but no guarantee could be given that he could do so; and if the canal were closed, the movement of troops would take at least four months instead of two. Another worry was the seamen (mainly Lascars and Chinamen amongst whom there had already been several strikes), whom Cunn-

59 Ibid.
60 Record of meeting ... 10.15 p.m. 6 Mar. 1941, FO Report, Avon FO 954, Yu/41/21. Wavell was not yet distracted by the prospects of German activity in North Africa. Latest information indicated that German armoured troops were estimated at a maximum of one armoured brigade group, in addition to the two Italian infantry divisions and motorised artillery regiments in Tripolitania. There was no evidence of additional mechanical transport landed, though eventually the two German divisions might be employed in a large-scale attack. See Wavell to war office, 2 Mar. 1941, PREM 3/309/2.
61 Cunningham to admiralty, 4 Mar. 1941, PREM 3/309/2.   62 Ibid.   63 Ibid.

ingham believed 'would not stand up to air bombardment'.[64] In addition, if the Germans mined the Greek ports 'it could not be guaranteed that we should be able to clear them'. With Longmore, Cunningham was under no illusion about the prospects of success; he warned that 'there was a risk of losing most of the convoy ships and most of our air forces in Greece'.[65]

Longmore, who agreed that the decision adopted in Athens was 'the only possible one', none the less also envisaged a series of risks and difficulties. The 'inadequate' British air forces operating in Greece 'might be eliminated if the Germans brought to bear the weight of the air forces ... they were believed to have ... in Roumania and Bulgaria'.[66] There would be inevitable delays in replacement. A four-month delay should be expected on the Takoradi route, before aircraft authorised for replacement by wastage could arrive.[67] Given that the RAF was engaged with the Italian air forces in Albania and with an increasing weight of German attack in other theatres, Longmore had 'grave doubts' about his ability 'to take on the German air force in Greece as well'.[68] With Cunningham he pointed to the danger of losing most of the convoy ships 'and most of our air forces in Greece'. He could not match the German and Italians in Greece. Their air forces in the Balkans could easily be reinforced – with increasing strain on British forces – but he could send no further fighter squadrons to Greece, for he 'simply had not got them'.[69] But Eden, once bound by the agreement, took the line that they had no choice but to proceed and that matters were not so black. He had the support of Smuts – who thought it would be worse to abandon Greece than to go down – and Palairet, who thought they had no choice. Moreover the soldiers, Dill and Wavell, for a variety of reasons supported this course, and urged that a reasonable fighting chance existed. Longmore and Cunningham also supported such a course – also for a variety of reasons – but did not conceal their pessimism about the risks and prospects.

This then was what constituted the feeling of those 'on the spot' to which the cabinet in London alluded in support of a formal decision to go

[64] Record of meeting ... 6 Mar. 1941, 5 p.m., FO Report, Avon FO 954 Yu/41/21.
[65] Ibid.
[66] Ibid.
[67] Ibid.; according to Longmore, the capacity of the Takoradi route at present did not reach 100 machines a month. Altogether 277 fighters, 256 medium bombers and 55 heavy bombers had been authorised. 500 Tomahawks had been promised, but it was now learned that only 190 were to be expected. See 'Brief appreciation of air situation', 6 Mar. 1941, attached to Longmore to Portal, 18 Mar. 1941, Portal, Box D 1b.
[68] Record of meeting ... 6 Mar. 1941, 5 p.m., FO Report, Avon FO 954 Yu/41/21.
[69] Ibid.; Record of meeting ... 10.15 p.m. 6 Mar. 1941, FO Report, Avon FO 954 Yu/41/21.

ahead. At no stage had the criterion for proceeding been limited to whether or not it had a chance of success in stopping Hitler. But other grander, more ephemeral goals continued to confuse the issue for those on the spot, even more so than for those at some remove in London. By 7 March there was no room to take account of the confusion; and the issue was resolved partly because the combined confusions had been artificially clarified and and the issue put in sharp relief.

The foreign office after Eden's departure

At the foreign office, the uncertainties about the changing circumstances in Greece, the Balkans and Turkey continued to affect views about intervention. There were varying reactions. They included the original feeling that they could not 'force assistance down [the Greek] throat' and, later on, that intervention must in the end be a failure, particularly given the refusal of the Turks to join in and the failure to get the Yugoslavs to commit themselves; a sense of amazement, not to say horror, at Eden's progress – or lack of it; and resentment at the formal commitment. All along there was both a hope that it might turn out all right, and a sense that it could not.

At the outset Cadogan agreed with Churchill that 'we ought to do all we can to help Greece'. He did not concede that 'our first obligation [was] to Turkey'. Greece was fighting, whereas Turkey was 'doing nothing'; but in any case, helping the Greeks 'may encourage Turkey'.[70] The initial reaction to Greek refusal had been that they could not force assistance on the Greeks and though the Balkan countries were 'wrong' they were were evidently terrified.[71] Failure here prompted reflections on other possibilities – such as North Africa or a peace between Greece and Germany.

The ambivalence displayed by the Turks before Eden's departure did not seem to change as a result of his visit – if anything, there seemed to be even less reason to count on them. The Turks would not, before Eden left, commit themselves but though their attitude was equivocal, their preliminary reply had not been 'too discouraging'.[72] Nor did Eden seem to make much difference when he saw them. Though he wired of their '"frankness" ... "friendliness" and "realism"' they seemed to have said 'quite flatly that they will only fight if attacked (which of course they

[70] Dill's view was that the first obligation was to Turkey, Cadogan diary 10 Feb. 1941.
[71] Cadogan diary, 16 Jan. 1941. There was also the possibility that Hitler was hoping to lure a small British force to the Balkans to destroy it.
[72] Cadogan diary, 3, 8, 10 Feb. 1941.

won't be – yet)'.[73] There was a fear that Eden would 'get nothing out of the Turks; and ... his prestige and ours ... [would] slump'. The Turks would 'do nothing unless attacked', and there was no reason for Hitler to attack yet.[74] Cadogan had doubts about 'the wisdom of Eden's visit'; he did not believe that 'either the Turks or the Yugoslavs [would] move'. Putting in troops 'would be a different matter if they did'.[75] By 1 March Eden appeared to have 'got nothing out of the Turks'.[76]

With the other Balkan countries it seemed, at the foreign office, to be the same story. Cadogan held out little hope for Bulgaria, whose minister was urged to fight the Germans, 'and thus join those small nations who had assured their own future in this manner'.[77] But as late as mid-February it was not clear that they would; and the attitude of the minister did not seem to tally with the action of his government. M. Montchiloff claimed that he himself had warned his government that 'things would not work out as they had in Norway'; that he 'still hoped his country would put up at any rate a modicum of resistance to the Germans'. At the same time, he regretted 'the tone of the British press' and found the propaganda 'offensive'. Bulgaria did not intend, he maintained, to play the jackal but was solely preoccupied with avoiding being 'overrun and destroyed'. He thought this would be best achieved 'through resistance', which course he was pressing on his government.[78] None the less, on 1 March the news came of Bulgaria's signing the Axis pact and the entry of German troops. The British minister at Sofia could 'break off diplomatic relations and ... leave Bulgaria' as soon as he considered his position impossible.[79] The Yugoslavs, too, seemed unlikely to co-operate. If they did move – or if the Turks did – that would change prospects but Cadogan held out little hope and was, as he told the Yugoslav minister, disappointed with their 'backwardness'. Butler, standing in for Eden, was gloomy and disappointed with the recent attitude of the Yugoslav regent: the 'only hope for [the] Balkans lay in their getting together'. Failure to get anything from the Turks would have bad results for the Yugoslavs who would now 'curl up' and he urged Yugoslavia to have closer links with Turkey.[80] He

---

[73] Cadogan diary, 28 Feb. 1941. The 'reality', according to Cadogan, was that 'they won't do a damned thing'.
[74] Dalton diary, 19 Feb. 1941.   [75] Ibid.   [76] Cadogan diary, 1 Mar. 1941.
[77] Cadogan diary, 14 Feb. 1941; Cadogan did think it a 'grim prospect for his country'. Butler account of conversation with Bulgarian minister, 15 Feb. 1941, Avon FO 954/1 Bul/41/2.
[78] Butler, account of conversation with Bulgarian minister, 15 Feb. 1941, Avon FO 954/1, Bul/41/2.
[79] Cadogan diary, 1 Mar. 1941; cabinet, 3 Mar. 1941, WM(41)22, CAB 65/18.
[80] He urged closer links with Turkey rather than visits by their prime minister and foreign secretary to Berchtesgaden; Cadogan diary, 17, 28 Feb. 1941; Channon diary, 20 Feb.

thought the Yugoslav position, by 24 February, 'obscure' and he did not rate highly the prospects of Yugoslavia's making a stand against Germany.[81]

At the foreign office, therefore, in the absence either of forming a Balkan front, or even of drawing individual countries in, and given the failure of either the Turks or the Yugoslavs to move, attention after mid-February shifted to other courses of action: should they concentrate on North Africa and drop the Greeks? Unless a 'good show in [the] Balkans' could be made, they had 'better clean up Africa and get the victorious "army of the Nile"' alongside Weygand in Tunisia.[82] Events in the Balkans might 'so move' that they might 'have to allow the Greeks, under pressure, to make a separate peace'. This might be better than having the country 'devastated to the last acre', or than 'putting in some of our own troops and having them, not even evacuated, but trapped and destroyed'. It would be 'a different matter' to put the troops in, if the Turks or the Yugoslavs moved.[83] As they were unlikely to do so, Cadogan set out the arguments for 'abandoning our friends and going on with Tripoli', which might encourage Weygand and the French 'to stand with us'.[84] On 19 February Cadogan put the case to Churchill ('advised the PM to have second thoughts about Libya'); and on the 20th Churchill, during a cabinet disquisition, left room for such a course.[85]

The news from the Balkans seemed, if anything, to get worse. Eden's failure either to bring in the Turks or to influence the Yugoslavs would mean 'we shall be alone with the Greeks to share their inevitable disaster'. By 1 March Bulgaria was definitely out and a bad shipping situation provided further argument 'against this Balkan expedition'.[86] By the 3rd 'everything look[ed] ... as black as black'. Cadogan did not see where they were to turn; was 'sure a folorn hope in Balkans w[ould] only do us harm in France and Spain' and wished they could have gone on into Tripoli and joined up with Weygand.[87] There was no further news from Eden on the 4th. His wires on the 5th convinced Cadogan he had 'run ahead of his instructions'; had 'agreed to things which [the] Greeks will take as commitments and on which they may make decisions ... in a

---

1941; Butler record of talk with Yugoslav minister (Soubbotitch), 21 Feb. 1941, Avon FO 954, Yu/41/5.
[81] Cabinet, 24 Feb. 1941, WM(41)20, CAB 65/21.
[82] Cadogan diary, 18 Feb. 1941. When the Greeks had first refused help, Cadogan's reaction, on 20 January, had been to 'go on in N[orth] Africa', Cadogan diary, 20 Feb. 1941.
[83] Dalton diary, 19 Feb. 1941. Cadogan felt sure that the Germans had been 'trying to entice us in force in Greece'.
[84] Dalton diary, 19 Feb. 1941; Cadogan diary, 19 Feb. 1941.   [85] Ibid., 20 Feb. 1941.
[86] Ibid., 27, 28 Feb., 1, 3 Mar. 1941.   [87] Ibid., 3 Mar. 1941.

critical moment'. Although Eden may have wished to prevent a collapse, Cadogan thought his head had been 'turned'. Cadogan would, on the 6th, have gone back on the agreement if he could 'see any better alternative'.[88]

But Cadogan did not see such an alternative. At the foreign office there had, throughout, been two cases. One was against intervention in Greece on the grounds that it would fail – particularly if there were no Balkan/Turkish front. The other was in favour of intervention because it was the right course and it might succeed. Neither view dominated absolutely. Although Cadogan, after Eden's departure, tended to turn against intervention (particularly as the neighbouring countries would not come in), and favoured, instead, going on in north Africa and abandoning the Greeks, he did not do so absolutely. For until early March there was always the chance that Eden would form a Balkan front; and it did not become clear until then that he had really failed to do so. When it did become clear that he had failed – and that the operation itself would end in failure – it was too late to abandon the Greeks, because Britain had been committed, in a formal agreement to military intervention, by Eden and Dill. In those circumstances there was nothing to be done but emphasise that the decision was right. Unlike Churchill – and unlike the opinion surrounding the cabinet decision – Cadogan had no feeling that the operation would succeed, or that the case should be made on those grounds. Whereas before the prospect of a Balkan front collapsed, that might have been possible, it was no longer so after 3 March. The case, therefore, was then made – as it had been partially throughout – solely on the grounds of right.

Cadogan had himself been distracted from opposing the scheme by the prospect of success, which Eden intimated existed and which the soldiers held out. He had been prompted by reports of Eden's discussions with Wavell, from which it seemed that about three divisions and one armoured one 'which might hold a "line" in Greece' could be spared. This gamble, Cadogan thought, was worth trying. But by 24 February, Cadogan thought that, though it was 'impressive that Wavell and Dill' endorsed Eden, it 'must' end in failure and reflected on the rightness of persisting.[89] Even if intervention were to fail, it was the right course. For example, when the wires on the 23rd suggested Eden had 'plumped for helping Greece', on the 24th Cadogan thought that was 'certainly respectable, but we must eventually be beaten there'. His reaction after reading the chiefs' report endorsing proposals for a Balkan expedition, was that, though right, 'it must in the end be a failure'; 'on all moral and sentimental (and consequently American) grounds, one [was] driven to the

[88] Ibid., 4, 5, 6 Mar. 1941.   [89] Ibid., 22, 24 Feb. 1941.

grim conclusion'. It was 'perhaps better to have failed in a decent project than never to have tried at all'. It was 'a nasty decision but ... on balance [he] agree[d] with it'.[90] By 5 March, without support for Greece from her neighbours, and with an inferior plan and fewer forces than anticipated at the outset, it seemed that they ought to go ahead. For, as Butler made the case at the cabinet, 'if we abandoned Greece, this might have a bad effect on the position in Spain which was uncertain, and in North Africa where German infiltration was increasing'.[91] They could not, Cadogan thought on the 6th, 'go back on [Eden] and Dill' when it emerged that they had formally committed Britain.[92] And when, on 7 March, the cabinet 'practically decided to go ahead in Balkans' Cadogan, on a 'nice balance', thought 'this is right'.[93]

The chiefs of staff and their advice to the cabinet

Although the general view at the time of Eden's departure was 'that it was essential ... to come to the assistance of the Greeks if they would have us', the issue was complicated. Dill, for example, thought 'our first obligation is to Turkey'; Eden, that the best way of ensuring that Turkey would fight, was to help Greece; Churchill, that it would be 'wrong' to abandon the Greeks so that 'later we could ... help Turkey, who was shirking her responsibility'. Despite an 'inclination' to concentrate on Turkey, the chiefs of staff did not distinguish Greece and Turkey categorically. They thought it was now essential 'to find out the Greek plan' and whether Turkey would regard a German ultimatum to Greece as 'cause to enter the war'. They intended to examine the issue on the assumption that the 'largest possible force' would be moved from Egypt to the European continent 'to assist the Greeks against a ... German attack through Bulgaria' and that steps should be taken 'to enable our plans to be concerted with the Greeks'.[94]

If the chiefs did not distinguish categorically between Greece and Turkey (and confusion between ends and means may have been increased by uncertainty of what to expect from each), nor did they abandon the prospect of continuing in North Africa. Their report would be made on the basis of a decision to divert to the Balkans to help the Greeks. But given the prospect of the Greeks refusing, 'it might then be necessary to consider whether an advance to Tripoli was justified as an alternative'.[95]

90 Ibid., 23, 24 Feb. 1941.   91 Cabinet, 5 Mar. 1941, WM(41)24, CAB 65/22.
92 Cabinet, 6 Mar. 1941; Cadogan diary, 6 Mar. 1941. Even to a plan previously considered inferior and with fewer Greek forces than anticipated.
93 Cadogan diary, 7 Mar. 1941.   94 Ibid.
95 Defence committee, 10 Feb. 1941, DO(41)7, CAB 69/2.

The chiefs' instructions were ready by 11 February, when the main point discussed at the defence committee was 'the size of the force which could be found from Egypt to Greece'. They must be in a position to send 'the largest possible land and air forces' from Africa to the European continent 'to assist the Greeks against a probable German attack through Bulgaria'. The 'only way of making sure ... the Turks do fight' was to give 'sufficient support to the Greeks to ensure that they fight'.[96]

Though forces were to be prepared for Greece, there was no certainty that the Greeks would take them; or that helping Greece could be distinguished from considerations about Turkey. Helping Greece was (for the chiefs) complicated by the shortages of those very supplies most needed by the Greeks and by the feeling that, in any case, nothing could be done militarily to stop the Germans; by the traditional place of Turkey in Middle East defence; by the changing position of the Greeks themselves – from being reluctant to take help, to looking to Britain to provide the bulk of forces to defend against a German invasion; and by what mattered to the individual services.

It may be that the despatch of troops from Egypt was partly designed to deflect demands for direct assistance in artillery. There had been the view among the chiefs that the artillery supplies the Greeks most needed could only be found by disarming British troops and thus taking 'the gravest risks in this country' – particularly in regard to artillery, their 'immediate need ... on the scale say of 144 field guns and 48 medium guns with substantial ... ammunition'. These guns could only be provided by withdrawing from the hands of the troops and such a diversion 'would be the equivalent of the disarming of two of our own divisions'.[97] But Churchill insisted that it was essential to send some help to the Greeks; and that 'a definite proposal should be put forward for the supply of weapons and ammunition from this country'. He suggested 'as a start 50,000 rounds of 75mm ammunition and another 50,000 rounds at a later date'; and a statement of 'definite proposals for the release to the Greeks of weapons and ammunition from the UK'. The chiefs would also consider 'the implications of releasing such equipment'.[98]

The offer to the Turks did not, therefore, resolve the question of priorities. The perplexities of deciding between the Middle East and the Balkans, and between Greece and Turkey, persisted – not only on account

---

[96] Defence committee, 11 Feb. 1941, DO(41)8, CAB 69/2; chiefs CsinCME, appended to DO(41)8, CAB 69/2.
[97] Chiefs of staff, 4 Feb. 1941, COS(41)41, CAB 79/9.
[98] Chiefs of staff, 6 Feb. 1941, COS(41)44, CAB 79/7. Wavell was to estimate, in addition, the captured material he could supply to Greece and a timetable of shipments; Dill to Wavell, 7 Feb. 1941; WO106/2144.

of the hovering of the Turks and the hopes for a Balkan front, but because of the changing views of where British interests lay and how central to these was military success.

The chiefs acquiesced in the decision to concentrate on Greece for a number of reasons – which continued to affect the changing emphases subsequently given to the Greek question and that of Turkey. When, on 10 February, the defence committee decided to send 'the largest possible ... force from Egypt ... to assist the Greeks against a ... German attack', the chiefs were not clear about the extent or nature of the commitment. A series of events had lent themselves to the decision: the 'unexpectedly early capture of Benghazi ... the Turkish refusal to accept ... immediate assistance ... The urgent request of the Greek government ... for information as to the size and composition of the British forces which we would send to Greece'.[99] They feared the effect on Turkey if Greece 'were to yield to Germany without fighting'; and claimed that 'the only way of making sure ... the Turks do fight is to give sufficient ... to the Greeks to ensure ... they fight'.[100] Furthermore, it was 'impossible to settle the precise size and composition of these forces, or their destination in Greece' until details of the Greek plan and forces were made available. They could not settle at this stage whether British forces would be based on Salonika (for which the Greeks would press), or the Piraeus. Even if the Greeks retracted their refusal to accept British forces before the Germans had 'actually marched' and even if 'we had sufficient forces available, it would be impossible for them to arrive in Salonika in time to be effective'. It was 'no longer possible to ... [send] an army to Salonika since the Germans ... could prevent us establishing ourselves there'.[101]

Although the feeling existed that they should have to keep something in hand with which to help the Turks, there was also the feeling that Greece excluded Turkey. No substantial acceleration or despatch to Turkey of war material would be possible 'unless the decision was taken to give Turkey higher priority than ... at present accorded'. 'No change in the existing order of priority' should be considered until after the discussions now about to be held.[102] Equipment which might be due for Turkey

---

[99] Defence committee, 10 Feb. 1941, DO(41)7, CAB 69/2; chiefs of staff to CsinCME, 11 Feb. 1941 appended to DO(41)8, CAB 69/2.

[100] Chiefs of staff to CsinCME, appended to defence committee, 11 Feb. 1941, DO(41)8, CAB 69/2.

[101] Ibid.; and defence committee, 10 Feb. 1941, DO(41)7, CAB 69/2. The draft telegram with minor amendments was approved on the 11th despite Dill's fear that it would be 'difficult ... to find four divisions in the immediate future to send to Greece'. Defence committee, 11 Feb. 1941, DO(40)8, CAB 69/2.

[102] Chiefs of staff, 15 Feb. 1941, COS(41)56, CAB 79/9; defence committee, 10 Feb. 1941, DO(41)7, CAB 69/2.

would be kept in hand pending the discussions; though that 'would not preclude the despatch to Turkey of a handful of army and RAF specialists in plain clothes if necessary – to ensure that the Turks were making full use of the equipment already supplied to them'.[103] Turkey's not having accepted complete units was regarded 'as a refusal of our offer [and] to send further equipment without personnel would be wasteful and unsatisfactory'; it might lead to loss of control over equipment 'which might be better used in Greece'.[104]

At no stage did the chiefs throw their collective weight against proceeding with help to Greece. Their advice, as conveyed to the cabinet on the 24th (which also heard that Dill thought 'we had a reasonable chance of resisting a German advance'), was that 'on balance ... the enterprise should go forward'.[105] And in early March they seemed to make light of the worsening conditions, to insist that those 'on the spot knew best' and to suggest, in any case, that as far as the troops went, all would be just about all right. Despite reservations expressed by Churchill at the cabinet and his suggestions (on 4 March) that a 'final view' might be taken in the light of fresh information which might be received (and despite his view at the cabinet (on the 5th) that it was still open to them to liberate the Greeks from any undertaking), the chiefs did not decide definitely against proceeding. On the contrary, they implied that it was a matter to be decided locally – in that they were not 'as yet in a position to question the military advice of those on the spot'. In their commentary – appended to Churchill's wire to Eden (that they must 'liberate Greeks from feeling bound to reject a German ultimatum') – they stated that 'the hazards of the enterprise ha[d] considerably increased' but added despite 'misgivings ... we are not as yet in a position to question the military advice of those on the spot'.[106] They recognised, therefore, that the situation had clearly changed for the worse (as it had by 5 March) but would not categorically advise a halt. For example, Papagos was now 'unaccommodating and defeatist' which was 'bound to react unfavourably on the fighting spirit of his army'; the Greeks had failed 'to withdraw to the line which we should have to hold if the Yugs were not willing to come in'. Of the thirty-five Greek battalions to hold that line, there would now only be twenty-three

---

[103] Ibid.
[104] Chiefs of staff to commanders in chief, no. 59, 17 Feb. 1941, PREM 3/309/2.
[105] Cabinet, 24 Feb. 1941, WM(41)20, CAB 65/21. The chiefs of staff paper before the cabinet added that 'even the complete failure of an honourable attempt ... would not be disastrous to our future ability to defeat Germany', a point which was recalled at the cabinet on 5 March. WM(41)24, CAB 65/22.
[106] Cabinet, 4 Mar. 1941, WM(41)23, CAB 65/22; defence committee, 5 Mar. 1941, DO(41)9, CAB/2 and annex Churchill to Eden, 5 Mar. 1941, with chiefs of staff commentary; cabinet, 5 Mar. 1941, WM(41)24, CAB 65/22.

at most – and even these might not all arrive 'since their withdrawal ha[d] been prejudiced by the rapidity of the German advance'.[107] In addition to the changed plan and reduced number of forces available, there would be a further shortage in the air: for given that Mandibles could not be completed before the operation 'all available air forces [could not be concentrated] against the German advance' while the mining of the Suez Canal had made the transportation of personnel more difficult.[108] None the less – and despite all that the chiefs maintained – 'the Greek enterprise ha[d] always been regarded as a hazardous operation', though not [by Eden] as hopeless even though more hazardous than the previous week. But 'even the complete failure of an honourable attempt to help Greece need not be disastrous to our future ability to defeat Germany' and in their view 'a weighty consideration in favour of going to Greece is to make the Germans fight for what they want ... on balance we think that the enterprise should go forward'.[109] Reluctance to abandon the operation was implied to be justified by deferring to those on the spot. Though 'the hazards of the enterprise ha[d] considerably increased' and despite a worsening of the general situation 'we are not yet in a position to question the military advice of those on the spot, who in their latest telegram describe the enterprise as not by any means hopeless'.[110]

The chiefs implied also that the time factor justified proceeding and sought to calculate the respective times of arrival of the German troops against that of their own. The Germans could reach the Veria line with two divisions by 15 March and with five by 22 March, whereas 'at best we should have one armoured brigade and one New Zealand brigade to oppose the first two German divisions on the Veria line'.[111] Moreover, 'three Greek divisions could get to the Aliakmon line in plenty of time'; that it was 'probable that our forces would arrive there at about the same time as the Germans'.[112] On the 7th, when they wired the commanders of their estimate, asking whether they agreed, they stressed that time was the 'obviously dominating factor in Greek enterprise'.[113] The cabinet was not

107 Chiefs of staff commentary, appended as *aide-memoire* to Cabinet, 5 Mar. 1941, WM(41)24, CAB 65/22. The text differs slightly to that annexed to DO(41)9, CAB 69/2.
108 Ibid.
109 Ibid.; and extract from chiefs of staff report to the cabinet, of 24 Feb. 1941, recalled at the cabinet on 5 March, WM(41)24, CAB 65/22.
110 Defence committee, 5 Mar. 1941, DO(41)9, CAB 69/2; chiefs of staff commentary in Churchill to Eden, 6 Mar. 1941, PREM 3/309/2.
111 Chiefs of staff, 3 Mar. 1941, COS(41)81, CAB 79/9; Chiefs of staff commentary appended as *aide-memoire* to cabinet, 5 Mar. 1941, WM(41)24, CAB 65/22.
112 Cabinet, 6 Mar. 1941, WM(41)25, CAB 65/22. The chiefs thought it also probable that the German force might consist of one armoured division plus three motorised divisions, and one infantry division.
113 Chiefs of staff to CsinCME, 7 Mar. 1941, appended to WM(41)26, CAB 65/22.

in any case to make a decision on the 6th, pending a reply from Eden – though Churchill's view was clear 'that we could not now go back on the agreement signed by ... Dill and ... Papagos, unless the Greeks released us'.[114]

When on the 7th after Eden's telegrams had come in insisting on going on and the final decision was reached, the chiefs again made much of the military judgement of those on the spot. Eden's wires made it clear that he, Dill and the commanders-in-chief had re-examined the matter and were 'unanimously agreed that despite the heavy commitments and grave risks ... the right decision had been taken in Athens'.[115] The chiefs maintained that the Greek campaign should go ahead despite deteriorating conditions, alluding in support to the views of the military on the spot. The principal new factors since their appreciation of 24 February were the intention of Yugoslavia and Turkey 'to keep out of the war' and the exacerbation of shipping difficulties, the Suez Canal being out of action for considerable periods, and Mandibles not being carried out before the opening of the campaign. Yet the Middle East command, according to the chiefs, claimed they had 'made due allowance for these difficulties in their recommendation that the Balkan campaign should go forward'; and thus they took the view that the chiefs had 'underestimated by from one to four days the time which it would take the Germans to reach the Aliakmon line'. The conclusion of the whole matter, in their view, was 'that our military advisers on the spot were convinced that the Greek campaign would not be a hopeless venture' and they were 'prepared to accept their judgement. Accordingly they adhered to their former opinion that the campaign should go forward.' And, in reply to a question, they added that their opinion was 'based mainly on the views of the commanders in chief in the Middle East, reinforced by the replies they had sent to the searching questions to them'.[116]

Churchill's reaction to Eden's mission

After Eden's departure, the respective importance of Greece and Turkey remained a matter of ambiguity – as the prospect of getting out of a Greek commitment and doubts about military success continued to be entertained. Churchill continued to change the emphasis on priority for Greece or for Turkey. While the publicly and privately reiterated view was that Greece must come first, that preparations for the despatch of troops and

---

[114] Cabinet, 6 Mar. 1941, WM(41)25, CAB 69/22; Cadogan diary, 6 Mar. 1941. Cadogan did not think so either, but Wood, Alexander and Anderson were 'out for A's blood'.
[115] Cabinet, 7 Mar. 1941, WM(41)26, CAB 65/22.   [116] Ibid.

RAF be made, that Eden's visit to Cairo, Athens and Angora had that aim, Churchill could not stake all on the Greeks. Nor need he. His interventions, after Eden's departure, suggest that the offer was made in the hope, if not the certainty, that it could not be taken up. The Germans would move too quickly for British troops to be there and the Greeks would accept terms without fighting. Britain would then avoid having wasted resources on the Greeks, but would have been seen to make the offer to help; and be seen to have meant it by virtue of the preparations, by the despatch of Eden, by the instructions to Wavell to make all arrangements for diversion. The offer had been made and could have been taken up. The Greeks must not, therefore, be stopped from making peace; and the only danger to all this was Eden.

Churchill did continue to maintain that the Greeks must have first refusal, though they might not take up the offer or else would fail to stop the Germans. On 20 February he told his colleagues that Eden and Dill had now reached Cairo on their way to Athens and Angora; that the 'object of this visit was to see what help could be given to the Greeks and Turks in the event of a German advance south through Bulgaria';[117] Eden would see the Greeks before going to Angora. Otherwise 'commitments might have been made to Angora which would tie your hands about Greeks who are actually fighting'.[118] It may be that the Germans could not be stopped, that a German thrust towards Salonika 'would be irresistible; but if the Greeks decided to fight we should do what we could'. If they decided to oppose a German advance into their country 'we should have to help them to the full extent of our power'.[119]

It is not clear how far Churchill expected they would be called on to help. He 'hoped [at the cabinet on the 20th] we should not have to put any large part of our army into Greece'.[120] Or it might be that the Greeks would make terms and that they would not regret such a development. The Germans might offer 'before ... their advance ... such attractive terms that [the Greeks] would feel bound to make peace'.[121] In that case we could not very well blame them, 'nor should we take such a decision on the part of the Greeks too tragically. We should have done our duty'.[122] Above all, Eden must not press the Greeks if the outcome of action was to be failure – which from the start it had fairly consistently been thought it would be. If the Greeks were reluctant to resist a German advance, then Eden must not press them to do so; and Churchill warned Eden in Cairo they should 'not consider [themselves] obligated to a Greek enterprise if in

---

[117] Cabinet, 20 Feb. 1941, WM(41)19, CAB 65/21.
[118] Churchill to Eden, 21 Feb. 1941, PREM 3/309/1.
[119] Cabinet, 20 Feb. 1941, WM(41)19, CAB 65/21.   [120] Ibid.   [121] Ibid.
[122] Ibid.

[their] hearts they [felt] it [would] only be another Norwegian fiasco'.[123] If no good plan could be made, then they must say so, though 'how valuable' success would be.[124]

Churchill's confidence about taking the Greek decision was bolstered by the sense that whatever happened, there was much to play for, and something to gain. In the series of overlapping considerations throughout the January–March period which informed his changing emphases, the decision to offer help should be seen in a multitude of contexts: from Greece's role in imperial defence and the need for bases in the Balkans, to the prospect of the Greeks not fighting and the force being released for other tasks – Tripoli or the Greek islands.

Strategically Greece could be seen as an 'advance position' to Egypt – the 'enterprise in Greece was an advance position, which we could try to hold without jeopardising our main position'.[125] The force could be put to other uses. In the event of its 'proving impossible to reach any good agreement with the Greeks and work out a practical military plan', they must save 'as much from the wreck as possible ... keep Crete ... take any Greek islands ... [useful] as air bases ... [and] reconsider the advance on Tripoli'.[126] On the 20th Churchill reviewed the questions Eden would have to settle 'leaving room ... for the possibility of Tripolitania'.[127] Or, intervention might help secure bases in the Balkans from which to bomb the Germans in Romania and in Italy – for which Portal had argued.[128] In any case, if the Greeks decided to make peace, the decision should not be taken 'too tragically'. 'We should have done our duty and should then have to content ourselves by making our position in the Greek islands as strong as possible.' From these 'we could wage air war against Germany, which might eventually turn in our favour'. If Greece were 'in the enemy's hands' and Turkey 'an honest neutral', then it would remain for consideration 'what we should do with our strong forces now in the Delta ... [and] the question of advancing into Tripoli would again arise'. Moreover, whatever ultimately happened, Churchill believed that Britain could

---

[123] Churchill to Eden, 20 Feb. 1941, PREM 3/309/2.   [124] Ibid.

[125] Cabinet, 24 Feb. 1941, WM(41)20, CAB 65/21. He told the cabinet that the war turned on '(1) holding England, (2) holding Egypt, (3) retaining command of the sea, (4) obtaining command of the air and (5) being able to keep open the American arsenals'.

[126] Churchill to Wavell, 11 Feb. 1941, appended to DO(41)8, CAB 69/2, although he also suggested the alternatives might be as 'consolation prizes after the classic race had been lost'.

[127] Cadogan diary, 19 and 20 Feb. 1941. Cadogan had minuted him the previous day 'setting out arguments with bias in favour of abandoning our friends and going on with Tripoli'.

[128] Churchill to Eden, 27 Feb. 1941, PREM 3/309/2. Dill thought Churchill regarded Portal as the real strategist of the chiefs of staff; and Portal had argued that the airforce should be given a 'platform' in Greece. Kennedy, *Business of War*, pp. 75–6.

hardly lose: even if the Greeks accepted the offer, 'in fact it was unlikely that it would be possible for a large British force to get there before the Germans'[129] – a point which continued to help his more cavalier attitude to failure.

By 24 February Churchill did not rate highly the prospects of success in Greece, and would not reassure the Australians. If pressed back, 'our troops might well have to be evacuated; but ... we ought to be able to evacuate safely all but the wounded'.[130] He could not assure Menzies that the venture 'had a substantial chance of success'. In his (Churchill's) opinion 'the enterprise was a risk which we must undertake. At the worst ... the bulk of the men could be got back to Egypt, where new equipment could by then be provided.' He was warned by Beaverbrook that the enterprise would involve 'a serious strain on our shipping, particularly if it should prove necessary to withdraw our forces from Greece'.[131]

Yet Churchill was, simultaneously, led by Eden partially to abandon his doubts. He was tantalised by the prospect of success and affected by Eden's plans in Cairo, by his resolution to proceed, and by his confidence – though he was never absolutely sure and continued to waver. From the Cairo reports of Eden's discussions with Wavell it seemed that 'about three divisions and one armoured which might hold "a line" in Greece' could be spared. It also seemed that Eden, by the 23rd, had 'plumped for helping Greece'. And the feelings of the chiefs by the 24th as relayed to the cabinet (which heard Dill's view that 'we had a reasonable chance of resisting a German advance') was that 'on balance' the enterprise should go forward.[132]

Eden's decision led Churchill in turn partially to abandon his doubts about Greece. Churchill, who intended to have the Cairo proposal 'studied', prepared to allow Eden his head 'in the meantime ... on the assumption that full approval will be given'.[133] He was struck by the 'impressive' telegrams in favour of the operation and by the optimism about the prospect of success.[134] By contrast with his own earlier warning against 'another Norwegian fiasco', he now referred to the support of the generals and to the recommendations of Dill and Wavell to send armed forces to Greece, and their 'impressive' telegrams. Wavell's being 'in favour of action in Greece must have considerable weight' given his tendency to 'understatement', and his wish to complete the campaign in

129 Cabinet, 20 Feb. 1941, WM(41)19, CAB 65/17; CAB 65/21.
130 Cabinet, 24 Feb. 1941, WM(41)20 CAB 65/21.
131 Cabinet, 24 Feb. 1941, WM(41)20, CAB 65/21. Cadogan diary, 24 Feb. 1941.
132 Cabinet, 24 Feb. 1941, WM(41)20, CAB 65/21; Cadogan diary, 22, 23, 24 Feb. 1941.
133 Churchill to Eden, 24 Feb. 1941, PREM 3/309/2.
134 Cabinet, 24 Feb. 1941, WM(41)20, CAB 65/21.

North Africa. Indeed, so must Dill's – for Dill 'always doubted whether Germany could be ... resisted on the mainland and had always taken a restrained view about our going to Greece', but now thought 'we had a reasonable chance of resisting a German advance'. Churchill's allusions to the military support for the operation (in Cairo and among the chiefs of staff, who had reported that 'on balance the enterprise should go forward') made it seem that intervention was now all the more attractive given the military appreciations of the prospects of success. Not only were there political reasons, the prospects of bringing in Turkey and Yugoslavia, of forcing the Germans to bring more troops from Germany, the factor of the Unites States reaction, but there was, or so it seemed, more than a chance of success.[135]

Churchill may have been tantalised by, though unsure of, the prospect of success but it is unclear whether he still envisaged that the troops would arrive too late. Simultaneously with stating that the military entertained hopes of success, he explained that he did not anticipate the German advance to take place until mid-March, 12 to 15th, and 'our troops would arrive at their positions at about the same time'.[136] Moreover he continued to allude to the difficulties and risks, even after the case had been made and accepted for going ahead and his confidence about numbers tended to be based on speculation. On the 27th he felt 'no doubt that the decision taken [i.e. to go ahead] ... had been right' but referred to the many difficulties which 'would attend the opening of a new theatre of war in Greece'. The decision had been reached 'in full knowledge' of these difficulties – the need to supply the forces by the long Cape route, the danger of the Suez Canal being blocked by enemy action, the 'heavy attacks now being made on our shipping'.[137] The difficulties were not offset by calculations about the number of reinforcements and troops – the 6th Division would be available in two months' time and possibly the 50th division could be sent to Greece from the UK while 'a considerable Empire force ... now engaged in East Africa ... might be available.[138] In addition to such speculation, he also calculated that intervention would increase the number of troops fighting the Allied cause. Intervention was the policy 'best calculated to retain the military co-operation not only of the 18 Greek divisions now in the field but also to secure the 27 Turkish divisions now in Thrace'. Together with 'our own', these forces would be 'larger than any which the Germans could put into the field against us for several months'.[139]

[135] Ibid.   [136] Ibid.   [137] Cabinet, 27 Feb. 1941, WM(41)21, CAB 65/21.
[138] Cabinet, 27 Feb. 1941, WM(41)21, CAB 65/21.
[139] Ibid.

Churchill's support for intervention was, therefore, argued by reference to the military case made by juxtaposing the views of the generals in the light of their 'impressive' telegrams; by calculating hypothetically the numbers of armed forces; by referring to the prospects of success – all in addition to the diplomatic and political considerations which had been developed since November. By the 24th he had, it seemed, 'made up his mind' and was, possibly, all the more convinced because he continued to take account of the dangers as well as the political advantages of acting whatever the outcome. In view of 'the evidence before them ... [he was] in favour of the plan'; and after the cabinet that day he wired Eden 'full steam ahead'. He was keen to allude, as he did at the cabinet on the 27th, to the 'political value of the military steps now decided upon' and had 'no doubt that the decision taken at the last meeting had been right'.[140]

Despite the wording of the wire he sent Eden on the 24th February ('we all send you the order "full steam ahead"'), which suggested neither hesitation nor the absence of unanimity, Churchill was, as he put it, under 'no illusion'.[141] The very factors which made for confidence also served to undermine it. And in the absence of any progress by Eden in the Balkans, and as the shipping situation (which was 'very gloomy') provided further 'argument against this Balkan expedition',[142] Churchill's resolve faltered. By 27 February his buoyancy had been tempered to the extent of his referring to the 'grave and hazardous decision to sustain the Greeks and try to make a Balkan front'.[143] It was further undermined by Eden's wire of the 28th as a result of which Churchill would only go ahead if there were a 'reasonable chance'. He was 'absolutely ready to go in on a serious hazard if ... a reasonable chance of success [existed], at any rate for a few months', in which case 'all preparations should go forward at fullest speed'. But if there were not such a chance, they should not. Instead, Eden must so handle matters in Greece that 'if upon final consideration of all the factors ... [he felt] there [was] not even a reasonable hope [he should] still retain power to liberate Greeks from any bargain and at the same time liberate ourselves'.[144] Whereas at the outset Churchill had thought of intervention for its political advantages, and was willing to decide in the knowledge that it would fail, by late February it had to some extent become a matter of military success, and the omens did not look good.

---

[140] Ibid.; Cabinet, 24 Feb. 1941, WM(41)20, CAB 65/21; Cadogan diary, 24 Feb. 1941; Churchill to Eden, 24 Feb. 1941, PREM 3/309/2.
[141] Churchill to Eden, 24 Feb. 1941, PREM 3/309/2.
[142] Cadogan diary, 27 Feb. 1941.
[143] Churchill to Wavell, 27 Feb. 1941 in Connell, *Wavell*, pp. 345–6.
[144] Churchill to Eden, 1 Mar. 1941, Churchill, *Second World War*, III, p. 86. Eden to Churchill, 28 Feb. 1941, PREM 3/309/2.

Since the prospect of success had so hung on bringing in the Turks and the Yugoslavs, Churchill was less sanguine about the whole thing, when by 3 March Eden seemed to have failed to do so.[145] He told the cabinet on the 4th that 'prospects in the Balkans were not promising'; Bulgaria was under German control; and 'it looked as though Greece would have to fight for her life and as though Yugoslavia intended to take no action before she was surrounded'. But were the Yugoslavs to decide to act at once 'their armies might well wipe out the Italian armies in Albania'.[146]

Given the unlikelihood of success should the operation be called off? Should Eden be encouraged to get out of it? Churchill was, or claimed to be, 'disinclined' to issue the necessary orders countermanding the troop movements due to start that day. He thought the cabinet might 'wish to take a final view of the whole position in the light of the information to be received in the next few days'.[147] The cabinet considered on the 5th the three alternatives facing Eden: 'to dribble up our forces piecemeal to the Macedonian frontier ... which ... Papagos wished ... [but which] we had refused to consider'; to accept the Greek offer (far below what originally had been expected) for the Aliakmon line; or to withdraw the offer of support entirely. No immediate decision was called for, but no further commitments should be entered into until the Yugoslav government's answer to the message taken to them by Campbell was known. A telegram would be sent by Churchill to Eden 'setting out the doubts expressed in discussion in the ... cabinet as to the wisdom of proceeding'.[148]

Churchill seemed more set against going on. The situation in Greece had 'deteriorated considerably'; the Greeks had not yet moved their troops from Macedonia to the Aliakmon line, and had offered far fewer troops than 'we had been led to expect' (12 to 15 battalions short of 35).[149] He recalled at the cabinet that Eden's written instructions did authorise him 'to act on his own authority if the urgency was too great for reference home'; that he had been wired on 3 March to conduct negotiations 'on the basis that preparations for the despatch of troops to Greece should proceed'; that it had been decided to proceed with the despatch of forces; but that the situation in the Balkans had already deteriorated and Eden should 'so handle matters that it would still remain open to us to take a final decision on the despatch of forces to Greece and to liberate the

---

[145] Cabinet, 4 Mar. 1941, WM(41)23, CAB 65/22. Cadogan recorded on the 3rd that Churchill had authorised him to read to the cabinet Eden's telegram from Ankara, that 'everyone's reaction ... the same. How can one account for the jaunty ... recital of complete failure?' Cadogan diary, 3 March 1941.

[146] Cabinet, 4 Mar. 1941, WM(41)23, CAB 65/22.   [147] Ibid.

[148] Cabinet, 5 Mar. 1941, WM(41)24, CAB 65/18.

[149] Cabinet, 5 Mar. 1941, CA WM(41)24, CAB 65/22.

Greeks from their undertakings'.[150] Although Churchill agreed with Eden who saw no 'alternative to doing our best to see it through', in his case 'going through with the plan' was conditional upon the Greeks having 'taken any action, or entered into any commitments, on the strength of undertakings received from us'. But as the Greeks 'had taken no such action ... had not taken the steps which we had expected in withdrawing divisions from the Albanian and Macedonian fronts ... it was still open to us ... to tell the Greeks that we would liberate them from any undertaking ... to us'. It would follow, 'of course, that the Greeks would be free to make terms with Germany'.[151]

Churchill seemed, at the cabinet on the 5th, to want to abandon the expedition: the position in Greece had deteriorated; and while he did see that they must go on with the plan if the Greeks had taken any action as the result of commitments from us, he maintained that that was not the case, for the Greeks had done nothing. Militarily the position was graver than it had been and he pointed out that 'our forces would be engaged in an operation more hazardous than it had seemed a week ago'; and that the Australian and New Zealand Governments must be consulted again 'before we committed them to a Balkan campaign'.[152] Moreover the international implications of failure would be worse than those of standing by: the effect in Spain and North Africa would be worse 'if we landed in Greece and were driven out than if we remained masters of the Delta and seized the Dodecanese'. Churchill would draft a wire to Eden 'setting out the doubts expressed in [the] discussion ... as to the wisdom of proceeding with the enterprise'.[153]

That evening, the 5th, Churchill set about pressing (though not directing) Eden to abandon the whole thing and preparing the ground for a formal decision to do so. He made it clear that nothing could be done 'to avert the fate of Greece' and they must not 'urge Greece against her better judgement into a hopeless resistance'. In face of a German ultimatum, 'the Greeks would find it impossible to carry on the struggle'. There was 'little or nothing ... we could do to assist them in time'. It was, as he said in the wire which he had drafted and which he thought should be sent, difficult to believe 'that we now have any power to avert fate of Greece'. All possible had been done to promote a Balkan combination against Germany and they must 'be careful not to urge Greece against her better judgement into a hopeless resistance alone, when we have only handfuls

---

[150] Ibid.   [151] Ibid.   [152] Cabinet, 5 Mar. 1941, CA WM(41)24, CAB 65/22.
[153] Cabinet, 5 Mar. 1941, CA WM(41)24, CAB 65/22.

of troops which can reach the scene in time'.[154] As Eden himself pointed out, the enterprise had become 'even more hazardous'. Churchill did not see 'any reasons for expecting success'. Moreover, 'grave imperial issues' were raised by committing the Australian and New Zealand troops.[155] He did not now want the Greeks to feel they had to fight, nor Eden and the command to think that Greece really mattered. They must 'liberate Greece from feeling bound to reject a German ultimatum'; and the 'loss of Greece and Balkans [was] by no means a major catastrophe for us provided Turkey remain[ed] an honest neutral'.[156] He wanted Eden to go no further, not to press the Greeks and not to stop them making peace with Germans – for any operation would be a failure.

Churchill had, until then, alternated between reluctance to intervene in Greece and confidence that they should intervene. His confidence had been prompted by the unexpectedly optimistic military appreciations and had been combined with his own case – made on military grounds. But the military case and military prospects had been undermined by Eden's failure to form a Balkan front or to have any effect on Turkey; and by the deterioration of the position in Greece itself. By 5 March Churchill did not see much likelihood of success. He had come to support the operation because he thought of it in the context of success – of the effect which support would have on the Balkan countries and on Turkey particularly, and of the prospect of delaying considerably any German march south-wards. He did not now see that that could be done. He resolved, therefore, to warn Eden, who must not press Greece against her judgement, off the operation; and to advise that far from being impossible to abandon the project, it was not only necessary but honourable to do so, given that the Greeks had done nothing at all, either on their own or at Britain's instigation. It was difficult 'to believe that we now ha[d] any power to avert fate of Greece unless Turkey and Yugoslavia come in which seem[ed] most improbable'. The loss of Greece and the Balkans was 'by no means a ... catastrophe ... provided Turkey remain[ed] an honest neutral'.[157] Although on the 5th Churchill did not instruct Eden defi-nitely, he had made up his mind and wired Eden 'to prepare [Eden's]

[154] Defence committee, 5 Mar. 1941, DO(41)9, CAB 69/2 and Churchill to Eden, annex 1, ibid.
[155] Ibid.
[156] Ibid. If the Greeks 'on their own' insisted on fighting, 'We must to some extent share their ordeal, but rapid German advance will probably prevent any appreciable British Imperial force from being engaged.'
[157] Churchill to Eden, annex 1, DO(41)9, 5 Mar. 1941, CAB 69/2.

mind' for the views which would 'probably be expressed in cabinet tomorrow'.[158]

By the next day, however, everything was changed. Churchill was presented with a *fait accompli* – the news that Eden had already signed an agreement with the Greeks on the 4th.[159] Although feeling against Eden ran high, Churchill's line was that they could not go back on the agreement signed. In addition, he set out to suggest that the feeling hitherto against proceeding had not arisen from any reluctance to help but from a proper desire not to force help on a weak, or unwilling, Greece. Besides, they had had no choice about helping; and in any case they were going in with a good fighting chance.

He explained that the Greeks might feel that 'we had put undue pressure on them and had persuaded them against their better judgement to put up a hopeless resistance'. He wished to avoid the charge 'that we had caused another small nation to be sacrificed without being able to afford effective help'. For 'this reason' he had, he explained, urged that they must 'liberate the Greeks from feeling bound to reject the German ultimatum'.[160] Besides, they had had no choice but to go ahead and if the Greeks were 'really determined to fight ... then we had no choice but to carry out the agreement reached at Athens'. In any case, the prospects were good enough: 'the chances of success ... must be greater than would appear from Telegram 313 from Athens' and it was 'inconceivable that [Dill] could have signed the military agreement ... if he regarded the chances of success ... as hopeless'.[161] Although there could be 'no decision' until the further information requested arrived, Eden and the military advisers would probably reply that there was 'no question of "liberating the Greeks from feeling bound to reject the ultimatum"' but rather that they had decided to fight Germany alone if necessary 'and the question was whether we would help them or abandon them'. Churchill gave his own view – 'we could not now go back on the agreement signed ... unless the Greeks themselves released us'; though he would wire Eden saying that no cabinet decision would be taken until they had his views.[162]

Churchill once again prepared to stand by the Greeks and to put as good a gloss on the prospects of the operation as he could. Although they

---

[158] Churchill to Eden, 5 Mar. 1941, annex 1, DO(41)9, CAB 69/2.
[159] Cadogan diary, 6 Mar. 1941; cabinet, 6 Mar. 1941, WM(41)25, CAB 65/22. Included amongst the telegrams before the cabinet at 6 p.m. was 326 from Athens (giving details of the decisions reached with the Greeks at the meeting on 4 March, in the form of a translation from the French of the agreement). Palairet to foreign office, 5 Mar. 1941, no. 326 with Dill and Eden to Churchill and chiefs of staff, PREM 3/309/2.
[160] Cabinet, 6 Mar. 1941, WM(41)25, CAB 65/22.   [161] Ibid.
[162] Ibid.; Cadogan diary, 6 Mar. 1941.

must now wait for Eden's wire before taking a final decision Churchill had, on 6 March, no doubt what that would be. Although in his final message (sent in the early hours of 7 March) he made one last allusion to not 'urging Greeks against their better judgement to fight a hopeless battle and involve their country in probable speedy ruin', he was preparing to go in with them. If they resolved to fight to the death 'we must, as I have already said, share their ordeal'.[163] Prospects were not, he implied, hopeless. He was 'deeply impressed with steadfast attitude maintained by [Eden] and ... military advisers, Dill, Wavell and ... Wilson, on the broad merits, after full knowledge of local, and technical situation'.[164] He thought they must be in a position to emphasise for the Australian and New Zealand governments (whose troops would mostly be involved) that the hazard had been undertaken 'not because of any commitment entered into by a ... cabinet minister at Athens' but because Dill and the commanders on the spot were convinced 'that there [was] a reasonable fighting chance'.[165]

The cabinet on the 7th (which had Eden's reply) decided to go ahead. The politicians made much of the professional advice – the tone set by Pound (for the chiefs of staff) who referred to the 'military advisers on the spot [having been] convinced that the Greek campaign would not be a hopeless venture'. Bevin claimed that the advice from the commanders 'gained greatly in value for the reason that it had not been given under political pressure'. Indeed, 'the political pressure had been in the opposite direction'.[166] Churchill stressed the auspicious military prospects; 'we should', he thought 'go forward with a good heart' on the grounds, he seemed to imply, that the military prospects were good.[167] There was 'a fair prospect of reaching the Aliakmon line in time to check the German advance'. If the Anglo-Greek forces were 'compelled to retire from ... [that line] ... they would be retiring down a narrow peninsula, which contained a number of strong defensive positions'.[168] They would, in addition, 'shortly have strong air forces in Greece ... [and though] ... outnumbered by the enemy's air forces ... the odds would not be greater than they had been on many occasions in the last few months in which we

---

[163] Churchill to Eden, 7 Mar. 1941, D 2.55 AM, PREM 3/309/2; the cabinet on the 7th had a copy of this telegram before it, cabinet, 7 Mar. 1941, WM(41)26, CAB 65/22.
[164] Ibid.   [165] Ibid.
[166] Cabinet, 7 Mar. 1941, WM(41)26, CAB 65/22. Attlee had wondered on the 6th whether it would be possible to send 'even a token British force to strengthen the Greek resistance on the Nestos-Rupel line'. On the 7th he did not think that Britain should wait until Greece was technically at war with Germany – and that German seizure of Bulgaria was a sufficiently flagrant offence to justify retaliation. Cabinet, 6, 7 Mar. 1941, WM(41)25, 26, CAB 65/22.
[167] Cabinet, 7 Mar. 1941, WM(41)26,CAB 65/22.   [168] Ibid.

had been able to inflict heavy punishment'. Although the Yugoslavs were adopting 'a cryptic attitude ... we need not despair entirely of their entry into the war on our side'.[169] The cabinet confirmed the decision 'to give military assistance to Greece'.[170]

Churchill had, at the outset, been influenced by the political effects of intervention and had then made the military case – not only on account of the impact on Turkey and other Balkan countries, but because, as he suggested, there was a good fighting chance. He had come round to opposition because the military prospects were bad. But he now made his final appeal on the grounds that they were not so bad. He did so partly because he had come to look on supporting the Greeks not as a means to an end (of standing by an ally and stiffening her neighbours) but as an end in itself – that of holding up the Germans. But he also did so because he would have to be able to reassure the Australians and New Zealanders that their troops were not being despatched to a hopeless task of certain failure.

By 5 March Churchill had been more definite about failure than at any earlier time; and he also had, by that date, been unwilling to go ahead purely for reasons of political honour, irrespective of the consequences. He had hoped to dissuade Eden – as he had on and off since Eden's departure. But his hands had been tied by the agreement signed in Athens on the 4th, of which (on the 5th) he knew nothing. He made one final attempt to urge Eden to extricate Britain from intervention, but he knew by then that Eden's mind was set; and he therefore resolved to make the most of it – to appear to have been entirely in favour of intervention and to suggest that the doubts he had expressed had not been reservations at all. Furthermore he seemed to resolve his doubts about the military prospects not on account of reassuring information, but of being presented with a *fait accompli*. When he urged that they should 'go forward with a good heart' he may also have considered that whatever the outcome (and even if it were as unfavourable as his own views throughout may have led him to believe it to be), it could not militarily be a disaster. For he had also argued that Greece did not matter. (This was in the sense that there was at first no question that they would ever try to stop, or would succeed in stopping the Germans.) Even when he thought about making a stand with the Greeks, the number of troops which would reach Greece in time for the fighting would be minimal.

It may be that the whole episode had been spun out to encourage the Turks and the other Balkan countries to hold out against Hitler, or to form a front, or – especially in the case of the Turks – to be encouraged to

[169] Ibid.   [170] Ibid.

provide the kind of bases from which the air war and heavy bombing would be brought into the Danube lands and Baku. It may well be that Churchill came to believe his own arguments that there were grounds for hoping for success. But it is possible that he had tried to make the most of promises and preparations to encourage those concerned, intending that the amount in question might be minimal. If the agreement signed in Athens called his bluff, it only partly did so – so long as the numbers for diversion before the advance began were minimal. For that reason, though Eden upset his plans, he did no more than that and Churchill could advocate intervention 'with a good heart'.

Conclusion

When, in January 1941, British politicians, officials and military commanders began to react to the prospect of a German descent on Greece, they were affected by a number of considerations but did not entertain serious hopes of a quick military victory. Rather, the question was seen in wider political and military terms. To abandon a small nation (and one which Britain had guaranteed) to the Germans might have an undesirable effect on opinion in America and elsewhere. Moreover, supporting Greece might be a way of stiffening Yugoslavia, Bulgaria and Turkey against Hitler. Although, then, a decision had to be made about whether to move forces from the Middle East, support for Greece was not thought of as an alternative to support for Turkey (and an unresolved ambiguity about how such a policy would work out in practice remained). Indeed, it was possible both to accept priority for Greece and to continue to think of Turkey as the key to the British position in the Middle East, since helping the Greeks could be seen as the best way of bolstering the Turks.

When Eden, accompanied by Dill, left for the Middle East on 10 February, with the aim of seeing how best to succour Greece, he intended to form a Balkan Front and to bring in Turkey against Hitler. In fact, although he committed Britain to military intervention in Greece, he failed to form the Front: Yugoslavia and Bulgaria would not co-operate (later they joined the Axis) and Turkey resisted overtures to commit herself. On 22 February Eden agreed that Britain would stand with the Greeks on the Aliakmon line, and on 4 March he formally committed Britain to this arrangement, even though the military circumstances had in the meanwhile deteriorated. Eden's willingness to intervene in Greece seems to have been strengthened by finding the British military command in the Middle East no longer hostile to intervention there. Eden began to consider that the operation might be successful in holding back the Germans. Yet it is unclear to what extent the Middle East commanders, in advising Eden, were swayed by the assumption that the decision to intervene in Greece had already been made by the politicians on high political and strategic grounds; and were confirmed by Eden's own views.

In London, a great deal was made of the advice of those on the spot, and their apparent view that military success in the operation was not impossible. When, on 7 March, the cabinet endorsed Eden's decision, many of its members were impressed by the advice from the chiefs of staff, which suggested that defeat was not inevitable.

Churchill, having made the case for Greece at the outset, became a reluctant interventionist. By early March, he seemed to want to call off the expedition, but found himself forced to endorse intervention in Greece because of the formal agreement Eden had reached on the 4 March, without his knowing. It might seem as if Eden had called Churchill's bluff. But all along, Churchill had been attracted by the variety of different arguments for intervention, which were not superseded by the one strong argument against: the near certainty of military defeat. Moreover, it might not come to military defeat, since many of the troops would not have reached Greece before the Germans arrived. But, by 5 March, he thought it would be better to pull out of Greece. Yet, after his initial shock on hearing about Eden's agreement, Churchill was able to think himself into his wider position, in which the advantages of intervention overshadowed the disadvantage of defeat – even if it came to that.

Churchill was both less bombastic and more cautious about standing up to Hitler – in this case in Greece – than comparisons with his predecessors might suggest. Because of the context on which his political – and popular – strength rested, he could not abandon the guarantee or prohibit Eden, expressly, from doing so. In one mind he was as anti-appeaser and in his apparent desire to 'succour' Greece, appeared as such. But like his predecessors he too was concerned with Britain's interests. He would not compromise them for reasons of political sentiment. When he agreed, on 7 March, to back Eden's commitment to the Greeks and urged that they should go ahead with good heart, he was accepting with characteristic resolution a decision about which his attitude had all along been equivocal.

General conclusion

In reflecting on this book, the advocate of Churchill and Churchillian historiography might suggest that concentration on so short a period and so particular a subject misses the overall and sweeping perspective which Churchill brought to the war. Reappraisal of his role should address itself to his wider vision of the war, and the period of the Grand Alliance: the many decisions in each of the different theatres; the interventions on even the smallest or most arcane matters; relations with Roosevelt and Stalin when Britain, the United States and the Soviet Union fought as allies to defeat Germany and the Axis powers in a global war from the Atlantic to the Pacific. At no stage did Churchill abandon the grand and bold sweep which emerged in Churchillian historiography. By contrast this book may appear parochial, and unrepresentative, concerned as it is with the short period when Britain fought for the most part alone. By virtue of its narrow scope and timescale, such a book could not constitute an authoritative challenge to the broad Churchillian view.

It is certainly true that the book only considers the first ten months of Churchill's wartime leadership before America and the Soviet Union joined the war. And its concerns are particular. It begins with Churchill's becoming prime minister; examines how he established himself in that position; considers the dominant, but particular, strategic problems to which his government responded – the fall of France, the Battle of Britain, and the security of the Middle East in which the Balkans was to become implicated. And it is also so that these are considered individually rather than in the context of grand strategy and diplomacy. None the less this concentrated examination helps to illuminate the wider war by considering how the decisions and reactions of those involved on a given issue were both more complex and more diverse than the broad sweep might suggest. Indeed, without this kind of study, it would be difficult to piece together the apparent contradictions and confusions of this period – contradictions which even the grand sweep of Churchillian history fails to dispel. Moreover by close attention to the emerging, often contradictory views and decisions, the context of and later tensions in the Grand

Alliance, can be understood. For one thing the often hesitant and tentative nature of Churchill's strategic leadership in face of the different and conflicting advice of political and military colleagues was the corollary to the resolute pursuit of British interests. The problem was not one of identifying national interests. Rather, in face of so many conflicting views and demands, and given the scarcity of resources, it was how best they should be pursued. Churchill's position reflected the uncertainties, differences and vacillations of his colleagues, far more than appears from his own account.

This emerged initially during the debates and discussions as France was falling, about whether and how much to continue to send to France. Should Britain recognise the inevitable and stop all reinforcements to the French in order to concentrate on securing the island? Or should she regard the prolonging of French resistance for as long as possible as the best means of preparation, military and political, for Britain's resistance alone to Hitler? Taken with such matters as whether peace-feelers should be considered, the conditions under which the French would abandon the struggle, and whether Britain could survive, the story takes on greater complexity and less clarity than that of Churchillian history.

In the same way the debates and discussions which developed after the Battle of Britain about securing the Middle East, about the role of Turkey, Greece and the Balkans, and the changing views of, or conflict amongst, the principle protagonists, followed a course more complicated if less apparently contentious than that which Churchill or his critics were to describe. Moreover the substantive issues which dominated the later stages of the war – relations with the Soviet Union and the ultimate territorial settlement, can be better understood by considering in detail the different positions and nuances of these months.

Take, for example, one of the central subjects of this book – strategy towards the Middle East and the Balkans and the decision to send military support to Greece with which the account ends. Between November 1940 and March 1941 a number of different and changing views – political, diplomatic, strategic – affected how Greece was considered and whether to send troops. After the Italian attack obligations of honour were evoked, which were to recur in face of the German threat in early 1941. And though these may have encouraged, they did not supersede the wider strategic and diplomatic context in which Greece came to matter: in terms of the influence of Greece on its Balkan neighbours; the role of Turkey; its position as the first line of defence for Egypt; not to mention the military object of halting Hitler. For Churchill, Eden, the cabinet and defence committee, and for the chiefs of staff and their military advisers in the Middle East, different weight was given to the different perspectives at different times. Although the ultimate decision tended to reflect considerations of Greece as a legitimate military and strategic aim in itself, the wider arguments and differences were to affect the longer-term view of the role of Greece in terms of British interests. Without this it is difficult to comprehend how Churchill came to agree to the ultimate settlement of Europe foreshadowed in his percentages' arrangement with Stalin. Eden's appreciations of the diplomatic and strategic balance in the Middle East, Greece, Turkey and the Balkans help to illuminate not only the complications within the British position, but also their bearing on subsequent relations with the United States and the Soviet Union.

For example, in the immediate aftermath of the Soviet Union's joining the war in June 1941 as Britain's only fighting ally, the views which were to govern Britain's aid to, and relations with, the Soviet Union, owed much to the considerations of the previous phase of the war and to the long-term interest of all concerned in securing the Middle East. Churchill who publicly proclaimed all manner of support for the Soviet Union, was determined that nothing should interfere with the campaign proposed in the western desert to secure Egypt. Eden, whose sympathy towards and interventions on behalf of the new ally owed much to radical sentiment, remained preoccupied with preventing German encroachment in the Middle East and with maintaining a benevolent status quo in Turkey, Iraq, Iran. For neither politicians nor soldiers were the demands of the new ally to distract from or undermine the pursuit of these objects and of Britain's true interests. In reacting to Stalin's demands for the opening of a second front and requests for assistance, a balance was struck between heartening the Russians in order to keep them in the fight, and ensuring that Britain's interests in the Middle East would not be compromised or superseded. Churchill, for example, who appeared to be enthusiastically behind the Soviets, was more restrained in meeting requests – for raids in the west, a second front, elaborate assistance. He saw the invasion of the Soviet Union as an opportunity for an offensive in the western desert. Eden, more sympathetic to Soviet demands, also looked upon the new position as the opportunity to maintain the status quo in the Middle East from the Black Sea to the Persian Gulf. German influence would be kept at bay, though collaboration with the Soviets would not be at the expense of Turkey, to be guaranteed territorial integrity. The chiefs of staff were not individually nor collectively prepared to cede any but the most superficial Russian demands and resolved to pursue their respective interests, the war office most notably preparing for a fresh campaign in the Middle East.[1]

[1] See S. M. Lawlor, 'Britain and the Russian Entry into the War', in *Diplomacy and Intelligence during the Second World War, Essays in Honour of F. H. Hinsley*, ed. R. Langhorne (Cambridge 1985), pp. 168–83. This will be the subject of a subsequent volume.

Bibliography

UNPUBLISHED SOURCES

PUBLIC RECORDS IN THE PUBLIC RECORD OFFICE, LONDON

War cabinet files (CAB)
CAB 65 War cabinet conclusions and confidential annex
CAB 66 War cabinet memoranda
CAB 69 Defence committee (operations) conclusions and confidential annex
CAB 70 Defence committee (supply) conclusions and papers
CAB 79 Chiefs of staff committee conclusions
CAB 127, CAB 63 Private office collections

Foreign office FO 954 Eden's papers

Prime minister's office files (PREM)
PREM 3 Private office papers operational
PREM 4 Private office papers confidential

War office files (WO)
WO 106 Directorate of military operations and intelligence
WO 193 Directorate of military operations collation files
WO 201 War of 1939–45 military HQ papers
WO 208 Directorate of military intelligence
WO 216 CIGS
WO 217, WO 218, WO 219 Private diaries, war diaries
WO 258 Private office papers, permanent under secretary
WO 259 Private office papers secretary of state

PRIVATE PAPERS AND/OR DIARIES

Abbreviated throughout the footnotes to the author's name only, unless otherwise designated in brackets

Field-Marshal Lord Alanbrooke (Brooke), Liddell Hart Centre for Military Archives, King's College, London
1st Viscount Alexander of Hillsborough (AVAR), Churchill College, Cambridge
1st Lord Altrincham, Bodleian Library, Oxford

1st Earl Attlee, University College, Oxford; Churchill College, Cambridge
Field-Marshal Sir Claud Auchinleck, The John Rylands University Library of Manchester
1st Earl Avon, Birmingham University Library
1st Earl Baldwin (SB), Cambridge University Library
1st Lord Balfour of Inchrye, House of Lords Records Office
1st Baron Beaverbrook (BBK), House of Lords Record Office
Ernest Bevin, Churchill College, Cambridge
1st Baron Brabazon of Tara, Royal Air Force Museum, Hendon
Air Marshal Sir H. Brooke-Popham, Liddell Hart Centre for Military Archives, King's College, London
Sir Alexander Cadogan, Churchill College, Cambridge
Neville Chamberlain (NC), Birmingham University Library
1st Viscount Cherwell, Nuffield College, Oxford
Sir Stafford Cripps, Nuffield College, Oxford
1st Baron Croft, Churchill College, Cambridge
1st Viscount Crookshank, Bodleian Library, Oxford
Admiral of the Fleet, the 1st Viscount Cunningham of Hyndhop, British Library
1st Baron Dalton, British Library of Political Science, London School of Economics
Major-General F. H. Davidson, Liddell Hart Centre for Military Archives, King's College, London
17th Earl of Derby, Liverpool City Library
Air Chief Marshal Dowding, Royal Air Force Museum, Hendon
Sir James Grigg (PJGG), Churchill College, Cambridge
1st Earl of Halifax (HFX MCF), made available at York and on microfilm at Churchill College, Cambridge
  (Halifax), Additional papers and diary made available at York
1st Baron Hankey (Hky), Churchill College
Sir Patrick Hannon, House of Lords Record Office
Sir Basil Liddell-Hart (LH), Liddell Hart Centre for Military Archives, King's College, London
Sir Cuthbert Headlam, Durham County Record Office
1st Baron Ismay, Liddell Hart Centre for Military Archives, King's College, London
Lieutenant-General N.N.S. Irwin (IRW), Imperial War Museum
Admiral of the Fleet, 1st Baron Keyes, Churchill College, Cambridge
2nd Marquess of Linlithgow, India Office Library
1st Earl Lloyd George of Dwyfor (LG), House of Lords Record Office
Air Chief Marshal Sir Arthur Longmore (DC), Royal Air Force Museum, Hendon
1st Viscount Margesson, Churchill College, Cambridge
1st Viscount Monckton of Brenchley, Bodleian Library, Oxford
Field Marshal Sir Archibald Montgomery-Massingberd (MM), Liddell Hart Centre for Military Archives, King's College, London
Marshal of the Royal Air Force, 1st Baron Newall, Royal Air Force Museum, Hendon
Harold Nicolson, Balliol College, Oxford
Air Chief Marshal Sir Richard Peirse, Royal Air Force Museum, Hendon

1st Baron Ponsonby of Shulbrede, Bodleian Library, Oxford
1st Viscount Portal of Hungerford, Christ Church, Oxford
2nd Earl Selborne, Bodleian Library, Oxford
3rd Earl Selborne, Bodleian Library, Oxford
Sir Geoffrey Shakespeare (GHS), Imperial War Museum
Air Chief Marshal Sir John Slessor, Royal Air Force Museum, Hendon
Admiral of the Fleet, Sir James Somerville, Churchill College, Cambridge
Marshal of the Royal Air Force, 1st Baron Tedder, Royal Air Force Museum,
    Hendon
1st Viscount Templewood, Cambridge University Library
1st Viscount Thurso, Churchill College, Cambridge
Marshal of the Royal Air Force 1st Visount Trenchard, Royal Air Force
    Museum, Hendon
(David) Euan Wallace, Bodleian Library, Oxford
1st Baron Woolton, Bodleian Library, Oxford
2nd Marquess of Zetland (ZNK), India Office Library

PUBLISHED MATERIAL

Addison, Paul, *The Road to 1945: British Politics and the Second World War*,
    London, 1975
    'Churchill in British Politics 1940–55', in J. M. W. Bean (ed.), *The Political
        Culture of Modern Britain: Studies in memory of Stephen Koss*, London, 1987
    Churchill on the Home Front, 1900–1955, London, 1992
Andrew, Christopher, *Secret Service: The Making of the British Intelligence
    Community*, London, 1985
Andrew, Christopher and Jeremy Noakes, (eds.), *Intelligence and International
    Relations 1900–1945*, Exeter, 1987
Aster, Sidney, *1939: The Making of the Second World War*, London, 1973
Avon, the Earl of (Anthony Eden), *Facing the Dictators*, London, 1962
    The Reckoning, London, 1965
Barker, Elisabeth, *British Policy in South-East Europe in the Second World War*,
    London, 1976
    Churchill and Eden at War, London, 1978
Barnett, Corelli, *The Collapse of British Power*, London, 1972
    The Audit of War: The Illusion and Reality of Britain as a Great Nation, London,
    1986
Baylis, John, *Anglo-American Defence Relations, 1939–84: The Special Relation-
    ship*, London 1984
Bell, P. M. H., *A Certain Eventuality: Britain and the Fall of France*, Saxon House,
    1974
Birkenhead, The Earl of, *The Prof in Two Worlds. The Official Life of Professor
    F. A. Lindemann, Viscount Cherwell*, London, 1961
Berlin, Isaiah, *Mr Churchill in 1940*, London, n.d. (*c.* 1949)
Bond, Brian (ed.), *Chief of Staff. The Diaries of Lieutenant-General Sir Henry
    Pownall*, 2 vols., London, 1972, 1974
    France and Belgium 1939–1940, London, 1975
Brabazon of Tara, Lord, *The Brabazon Story*, London, 1956

Bryant, Arthur, *The Turn of the Tide 1939–1943*, London, 1957
Butler, Ewan, *Mason-Mac. The Life of Lt. General Sir Mason Macfarlane*, London, 1972
Butler, Sir James (ed.), *History of the Second World War. United Kingdom Military Histories*, London, 1952–
Butler, R. A., *The Art of the Possible*, London, 1971
Carlton, David, *Anthony Eden: A Biography*, London, 1981
'Cato' (Michael Foot, Peter Howard and Frank Owen), *Guilty Men*, London, 1940
Charmley, John, *Churchill: The End of Glory. A Political Biography*, London, 1993
Winston S. Churchill, *Into Battle. War Speeches by the Right Hon. Winston S. Churchill, C.H., M.P.*, compiled by Randolph S. Churchill, London, 1941
   The Unrelenting Struggle War Speeches by the Rt. Hon. Winston S. Churchill, compiled by Charles Eade, London, 1942
   The Second World War, vol. I: *The Gathering Storm*, London, 1948
   The Second World War, vol. II: *Their Finest Hour*, London, 1949
   The Second World War, vol. III: *The Grand Alliance*, London, 1950
   Winston S. Churchill. His Complete Speeches 1897–1963, 8 vols. (ed.) Robert Rhodes James, New York, 1974
Colville, John, *The Churchillians*, London, 1981
   The Fringes of Power: Downing Street Diaries, 1939–1945, London, 1985
Connell, John, *Auchinleck. A Biography of Field-Marshal Sir Claude Auchinleck*, London, 1959
   Wavell. Scholar and Soldier to June 1941, London, 1964
   Wavell. Supreme Commander: 1941–3, ed. and completed M. Roberts, London, 1969
Cooper, Duff, *Old Men Forget*, London, 1953
Cowling, Maurice, *The Impact of Hitler: British Politics and British Policy, 1933–1940*, Cambridge, 1975
Croft, 1st Baron, *My Life of Strife*, London, 1948
Day, David, *The Great Betrayal: Britain, Australia and the Onset of the Pacific War, 1939–1941*, London, 1988
Dilks, David, *The Diaries of Sir Alexander Cadogan 1938–45*, London, 1971
   'Appeasement Revisited', *University of Leeds Review* 15 (1972) 28–56
   'Allied Leadership in the Second World War: Churchill', *Survey*, 21, no. 1/2 (1975), pp. 19–21
   'Baldwin and Chamberlain', in Lord Butler (ed.), *The Conservatives. A History from their Origins to 1965*, London, 1977
   'The Twilight War and the Fall of France: Chamberlain and Churchill in 1940', in *Transactions of the Royal Historical Society*, 1978
   (ed.), *Retreat from Power: Studies in Britain's Foreign Policy of the Twentieth Century*, 2 vols., London, 1981
Feiling, Keith, *The Life of Neville Chamberlain*, London, 1946
Fuller, Major-General J. F. C., *The Second World War 1939–45*, London, 1948
   The Conduct of War, 1789–1961, London, HMSO, 1961
Gates, Eleanor M., *End of the Affair: The Collapse of the Anglo-French Alliance, 1939–1940*, London, 1981
Gibbs, N. H., *Grand Strategy*, vol. I: *Rearmament Policy*, London, 1975
Gilbert, Martin, *Finest Hour: Winston S. Churchill 1939–1941*, London, 1983

Road to Victory: Winston S. Churchill, 1941–1945, London, 1986

Gorodetsky, Gabriel, *Stafford Cripps' Mission to Moscow 1940–1942*, Cambridge, 1984

Grigg, P. J., *Prejudice and Judgement*, London, 1948

Halifax, The Earl of, *Fullness of Days*, London, 1957

Harris, Kenneth, *Attlee*, London, 1982

Harvey, J. (ed.), *The Diplomatic Diaries of Oliver Harvey*, London, 1970

Hinsley, F. H., with E. E. Thomas, C. F. G. Ransom and R. C. Knight, *British Intelligence in the Second World War: Its Influence on Strategy and Operations*, London, HMSO, 1979

'British Intelligence in the Second World War', in Andrew and Noakes (eds.), pp. 209–18, 1987

Howard, Anthony, *RAB. The Life of R. A. Butler*, London, 1987

Howard, Michael, *The Continental Commitment: The Dilemma of British Defence Policy in the Era of Two World Wars*, London, 1972

Ismay, Lord, *The Memoirs of Lord Ismay*, London, 1960

Jefferys, Kevin, *The Churchill Coalition and Wartime Politics, 1940–1945*, Manchester, 1991

Jones, Thomas, *A Diary with Letters, 1931–50*, Oxford, 1954

Keegan, John, *Churchill's Generals*, London, 1991

Kennedy, John, *The Business of War*, ed. Bernard Fergusson, London, 1957

Langer, William L. and S. Everett Gleason, *The Challenge to Isolation 1937–1940*, London, 1952

The Undeclared War 1940–1941, London, 1953

Langhorne, Richard (ed.), *Diplomacy and Intelligence during the Second World War: Essays in Honour of F. H. Hinsley*, Cambridge, 1985

Lash, Joseph P., *Roosevelt and Churchill 1939–1941*, ed. R. Langhorne, London, 1977, pp. 168–83

Lawlor, S. M., 'Britain and the Russian Entry into the War', in R. Langhorne, ed., *Diplomacy and Intelligence*

Lewin, Ronald, *The Chief Field Marshal Lord Wavell Commander-in-Chief and Viceroy 1939–47*, New York, 1980

Loewenheim, Francis L., Harold D. Langley and Manfred Jonas (eds.), *Roosevelt and Churchill: Their Secret Wartime Correspondence*, London, 1975 (first published in USA, 1975)

Lysaght, Charles Edward, *Brendan Bracken*, London, 1979

Macleod, R. and D. Kelly, *The Ironside Diaries, 1937–40*, London, 1962

Macmillan, Harold, *The Blast of War 1939–1945*, London, 1967

Middlemas, K. and J. Barnes, *Baldwin. A Biography*, London, 1969

Minney, R. J., *The Private Papers of Hore-Belisha*, London, 1960

Moran, Lord, *Winston Churchill. The Struggle for Survival 1940–65*, London, 1966

Newman, Simon, *March 1939: The British Guarantee to Poland: A Study in the Continuity of British Foreign Policy*, Oxford, 1976

Nicolson, N. (ed.), *Harold Nicolson. Diaries and Letters 1939–1945*, London, 1967

Overy, R. J., *The Air War, 1939–1945*, London, 1980

Parker, R. A. C., 'Economics, Rearmament and Foreign Policy: The United Kingdom before 1939 – a Preliminary Study', *Journal of Contemporary History*, 10 (1975), 637–47

'British Rearmament, 1936–1939: Treasury, Trade Unions and Skilled Labour', *English Historical Review*, 96 (1981), 306–43

'The Pound Sterling, the American Treasury and British Preparations for War, 1938–1939', *English Historical Review*, 98 (1983) 261–79

Struggle for Survival. The History of the Second World War, Oxford, 1989

Peden, G. C., 'Sir Warren Fisher and British Rearmament against Germany', *English Historical Review*, 94 (1979), 29–47

British Rearmament and the Treasury 1932–39, Edinburgh, 1979

'A Matter of Timing: The Economic Background to British Foreign Policy, 1937–1939', *History*, 69 (1984), 15–28

'The burden of imperial defence and the continental commitment reconsidered', *Historical Journal*, 27 (1984), 405–23

Pelling, Henry, *Britain and the Second World War*, London, 1970

Pimlott, Ben (ed.), *The Second World War Diary of Hugh Dalton, 1940–45*, London, 1986

Reynolds, David, *The Creation of the Anglo-American Alliance, 1937–1941: A Study in Competitive Co-operation*, London, 1981

'Churchill and the British "Decision" to Fight on in 1940: Right Policy, Wrong Reasons', in Langhorne (ed.), *Diplomacy and Intelligence*, pp. 147–67, (1985)

'1940: Fulcrum of the Twentieth Century?', *International Affairs*, 66 (1990), 325–50

Rhodes James, Robert (ed.), *Chips. The Diaries of Sir Henry Channon*, London, 1967

Churchill. A Study in Failure, London, 1970

Anthony Eden, London, 1986

Richards, Denis, *Portal of Hungerford*, London, 1977

Roberts, Andrew, *The Holy Fox. A Biography of Lord Halifax*, London, 1991

Roskill, Stephen, *Hankey Man of Secrets*, vol. III, *1931–1963*, London, 1974

Sherwood, Robert E., *The White House Papers of Harry L. Hopkins. An Intimate History by Robert E. Sherwood*, vol. I, *September 1939–January 1942*, London, 1948

Simon, Lord, *Retrospect*, London, 1953

Smyth, Denis, *Diplomacy and Strategy of Survival: British Policy and Franco's Spain 1940–1941*, Cambridge, 1986

Stuart, Charles (ed.), *The Reith Diaries*, London, 1975

Taylor, A. J. P., *My Darling Pussy. The Letters of Lloyd George and Frances Stevenson, 1913–41*, London, 1975

Templewood, Lord, *Nine Troubled Years*, London, 1954

Thorne, Christopher, *Allies of a Kind: The United States, Britain and the War against Japan, 1941–1945*, London, 1978

The Far Eastern War: States and Societies, 1941–45, London, 1986 (1985 title: *The Issue of War*)

Watt, D. C., 'Appeasement: The Rise of a Revisionist School?', *The Political Quarterly*, 36 (1965), 191–213

Watt, Donald Cameron, *How War Came: The Immediate Origins of the Second World War, 1938–1939*, London, 1989

Williamson, Philip, *National Crisis and National Government: British Politics, the Economy and Empire, 1926–1932*, Cambridge, 1992

Woodward, Sir Llewellyn, *History of the Second World War: British Foreign Policy in the Second World War*, vols. I and II, London, 1970–1

Woolton, The Earl of, *The Memoirs of the Rt. Hon. the Earl of Woolton*, London, 1959

Index